An Eye for Music

THE OXFORD MUSIC / MEDIA SERIES

Daniel Goldmark, Series Editor

oxford
music/media series

Tuning In: American Narrative Television Music
Ron Rodman

Special Sound: The Creation and Legacy of the BBC Radiophonic Workshop
Louis Niebur

Seeing Through Music: Gender and Modernism in Classic Hollywood Film Scores
Peter Franklin

An Eye for Music: Popular Music and the Audiovisual Surreal
John Richardson

An Eye for Music

POPULAR MUSIC AND THE AUDIOVISUAL SURREAL

JOHN RICHARDSON

OXFORD
UNIVERSITY PRESS

Oxford University Press, Inc., publishes works that further
Oxford University's objective of excellence
in research, scholarship, and education.

Oxford   New York
Auckland   Cape Town   Dar es Salaam   Hong Kong   Karachi
Kuala Lumpur   Madrid   Melbourne   Mexico City   Nairobi
New Delhi   Shanghai   Taipei   Toronto

With offices in
Argentina   Austria   Brazil   Chile   Czech Republic   France   Greece
Guatemala   Hungary   Italy   Japan   Poland   Portugal   Singapore
South Korea   Switzerland   Thailand   Turkey   Ukraine   Vietnam

Published by Oxford University Press, Inc.
198 Madison Avenue, New York, New York 10016

www.oup.com

Oxford is a registered trademark of Oxford University Press

Library of Congress Cataloging-in-Publication Data
Richardson, John, 1964–
An eye for music : popular music and the audiovisual surreal / John Richardson.
p. cm.
Includes bibliographical references and index.
ISBN 978-0-19-536736-2 (alk. paper)—ISBN 978-0-19-536737-9 (alk. paper)
1. Music—Philosophy and aesthetics.   2. Motion picture music—Philosophy and aesthetics.
3. Surrealism and music.   I. Title.
ML3849.R488 2011
780'.07—dc22   2010054094

1 3 5 7 9 8 6 4 2
Printed in the United States of America
on acid-free paper

In loving memory of my mother
Margaret Frances Richardson
1932–2009

Contents

Acknowledgments

The task of thanking all who had a hand in the success of a project spanning almost a decade is formidable. I emphasize success because I cannot blame anyone but myself for those areas in which my writing is deficient. If I have failed to acknowledge your contribution adequately please don't consider this a deliberate snub, but rather a sign of human fallibility. I would first like to express my unreserved gratitude to the two initially anonymous readers who gave this project their approval and provided numerous helpful comments and suggestions: Carol Vernallis and Annette Davison. In addition, a third anonymous reader commented on an earlier draft of the manuscript, which is a contribution deserving of appreciation. An immeasurable debt of gratitude goes to my commissioning editor at Oxford University Press, Norm Hirschy, whose positive outlook, professional acumen and unfailing patience left nothing to be desired. In addition, the series editor (and my former UCLA associate) Daniel Goldmark deserves heartfelt thanks for occasional messages of encouragement and ensuring that publication of this book has progressed smoothly. Similar plaudits are extended to all the staff at Oxford University Press. Four accomplices on recent and past book projects helped me in countless indeterminate ways simply by being part of my academic circle (often virtually, by e-mail or video chat) and by generously exchanging ideas and insights on a wide range of subjects. From the perspective of my current research interests, it is hard to imagine a more inspiring and distinguished group of academic associates than Claudia Gorbman, Stan Hawkins, Amy Herzog and Carol Vernallis. Claudia Gorbman should additionally be thanked for coming up with the main title of this book at a time when inspiration was running dry. I held positions at six different universities during the time it took to complete this book. Crucially for the success of the project, I benefited from a five-year Academy of Finland Research Fellowship starting in 2003 to conduct research at the University of Jyväkylä in Finland. There I pursued a line of research that would culminate in the writing of this book. There I led the research project, Contemporary Music, Media and Mediation, which provided a microcommunity of scholars supportive to work in this field. Stan Hawkins and Anne Sivuoja both made timely and important contributions to the success of this research project; as did project partners Erkki Pekkilä, Anahid Kassabian and Annette Davison. Additionally, I should like to express my gratitude to students and colleagues at the various universities where I have held positions for motivating me to become a better teacher and for asking suitably challenging questions (as well as sometimes supplying the answers). My thanks, therefore, to all who helped me at the Department of Music, City University (where this project was conceived); the subject of Music Technology and Innovation, DeMontfort University, Leicester (where I worked for a regrettably short period of time); the Department of Music at the University of Helsinki; the subject of Musicology at Åbo Academy, Finland; and, finally, the subject of Musicology and Department of History, Culture and the Arts at the University of Turku, Finland, where I currently hold a position. Colleagues I would like to thank for their support include Denis Smalley, Rhian Samuel, Simon Emmerson, Annegret Fauser and my most valued associate, the late Gerry Farrell, at City University; Leigh Landy and John Young at De Montfort University; Pirkko Moisala (who should be doubly thanked for appointing me substitute professor of ethnomusicology when she was on research sabbatical); Eero Tarasti, Alfonso Padilla and Kai Lassfolk at the University of Helsinki; Matti Vainio at the University of Jyväskylä, Johannes Brusila at Åbo Academy and Yrjö Heinonen and Kari Kallioniemi at Turku University. Additionally, Susanna Välimäki (Jyväskylä, Helsinki, Turku), Juha Torvinen (Helsinki, Turku) and Petri Kuljuntausta (Jyväskylä, Helsinki) have all offered support and stimulating conversation at more than one location. Readers of sections of this work, editors of earlier versions of the research included here, and people who have offered useful comments on presentations, include (but are not limited to) Philip Auslander, Steven Baur, Annette Davison, Caryl Flinn, Claudia Gorbman, Stan Hawkins, Raymond Knapp, Miguel Mera, Derek Scott, Anne Sivuoja, Pwyll ap Siôn, Robynn Stilwell, Philip Tagg, Juha Torvinen, Sheila Whiteley, Carol Vernallis, Susanna Välimäki and Jacqueline Warwick. My wife, Ulla, and daughter Lise, have endured a great deal over the years. For this I can never thank them enough. The past few years have brought more personal grief and misfortune than I could have anticipated. But they have also brought moments of relief, exhilaration (including the exhilaration of intellectual discovery), joy (including the joy of sharing knowledge with others and watching their abilities develop), and a growing sense of accomplishment.

For assistance with obtaining research materials and useful perspectives on their work, I thank the composer Glover Gill, Philip Glass and the staff at Dunvagen Music, and the team at Musion Systems. Earlier versions of some of the materials presented here have originally appeared as follows: "Resisting the Sublime: Loose Synchronisation in *La Belle et la Bête* and *The Dark Side of Oz*," in

Steven Baur, Raymond Knapp and Jacqueline Warwick, eds., *Musicological Identities: Essays in Honour of Susan McClary* (Aldershot: Ashgate, 2008), 135–48; "'The Digital Won't Let Me Go': Constructions of the Virtual and the Real in Gorillaz' 'Clint Eastwood,'" *Journal of Popular Music Studies* 17/1 (2005): 1–29; "Televised Live Performance, Looping Technology and the 'Nu Folk': KT Tunstall on *Later…with Jools Holland*," in Derek B. Scott, ed., *The Ashgate Research Companion to Popular Musicology* (Farnham and Burlington: Ashgate, 2009), 85–101; and "On Music Criticism and Affect: Two Instances of the Disaffected Acoustic Imaginary," in Stan Hawkins, ed., *Critical Musicology: Festschrift for Derek Scott* (Aldershot: Ashgate, 2011).

An Eye for Music

1

Introduction

In dreams begins responsibility.
—William Butler Yeats

Surrealist forms are merely analogous to dreams, not more. They suspend the customary logic and the rules of the game of empirical evidence but in doing so respect the individual objects that have been forcibly removed from their context and bring their contents, especially their human contents, closer to the form of the object… The dream, to be sure, does the same thing, but in the dream the object world appears in a form incomparably more disguised and is presented as reality less than it is in Surrealism, where art batters its own foundations.
—Theodor Adorno

Preliminaries

Strange things have been happening in audiovisual expression over the last couple of decades. The writing on postmodernism began to address the causes of this strangeness, although the instances investigated in this book were produced for the most part in the nineties and "noughties," by which time emerging tendencies were replacing older ones and the concept of postmodernism had already begun to lose some of its sparkle. These changes in the tone of cultural production gave rise to a need for corresponding new theoretical models and analytical strategies. The practices elucidated in this study share a general constructivist outlook with ideas about postmodernism.[1] They seem to require closer attention to matters of sensory detail and historical reference, however, than is currently evident in the writing on postmodernism in order to capture something of the unyielding complexity of audiovisual expression. This book is not the first study to have mined

---

Epigraph is from Theodor Adorno, "Looking Back on Surrealism" (1954), in *Notes to Literature*, vol. 1, trans. Shierry Weber Nicholson (New York: Columbia University Press, 1991), 86–90, 87.

[1] See, for example, the section "De-naturalizing the Natural," in Linda Hutcheon, *The Politics of Postmodernism* (London and New York: Routledge, 1989), 31–42.

this seam, but it does, as far as I am aware, make a unique contribution insofar as it focuses on a specific aesthetic tendency within a far larger field of practices, with a view to shedding new light on the contribution of this tendency to the general cultural ground-tone. The aim is not to map the entire audiovisual terrain, but to present more localized and culturally contingent observations that nevertheless reflect back onto bigger questions about the nature of life at the turn of the third millennium and beyond.

As the title of this book implies, much of what I will offer commentary on can be related in some way back to the artistic output of the historical surrealists. This is not to suggest that everything going on is a simple repetition of canonical surrealist works or the direct realization of principles expounded in writings on surrealism such as Breton's surrealist manifestos. Surrealism for me is at most a productive analogy; one that opens up a line of inquiry other writers have touched upon in passing, but that warrants, in my opinion, a more thoroughgoing consideration. By grouping together phenomena as diverse as those to be investigated, it is hoped that they will rebound against one another in unexpected ways—much like a surrealist collage, a *cadavre exquis* (exquisite corpse) drawing, or the elements of a montage sequence by Eisenstein or Buñuel. In this way, the writing will bring into sight connections that might otherwise go unnoticed. I am convinced about the integrity of materials presented in this book. They combine to form a composite "argument" that the necessary element of complexity in the analytical discussions, to some extent, masks. This argument is always present, in some shape and form, even when it momentarily accedes to the ground-level concerns of close critical readings. It is an argument made up of several interweaving threads rather than a single guiding proposition. Neosurrealism, as I call it, is in this consideration a cluster of loosely related practices rather than a single determining "code." My discussions will not attempt to gloss over this heterogeneity nor to braid together discursive threads that do not belong together. In this way, I hope to remain true to the irreducible otherness of my materials and to the phenomenal character of their appearances.

Important differences exist between present-day practices and those of the historical surrealists. This is reflected in my use of the term neosurrealism on many occasions and my avoidance of any such reference in others. Nowhere do I take for granted affinities between historical surrealism and the emerging forms that I discuss. Rather, the relationship I am proposing is in the nature of a family resemblance in the Wittgensteinian sense: implying overlap of several conceptual nodes rather than direct conceptual alignment—by this I mean that the essence of my argument has little to do with influence.[2] To prove that historical surrealism has influenced subsequent forms is, in fact, largely peripheral to the aims of this project. It is enough

---

[2] On families of resemblance, see also George Lipsitz, "Cruising Around the Historical Bloc: Postmodernism and Popular Music in Los Angeles," *Cultural Critique* 5 (1986): 157–77.

to demonstrate how the present-day practices discussed "work" on their own terms, how they afford meanings in similar ways to historical antecedents, and how they hook up with larger discursive formations in contemporary society and the theories that have been produced to explain them. New audiovisual expression in this view is unavoidably a cultural practice; one that connects with wider patterns of practices to produce sum effects that are always more complex than could be guessed on the basis of aesthetic considerations alone. In this respect, it is necessary to combine phenomenological with hermeneutical methods; observations about ontology with attention to how forms and practices are historically and humanly situated and derive their meanings from these connections. Aestheticism itself is in this view a cultural construct; it is never external to cultural practices but emerges within and in dialectical response to them. So when I speak of aestheticism in reference to the materials discussed in this book, I am not referring to something that is external to symbolic or cultural understanding, but very much implicated within it.

This book therefore tracks my attempts to fathom how neosurrealist ideas have been articulated in a variety of circumstances across an audiovisual terrain that can be broadly described as popular. The fact that these instances span everything from feature films to live stage performances, Internet mashups, and even the implicit visual encoding of music does not entail a desire on my part to provide comprehensive coverage of "new media." These are simply the instances that best illustrate the guiding ideas of this study. I make no apologies for omitting other emerging media forms, such as gaming, implementations of "virtual reality" (VR) and installation art, each of which could be thought of as encapsulating other core principles of neosurrealist aesthetics. Such exclusions are a necessary part of demarcating an area of study. And in defining my work in accordance with the popular, I choose to concentrate on those forms readily available in mainstream media contexts, which to a certain extent discounts forms such as installation art and VR. In fact, this focus on mainstream media contexts can be taken as an heuristic definition of the popular that is in many respects adequate to the needs of this project (in lieu of a more elaborately argued definition, which would require considerable page space and even then is likely to be inconclusive).[3]

Regarding the concept of the popular: the attitude adopted in this book resembles that of the historical surrealists, insofar as artistic production from both sides of

---

[3] Ideas about what constitutes the popular have changed over time. In current research, some scholars align the popular with commercialism, some with mass media modes of dissemination and consumption, some with ideas about a vernacular or common language, some with Marxist or quasi-Marxist ideas about "the people" or the working class, some with distinctions between cultivated or artistic forms and those that are less cultivated or "vulgar," some with literary versus oral traditions, while some hark back to the traditional distinction between popular, folk and art. The last of these is becoming increasingly hard to defend in light of the prominent role of popular music and the mass media in contemporary society. The second and third of the above categories are probably those that align most closely my theorizations.

the high-low divide is held to be equally suitable grist for the neosurrealist mill. In short, this book intentionally loiters in the gray area between popular and high, just as many of the artists discussed in these pages seem intent on destabilizing any such binary constructs. My alignment of this study with the popular is nevertheless defensible to the extent that the cultural forms scrutinized address sizeable constituencies via the mass media, and, further, to the extent that these instances draw on codes that are widely recognized as belonging to the sphere of popular culture (vernacular codes). Of particular interest is an alignment with a pop art sensibility that flirts with the concerns of the historical avant-garde (including the surrealists). A long tradition exists of this kind of symbiosis between the popular and the avant-garde, as commented on, for example, in Simon Frith and Howard Horne's groundbreaking study of the British art school movement, *Art into Pop*, and Bernard Gendron's panhistorical study, *Between Montmartre and Mudd Club: Popular Music and the Avant-Garde*.[4] Countless other recent studies could be cited that in different ways draw attention to the artistry of popular expression. I highlight these books as exemplars mainly because of the balanced light in which they present the commercial and the critical imperatives of popular music.[5] The critical and self-reflexive mode of address that characterizes expression of this type has been the subject of detailed consideration in some enclaves of academic writing. This line of criticism has spawned terms such as metapop, avant-pop, intelligent pop and crossover, all of which have some currency with respect to the subject matter of this book.[6] (The first of these categories is probably my personal favorite.)

Despite my interest in the popular audiovisual broadly considered, I will discuss music videos only in passing. The analysis of Gorillaz' "Feel Good Inc." in chapter 6 is a brief exception to this rule, although the chapters on contemporary cinema (3 and 4) both draw attention to the use of stylistic devices that originated in this audiovisual form. It is tempting to go so far as to assert that everything hap-

---

[4] Simon Frith and Howard Horne, *Art into Pop* (London: Routledge, 1987); Bernard Gendron, *Between Montmartre and the Mudd Club: Popular Music and the Avant-Garde* (Chicago: University of Chicago Press, 2002).

[5] A collected edition that views such migrations between high and low with some skepticism is Jim Collins, ed., *High-Pop: Making Culture into Popular Entertainment* (Malden, MA and Oxford: Blackwell, 2002). Taking a popular-culture-as-commerce perspective on the subject, the chapters of this book argue that crossover forms from *Shakespeare in Love* to the Three Tenors should be seen primarily as machinations of a cultural industry determined to cash in on the misguided desire of consumers to achieve higher social status through the accumulation of cultural capital. Suffice it to say that the choice of subject matter in these cases largely determines the analytical outcomes.

[6] See Michael Dunn, *Metapop: Self-Referentiality in Contemporary American Popular Culture* (Jackson and London: University Press of Mississippi, 1992). See also Larry McCaffery, *After Yesterday's Crash: The Avant-Pop Anthology* (New York: Penguin, 1997). Writers seem uncertain as to whether avant-pop came about in polemical response to postmodernism or whether it is somehow indebted to postmodernist aesthetics. In general, I prefer the designation metapop to avant-pop for reasons that will become apparent in the course of my later discussions of surrealism as an avant-garde artistic movement.

pening in audiovisual culture today is somehow related to music video aesthetics. This is a generalization but in some measure true. For this reason I end both chapters 3 and 4 with short concluding sections, or codas, in which I relate what I have discussed back to music video aesthetics. In addition, in chapter 5, I discuss the phenomenon of video mashups in reference to loosely synchronized audiovisual combinations,. In the final assessment, however, this book is more about *what music video aesthetics led to* (along with other impulses) than what it is *or was* in its own right. I had intended to cover music videos more extensively when beginning this study, but the materials ended up taking me in a different direction. As a result, the book in its present form probably makes a more coherent argument than it would have otherwise. I would advise readers with an interest in music videos to consult the numerous existing publications on the subject, including several of my own.[7]

Attention to the relations between media (intermediality) and matters of media convergence are both important aspects of this study. Several case studies in this book illustrate how these factors are shaping the audiovisual terrain to a surprising degree. Performances routinely contain or allude to prior performances designed for presentation in different media. Several theories in media studies, performance studies and cultural theory have begun to respond to this aesthetic shift. The writing on recent stage performances has addressed questions of intermediality with the greatest determination.[8] The term can refer to the relationship between different media within a performance (or work), to intertextual relationships to external performances and media, or to the transformation of performances designed for different media. A subclass of intermediality that has gained a certain amount of currency in recent writing is the idea of "remediation," defined by Bolter

[7] Noteworthy studies of music videos include E. Ann Kaplan, *Rocking Around the Clock: Music Television, Postmodernism, and Consumer Culture* (New York: Methuen, 1987); Andrew Goodwin, *Dancing in the Distraction Factory; Music Television and Popular Culture* (Minneapolis: University of Minnesota Press, 1992); Carol Vernallis, *Experiencing Music Videos: Aesthetic and Cultural Context* (New York: Columbia University Press, 2004); Stan Hawkins, "Perspectives in Popular Musicology: Music, Lennox and Meaning in 1990s Pop," *Popular Music* 15/1 (1996): 17–36; *The British Pop Dandy: Male Identity, Music and Culture* (Aldershot: Ashgate, 1999); John Richardson and Stan Hawkins, "Remodeling Britney Spears: Matters of Intoxication and Mediation," *Popular Music and Society* 30/5 (2007): 605–29; John Richardson, "Plasticine Music: Surrealism in Peter Gabriel's 'Sledgehammer,'" in Michael Drewett, Sarah Hill and Kimi Kärki, eds., *Games Without Frontiers: Peter Gabriel From Genesis to Growing Up.* (Farnham and Burlington: Ashgate, 2010), 195–2010; "Double-Voiced Discourse and Bodily Pleasures in Contemporary Finnish Rock: The Case of Maija Vilkkumaa," in John Richardson and Stan Hawkins, eds., *Essays on Sound and Vision* (Helsinki: Yliopistopaino/Helsinki University Press, 2007), 401–41; Alf Björnberg and John Richardson, "Music Videos," *The Grove Dictionary of American Music* (New York: Oxford University Press, forthcoming); and Henry Keazor and Thorsten Wübbena, eds., *Rewind, Play, Fast Forward: The Past, Present and Future of the Music Video* (Verlag, Bielefeld: Transcript, 2010).

[8] Freda Chappl and Chiel Kattenbelt, eds., *Intermediality in Theatre and Performance* (Amsterdam: Rodopi, 2007).

and Grusin as "the representation of one medium in another."[9] Both of these theories are concerned with the changes being wrought in contemporary artistic production in light of the digital turn. This idea is given special prominence in Philip Auslander's writing on mediatized live performance, which provocatively unpacks assumptions concerning the ontological "sencondariness" of mediatized communication in relation to assumed "primary" liveness. Bolter and Grusin propose that practices of remediation can be understood in terms of a continuum between those forms that strive to erase the boundary between predigital and digital forms; those that represent existing media in new digitalized forms without irony or critique; and, lastly, those that "seem to want to emphasize the difference rather than erase it."[10] The last of these categories is especially relevant when it comes to this book's subject matter, which speaks to an attitude of performative consciousness that effectively roots transformations of existing materials in the here and now. This consciousness has a critical edge since the relationship between media at any given time is not equal but reflects implicit cultural priorities and power relations.[11] In addition to this concern to reveal cultural priorities, the affective end results of intermediality interest me more than the fact that it is simply happening. It is only through understanding the pleasures afforded by media forms that we can better comprehend the power dynamics implicit in them. Intermediality in my view results in transformations of originals that push them toward the domain of neosurrealist aesthetics.

The frame of surrealism is one of several ways of coming to grips with these materials. Economic and technological factors (especially the digital turn) also impinge on the subject of this study at almost every step. This is reflected in the eclectic nature of my approach, which acts as a safeguard against the kind of reductionism that makes the products of popular culture appear to be nothing more than exchangeable commodities. Like other studies of popular music that are defined around specific styles, genres or aesthetic movements, I endeavor to take personal agency seriously by showing how artists adhering to the spirit of what

[9] Jay David Bolter and Richard Grusin, "Remediation," *Configurations* 3 (1996): 311–58, 339. Also Philip Auslander, *Liveness: Performance in a Mediatized Culture* (London: Routledge, 2008), 6–7. Bolter and Grusin stress the point that "remediation is a defining factor of the new digital media." Jay Bolter and Richard Grusin, *Remediation: Understanding New Media* (Cambridge, MA: MIT, 1999), 45. Intermediality and remediation are related to, although not entirely synonymous with, a concept that has stimulated much discussion in literary criticism: adaptation. This term is found also in the recent writing on audiovisuality. See Miguel Mera, "Invention/Re-invention," *Music, Sound, and the Moving Image* 3/1 (Spring 2009): 1–20. I will reserve this concept for specific instances where an existing work (e.g., a book, a television series) has been adapted in a fairly straightforward way for use in a different media (e.g. film, gaming). The transformations that are the subject of the present study operate mostly on a more general level.

[10] Bolter and Grusin, *Remediation*, 46.

[11] See Philip Auslander, "Liveness, Mediatization, and Intermedial Performance," *Degrés: Revue de synthèse à orientation sémiologique* 101 (Spring 2000): 1–12. Available online, http://www.lcc.gatech.edu/~auslander/publications/liveness.pdf, retrieved December 12, 2010.

I call neosurrealist aesthetics respond dialectically to cultural givens; in other words, how they do more than simply reflect prevailing cultural conditions (economic or otherwise).[12] Technologies provide the material preconditions for "user responses" (including those of cultural producers or artists), but they never fully determine the uses nor the meanings that will be attributed to artistic performances in different contexts. Recent research on the cultural significance of music technologies has extolled the virtues of caution when it comes to claims concerning the determining impacts of technological change.[13] The historical scope of this study coincides quite neatly with the emergence of the dominant cultural position of what some have called the digital turn. This has undeniably brought with it both marked changes in audiovisual practices and dialectical responses to these changes (such as the approach of the Dogme 95 school of filmmaking). Each chapter of this book in one way or another addresses the repercussions of ongoing technological transformations. I offer a new angle on the causes of these changes, however, by directing attention toward factors that are usually omitted from analytical models. An emphasis on surrealist aesthetics does precisely this: it complicates existing theoretical formulations by detaching the object of study momentarily from its technological or more expansive sociocultural contexts (such as postmodernism, modernity, or advanced capitalism) before returning it to these contexts with a view to deepening exegetical inquiry.

Close reading is a necessary part of my methodological apparatus. This approach more than any other reveals the extent to which audiovisual performances connect with neighboring discursive formations. Equally, the materials themselves can be understood as constituting their own phenomenal reality, which to some extent always resists incorporation within overarching theoretical models. Expressed differently, cultural production can never be fully assimilated within *any* explanatory model; its very substance or *materia* bearing testimony to the gap that will always exist between the intentions that propelled it into existence and the alignments and recognitions that are called into play by those on the "receiving" (or activating?) end of the expressive contract. This distance between production and what I hesitate to call consumption is addressed in Paul Ricoeur's writing on hermeneutics with the help of the term "appropriation," this concept implying more than simply practices

    [12] See, for example Stan Hawkins, *The British Pop Dandy*; Michael Veal, *Dub: Soundscapes & Shattered Songs in Jamaican Reggae* (Middletown, CT: Wesleyan University Press, 2007); Tricia Rose, *Black Noise: Rap Music and Black Culture in Contemporary America* (Hanover, NH: Wesleyan University Press, 1994); and Matthew Bannister, *White Boys, White Noise: Masculinities and 1980s Indie Guitar Rock* (Aldershot: Ashgate, 2006).

    [13] See, for example, Mark Katz, *Capturing Sound: How Technology Has Changed Music* (Berkeley: University of California Press, 2004), 156; Timothy D. Taylor, *Strange Sounds: Music, Technology and Culture* (New York and London: Routledge, 2001); René Lysloff and Leslie Gay, eds., *Music and Technoculture* (Middletown, CT: Wesleyan University Press, 2003).

of disingenuous decoding.[14] For Ricoeur, appropriation is unavoidably present in all communicative acts. The upshot is that reading from any theoretical position can never be exhaustive or definitive in a final sense; it can only present an argument whose authority rests in the final evaluation upon the strength and density of the evidence called upon in its defense. The very density of my readings is in this respect represents a further safeguard against theoretical reductionism.

The concept of surrealism brings into sight a central proposition of this book: namely, that the cluster of ideas that define the terrain of the surreal provide a productive framework for inquiry into a significant (under)current within the broader (main)stream of audiovisual practices on either side of the third millennial turn. The materials of this study cannot be classified as belonging to a homogenous artistic movement or "scene," in the same sense as might be said of works by the historical surrealists. The performances and works (I should stress at this point that I view "works" to be nothing more than encapsulated performances) included in this study were produced by a collection of artists and cultural producers bonded only by a loosely comparable aesthetic outlook that surfaced in similar cultural conditions (those of the late modern or postmodern industrialized, and in a limited sense "postindustrial," contemporary world). In some cases, an influence from surrealism is directly indicated and almost unavoidable. Mostly it is not. Regardless, the cultural artifacts discussed collectively represent a recognizable neosurrealist *esprit* that takes different shapes in different contexts. This corpus of work suggests a dialectical relationship with the cultural mainstream that sets it apart from the more direct oppositional positioning of those who purport to continue the legacy of the historical avant-garde (including surrealism). An independent (or indie) frame of mind characterizes the approaches in these works and performances, which in turn implies critical agency and an auteurist attitude that is reflected also in reception. Outright opposition or shock tactics are not typical to the modes of expression discussed here, although readers drawn to significant details might detect more subtle forms of resistance in the gap between encoding and decoding.

Academic Criticism and Phenomenological Awareness

This book addresses a broad interdisciplinary readership. The academic reader is always my principal addressee, although I aim to make this book accessible to the

---

[14] See Paul Ricoeur, "Appropriation," in *Hermeneutics and the Human Sciences*, trans. John B. Thompson (Cambridge: Cambridge University Press, 1981 [1972]), 182–93. On discrepancies between intentionality and attributions of cultural meaning, see also Stuart Hall, "Encoding/decoding," in Centre for Contemporary Cultural Studies, ed., *Culture, Media, Language: Working Papers in Cultural Studies, 1972–79* (London: Hutchinson, 1980 [1973]), 128–38.

general educated reader—particularly a reader with some background in aesthetics (through artist activities, for example) who possesses a college or university level of education. My background is in music research and the discussions presented undoubtedly benefit from disciplinary training in the field of musicology. The premium I place on discipline-specific skills is relatively low, however. Instead, my deployment of academic criticism as the primary research method of this study allows for significant mobility across disciplinary boundaries. This might be considered prerequisite in an approach to the audiovisual that has anything of note to say about matters of aesthetics and cultural meaning. Much of my research will draw liberally on research from the neighboring fields of art criticism, film criticism and cultural criticism. Without the perspective the writing in these fields brings to the subject, the interpretative work undertaken here would be noticeably impoverished.

What, then, do I mean by academic criticism? Scholars of all stripes working under the banner of criticism take an interest in the cultural and material conditions in which the production of artworks happens, how they are experienced, what meanings they afford, and what uses audiences make of them. Insofar as this is a musicological study, it is one of many responses to Joseph Kerman's call in the 1980s for the foundation of a new paradigm of musicological research geared more toward criticism than traditional historical and analytical methods.[15] The type of academic criticism Kerman espoused implies a mode of writing about music that does not hesitate to relate musical sounds to surrounding discursive formations. Such writing shares a fundamental expository function with journalistic criticism, but it responds to different reader expectations concerning the requirement of acknowledging sources and the evidentiary bases of academic inquiry. In addition, a level of thoroughness is expected in academic writing that ordinarily (but not invariably) surpasses that found in journalistic writing. Criticism implies a methodological outlook more than it does a theoretical disposition, although the extent to which it overlaps with the concept of "cultural criticism" brings a different set of assumptions to bear on the subject (to which I return later). In general, it might be said that critical methods require the ability to write from experience, to apply knowledge of cultural codes to primary research materials, and to extrapolate from theory when undertaking interpretations. Finally, critical writing in the hermeneutical sense requires the writer to reflect on taken-for-granted assumptions and to interrogate them when necessary (often through applications of critical theory; this is where critical theory and criticism overlap most significantly).

---

[15] See Joseph Kerman, *Musicology* (Fontana, London, 1985), 17. (British title; published in the United States as *Contemplating Music: Challenges to Musicology*.)

Criticism as a method can be parsed into a number of interrelated activities, including description (or elucidation), analysis, interpretation and evaluation.[16] Research in the 1990s in cultural studies placed a strong emphasis on interpretation and hermeneutical methods. Concurrent with the turn of the third millennium, researchers have taken a noticeable turn toward matters of experience and performance, as indicated by terms such as the performative turn, the phenomeno-logical turn, and the affective turn. This has brought with it a heightened interest in the first of the above categories, *description*, which has traditionally occupied a prominent position in writing on phenomenology.[17] Here I will combine the inter-pretative direction of critical writing with an appreciation of ontology and perfor-mative detail that comes through closer attention to how performances are experienced. My intention in drawing on phenomenological perspectives is not to steer my work toward a naïve approach to phenomenological inquiry; in other words, one that would use Husserlian "reduction" as a pretext for the dismissal of all discursive understanding. In music research, spanning several decades, steps have been taken to combine the intuitive and myth-busting properties of phenomeno-logical inquiry with a more eclectic palette of methods that bring intuitive readings into dialogue with prior knowledge of musical semantics and cultural context. Lawrence Ferrara's writing provides a useful point of reference in this regard. Some years before Rose Rosengard Subutnik offered parallel viewpoints on pieces of music by alternating between deconstructive and more traditional analytical read-ings, Ferrara attempted something similar by furnishing not one but several read-ings, or reflections, on a piece of music, Edgard Varèse's *Poem électronique,* in one of the earliest detailed applications of phenomenology in musicological inquiry.[18] In these reflections, he allows an initial intuitive understanding of the music to inform subsequent readings in which musical syntax, semantics and cultural context are given closer attention.[19] Even while he champions phenomenology, Ferrara warns against "solipsistic subjectivism," which can be avoided by the discerning use of hermeneutical procedures alongside the "sheer sound-in-time dimension" of

---

[16] Bordwell employs these categories in his discussion of academic film criticism. See David Bordwell, "In Critical Condition," *David Bordwell's Website on Cinema,* May 14, 2008, http://www.davidbordwell.net/blog/?p=2315, retrieved October 19, 2010. Similar ideas about criticism are found across studies of the arts.

[17] Merleau-Ponty argues, for example, that phenomenology implies "description, not explanation or anal-ysis." Maurice Merleau-Ponty, *Phenomenology of Perception* (London and New York: Routledge, 2002), x. For an overview of the concept of description in phenomenology, see Simon Glendinning, *In the Name of Phenomenology* (Abingdon, Oxon: Routledge, 2007), 16–17.

[18] Rose Rosengard Subotnik, *Deconstructive Variations: Music and Reason in Western Society* (Minneapolis: University of Minnesota Press, 1996).

[19] Lawrence Ferrara, "Phenomenological Analysis as a Tool for Musical Analysis," *Musical Quarterly* 70 (1984): 355–73.

musical sounds.[20] For Ferrara and Elizabeth Behnke, recurring themes in the phenomenology of music include

> an abiding commitment to addressing the experienced musical sound itself… a persistent focus on music as a temporal formation… [attention to] historical situatedness and interpretation; some emphasis on bodily, kinaesthetic, and intersubjective/communal dimensions of music making; and an emerging concern for music in the context of its world.[21]

Such a description closely matches the aims of the present study. Phenomenology in this view does not imply "desituating" musical performance from its textual encoded actuality or its cultural context. The phenomenological approach does involve some degree of "bracketing" as an exploratory method, but only, ultimately, to facilitate bringing the experience of sound and corresponding visual images into dialogue with underlying historical assumptions.[22] This bridging function could in fact be thought of as the tacit agenda of certain branches of phenomenological inquiry.

In this view, the idea of musical sound removed from its attendant performative (or emergent) and other crossmodal sensory dimensions holds little promise for research purporting to address audiovisuality. The idea of "resisting the visual" has long been a call to arms in certain enclaves of phenomenological study, and this attitude has been revisited to some extent in soundscape research and writing on the cultural history of sound.[23] In chapter 7, I will touch on what is at stake in setting up music in this way as discrete from the other senses. Bracketing of various kinds can be useful as an analytical tool in audiovisual analysis, but it has little to do with the realities of *audiovisual* experience, which unavoidably implies experiences that traverse modalities. One might go so far as to say that the term audiovisual is inadequate for many experiences conveyed in the media to which it is conventionally applied. A more accurate designation might include also olfactory, gustatory and somatosensory experiences. The obligatory box of popcorn at the cinema represents just the tip of the iceberg. Once sensory memory is taken into consideration, the plot thickens considerably.

Phenomenology in the present study is closely bound up with the notion of close reading. So as not to confuse close reading with the *closed readings* of autonomous texts espoused by New Critics in literary criticism, let me be clear that I am referring

---

[20] See Lawrence Ferrara and Elizabeth Behnke, "Music," in Elizabeth Behnke, David Carr et al., eds., *Encyclopedia of Phenomenology* (Dordrecht and Boston: Kluwer Academic Publishers, 1997), 467–73, 470.

[21] Ibid., 471.

[22] Ibid., 472.

[23] Ibid., 469; for more on this subject, see also Jonathan Sterne, *The Audible Past: Cultural Origins of Sound Production* (Durham, NC: Duke University Press, 2003), 342–45.

to something resembling what Clifford Geertz's calls "thick description," which is intended to "inscribe social discourse" through the very action of writing it down.[24] This is not equivalent to the initial act of enunciation—not a direct translation of the perceived performative actions—but an approximation of their meaning that might be thought of as a kind of phenomenological representation.[25] In this respect, I align my work with cultural musicologists like Lawrence Kramer and Gary Tomlinson, whose writing invokes an anthropological attitude that reflects a determination to interpret musical activities as cultural practices.[26]

The presence of a chapter on Geertz's thick description in the edited collection *The Cultural Study of Music* (2003) hints at the importance this concept is garnering in recent musicological thinking.[27] A second chapter in the same collection approaches the concept of description in a different but nevertheless commensurate sense; one that is informed both by phenomenological and ethnographical views. Namely, Lawrence Kramer uses the term "constructive description" to address how musical meaning is reconstituted in the act of interpretative writing.[28] Striving to convey the truth of musical experience, Kramer's vivid descriptions might be said to articulate cultural experiences to the extent that language itself is saturated with cultural assumptions.[29] Writers undertaking constructive descriptions should be cognizant of this encoding function and the distance that exists between firsthand experiences and recounting those experiences in writing. By minding the gap between expression and re-expression, constructive descriptions have the power to capture something of the qualitative richness of musical experiences while nesting them within a discourse that inscribes its own historicity.[30] The methodological framework employed in the present study falls somewhere between thick description in the Geetzian sense and Kramer's idea of constructive description. The former seeks to convey the performed realities of a culture; the latter does much the same thing while exposing how subjectivity has been culturally encoded.

---

[24] Clifford Geertz, *The Interpretation of Cultures: Selected Essays by Clifford Geertz* (New York: Basic Books, 1973), 19.

[25] Ibid.

[26] These writers have been around for some time, but I find their contributions to the recent edited collection *The Cultural Study of Music* to be especially valuable in terms of current directions in musicological research. Martin Clayton, Trevor Herbert and Richard Middleton, eds., *The Cultural Study of Music: A Critical Introduction* (New York and London: Routledge, 2003). Close reading has been advocated by several other musicologists, including Lori Burns, *Disruptive Divas: Feminism, Identity and Popular Music* (New York: Routledge, 2002), 31–51; and Stan Hawkins, "Musicological Quagmires in Popular Music: Seeds of Detailed Conflict," *Popular Musicology Online* 1 (2001), http://www.popular-musicology-online.com/, retrieved October, 26, 2010.

[27] Jeff Todd Titon, "Textual Analysis or Thick Description?" in *The Cultural Study of Music*, 171–80.

[28] Lawrence Kramer, "Music, Hermeneutics, and History," in *The Cultural Study of Music*, 124–35.

[29] Ibid., 128–29.

[30] Ibid., 129.

Description of the type described requires the mapping of experiences across a terrain that is always intersubjective. The writer's individual experiences are generalized to the extent that evidence is forthcoming to support such claims, which implies the deployment of inductive reasoning.[31] A tendency to argue from the particular to the general is the greatest strength of phenomenological approaches when compared to the theory driven approaches that have dominated critical theory.[32] Phenomenology in this understanding requires the utilization of what Eve Kosofsky Sedgwick (drawing on the writing of Silvan Tomkins) calls "weak theory." In weak theoretical alignments, affective response is viewed as being paramount and much stock is given to local, transitory and conditional modes of structuring experience. Weak theory can be contrasted with "strong theory," which has long influenced writing in sociology and cultural criticism due to its amenity to generalizations—the flip side of which is nevertheless a tendency toward monolithic and tautological formulations. Weak theory in this sense becomes an ameliorative descriptor, the inference of "weakness" belying the strength such a mode of address wields to contour itself around the experiences of those whose consciousness it tracks.[33] For the present purposes, it is significant that Sedgwick considers "imaginative close reading" to be a defining feature of the weak theoretical approach (a near synonym of Kramer's "constructive description"), but at the same time she hastens to add that weak and strong theory have always "interdigitated" in scholarly work.[34] In any convincing or plausible critical approach these modalities might be thought of as mutually implicated.

The aim when doing theoretically "weak" thick descriptions is not to describe every single event in painstaking detail for the sake of pedantic thoroughness (in something resembling Philip Tagg's impressive but in retrospect overdetermined analysis of fifty seconds of title music from the television series *Kojak*). Rather, the

---

[31] Juha Torvinen, "Fenomenologinen tutkimus: lähtökohtia kriittiseen keskusteluun," *Musiikki* 1 (2008): 3–17, 11.

[32] To the extent that popular music studies has long neglected musicological and ethnographic evidence and relied upon sociological theories as a means of arguing from the general to the particular, it might be said to contradict the phenomenological impulse, which demands inductive reasoning. For a staunch defense of theory-driven sociological popular music studies that is overly critical of textual and phenomenological approaches to musical interpretation, see John Shepherd and Peter Wicke, *Music and Cultural Theory* (Cambridge: Polity Press, 1997). Writing in popular musicology that pays adequate attention to musical performance and experience has to some extent resisted the dominant theory-driven approaches of popular music studies. See the introduction and many of the chapters in Derek Scott, ed., *The Ashgate Research Companion to Popular Musicology* (Farnham: Ashgate, 2009).

[33] Eve Kosofsky Sedgwick, *Touching Feeling: Affect, Pedagogy, Performativity* (Durham, NC: Duke University Press, 2003), 133 and 145; Eve Kosofsky Sedgwick and Adam Frank, eds., *Shame and its Sisters: A Silvan Tomkins Reader* (Durham, NC: Duke University Press, 1995), 165–72. Raymond Williams's concept of "practical consciousness" refers to something similar. See Raymond Williams, *Marxism and Literature* (Oxford: Oxford University Press, 1977), 35–42. See also Lawrence Kramer, *Music as Cultural Practice, 1800–1900* (Berkeley: University of California Press, 1990), 14.

[34] Sedgwick, *Touching Feeling*, 145.

woods should always be differentiated from the trees; choices made about the inclusion of "significant details" should be weighed against considerations concerning their import as carriers of experiential substance or meaning. Close reading offers an elegant way to fish for telling details in the course of an elucidatory exposition, with a view to disclosing "meanings" that will bring the cultural dimensions of music into sight.[35] A special case of musical details conditioning the terms of interpretations is addressed in Lawrence Kramer's pathbreaking study of musical hermeneutics, *Music as Cultural Practice*, where he notes how interpretation "takes flight from breaking points, which usually means from points of under- or overdetermination: on the one hand, a gap, a lack, a missing connection; on the other, a surplus of pattern, an extra repetition, an excessive connection."[36] Without thinking consciously about Kramer's formulation, I have found this to be true on countless occasions. Accordingly, I have learned from experience to play close attention to this deconstructive function (for that is what it is) whenever it surfaces in the course of a critical reading. Cases in point in the present study are the role that silence plays in so-called acoustic music (chapter 7) and dissynchronization in Glass's film opera, *La Belle et la Bête* (chapter 5). The transitions between narrative film form and musical numbers in Tsai Ming-Liang's *The Wayward Cloud* (chapter 4) can be understood as similar points of interpolation. The nub of the matter is that meaningful transactions can often be located on the edges of discourse, where things appear to break down rather than where everything is running smoothly. A case could be made, and is by the art critic Rosalind Krauss in reference to the visual arts, that such moments of rupture take on a special significance in surrealist discourses.[37] In the discussion of audiovisual neosurrealism that follows, I address the role of sound in precipitating this sense of "being on (the) edge." Such an awareness of inside-outside relations reflects back on the very nature of the discourse itself, allowing it to be seen from a different and expository angle.

Simon Glendinning argues that the emphasis on interruption in Jacques Derrida's ideas about deconstruction serves a function that is closely, if dialectically, related to the phenomenological project.[38] I will return to this matter, but for now let it suffice

[35] In recognizing the salience of detail in producing expressive meanings in music, my argumentation follows that of McClary and Walser. Susan McClary and Robert Walser "Start Making Sense! Musicology Wrestles with Rock," in Simon Frith and Andrew Goodwin, eds., *On Record: Rock, Pop, and the Written Word* (London and New York: Routledge, 1990), 267–92, 279–80. See also Hawkins, "Musicological Quagmires in Popular Music." The idea of scripts rather than texts as underlying the audience encounter with music comes from Nicholas Cook, "Music as Performance," in Martin Clayton, Trevor Herbert and Richard Middleton, eds., *The Cultural Study of Music: A Critical Introduction* (New York and London: Routledge, 2003), 304–214.

[36] Kramer, *Music as Cultural Practice*, 12.

[37] Rosalind Krauss, *The Originality of the Avant-Garde and Other Modernist Myths* (Cambridge, MA: MIT Press, 1985), 110.

[38] Glendinning, *In the Name of Phenomenology*, 5, 178–211.

to state that I believe this to be the case with respect to many of the materials discussed in the present study. Derrida's attention to the concept of performativity arguably harbors a similar proclivity, particularly his notion of iterability, which provided the conceptual cornerstone to the writings of Judith Butler and others on the subject (discussed in chapter 4). Performance and performativity, although they are discrete concepts, both in different ways presuppose the "presentness" of experiences. These concepts will be explored in greater detail in the following section.

From Performance to Performativity

Recent writing in musicology has paid greater heed to matters of performance than was the case in much of the twentieth century research. With the turn toward cultural or critical musicology has come a new willingness to address meanings that are bound up with performance and cultural context. Attention to audiovisuality is inseparable from this orientation, since musical performances are unavoidably also visual performances. Anthropological awareness (often via the mediating hand of ethnomusicology) has also impinged on cultural approaches to music, for thick descriptions as theorized by Geertz are implicitly multimodal. The direction of ethnomusicology which studies "music in culture" or "music as culture," encompassing the work of Alan Merriam, John Blacking, Marcia Herndon and others, has long argued for an understanding of musical meaning as arising directly out of the cultural and material conditions of performances. In the introduction to the textbook *Worlds of Music*, Mark Slobin and Jeff Todd Titon express this attitude visually, in the form of a diagram comprising concentric circles in which music/affect is placed at the center and the category of performers/performance occupies the next level.[39] A third ring is allocated to communities/audiences, a fourth to historical space and time where all of the above categories are embedded. Slobin and Titon thus offer a phenomenological perspective on musical performances, as can be seen from the alignment of musical sound with affect and the category of performance with performers. In other words, the central analytical categories of the model are viewed as being connected to emotional and embodied responses.[40]

More recently, ethnomusicologists have studied those forms of mediated performance distinct to the digital world. This is seen in recent ethnomusicological collections and monographs in which the concept of performance is extended to the electronic domain and traditional ideas of fieldwork are revised to encompass every

---

[39]   Mark Slobin and Jeff Todd Titon, "The Music-Culture as a World of Music," in Jeff Todd Titon et al., ed., *Worlds of Music: An Introduction to the Music of the World's Peoples*, 2nd ed., (New York: Shirmer Books, 1992), 1–15, 3–4.

[40]   Ibid.

facet of modern life, from reading music-technology periodicals to perusing YouTube and MySpace sites via computer.[41] The latter become performances in an extended sense, to the extent that they are concerned with the material situations in which artistic production and its correlative cultural performances reach audiences. The research conducted here overlaps with ethnomusicological methods to the extent that it incorporates some of the approaches just delineated. (More traditional ethnographic methods supplement the primary critical method of this study, insofar as my approach involves qualitative methods such as interviewing and the participant-observation ethnography of attending performances and even performing music myself.)

An anthropological emphasis on performance has been felt also in the cross-disciplinary field of performance studies. Richard Schechner's *Performance Theory* set an inclusive agenda for studies of this type, when he described performance analysis as tracking "horizontal relationships among related forms."[42] More recently this approach has been followed up in studies such as Peggy Phelan's *Unmarked: The Politics of Performance*, where this theorist makes a case for a mimetic approach to the politics of performance as necessarily unfolding in shared space and time.[43] Against the grain of this understanding, Philip Auslander argued for a revised notion of performance and performance studies in which the unavoidably mediated nature of contemporary experience is highlighted.[44] More recently, Auslander extended this line of research by showing how the staged personae of performers became an issue in the performances of the self that were a part of the British glam rock movement in the 1970s.[45]

Nicholas Cook has written of the performative turn in musicology in recent publications, where he shows how meaning is negotiated across time in performances of canonical works. Importantly, Cook argues for a revised notion of classical music in which musical notation is defined as a "script" more than a fixed "text."[46] Cook

---

[41] For perspectives on new ethnomusicological methods addressing contemporary digital culture, see Taylor, *Strange Sounds*; Lysloff and Gay, eds., *Music and Technoculture*; and Gregory Barz and Timothy Cooley, eds., *Shadows in the Field: New Perspectives for Fieldwork in Ethnomusicology* (Oxford and New York: Oxford University Press, 2008).

[42] Richard Schechner, *Performance Theory* (New York and London: Routledge, 1988), 28.

[43] Peggy Phelan, *Unmarked: The Politics of Performance* (London and New York: Routledge, 1993).

[44] Auslander, *Liveness*.

[45] Philip Auslander, *Performing Glamrock: Gender and Theatricality in Popular Music* (Ann Arbor: University of Michigan Press, 2006).

[46] See Nicholas Cook, "Analysing Performance and Performing Analysis," in Nicholas Cook and Mark Everist, eds., *Rethinking Music* (Oxford and New York: Oxford University Press, 1999), 239–61; Nicholas Cook, "Music as Performance," in Clayton, Herbert and Middleton, eds., *The Cultural Study of Music*, 204–14. See also the collected volume, John Rink, ed., *The Practice of Performance: Studies in Musical Interpretation* (Cambridge: Cambridge University Press, 1995). It should be stressed that much of this research concentrates on the expressive choices made by performers more than reflecting upon the act of performance as experienced by audiences. The field of performance studies in musicology has traditionally concentrated on faithful adherence to the intentions of revered composers.

gives voice to an emerging tendency in musicological writing in which the authority of the written score is challenged through the recognition of how interpretations vary in concord with implicit and performed knowledge. Richard Leppert was one of the first scholars to express such concerns in his book, *The Sight of Sound,* where he noted how the "visual-performative" aspects of music should be as central in discussions of cultural meaning as they are in reference to aesthetic forms such as dance or theater.[47] Research on "everyday life" is the measure of how far this line of reasoning can be taken, through the attention this line of research devotes to discrepancies between compositional intention and actual uses of music in "the real world." Studies on soundscape, following the prescriptions of the Canadian composer Murray Shafer, offer another example of the outermost limits of a kind of applied performance analysis. A connection exists, moreover, between the aesthetics of surrealism and everyday life that I will return to in later chapters. This connection comes primarily through the contingencies of performance and the juxtapositions they occasion between the sonic realities encoded in recorded musical performances (concerning temporal and spatial situation, among other things) and those that exist in the external world. An element of surrealism comes into play when these elements come into conflict with one another, as is evidenced in instances of so-called elevator music and uses of portable stereos to create inner (cinematic) worlds that are formally incongruous with surround lived realities. In both cases the incongruities that arise can occasion transformed perceptions of "the real world."[48] These everyday performances capture something essential about surrealist aesthetics.

Nowhere is "the performative turn" more in evidence than in research on audiovisuality. This line of research more than any other has brought an appreciation to music studies of how visual context moderates and modulates auditory meanings. The pathbreaking research in this area of study is that of scholars with a dual background in musicology and film studies, including Claudia Gorbman, Kathryn Kalinak and Caryl Flinn.[49] The writing of Kalinak and Flinn is particularly important to the orientation of this study for the attention both authors give to gender

[47] See Richard Leppert, *The Sight of Sound: Music, Representation, and the History of the Body* (Berkeley: University of California Press, 1993), xxi.

[48] On portable music players, see Michael Bull, *Sounding out the City: Personal Stereos and the Management of Everyday Life* (Oxford: Berg, 2000), 85–96. On the surrealism of canned music, see Joseph Lanza, *Elevator Music: A Surreal History of Muzak, Easy-Listening, and Other Moodsong* (New York: Picador, 1995). See also Tia DeNora, *Music in Everyday Life* (Cambridge: Cambridge University Press, 2000); and Anahid Kassabian, "Ubiquitous Listening and Networked Subjectivity," *Echo* 3/2 (Fall 2001), online journal: www.echo.ucla.edu, retrieved 26 July, 2010.

[49] Caryl Flinn, *Strains of Utopia: Gender, Nostalgia, and Hollywood Film Music* (Princeton, NJ: Princeton University Press, 1992); Kathryn Kalinak, *Settling the Score: Music and the Classical Hollywood Film* (Madison: The University of Wisconsin Press, 1992).

representation in film music.[50] This is especially relevant to the discussions of camp aesthetics and gender representation in relation to metamusicals (chapter 4). In the Anglophone world, Claudia Gorbman undoubtedly set the gold standard for research on the relationship between cinematic images and musical sounds in an approach indebted to the writing of the French electronic composer and film critic Michel Chion (whose output she has since translated extensively). The relevance of Gorbman's writing to this study extends beyond theoretical models to the films that are the subject matter of her research. This is evident in her explanations of how the audiovisual implies processes of mutual implication, the most obvious example being the surrealists' delight in unorthodox combinations.[51] Her choice of *King Kong* and *Zéro de Conduite* as case studies evidences a surrealist strain in cinematic tradition that pays little heed to distinctions between experimental and mainstream forms. Gorbman's more recent work on films like Kubrick's *Eyes Wide Shut* (1999), Tsai Ming-Liang's *Dong* (*The Hole*, 1998) and Zhang Ke Jia's *Shijie* (*The World*, 2004) has extended this line of research, the surreal in film serving as a benchmark for how to push the conventions of film to their limits, with implications that reflect back on theories about the audiovisual.[52]

The reference to the audiovisual in the title of this book refers above all to Chion's understanding of the term as a mode of experience that encompasses both sound and vision. Chion's idea of "synchresis" has important implications when studying surrealist aesthetics. A neologism made up of the words synchronism and synthesis, the concept illuminates how sounds become naturalized in film through audiovisual synchronization. Synchresis is "the spontaneous and irresistible weld produced between a particular auditory phenomenon and visual phenomenon when they occur at the same time."[53] Related to this assertion is the more general observation that images in mixed-media contexts "only take on consistency and materiality through sound."[54] Statements such as these offer some important premises for the analyses conducted in this book. Two conclusions follow from these premises: First, intermodal synchronization is essential to our understanding of audiovisual performances. Consequently, where synchronization fails or diverges from the norm, something interesting is likely to happen. Second, enduring assumptions about the

[50]   For a more recent appraisal of gender in film, see Heather Laing, *The Gendered Score: Music in 1940s Melodrama and the Woman's Film* (Aldershot: Ashgate, 2007).

[51]   Gorbman, *Unheard Melodies*, 15.

[52]   See Claudia Gorbman, "Auteur Music," in Daniel Goldmark, Lawrence Kramer, and Richard Leppert, eds., *Beyond the Soundtrack: Representing Music in Cinema* (Berkeley: University of California Press, 2007), 149–62; and "Ears Wide Open: Kubrick's Music," in Phil Powrie and Robynn Stilwell, eds., *Changing Tunes: The Use of Pre-Existing Music in Film* (Aldershot: Ashgate, 2006), 3–18.

[53]   Michel Chion, *Audio-Vision: Sound on Screen*, trans. Claudia Gorbman (New York: Columbia University Press, 1994), 63.

[54]   Ibid., 5.

transcendental nature of music are apparently reinforced by the visual absence of sound sources in nondiegetic music. On a more fundamental level, however, they are also destabilized: sound more than moving images draws the audio-viewer into an embodied understanding of audiovisual experience. Sounds give substance and multidimensional depth to two-dimensional screen images. They do this through the bond that is effected in processes of audiovisual synchronization, in which sound more than moving images is propelled forth more tangibly into the audience's world.[55]

This has implications for theorizations about the phenomenology of audiovisuality, as distinct from the image-centered theorizations that have dominated film studies and philosophical writing about postmodernism. For Chion, synchretic experience does not imply a naturalistic understanding of the real world. Rather synchronization produces audiovisual configurations that have no place in the world beyond cinematic experiences. In a tangible sense these configurations are surreal, or in some cases hyperreal (a concept that is closely related to the surreal, if not entirely overlapping; implying heightened experience rather than heightened *and* dislocated experience). The conventional nature of such associations is further addressed in Chion's use of the term "rendering." In this view, the audiovisual totality of film is understood to be a rendering of the external physical world, a representation, rather than its unmediated reflection.[56] From this it follows that film (and other audiovisual expression) is always first and foremost a singular and unique performance, even when it is a repetition or a transformation of things that existed prior to its coming into being. Audiovisual performances are consequently something we can recognize as having been put together in a certain way and therefore can imagine being assembled differently.

Implicit, as well, in Chion's position is the assumption of experiential unity in the soundtrack, which is addressed in his use of the term "superfield." This perspective would seem to be increasingly indisputable in the digital age when quieter sounds can be perceived more readily. Terms like *mise-en-bande* and "the musicalization of the soundtrack" in recent research highlight the extent to which interaction between the various components of the soundtrack is receiving a greater share of attention in the methods of audiovisual analyses.[57] As the soundtrack becomes more overtly aestheticized, sound effects and dialogue are more closely integrated with

---

[55] See also See Mary Anne Doane, "The Voice in Cinema: The Articulation of Body and Space," in Elisabeth Weis and John Belton, eds., *Film Sound: Theory and Practice* (New York: Columbia University Press, 1985), 162–76, 166.

[56] Ibid., 107–14.

[57] See Kevin Donnelly, *The Spectre of Sound: Music in Film and Television* (London: BFI, 2005); Rick Altman, McGraw Jones and Sonia Tatroe, "Inventing the Cinema Soundtrack: Hollywood's Multiplane Sound System," in James Buhler, Caryl Flinn and David Neumeyer, eds., *Music and Cinema* (Hanover, NH: Wesleyan University Press, 2000), 339–59; Chion, *Audio-Vision*, 152–54.

soundtrack music, and narrative feature films resemble film musicals in their modus operandi (as I contend in chapters 3 and 4): it could be said that the entire audiovisual field is undergoing a geological shift in a surreal direction.

Chion was the first theorist to use the term "acousmatic" (from the Greek *akousmatikoi*) in writing on the audiovisual. The term designates sounds that have no visible originating cause and is associated with the founder of *musique concrète* Pierre Schaeffer. Both offscreen diegetic sounds and nondiegetic sounds are acousmatic.[58] Chion aligns the concept of the acousmatic with the neologism *acousmêtre* (a compound of spectre and acousmatic). "Invisible sounds" in this category carry a specific affective charge, attracting to themselves connotations of otherworldliness and godly omnipotence.[59] Other writers have similarly aligned acousmatic sounds with an irrational function (because the sounds have no rational justification in the visual sphere), or have designated sounds "fantastical" when they assume an ambiguous function between the diegetic and the nondiegetic because they break the rules governing the behavior of sounds in the empirical world, occupying an imaginary or hypothetical position in relation to the fictional world of the story.[60] Gorbman's work is once again prescient in this respect. Her modeling of scoring practices in early Hollywood films highlights three senses in which classical underscoring can convey a sense of elevated emotionalism and implied otherness. Associated with the irrational, the representation of women, and epic function, nondiegetic music conveys experiences intentionally set apart from everyday reality. "Unseen" nondiegetic music therefore could be aligned with an unconscious or sublimated function that has a certain affinity with surrealist thinking. To the extent that it is "unheard" or naturalized, however, I would argue that classical film scoring does not challenge our ideas about the nature of reality in the same way as surrealist discourse. Instead, denaturalization through dislocation and fragmentation plays an important part in surrealist aesthetics; as does a sense of audiovisual flow that transcends the diegetic-nondiegetic divide, being closer to what Rick Altman calls the "supradiegetic."

In addition to the writing of Chion and Gorbman, Annette Davison's book on auteur films, *Hollywood Theory, Non-Hollywood Practice: Cinema Soundtracks in the 1980s and 1990s*, sets an important precedent for the present study because of its contemporary focus and how it positions "indie" directors in a dialectical relation-

---

[58]   Chion, *Audio-Vision*, 72.

[59]   Chion, *Audio-Vision*, 76–78; Michel Chion, *The Voice in Cinema*, trans. Claudia Gorbman (New York: Columbia University Press, 1999), 62.

[60]   See Donnelly, *The Spectre of Sound*, 23; on the irrational function of Bernard Herrmann's music in Hitchcock's films, see also Royal Brown, *Overtones and Undertones: Reading film music* (Berkeley: University California Press, 1994), 174; and Claudia Gorbman, *Unheard Melodies: Narrative Film Music* (Bloomington: Indiana University Press, 1987), 79–80. See also Robynn J. Stilwell, "The Fantastical Gap between Diegetic and Nondiegetic," in Daniel Goldmark, Lawrence Kramer and Richard Leppert, eds., *Beyond the Soundtrack: Representing Music in Cinema* (Berkeley: University of California Press, 2007), 184–202.

ship with the Hollywood mainstream.[61] Other significant work on audiovisuality includes writing on music videos by Carol Vernallis, Stan Hawkins, E. Ann Kaplan, and Andrew Goodwin. Various edited collections covering uses of popular music in film also stand out, as well as important studies on popular music and audiovisuality by scholars like Philip Tagg, Anahid Kassabian, Miguel Mera, Kay Dickinson and Robynn Stilwell.[62] Writing on musicals by the likes of Rick Altman, Richard Dyer, Caryl Flinn and Amy Herzog informs my work in chapter 4. Research on new media and audiovisuality in general is almost too copious and variegated to discuss in this context. This will be called upon when relevant to support specific arguments. Above all, my approach is defined by a determination to understand how experience is shaped with reference to sensory input that crosses modalities. This crossing of modalities most likely happens within an affective register. Indeed, it is the very affective valence of sounds combined with images that allows them to coalesce in configurations that defy understanding when considered discretely.[63]

Returning to the underlying theme of performance but moving in the direction of performativity, approaches in cultural studies broach several issues that seem in keeping with this emphasis. Stuart Hall's concept of articulation attends to the performative aspect of cultural expression: culture as expressed through articulated and rearticulated actions that reflect social contexts more than words. Mikhail Bakhtin's concern with tracing intersecting cultural discourses back to "utterances" similarly attends to the singular actuality of performative actions, albeit with an emphasis on strategies of citation in relation to the written word. In semiotics, C.S. Peirce was a forerunner in meticulously theorizing the symbolic aspects of human experience, but not without placing a strong emphasis on linguistic iconicity and phenomenological "firstness." It remains a matter of debate whether Derrida was so caught up in the effects of written language *on language,* and so distrustful of "the metaphysics of presence" as to be blind to phenomenal actuality. I would nevertheless side with Glendinning in maintaining that Derrida's ideas about performativity illustrate more convincingly than prior theorizations the empirical conditions that effect the separation of language and experience. Through the concept of

[61] Annette Davison, *Hollywood Theory, Non-Hollywood Practice: Cinema Soundtracks in the 1980s and 1990s* (Aldershot: Ashgate, 2004).

[62] Important collected editions include James Buhler, Caryl Flinn and David Neumeyer, eds., *Music and Cinema* (Hanover, NH: Wesleyan University Press, 2000); Kevin Donnelly, ed., *Film Music: Critical Approaches* (New York: Continuum, 2001); Ian Inglis, ed., *Popular Music and Film* (London: Wallflower Press), 2003; Phil Powrie and Robynn Stilwell, eds., *Changing Tunes: The Use of Pre-Existing Music in Film* (Aldershot: Ashgate, 2006); Pamela Robertson Wojcik and Arthur Knight, eds., *Soundtrack Available. Essays on Film and Popular Music* (Durham and London: Duke University Press, 2001); and Goldmark, Kramer and Leppert, eds., *Beyond the Soundtrack.*

[63] For a defense of the multiplicity of embodied and therefore also cross-modal musical experience, see Ruth Finnegan, "Music, Experience and the Anthropology of Emotion," in Clayton, Herbert and Middleton, eds., *The Cultural Study of Music,* 181–92.

iterability, Derrida above all acknowledges the singularity of experience at any given moment, with each manifestation of a repeated element implying a transformation that in turn signals performativity. Derrida's idea of "hauntology," which I will return to in later chapters, is essentially a theory of the performative that draws attention to how the residue of past actions, previous performances, impinges on how we relate to objects in the here and now, superimposing a reality that is imminent onto specters of a different reality that has passed.[64] Presence and absence become caught up in an exchange of values in which meaning can never be entirely separated from nascent experiences, but whose immanent presentations nevertheless leave a great deal untold. This duality has an undeniable surreal aspect that resonates with the writing of cultural theorists like Adorno and Benjamin about the aesthetics of surrealism. In a sense, Derrida theorizes a ground plan for living on the edge of reality; which brings his conception close to the idea of *sur*-reality.

The term performativity has met with its most enthusiastic response in research on gender identity and sexuality. The writing on gender performativity is particularly concerned with how entrenched structures of gendered socialization can be subverted through the agency of performative reenactments. Judith Butler's theorizations in this regard have been hugely influential, although she has been widely criticized for her apparent preoccupation with language and relative neglect of corporeality.[65] Others feminist thinkers, like Judith Halberstam and Eve Kosofsky Sedgwick, have theorized performativity in a manner that is more finely attuned to questions of physical embodiment, human agency and affective pleasure. In this respect, their approaches to performativity are of considerable value to the present study, which is concerned not only with gender performativity in the Butlerian sense, but the full spectrum of performed social activity in embodied and human contexts.[66] The theoretical rubric of performativity offers one convincing path toward understanding the dynamic between the here and now aspects of the materials discussed in this study and an aspect of citational practice that goes to the very heart of definitions of the surreal and, in this context, the neosurreal.

Between Cultural Criticism and Affect

So far I have postponed entanglement in the question, what does criticism (in the sense of cultural criticism) entail in the context of the present study? The reason

---

[64]   See Jacques Derrida, *Specters of Marx*, trans. Bernd Magnus (New York and London: Routledge, 1994), 10–15.

[65]   Judith Butler, *Gender Trouble* (London and New York: Routledge 1990), 43–44.

[66]   Eve Kosofsky Sedgwick, *Touching Feeling: Affect, Pedagogy, Performativity* (Durham, NC: Duke University Press, 2003). On gender performativity in popular music, see Stan Hawkins, *Settling the Pop Score: Pop Texts and Identity Politics* (Aldershot: Ashgate, 2002); and Auslander, *Performing Glamrock.*

for this has been my concern to address how academic criticism *as a method* can be useful as a means of tracking culturally encoded experiences. Criticism, of course, has another meaning inseparable from the identity of cultural studies as an interdisciplinary field of study. Few in this field would contest that cultural studies as a research orientation owes much to early writing on the subject by the Frankfurt-school theorists Max Horkheimer, Theodor Adorno and Walter Benjamin. Horkheimer was the first to apply the term *criticism* to his orientation, in the essay "Traditional and Critical Theory" (1937), where he contrasted the position of the theoretically orientated (and critical) scholar with those who pay greater attention to empirical data (a standpoint he finds naïve and overly compliant). Adorno and Benjamin followed Horkheimer's lead in defining their approaches to cultural studies around this concept.[67] Criticism implies a lineage that extends back to the transcendental idealism of Kant (his *Critique of Pure Reason*). More imperatively for these writers, it is grounded in Marx's "critique of political economy." It is motivated, therefore, by a concept of social justice bound up with assumptions about economic equity based on everyone working for the common good. This framework is so complex as to defy categorization in this context. For the present, let it suffice to note that criticism in this view implies an action-based form of social critique that strives to unveil the capitalist world order's "false consciousness" by means of critical reflection and thereby to motivate change. The idea of criticism in this arrangement assumes a certain position of exteriority with respect to society.

To his credit, Adorno was well aware of the conceit of this positioning, which Horkheimer was the first to identify. Criticism in Adorno's view required an act of detachment into reflective (or philosophical) consciousness, which itself becomes symptomatic of the very processes of abstraction that are the primary object of his Marxist critique. To be a critic, Adorno wrote, is to play at being more cultured.[68] This external positioning did not help him overcome his own well-documented cultural prejudices. It does, however, reveal the complexity of, and some inherent contradictions in, his overview of cultural life, which comes to the fore in different ways in his essay on surrealism (discussed later and the second epigram of this chapter).

Indirectly related to this position of critical "outsiderness" is the attitude I identified above in anthropologically orientated cultural studies: the idea that there is

---

[67] A translation of Horkheimer's original definition of cultural criticism can be found in Max Horkheimer, *Critical Theory: Selected Essays,* trans, Matthew J. O'Connell (New York: Continuum, 1972). Benjamin's views on criticism can be found in the two essays, Walter Benjamin, "The Concept of Criticism in German Romanticism" and "The Theory of Criticism," both in *Walter Benjamin: Selected Writings, Vol. 1* (Cambridge: Harvard University Press, 1996), 116–200; 217–19.

[68] See Theodor Adorno, "Cultural Criticism in Society," in *Prisms* (Cambridge, MA: MIT Press, 1983), 19–34.

value in approaching your culture(s) in much the same way as you would approach the cultures of others, and the corresponding importance of some notion of thick description as a means of attributing meaning through critical consideration of how the various pieces of a cultural jigsaw puzzle interconnect. Implicit in the above is the idea of culture as a discursive entity—a connective web of culturally invested meanings and interactions. Such a view can provide profound insights into the mechanisms of human subjectivity and, in a more Foucauldian view of things, epistemological connections across discourses that harbor also regulative propensities. In this way, the historical situatedness of aesthetic actions is given prominence. Not unlike Foucault's "epistemes" (overarching structures of knowledge that provide the strictures within which discourses operate) are literary critic Raymond Williams's "structures of feeling," which connect the social with the affective in a way that seems particularly useful in discussions of aesthetics. Williams's term refers to discursively defined realities that are understood to resonate across material and affective planes.[69] The value of a discursive-critical view to the present study is to some extent proportional to the extent to which it is implicated in the cultural formations discussed. When it comes to the historical surrealists, such a relationship is most obviously indicated in Breton's troubled relationship with the Communist Party, but also in the more general desire of surrealist artists to shock mainstream (middle-class) sensibilities and thereby to effect change.

Things are less polemical in the cultural formations that are the primary subject of this book. Nevertheless, an aspect of resistance (to the mainstream) underlies the intentions and the performative actions of many of the producers whose works and performances will be discussed, including such figures as Richard Linklater, Sally Potter, Damon Albarn, and KT Tunstall. Independent cinema and "alternative music" understood as discursive constructions both imply an aspect of outsiderness in relation to mainstream formations that to some extent belies the actual socioeconomic conditions that inform the lived realities of production and consumption. The attitudes adopted by artists and other cultural producers in these spheres of activity are

---

[69] Williams, *Marxism and Literature*, 128–35; see also Fred Pfeil, "Postmodernism as a 'Structure of Feeling,'" Cary Nelson and Lawrence Grossberg, eds., *Marxism and the Interpretation of Culture* (Urbana: University of Illinois Press, 1988), 381–403; Susan McClary, *Conventional Wisdom: The Content of Musical Form* (Berkeley: University of California Press, 2000). The term was initially coined by Raymond Williams, who toyed with the idea of calling it "structures of experience," an option he rejected because it seemed to imply "past tense consciousness." Structures of feeling are those indistinct and not always fully formed means of structuring things that evidence a certain stylistic consistency which changes subtly across time. Williams refers specifically to "manners, dress, building, and other similar forms of social life." (Williams, *Marxism and Literature*, 31.) Structures of feeling are always affectively freighted and derive their effectiveness as social intervention from this very quality. Williams comments thus: "[w]e are talking about characteristic elements of impulse, restraint, and tone; specifically affective elements of consciousness and relationships: not feeling against thought, but thought as feeling and feeling as thought: practical consciousness of a present kind, in a living and interrelating continuity" (ibid., 32).

remarkably similar in certain cases to the critical stance of the modernist cultural theorist (the chapter on Gorillaz strongly supports this assertion). Accordingly, a tentative hypothesis might be extended about a resemblance in both intentionality and effect between the activities of the cultural critic and the imminent cultural critique that is produced in surrealist performances. Much the same could and has been said about Bertolt Brecht's epic theater; or, perhaps more fittingly given the agenda of the present study, Antonin Artaud's surrealist theater of cruelty. Both of these theatrical players wanted to transform society as much as "to entertain," although it has to be noted that the furrowed brow of modernism is not an expression all of the artists examined in these pages would be comfortable to adopt.

The adoption of position of default outsiderness and inherent suspicion does have its shortcomings, not least of which is a certain tautological strain of reasoning when it comes to interpreting performances. If the theories employed in academic discourse are given to us in preassembled form, as would appear to be the case in some of the theoretically driven cultural studies writing (Horkheimer strenuously defends this tautological attitude, considering it a virtue rather than a vice),[70] what are the chances of finding anything other than what the researcher is looking for? The advantages, once again, of something resembling what Sedgwick calls a weak theoretical positioning will be evident. Existing cultural theory will and should be administered in a study aiming to adopt a critical attitude, if nothing else for the historical sense of grounding it provides. Better perspective can be gained, however, by weighing the perspectives such theories bring against the more directly personal and experiential orientation that alignment with phenomenological induction and Sedgwick's "weak theory" have to offer. What I propose is a mode of critical distancing from critical distanciation theory. The descriptive activity of close reading itself in this approach is the primary means by which entrenched theoretical configurations and epistemological reductionism might be challenged. In others cases, however, a theory might be supported and reinforced by the constructive or imaginative readings the analyst undertakes. Whatever the outcome of a critical account, an automatic position of opposition is as unbefitting in phenomenological studies as it is in theoretically orientated writing. Perspective can be gained only by alternating between these two modalities.

This brings us to another "turn" registered in recent academic writing, which is arguably closely related to the others previously discussed. Designated "the affective turn" by some scholars, writing of this predisposition represents a shift toward greater attention to embodied and sensory responses to the world as experienced.[71]

---

[70] Horkheimer, *Critical Theory: Selected Essays.*

[71] See, for example, Patricia Ticineto Clough with Jean Halley, *The Affective Turn: Theorizing the Social* (Durham, NC: Duke University Press, 2007). See also Eve Kosofsky Sedgwick and Adam Frank, eds., *Shame and its Sisters: A Silvan Tomkins Reader* (Durham, NC: Duke University Press, 1995); Brian Massumi, *Parables for the Virtual: Movement, Affect, Sensation* (Durham, NC: Duke University Press, 2002).

Affectivity is discussed in some detail in various chapters; most notably, chapters 4 and 7. The idea of affective response as primary and ever-present underlies many of the claims of this study. If I have chosen in some readings to highlight the discursivity that envelops affective responses, it is to help the reader to situate them in the contexts in which they are experienced, as part of the totality of meaningful human actions and social interactions. The aim is therefore to combine and to move freely between a critical-discursive orientation and one that attends to corporeal experience, rather than seeing these two approaches as diametrically opposed.

When it comes to the ontological nature of audiovisual experience, it should be clear that in this view it makes little sense to approach the subject in a way that focuses on one discrete modality at a time. The current research on intermodal exchange in the field of psychology suggests a more complex understanding, in which experience is understood as being configured with reference to complementary cues apprehended in different senses.[72] The audiovisual is assumed to overspill the senses to which it is usually thought to belong. Moreover, to the extent that memory is implicated in sensory perception, a cue given in one modality or medium is likely to invoke a response in another. Sight invokes smells, sound invokes visions, writing invokes sounds, combinations of sound and image can invoke touch or hapticity. Such is the intermodal nature of the reality in which we live. It is a reality inhabited by the ghosts of neighboring senses. Present senses invoke those that are absent, and these in turn resonate with cultural memories. We are surrounded by banal examples of such sensory interdependency. We only have to see, hear *and feel* (and arguably also to taste and smell) the latest blockbuster movie at our local cinema multiplex to understand the logic behind crossmodal exchange firsthand. New media forms from gaming to VR often play with our expectations in this regard. On a more banal level, speech comprehension and the thought processes required to identify and locate objects in the world both rely heavily upon crossmodal interchange. Conversely, the absence of expected complementary cues or the presence of dissynchronization in multimodal contexts can be disorientating and affectively upsetting to those who encounter it unprepared, such as infants.[73] Such perceptions occupy a privileged position in neosurrealist audiovisual expression, however. Surrealist realignments and imaginative embellishments of the senses, I argue, reconfigure the audiovisual contract in similar ways, which may well open up new possibilities for previously unenvisaged experiences. Surrealism, if anything, is about reconfiguring our expectations about the nature of experience. It is about challenging comfortable familiarity with unexpected realignments and mediations.

---

[72] See Lawrence Marks, *The Unity of the Senses: Interrelations among the Modalities* (New York: Academic Press, 1988), 185. See also Charles Spence and Jon Driver, eds., *Crossmodal Space and Crossmodal Attention* (Oxford and New York: Oxford University Press, 2004).

[73] Spence and Driver, eds., *Crossmodal Space and Crossmodal Attention*, 2–3.

The organization of this book is intended to take the reader on a journey across the variegated terrain of neosurrealist expression, where each chapter reflects back on that which preceded it, and at the same time signals a line of thinking that will project forward onto subsequent writing.

Chapter 2 will set the main agenda of the book by addressing the relationship between current practices and those that surfaced under the aegis of historical surrealism, providing a road map that will inform subsequent readings of neosurrealist practices. A central part of this chapter is a comprehensive review of existing definitions of surrealism.

Chapter 3 continues by tracking how neosurrealist aesthetics has permeated audiovisual practices in so-called independent films. The chapter begins with a review of theories on recent cinema, included the new "smart film," digital cinema and the impact of MTV's accelerated or "intensified" aesthetic. The two case studies discussed are Richard Linklater's *Waking Life* (2001) and Michel Gondry's *Be Kind Rewind* (2008). The first of these addresses how Glover Gill's nuevo-tango score works with corresponding rotoscoped images to produce an experientially rich and immersive filmic world. The second highlights how Gondry's *Be Kind Rewind* can be interpreted as metafilmic commentary on recent technological changes. In each film, an element of wonder is conveyed through the use of audiovisual devices that blur the boundaries between narrative levels, combined with an aesthetic of "repurposing" that draws attention to the cultural memory of objects.

Chapter 4 teases out a tendency toward modes of expression resembling those found in the classic film musical. Drawing on two case studies of independent films, Sally Potter's *Yes* (2004) and Tsai Ming-Liang's *The Wayward Cloud* (2005), the chapter explains two very different ways in which the adoption of a sensory cinematic language can be turned to critical ends. Sally Potter employs an audiovisual language that falls halfway between cinematic realism and the fantasy of the musical number to suggest a mode of "becoming" that communicates a reparative message. The dominant modality in Tsai's film is more deconstructive, with different audiovisual genres such as the film musical and hardcore pornography reflecting on one another in ways that are surprising and yet somehow seem disarmingly natural. This chapter addresses, above all, the affective and affected nature audiovisual flow and the consequences of its interruption through theories of performativity, flow and camp aesthetics.

Chapter 5 examines practices of loose audiovisual synchronization that speak to an aesthetic of repurposing in contemporary audiovisual expression. The two case studies are Philip Glass's cinematic opera *La Belle et la Bête*, an operatic adaptation of Jean Cocteau's original film, and the Internet phenomenon of "syncing," represented by the synchronization of the classic film *Wizard of Oz* with Pink Floyd's *Dark Side of the Moon*. Both forms are seen in the light of an avant-garde lineage that destabilizes the binary opposition of art and life. Both, in different ways, become forms of audiovisual dialogue that draw attention to new forms of technological estrangement in advanced modernity.

Chapter 6 introduces several new themes and concepts. Revolving around mediated performances by the cartoon band Gorillaz, the first case study approaches the hit song "Clint Eastwood" from narratological and phenomenological angles in light of the group's heavily publicized media-critical agenda. Issues of originality and artistry are broached in a second study on the music video of "Feel Good Inc." In references to the band's evasive modes of performance, Manuel Castells's concept of "real virtuality" and Katherine Hayles's similar idea of "embodied virtuality" are offered as alternatives to the widely cited Baudrillardian concepts of hyperreality and simulacra. Commentary on Gorillaz asserts that the group resembles the media realities they critique to such an extent that any critical content is bound to be irretrievably compromised. My analysis emphasizes the point that without resemblance there can be no effective critique.

Chapter 7 explores the boundaries of audiovisual experience by examining how anxieties about the visual in acoustic music are articulated in live and recorded performances. The first case study investigates KT Tunstall's breakthrough performance of the song "Black Horse and the Cherry Tree" on BBC television's *Later…with Jools Holland*. Most distinctive about this performance is how Tunstall employs looping technology to simulate multitrack recording techniques in "real time," resulting in an apparent schism between traditional musical influences and their experimental means of organization. Outwardly eschewing the visual trappings of mainstream media culture, Tunstall's performance, in fact, depends heavily on visual reinforcement to convey its critical effects. The following two case studies, Paul Buchanan's "Because of Toledo" and Suzanne Vega's "Night Vision," both, albeit differently, highlight how transmodal experience can play a key role in musical production and listening, even in the absence of an obvious visual text. Like the chapters on neosurrealist cinematic forms, this chapter advances the view that the imaginative faculties are key in permitting producers to "envision" new forms that allow audiences to reflect on the nature of contemporary mediatized experience. A final case study on the Sigur Rós song "Heysátan" brings this point home.

Might a more elevated theoretical agenda be found in this study? Put differently, is the approach I take amenable to emulation by future researchers interested in similar phenomena? Such an attitude might seem conceited in light of the wealth of models and theories on music and visual media that are currently in circulation. For this reason it is probably judicious to concentrate on the more modest aims of the individual cases that make up this book and its broader thesis about the prevalence of neosurrealism in the contemporary audiovisual sphere. However, there is another quite sweeping theoretical agenda that might be perceived as integral to this project. It resembles that which Robert B. Ray puts his name to in the book *How a Film Theory Got Lost and Other Mysteries of Cultural Studies*.[74] Ray argues for the

---

[74] Robert B. Ray, *How a Film Theory Got Lost, and Other Mysteries of Cultural Studies* (Bloomington: Indiana University Press, 2001).

resurrection of a mode of film theory built on different priorities than those that have dominated the landscape of research in recent years. Taking a stand against the "path dependence" of conventional rationally biased models, Ray extols the virtues of an impressionist-surrealist attitude when it comes to discussions of aesthetics, in which the unshackled imagination is accorded higher status and the sensory dimension of experience is attended to with greater focus. My book, like his, overflows its pages with questions and evocations; it incites readers with its own series of interruptions and unlikely combinations, demarcating a surreal journey in its own right. The materials examined here might be considered intrinsically resistant to clean-cut or definitive interpretations. Such is the nature of surrealist expression, which seems designed to evade easy categorization.[75] Nevertheless, I hope to demonstrate that both a form of content analysis—albeit one that pays close attention to phantoms of meanings and sensory memories more than explicit signification—combined with an approach that understands neosurrealist performances to be cultural practices, both embodying and mimetically repeating more extensive cultural formations (structures of feeling, structural tropes), hold the greatest promise for deepening our understanding of these emerging forms and practices. I can only hope therefore that the methodological and interpretative choices I made when writing this book are equal to the formidable task of tracking a significant and often overlooked tendency in recent cultural production in the audiovisual sphere.

---

[75] This concern is eloquently addressed in Phil Powrie's discussion of surrealism film criticism, which in turn draws on the writing of Linda Williams. Phil Powrie, "Masculinity in the Shadow of the Slashed Eye: Surrealist Film Criticism at the Crossroads," *Screen* 39/2 (Summer 1998): 153–63, 153.

2

Navigating the Neosurreal: Background and Premises

Then and Now: Toward an Appreciation of Surrealism in the Digital Age

Historical surrealism has been located, with a fairly broad consensus, between the two World Wars, for the most part revolving around the activities of the Parisian writer and theorist André Breton. The movement waned noticeably in the years following World War II. Whether this was due to a desire to embrace rational thinking in response to the devastation of two world wars or because of some more complex set of circumstances, there can be no denying that surrealism as an artistic movement no longer occupied center stage in artistic life after this time. A move toward realist forms of representation in several countries, including France, Italy, Britain and the Soviet Union, in the years that followed is well documented in research. This impulse more than anything demonstrates the extent to which the surrealist sensibility was in decline, notwithstanding some significant enclaves of surrealist activity that bridged the gap between historical surrealism and what I call neosurrealism.

Regarding the formative years of the surrealist aesthetic, Hal Foster suggests a vision of French consumer society in the interwar years as a culture haunted by its recent history.[1] The aspirations spurred by the industrial revolution exhausted themselves in the years leading up to the First World War, the aftermath of which saw a rapid accumulation of material wealth and technological innovation. Modernization intensified to unprecedented levels, prompting an ever faster turnover of commodities as well as a proliferation of utopian discourses. In a sense, surrealism became the postmodernism of its day, commenting on changes in society and the arts through the adoption of a self-reflexive attitude. Factors such as the economic ascension of the baby boomers generation, the dawning of the information age, and accelerated movement toward what Castells calls "the network society" in recent

---

[1] Hal Foster, *Compulsive Beauty* (Cambridge, MA: MIT Press, 1993), 165.

postwar decades all resonate with the optimism and proliferation of industrial production that took place in the interwar years. Comparable circumstances therefore
define the historical periods in which both surrealism and neosurrealism have
flourished.

The impetus toward neosurrealist approaches was indicated already in the hippie
movement's taste for psychedelia, which as Auslander commented would later
metamorphose into the highbrow-lowbrow dichotomy of progressive rock/glam
rock.[2] Elements of surrealism would also crop up, however, in concept art,
performance art, pop art, the boundary-crossing "underground" movement, and
various forms of experimental film and theater. In retrospect, these tendencies can
be held to have adumbrated postmodernism, in which a taste for the surreal has
often been perceived. As an aesthetic movement, postmodernism has been described
as celebrating an aesthetic of fragmentation, semantic abstention, and cultural
leveling, a kind of anti-aesthetic (Foster), which was thought to reflect the conditions of production in the late capitalist era (Jameson, Baudrillard) or to repudiate
(through techniques of denaturalization and deconstruction) the dominant master
narratives (Lyotard) and hierarchies of Enlightenment thinking as they impacted
twentieth-century life (Hassan, Bauman, Jenks, Huyssen, Hutcheon, hooks).[3]
A defining feature of both surrealist and postmodernist structures of feeling is to be
found in montage practices. In this respect it is instructive to compare Adorno's
"world-rubble of Surrealism" to Susan McClary's characterization of postmodernist
composers as "reveling in the rubble."[4] What is at stake is a similar desire "to uncover
childhood experiences by means of explosions."[5]

While it is possible to identify a line running through historical surrealism and
postmodernism to the more recent practices addressed in this chapter, the affective
tone of artistic production has undeniably changed in concord with changing cultural
and technological circumstances in the nineties and noughties. Consider, for example,
the profound cultural and technological transformations those decades witnessed,
including rapid advances in CGI technologies in film production, the proliferation of
digital recording technologies in audio production, and more sweeping technological changes from broadband Internet and smartphones to increasingly realistic or
hyperrealistic gaming experiences. These technological developments coincided with
a general textural thickening of expressive means and ends, combined with a noticeable thawing of the "cool" and "mechanical" tone favored in the previous two decades,
aspects that were held by many commentators to be distinctive of postmodernism. In

---

[2] Philip Auslander, *Performing Glamrock: Gender and Theatricality in Popular Music* (Ann Arbor, MI:
University of Michigan Press, 2006).

[3] It is unnecessary to cite all of the relevant literature in this context.

[4] Theodor Adorno, "Looking Back on Surrealism" (1954), in *Notes to Literature*, vol. 1, trans. Shierry Weber
Nicholson (New York: Columbia University Press, 1991), 86–90, 87; Susan McClary, *Conventional Wisdom:
The Content of Musical Form* (Berkeley: University of California Press, 2000), 141.

[5] Adorno, "Looking Back," 88.

earlier writing, I compared this aesthetic tendency to Michel Foucault's scholarly method of archaeological inquiry, which requires a mode of production concentrating on the relationships between fragmentary texts (archive materials) and has little to say about the human actions or the intentionality that put them there in the first place.[6] The new directions addressed here are less self-contained and more historically bound in a manner resembling the turn toward Nietzschean genealogy in Foucault's later writing. Although, the practices elucidated here imply critical agency and heightened sensory responses in a manner not easily reconciled with the frames of reference of either paradigm. Greater levels of narrative complexity, textural density and temporal volition are all factors conducive to the emergence of neosurrealist discourses. Affective (or disaffected) coolness and a certain mode of techno-aesthetics continue to be markers of the new aesthetic outlook, but they are framed within an ontological context that Katherine Hayles refers to as "embodied virtuality."[7] We will see ample evidence of this sensibility in the chapters on Glass's *La Belle et la Bête*, "virtual band" Gorillaz, and Richard Linklater's rotoscoped film *Waking Life*. More surprisingly, we will see evidence of this sensibility in the chapter discussing performances by musicians working in the acoustic domain of nu-folk.

One particular comment on the writing on postmodernism seems especially germane to the subject of this study: Fredric Jameson's characterization of postmodernism as "surrealism without the unconscious."[8] Although incorporated as a chapter title in Jameson's seminal expository text on postmodernism, nowhere is the term adequately explained. Surrealism for Jameson would seem to imply disorientation caused by the avoidance of conventional narrative forms and the widespread use of montage techniques. This aspect of surrealism is applicable to many of the examples discussed below, although to apply existing theories of postmodernism to the corpus of materials compiled here without in some way revising them would be to miss much of what is distinctive about the new forms. These forms are not "psychological" in the same sense as surrealism is often held to be. Nor are they narratively motivated in the sense that they seek to lure audio-viewers into a closely synchronized bond with the narrative actions and subjective point of view of characters. Instead they articulate psychological concerns on a different plane, by reflecting on areas of experience such as cultural memory, existential loss and sensory perception. In general, they do not imply a repressed sexuality arising from the unconscious, but they are erotic in the more general sense of pointing toward a heightening of the sensory

    [6] See John Richardson, *Singing Archaeology: Philip Glass's* Akhnaten (Hanover, NH and London: Wesleyan University Press and University Press of New England, 1999).

    [7] Katherine Hayles, *How We Became Posthuman: Virtual Bodies in Cybernetics, Literature, and Informatics* (Chicago: University of Chicago Press, 1999), 1.

    [8] Fredric Jameson, *Postmodernism or The Cultural Logic of Late Capitalism* (Durham, NC: Duke University Press, 1991), 67.

dimension of audiovisual experience (Susan Sontag's "erotics of art").[9] This erotics does not unfold on a purely abstract or aesthetic plane, however; it connects loosely with homologous social structures to do with the changing nature of experience in the digital age. Contrary to Jameson's contentions about postmodernism, the forms discussed here *are* characterized by a strong affective impulse. If the above characteristics of historical surrealism are absent, what is retained is an enticing sense of mystery that transforms ordinary perceptions.

Essential to this idea of the neosurreal is a principle the historical surrealists consistently expounded: the capacity of surrealist acts, performances, or objects to bring about altered perceptions of the world—to help us to imagine afresh. It is no coincidence that this sensibility arose at a time when questions were being asked about the role of immersion in the arts across "new" and "old" media: the idea of getting lost, caught up in parallel worlds or realities in the context of proliferating new media and their correlative forms, some of which offer previously unforeseen possibilities for participatory involvement. To the extent that those forms that afford the deepest levels of immersion could be said to model modern life most faithfully, they might also be considered to possess the greatest potential to bring into sight (and *sound*) the conditions of modern life.

This principle is most elegantly illustrated in the so-called oneiric film, which constructs a dreamlike alternative reality as a means of augmenting and commenting on everyday lived reality: thus *sur*-realism (above realism). An indistinct line separates fantasy genres and surrealism, but it is an important one for most specialists on surrealist aesthetics. In fantasy, the perceiver/participant gets lost in a fictive other world and essentially stays lost; and this experience serves as an antidote to difficulties encountered in everyday reality. Fantasy forms sustain an impression of internal believability (through suspension of disbelief) that effectively locks audiences into undialectical responses. Rick Altman cites this mode of escapism as a significant factor behind the rise of the American film musical concomitant with the era of the Great Depression, particularly when it comes to so-called folk musicals.[10] In surrealist and neosurrealist forms the escapist impulse is not as evident. The oneiric film provides a typical example of the kind of "escape" one finds in surrealist films, in which a dreamlike logic alters the normal codes of behavior and the forms of representation that govern the interior world of the film and its characters. In this mode of address, an allegorical function can easily replace the established narrative forms and identificatory mechanisms of classic cinematic naturalism. This principle applies as much to the intermedial audiovisual worlds created by the animated band Gorillaz as it does to the inner landscapes of a film such as Michel Gondry's *La science des rêves* (*The Science of*

---

[9] Susan Sontag, "Against Interpretation," in Elizabeth Hardwick, ed., *A Susan Sontag Reader* (New York: Vintage, 1983), 95, 104.

[10] Rick Altman, *The American Film Musical* (Bloomington and Indianapolis: Indiana University Press, 1987), 62–69, 272.

Sleep, 2006). In such instances, the audiovisual dreamscape refracts back on the everyday world, even while it is subject to its own interior laws. In other words, the audio-viewer is provided with clues that everything is not right or, scientifically speaking, plausible (David Lynch's *Lost Highway*, 1997, contains many such clues, such as characters appearing in two different locations at once). Works of this kind are often inscribed with of high level of perceptible artifice, which draws attention to underlying production techniques and reveals ruptures, breaches or incongruities; excesses of repetitive patterning; silences, gaps, and instances of narrative open-endedness; implausible coincidences and unexpected juxtapositions between media or codes. The instances discussed in this book furnish numerous examples of such approaches, turning them into audiovisual riddles of a kind—strange and beguiling artifacts that are just as likely to inspire bewilderment as wonder.

Definitions of Surrealism

Looking beyond the vernacular understanding of surrealism as strange or fantastical, both the movement itself and its later transformations are notoriously difficult to pin down to a fixed stylistic agenda. Because surrealism is an idea conceived with reference to competing discursive formations, it would make little sense to go in search of a definition of a term that is all encompassing. Instead, each of the theories about surrealism enumerated below will be shown to have greater relevance in different circumstances. These categories in my view summarize some of the most important facets of surrealism to have arisen in relation to the concept since its early usage.

i) Semiotic and linguistic definitions: Early commentary on surrealism was largely concerned with defining the nature of the "surrealist object." For André Breton, founder of the movement, the surreal was defined by "the fixing of dream-images through tromp-l'oeil."[11] Citing the painter Salvador Dalí, Breton goes on to suggest that visual doubleness is key in determining surreal status: a surreal object is one that "without the least figurative or anatomical modification is at the same time the representation of another object that is absolutely different, one that is also free of any type of deformation or abnormality that would reveal some sort of artificial arrangement."[12] Breton's apparent aversion to artifice is worth highlighting at this early stage: contrary to popular belief, surrealist art *does not* stand in diametric opposition to realism. It might even depend upon some notion of realistic representation, implying a mimetic relationship to the natural world, in order to produce some of its most powerful effects.

---

[11] André Breton, *Manifestoes of Surrealism*, trans. Richard Seaver and Helen Lane (Ann Arbor, MI: University of Michigan Press, 1972), 274.

[12] Dalí quoted in Breton, *Manifestoes*, 274.

Roland Barthes builds on the foundations of these earlier definitions in his discussion of the Georges Bataille novel *Histoire de l'oeil* (*Story of the Eye*, 1928).[13] Eschewing the obvious Freudian implications of the book's subject matter, he comments on the interchangeability of objects of similar size and shape—eyes, eggs and testicles. Drawing on Roman Jackobson's understanding of Saussurean linguistics, he asserts that the primary mode of expression in Bataille's writing is metaphorical and "virtual," in contrast to the predominantly metonymic and realist orientation of novelistic discourse. Thus, his writing suggests experiences of shifting paradigmatic relations in which the linguistic sequence (or syntagma) is broken vertically by the insertion of a "false" metaphorical element: "break an egg" becomes "break an eye" (or an ear for music becomes an *eye* for music, as in the title of this book). Because of this disruption of narrative continuity, surrealist discourse for Barthes is "poetic" and metaphorical more than it is realistic.[14] The more distant the relationship between the original object and the object that substitutes for it paradigmatically, the more shocking or convulsive the end result will be.[15] Bataille's writing therefore implies a destabilizing semantics of displacement, the presence of a consistent "motif" throughout the novel (in this case globular objects) belying its transformations into functionally discrete entities, which because of their unfixed status take on the appearance of "avatars."[16] Bataille's transgressive eroticism in this way implies an oppositional stance toward conventional linguistic operations as much it does a flouting of bourgeois values on the level of content, due to the novel's coarse and sacrilegious imagery.[17] The sum effect is "a general contagion of qualities and actions" that brings about a blurring of the material world.[18] Barthes perceives in surreal objects an ameliorative tremulous quality combined with nonhierarchical shallowness. Foremost in his interpretation is the regenerative power of language gone askew (*devoyé*). If this interpretation seems to go against the grain of surrealists' interpretations of their own works, including Bataille's Freudian account of his own novel, then it should be understood as conditioned in large measure by the textual priorities of emerging poststructuralist critical theory, which would later be appropriated in

[13] Roland Barthes, "The Metaphor of the Eye." trans. J. A. Underwood, in Georges Bataille, *Story of the Eye*, by Lord Auch [pseudonym] (London and New York: Penguin, 1982), 119–27.

[14] Ibid., 125–27.

[15] Ibid., 124.

[16] Ibid., 125.

[17] Ibid., 125–26. See also Georges Bataille, *Erotism: Death and Sensuality* (San Francisco: City Lights Books, 1986), 63–70. A fundamental principle in Bataille's writing is often said to be his alignment of sexuality with death. See also Susan Sontag, "The Pornographic Imagination," in Bataille, *Story of the Eye*, 82–118, 106. Bataille's idea of sexual transgression brings other useful ideas into play, including the interdependency of sacred and profane, an aspect of his writing that adumbrates Derrida's deconstruction. Bakhtin's carnivalesque operates in accordance with similar principles.

[18] Barthes, "The Metaphor," 125–26.

debates on postmodernism, not least Fredric Jameson ideas about postmodern flatness and pastiche.[19]

Subsequent poststructuralist theories on surrealism complicated this view by asking difficult questions about the boundaries of discourse. Art historian Rosalind Krauss's understanding of photographic surrealism as giving expression to the Derridean idea of "spacing" is one of the more noteworthy applications of poststructuralist theories. Spacing effects are produced through the doubling of images in photographic "special effects," including negatives images, techniques of solarization, Man Ray's rayograph technique, and photographic doubling, a technique that "marks the first [image] in the chain as signifying element."[20] Surrealist photographs in this understanding bring about a cleavage in reality that makes the perceiver more aware of the photographic image as sign. More than transcendence, spacing indicates a rupture that is constitutive of the object and signals its demarcation as an object. It registers the moment at which the indexical presence of the photograph is accommodated within the symbolic sphere. In this sense, photographic surrealism gives expression to the Derridean concept of *différance*, a concept that evokes two discrete meanings of the French verb *différer*: deferral and difference. Deferral refers to the temporal aspects of language, the definition of any word depending on the recognition of other previously defined words. Difference refers to the spatial organization of words, syllables and letters on the page. The latter of these elements is the most salient here. An element of emptiness *or silence* resides in this domain, conveyed through the spatial presentation of words on the page (hence, spacing). Gaps between the words and letters do not for Derrida convey an exteriority that precedes language but instead point toward an inbuilt feature of it, a precondition for its existence. The primary function of spacing is thus to expose the conventional nature of artistic materials and thereby to introduce them into the operational domain of the symbolic. It has to be noted, however, that the very possibility of this dialectic hints at something that lies beyond the boundaries of the representable—a domain Lyotard aligned with the Romantic notion of the sublime. Moreover, when spacing is construed as a form of intervention available to producers more than as a means of derailing the conventional strategies of interpretation available to readers, it offers a potentially useful starting point for discussions that look beyond the obvious level of referential meaning toward a more stratified and dialectical appreciation.

In Krauss's deliberation, photographs are the most efficacious transmitters of such messages due to their close indexical relationship to the real: they carry within them the direct ontological imprint of events in the world. Precisely because of how the photographic image extends directly from reality, disjunc-

[19]   Bataille, *Story of the Eye*, 69–74.

[20]   Rosalind Krauss, *The Originality of the Avant-Garde and Other Modernist Myths* (Cambridge, MA: MIT Press, 1985), 110.

tions caused by its removal from this context become all the more striking.[21] Krauss's understanding of surrealism in photography as a mode of deconstruction provides some rich avenues for interpretative inquiry that are explored more fully below. The fact that her analyses remain locked within an essentially intralinguistic conception of reality does not detract from the usefulness of her apparatus. This aspect does, however, seem ironic in light of the overarching claim of her study, to unpack *The Originality of the Avant-Garde and Other Modernist Myths*. Myths of abstraction and autonomy in this account could evidently still use some unpacking.

The mediating potential of techniques and technological inscriptions *recognized as such* can fruitfully be brought to bear on the naturalized conventions of audiovisual expression. This perspective is germane to several of the cases included in this study.[22] More interesting than the simple fact of denaturalization, however, is to consider the relationship that pertains between this fragmented mode of presentation and what is represented mimetically through techniques of photographic inclusion. Abstraction as such is interesting, but what is being abstracted and to what ends? What is being (re)presented at the point of interruption, when auditory or visual spacing comes into sight? And how, with reference to what affective means? The penultimate chapter of this book sheds light on both of these questions. Suffice for now to say that it is essential to look beyond language and to address questions of cultural context and historical memory in order to provide readings that adequately address the affective nature of these practices.

ii) Psychoanalytical and affective definitions: Any view that interprets the surreal as an expression of the Freudian unconscious or that places an emphasis on psychoanalytical concepts like the uncanny falls under this heading. Those who have trouble entertaining Freud's idea of the unconscious are likely to have difficulty with surrealist works or analytical accounts that take its existence for granted. Because of their preoccupation with inner experience, the surrealists have been accused of solipsism: of focusing too much of their attention on the internal resolution of psychological conflicts, while allowing the relationship of the subject with real objects in the world (not least, fellow human beings) to

---

[21] Ibid., 112.

[22] Derrida notes that the concept of différance calls attention to "an interval, a distance, spacing…produced between the elements other, and . . . produced with a certain perseverance in repetition." Jacques Derrida, "Différance," in *Margins of Philosophy*, trans. Alan Bass (Chicago: University of Chicago Press, 1982), 1–27, 8. An illuminating discussion of Derrida's concept of spacing in relation to current theory on sound and embodiment is found in Frances Dyson, *Sounding New Media: Immersion and Embodiment in the Arts and Culture* (Berkeley: California University Press, 2009). A useful application of Derridean spacing to musical meaning, theorized with reference to Derrida's concept of the remainder, is found in Lawrence Kramer, *Musical Meaning: Toward a Critical History* (Berkeley: University of California Press, 2002), 174. The most convincing exposition of spacing in the visual arts is found in Krauss, *The Originality of the Avant-Garde and Other Modernist Myths*, 110.

become atrophied. This criticism could easily be applied to oneiric forms of surrealist discourse. From the outset, surrealism set out to blur the boundaries between sleeping and waking life, external reality and imagination, presence and absence, life and death, the organic and the inorganic.[23] Surrealism adheres to the aggregative logic of dreams rather than the dialectical logic of rational thinking. As Freud wrote in *The Interpretation of Dreams*: "The attitude of dreams to the category of *antithesis* and *contradiction* is very striking. The category is simply ignored; the word 'No' does not seem to exist for the dream. Dreams are particularly fond of reducing antitheses to uniformity, or representing them as one and the same thing."[24] This affirmative function of dream consciousness is particularly evident in the case study of Sally Potter's *Yes*, presented in chapter 4, which embodies another central principle of psychoanalytical thinking: the idea of stream of consciousness or random association. Associative thinking was a central method in Freud's psychoanalytical practices, and it found expression in surrealism through the surrealists' interest in "automatic writing" (writing without conscious intervention or censorship by the rational mind).

Breton's "surreal objects" find a direct counterpart in Freud's descriptions of dream imagery: "The possibility of creating composite formations is one of the chief causes of the fantastic character so common in dreams, in that it introduces into the dream-content elements which could never have been objects of perception."[25] In addition to a concern with dream imagery or reverie, other affectively conditioned psychological concepts are found extensively in the writing on surrealism, including melancholia, abjection, the uncanny, the sublime and the oceanic. Slogans associated with the movement, such as Breton's "convulsive beauty" and "the marvelous" are similarly driven by affective qualities.[26] Regarding the uncanny, Hal Foster goes so far as to assert that almost all of the defining features of surrealism are present in Freud's description of the uncanny. These include "indistinction between the real and the imagined," "confusion between the animate and the inanimate," and "usurpation of the referent by the sign or of physical reality by psychic reality."[27] Uncanny transformations occur in several examples examined in this book; indeed, it is an integral affective component of the forms of auditory repurposing that play a prominent role in uses and reuses of music

---

[23] See Breton, *Manifestoes*, 140.

[24] Sigmund Freud, *The Interpretation of Dreams*, trans. A. A. Brill (Wordsworth Editions: Ware, Hertfordshire, 1997), 202.

[25] Ibid., 207.

[26] The final line of Breton's novel *Nadja* reads: "Beauty will be convulsive or it will not be at all." André Breton, *Nadja*, trans. Richard Howard (London: Penguin, 1999 [1928]); also Krauss, *The Originality of the Avant-Garde*, 112; and Foster, *Compulsive Beauty*, 57–98. In *Le Paysan de Paris*, Aragon writes: "How long shall I retain this sense of the marvellous suffusing everyday existence." Luis Aragon, *Paris Peasant*, trans. Jonathan Cape (Boston: Exact Change, 1994 [1926]); see also Breton, *Manifestoes*, 16.

[27] Foster, *Compulsive Beauty*, 7.

encountered throughout the book. Foster's theorization via Freud is therefore relevant to many of the interpretive discussions.

iii) Stylistic definitions (or technique- and production-orientated definitions): Attempts to define surrealism as a style have revolved around two main poles: automatism and dream imagery.[28] What Breton calls "pure psychic automatism"[29] is the utilization of the psychoanalytical technique of free association (sometime called psychodynamic theory) in creative practices. Freud was exclusively concerned with the therapeutic implications of the technique, but Breton's principal concern was to unshackle the imagination with a view to subverting bourgeois morality. Not unrelated to the idea of free association, collage and montage techniques are widely found in surrealist forms, although without the explicit political motivation of a Dada photomontage or the level of abstraction found in cubist painting.[30] Many commentators consider surrealism to be too stylistically diverse or "universal" in its essential outlook to be easily amenable to overarching stylistic definitions.[31] Peter Bürger, for example, maintains that the nature of the Dada/surrealist aesthetic exempted works of this type from incorporation in a definitive style. In his view, "these movements liquidated the possibility of period style when they raised to a principle the availability of artistic means of past periods."[32] This suggests that the interest in montage in these movements elevated avant-garde art to a level of generality that transcended history. Or perhaps Bürger is implying that surrealism announced the end of history, much like deconstruction and millennial postmodernism were thought to do in later years. While I would concur that practices of incorporation loosen the bond between intentionality and effect, Bürger's position is irretrievably idealistic in its failure to recognize the historical contingencies that obtain in the production and consumption of the surrealist style.

iv) Aesthetic definitions: Definitions in this category extol the idea that the removal of an object from its everyday functionality casts it as surreal: examples range from Duchamp's found objects to Magritte's pipe. Quoting Duchamp, Breton proposes the creation of "objects that one approaches only in dreams that appear to be just as indefensible from the standpoint of their utility as from the standpoint of the pleasure they afford."[33] This sensibility is evident also in the

---

[28] See Krauss, *The Originality of the Avant-Garde*, 91–92.

[29] Most specifically in Breton's "First Manifesto of Surrealism" in Breton, *Manifestoes* [1924], 26, although he refines the concept throughout his work, including the lecture, "Surrealist Situation of the Object," ibid., 267–68 and the "Second Manifesto of Surrealism," ibid. [1946], 157–59.

[30] Peter Bürger, *Theory of the Avant-Garde*, trans. Michael Shaw (Minneapolis: University of Minnesota Press, 1984), 73–79; Krauss, *The Originality of the Avant-Garde*, 102–05.

[31] Krauss, *The Originality of the Avant-Garde*, 91–92; Michael Richardson, *Surrealism and Cinema* (Oxford: Berg, 2006), 3.

[32] Bürger, *Theory of the Avant-Garde*, 18.

[33] Duchamp quoted Breton, *Manifestoes*, 275.

reportage techniques drawn on in the surrealist novels of Louis Aragon (particularly *Le Paysan de Paris*, 1926) and André Breton (*Nadja*, 1928). In both of these novels, direct textual incorporation features prominently, including the use of photographs, newspaper cuttings and textual citations from shop-window banners and postings (techniques that are now widely interpreted to be postmodernist). Benjamin's extensive unfinished study of the Parisian shopping arcades, *Das Pasagen-Werk*, was strongly indebted to the techniques and general artistic ethos of the surrealist writers.[34] The attitude of Baudelaire's *flâneur* falls into this category, as does camp aesthetics to the extent that it is concerned with aestheticization of everyday experience. As Sontag noted, a conceit of the surrealists was to imagine that their research on daily life fell outside of the social sphere.[35] "Surrealism," in her view, "is a bourgeois disaffection; that its militants thought it to be universal is only one of the signs that it is typically bourgeois."[36] Notwithstanding these reservations, the attitude of the *flâneur* is fundamentally one of sympathy with the downtrodden fused with a desire to elevate their plights into the spotlight. He (in the case of the historical surrealists, the male personal pronoun is usually justified) *feels* popular culture more profoundly than he does refined middle-class culture, despite possessing a cultivated upbringing. In this respect there is an important leveling function in his attitude that belies the *flâneur's* distancing aestheticism. Thus, while his actions might on one level be perceived as betraying an attitude of condescension toward the world, his role as archivist of the unseen in the everyday reveals "a promiscuous acceptance *of* the world."[37]

Stan Hawkins's recent study of the British pop dandy elevates a more sympathetic reading of the *flâneur* than emerges in Sontag's writing, primarily in relation to Baudelaire's original conception.[38] In the context of British pop performance, the emphasis on style and aesthetic exteriorization provides a convincing example of the effectiveness of this kind of positioning as an element contributing to the destabilization of normative cultural formations. In Hawkins's theorization, Baudelaire's idea of "temperament" allows the dandy to rise above the crowd and to assert a mode of resistance through the dynamic assertion of the self. An additional relevant concept is audiovisual "masking." Most obviously applicable to the act of physical self-display, it is how masking translates into sound in the work of the record producer, as well as the dandy's inflections of linguistic accent in vocal performances, that provides some of the most productive lines of inquiry offered in the

---

[34] Walter Benjamin, *The Arcades Projects*, trans. Howard Eiland (Cambridge, MA: Harvard University Press, 1999).

[35] Susan Sontag, *On Photography* (London: Penguin, 1971), 53–54.

[36] Ibid., 53.

[37] Sontag, *On Photography*, 81. The emphasis is in the original text.

[38] Stan Hawkins, *The British Pop Dandy: Masculinity, Popular Music and Culture* (Farnham: Ashgate, 2009), 40–47.

study. Hawkins's attention to the craft of the producer demystifies musical production by showing how it can be used to modulate the artist's "temperament." Examples are Toni Visconti's painstaking attention to vocal multilayering and experimental miking techniques in his work with David Bowie (on the album *Scary Monsters*), and Steven Hague's revealing observation that British artists "don't want to sound like somebody else."[39] Accent is a further area where masking is implicated in dandified performance, whether one considers Bowie's and Damon Albarn's mockney affectations, the Gallagher brothers' northern drawl, Neil Tennant's understated and characteristically aloof RP, or the Americanized crooning of Robbie Williams and Rod Stewart. Common to all of the above is an element of affectation through masking that betrays a desire to conceal while reflecting back on earlier practices mimetically. Philip Auslander raises similar issues concerning the staging of personal identity in pop performances in the critically undervalued genre of glam rock.[40] Like Hawkins, Auslander attends to the theatricality of the star persona by concentrating on the manifold ways in which it can be modified creatively. Both of these studies reveal a taste for surreal transformations that has characterized the British music landscape, in particular, since the late 1960s and psychedelic movement into the 1970s and the binary divide between progressive rock and its more high-spirited distant cousin, glam rock. Performative modifications of the singing voice are encountered in several chapters in this book, including case studies on Gorillaz, KT Tunstall and The Blue Nile. An element of musical and technological masquerade in each of the above cases brings into sight the performer's modifications of the projected self, which in turn has a destabilizing effect on conventions resembling the effects produced in surrealist photographic representations of the human body. One only has to consider the extremes to which such measures can be taken in performances by the likes of Scissor Sisters and Lady Gaga to appreciate how close such strategies are to the colloquial meanings of surrealism.

Gendered queering, bisexuality, and camp are issues that extend across the terrain of 1970s gender bending and constructions of the pop dandy. The camp or queering function of aestheticism (implying a leveling of conventional or heteronormative binary gender coding) is prominent also in Eve Kosofsky Sedgwick's theorization of performativity and affective consciousness.[41] In chapters 3 and 4, a case is made that this sensibility is powerfully articulated in recent independent cinema. The performative conventions of recent cinema paint a picture of an intoxicating affectively conditioned world that resists the hierarchical norms of "straight" and aesthetically unconditioned society.

v) Ontological/perceptual definitions: According to some theories, surrealism is recognizing juxtapositions that are present in daily life but which our cultural

---

[39] Ibid., 158–169.

[40] Auslander, *Performing Glamrock*.

[41] Eve Kosofsky Sedgwick, *Touching Feeling: Affect, Pedagogy, Performativity* (Durham, NC: Duke, 2003).

conditioning has made invisible to us.[42] Surrealism, in this view, is an attitude of willed detachment from banal consciousness that precipitates greater awareness of the world as it actually is—or as it is actually is *experienced*—with an emphasis placed on its inequalities, injustices and material imperfections. An attitude of detachment is deployed to bring into sight surprising juxtapositions embedded in the everyday, with occasional shocks of recognition that allow us to see the capitalist and/or existential "real." This idea was espoused by the surrealists themselves, as well as by the French Second Situationist International political movement of the 1960s, including its figurehead, Guy Debord. More recent writing on "everyday life" in sociology and cultural studies, including that of Lefebvre and De Certeau, is indebted to the reportage techniques of the early surrealist writers and filmmakers.[43] A powerfully idealism infuses this line of thinking, which seems incommensurable with (among other things) the commercial tenets of current popular culture. Nevertheless, it is a factor that undoubtedly impinges on the modes of deconstruction found in several of the instances investigated later. The extent to which the realizations occasioned by these surrealist shifts in consciousness can be thought of as politicized varies according to context. For certain, the cases discussed in the penultimate chapter bring into sight an implicit ecological or environmentalist agenda that reflects back on the dominant structures of capitalism. Elsewhere such positioning is not so easily perceived.

Shock tactics are an element of surrealist expression that is easily associated with ontological/perceptual categorizations.[44] These are found in relation to definitions of historical surrealism to the extent that it might be considered an avant-garde movement. Several problems have been voiced with regard to shock tactics in art, which are undoubtedly as relevant in discussion of films by Lynch, von Trier or Tarantino as they are in reference to the historical surrealists. First, shock as such is indeterminate in terms of its political effects: it disrupts a line of thinking but does not always direct it. Second, it is easily conventionalized, repeated, repackaged and therefore accommodated within the structures of capitalist consumption.[45] Third, shock tactics may effectively challenge middle-class hypocrisy and/or complacency but they may also lack a sound ethical footing. The absence of ethics (on a personal rather than a directly political level)

[42] Ben Highmore, *Everyday Life and Cultural Theory* (London: Routledge, 2002), 50–51.

[43] Ibid., 113–73.

[44] The concept of shock is most forcefully illustrated in Benjamin's description of the activities of the flâneur in the essay "On Some Motifs in Baudelaire" in Walter Benjamin, *Illuminations: Essays and Reflections*, trans. Harry Zohn (New York: Schoken, 1968), 175. Typical of urban existence, the shock of surreal juxtapositions in daily life in the mechanized context of the modern city represented for Benjamin a means of achieving loss of the self, which he viewed ambivalently as potentially liberating but also as a symptom of social alienation.

[45] Bürger, *Theory of the Avant-Garde*, 80–81.

is written into the tenets of surrealist aesthetics in Breton's wish that surrealism should be "exempt from any esthetic or moral concern."[46]

Instead of shock, a continuous frisson (or static electrical charge) would probably come closer to the (post-avant-garde) forms of interference mapped in the greater part of this book; as well as interruptions in the flow of discourse that serve as reminders (or Derridean remainders) of the status of discourse as discourse. Combining hypothetical reasoning and pure aesthetic grace, new audiovisual practices challenge audiences to frame the world differently rather than shocking them into recognizing a reality their conscious minds had denied them. One exception to this rule is the Tsai Ming-Liang film *The Wayward Cloud*, discussed in chapter 4, which employs the cinematic techniques of hardcore pornography but with a distinct surrealist twist, whereby the image is rendered intentionally base in a Bataillean way. The effects of this juxtaposition are intended to shock but the deconstructive intent of the images and sounds is a long way from being exempt from ethical considerations.

vi) Institutional definitions: The presence of such a category will probably seem objectionable to those who take the anti-institutional rhetoric of the historical surrealists at face value. The surrealists resist societal norms and strictures. Over several decades, however, leading surrealist artists have both striven for integration with existing institutions (artistic and political) and formed and regulated their own. The primary institutional definitions relate to the figurehead of the movement, Breton, who founded the first surrealist group, edited the first periodical of the movement, *La Révolution surréaliste* (founded in 1924), and wrote two manifestoes and a prolegomena for a third. Acceptance as an artist working within the surrealist idiom in the early years of the movement was largely contingent on approval by the autocratic and whimsical Breton. Several key figures were expelled (or "excommunicated," as critics have put it) after disagreements with Breton, including Cocteau and Bataille. The French intellectual, philosopher and feminist Simone De Beauvoir named Breton "a pope."[47] Her alignment of surrealism with its main adversary, institutionalized religion, extends back to the rift between Bataille and Breton when the former characterized the latter as a priest and architect of the surrealist religion.[48]

Conflicting views of Marxist political theory were closely linked with surrealism in its later manifestations; a factor that was a source of some controversy amongst its exponents. Tensions between orthodox Leninist-Marxism and the more loosely egalitarian principles of surrealism are perceptible in the defensive tone of Breton's writing in the *Second Manifesto of Surrealism*, where he attempts (in vain?) to reconcile the emphasis on imaginative free-play and psychological self-exploration in

---

[46] See Breton, *Manifestoes*, 26.

[47] Simone de Beauvoir, *The Ethics of Ambiguity* (New York: Citadel Press, 1994 [1948]), 55.

[48] See, for example, the short essay "The Castrated Lion" in Georges Bataille, *The Absence of Myth: Writings on Surrealism* (London: Verso, 1994), 28–29.

surrealism with the tenets of historical materialism and its officially sanctioned artistic outlet, socialist realism.[49] As Sontag expressed the matter, "Surrealists, who aspire to be cultural radicals, even revolutionaries, have often been under the well-intentioned illusion that they could be, indeed should be, Marxists. But Surrealist aestheticism is too suffused with irony to be compatible with the twentieth century's most seductive form of moralism."[50] The history of surrealism is to some extent a history of the movement's failure to find an institutional home within the political and intellectual currents of its time. Surrealism continues to be institutionally supported insofar as galleries and publications on the subject are funded by national institutions; including, in Britain, the AHRC Research Centre for Studies of Surrealism and the Tate Gallery in London. Comparable organizations exist in other countries. Of the research on audiovisual surrealism, Michael Richardson adopts a position that falls perilously close to institutional definitions of surrealism and with the assumptions behind institutional theories of art in general.[51] Surrealism in his view is attainable either "by means of a direct link with surrealist activity or through a convergence of themes or an affinity of intention."[52] Otherwise a workable and historically attuned definition, the main problem here lies in what is meant by the term "direct link." Namely, when it comes down to the crunch, a formal affiliation with an "accredited" surrealist movement (one accepted by Breton and his followers) appears in his discussion to be the most reliable litmus test of an artist's surrealist credentials and implicitly their seriousness as an artist. Writing of the avant-garde animator Jan Švankmajer, he remarks that this is "the only major filmmaker whose work fully belongs to surrealism, in so far as he has conceived and realized the majority of his films in the heart of the Czechoslovak Surrealist Group."[53] (I should add as an aside that the Czech group was visited by "the pope of surrealism," Breton, and officially endorsed by him.) This writer has many instructive things to say about surrealist cinema, but his doting on the authority of official groups seems out of kilter with the anti-authoritarian tenets of much surrealist writing and artistic practice.

SurREALISM or SURrealism? Different Times and Different Media

A seam running through many of the above definitions is the idea that surrealism is not the antithesis of realism but rather its extension and transformation. In this respect it might be more closely related to the concept of "hyperrealism" than

---

[49] See Breton, *Manifestoes*, 142–57.

[50] Sontag, *On Photography*, 81–82.

[51] See, for example, George Dickie, *Art and the Aesthetic: An Institutional Analysis* (Ithaca, NY: Cornell University Press, 1974). In a broader sense, the theories of Pierre Bourdieu could be regarded as institutional.

[52] Richardson, *Surrealism and Cinema*, 10.

[53] Ibid., 11.

some academic writers realize—a term used in reference to the intensified experiences afforded by cinema and computer-generated virtual reality. "Intensified realism" is another term found in reference to works of Dada and protosurrealism, but also employed to describe the effects of contemporary technologies in the audiovisual field.[54] Similarly, the term "magical realism" is loosely intertwined with the history of surrealism and is suggestive of a halfway semantic territory between surreal fantasy and reality, imagination and perception. A strained relationship between experienced reality and the unbounded imagination is key to understanding much of what I unpack below. It is no accident that painters such as Dalí adopted a heightened representational style; surrealism depends on accurate (re)presentations of reality in order to discharge some of its most powerful (and uncanny) effects. In much the same way, the photography of Man Ray, Hans Bellmer and others came to occupy a central position in the surrealist aesthetic. This point did not go undetected by one of the most noteworthy proponents of realism in cinema, André Bazin:

> For [the surrealist] the logical distinction between what is imaginary and what is real tends to disappear. Every image is to be seen as an object and every object as an image. Hence photography ranks high in the order of surrealist creativity because it produces an image that is a reality of nature, namely, an hallucination that is also a fact. The fact that surrealist painting combines tricks of visual deception with meticulous attention to detail substantiates this.[55]

In Bazin's writing this statement is deployed at the service of his argument concerning the primacy of realist cinematic forms. It is not necessary to subscribe to the general point, however, to appreciate the more particular one: that some notion of realism underlies the most effective forms of surrealist expression.[56] Breton himself articulated this relationship most directly when he stated in his first *Manifesto of Surrealism* (1924): "I believe in the future resolution of these two

[54] See David Hopkins, *Dada and Surrealism: A Very Short Introduction* (Oxford: Oxford University Press, 2004), 27.

[55] André Bazin, *What is Cinema*, vol. 1, trans. Hugh Gray (Berkeley: University of California Press, 2005 [1967]), 15–16.

[56] Lowenstein makes a persuasive case that the aesthetic views of Barthes and Bazin converge around the question of surrealism. This view is better justified in the case of Barthes, however, whose notion of the *punctum*, or significant detail in a photograph, resembles the surrealists' attention toward isolated body parts. Barthes's interest in the retrospective quality of the photographic signifier can similarly be related to surrealist aesthetics. Bazin's realism on the other hand seems narrower than anything the surrealists envisioned in their photographic perversions of the real. Of greatest value in Lowenstein's discussion is how he equates the forms of representation associated with intermediality and the digital reproduction of films (through uses of DVD technology) with a nascent surrealist impulse. See Adam Lowenstein, "The Surrealism of the Photographic Image: Bazin, Barthes, and the Digital Sweet Hereafter," *Cinema Journal* 46/3 (Spring 2007): 54–82.

states, dream and reality, which are seemingly so contradictory, into a kind of absolute reality, a surreality, if one may so speak."[57] Sontag too notes how surrealism "lies at the heart of the photographic enterprise: in the very creation of a duplicate world, of a reality in the second degree, narrower but more dramatic than that perceived by natural vision."[58] More than this, it is the distance—imposed and bridged—between the imprint of reality found in the photographic still and the surrounding lived reality that is most directly productive of surreal effects. This distance for Sontag is demarcated in a parallel social stratification between the supposed middle-class photographer and the subjects of the photographs. Most fundamentally, it is expressed in the difference between the moment of registration (or image capture) and the viewer's experienced time.[59] In this way, photographs become "an inventory of mortality," documentary proof of a world that is slipping away.[60] This subtext of melancholy is an aspect that infects almost all of the early writings on surrealism, from Breton to Benjamin. But it is a melancholy that harbors a subtle transformative power, as the marked object is made to speak again in present-day discursive contexts.

Strikingly similar in this regard are Roland Barthes's observations concerning a second *punctum*, or photographic interruption. As such, the concept of the punctum in Barthes's discussion approaches surrealist aesthetics in its insistence on detaching photographic details from their meaningful (and sensible) context in the photographic composition. This is contrasted with the *studium*, which conveys the obvious symbolic meaning of the photograph. In the book *Camera Lucida*, however, Barthes writes of "another punctum . . . than the 'detail.' This new punctum, which is no longer of form but of intensity, is Time, the lacerating emphasis of the noeme ('that-has-been'), its pure representation."[61] This second punctum refers above all to the affective quality of photographs to imply absence by shifting attention toward the registration of physical presence at the moment when the image was captured. Readings such as this have special resonance with the primary materials of this study, although my main focus is on auditory rather the visual temporal breaks and the melancholy such registrations of absence occasion on the reflective listener or audio-viewer.

Claims regarding the primacy of photography in surrealism have been countered by writing on film. Responding to Bazin's advocacy of cinematic realism, Ado Kyrou argued that cinema is of its essence surrealist.[62] His discussion of surrealist cinema ranged from early experimental films (those of Méliès and Feuillade) to popular films of that time, especially those in which the surreal categories of "love," "revolt," "elsewhere," and "the impossible" find expression. J.H. Matthews (1971) similarly

[57]   See Breton, *Manifestoes*, 14.
[58]   Sontag, *On Photography*, 54.
[59]   Ibid., 58.
[60]   Ibid., 70.
[61]   Roland Barthes, *Camera Lucida: Reflections on Photography* (London: Vintage, 1993), 96.
[62]   Ado Kyrou, *Le Surréalism au cinema*, 3rd ed. (Paris: Le Terrain Vague, 1985).

extends his discussion of surrealism beyond surrealist film proper to include genres in commercial cinema such as horror, slapstick comedy and, once again, romantic genres.[63] While acknowledging that all films can be understood in part to be surreal, his primary focus is the canonical surrealist filmmaker, Luis Buñuel. The point cannot be made strongly enough that not only films produced with surrealist aesthetics in mind are open to surrealist decodings. In this way, the aesthetics of surrealism is amenable to readings that subvert conventional distinctions between high and low. Breton's cinematic experiences can be seen in this light; in the early days of the movement, a common practice was to visit cinemas at random and then move to a neighboring cinema the minute the film began to make conscious sense.[64] It is not difficult to perceive an affinity between this mode of spectatorship and the emphasis on multifocus and fragmented narrative structures in recent cinema, which arguably have similar disorientating effects on audiences.

Michael Richardson likewise holds cinema to be fundamentally surreal, but for different reasons.[65] For him, the environment where films are screened is a decisive factor. The fact that people watch and listen to films in darkened spaces among unknown groups of passive spectators is suggestive of an aesthetic geared toward ritual, which in turn is conducive to experiences of reverie and wonder. The sense of disorientation filmgoers experience on leaving a theater lends credence to such a proposition, although psychoanalytical theories of spectatorship might offer different explanations as to the causes of this disorientation.[66] Certainly, when it comes to films that construct unlikely other worlds (those of Buñuel, Lynch, Tarkovsky, Kubrick, von Trier, Kieslowski and others), it is easy to imagine how the phenomenal and affective impact of surrealism might become intensified in a darkened theatrical setting. Decisive here is the question of realism and whether fictional reality is understood, on some level, to stand in for lived reality, even while it is obviously differentiated from it because of the two-dimensional constraints of the form (which admittedly are breached through the three-dimensional and embodied qualities of sounds). In this respect, it is noteworthy that the directors I listed seem to invest their imagery (and sounds) with an intensified realism, sometimes to the point of Bataillean grotesqueness. This mode of consumption obviously has little to do with audience's experiences of music videos, which are principally a televisual form, although this is rapidly changing as computer screens, portable media players and smartphones are produced with video-playback capability. The sensory impact

[63]   J. H. Matthews, *Surrealism and Film* (Ann Arbor: University of Michigan Press, 1971).

[64]   André Breton, "As in a Wood," Paul Hammond, ed. and trans., *The Shadow & Its Shadow: Surrealist Writings on the Cinema* (San Francisco: City Lights Books, 2000), 72–77, 75.

[65]   Richardson, *Surrealism and Cinema*, 2006, 8–9.

[66]   This sense of disorientation was commented on implicitly in Jacques Rivette's *Céline et Julie vont en bateau* (1974, *Céline and Julie Go Boating*). In this film two female friends stumble in and out of a 1940s style melodrama film before eventually realizing that they can influence its dramatic outcome through their actions. In this way the film becomes a contemplation of the act of spectatorship. This film is often called surrealist.

of cinematic screens and sound is more profound and therefore arguably more conducive to the surreal, since this mode of address encourages more convulsively
embodied responses.

Despite the limitations of television as a medium, modes of expression that
resemble surrealism have taken a firm hold in the music videos of certain directors in
the past three decades. There is no easy answer as to why this might be the case, but
there seems to be something about the constraints and possibilities of music videos as
a form that is conducive to surrealist expression. Videos are usually viewed more than
once, thereby inviting closer scrutiny of repeated gestures and their transformations.
In this respect they are "poetic" more than "novelistic," if we adopt Barthes's dichotomy
that was invented to explain literary surrealism—guided more by musical structure
than to a clear expository narrative function. The research on videos starting from
E. Ann Kaplan's influential study undoubtedly got it right in this respect, although to
judge popular performance by the yardstick of cinematic theories of spectatorship is
undoubtedly something that should be done with caution.[67] The fact that videos are
driven primarily by music makes it possible to incorporate visual imagery that is
implausible, eccentric or abstruse without alienating listeners whose primary
investment is, after all, in the song and its performing star(s). This permits weird or
"arty" imagery to be more easily accommodated in music videos than in other mainstream audiovisual forms. Painting or poetry have no comparable anchoring in the
popular sphere, and the tradition of the independent oneiric film (which I referred to
briefly and return to in chapter 3) teeters on the brink of "art film" status, although
there is some evidence that this situation is changing—not accidently, but through the
influence of directors who started out by working on music videos. A case could be
made (and will be made in chapter 6) that there is something in the sounds of certain
styles of music (electronic dance, psychedelic, progressive rock) that is homologous
with the surrealist visual aesthetic, and this might translate into audiovisual expression
with greater effectiveness than other musical styles. In any case, the presence of popular
songs set to synchronized images instantly removes such experiences from everyday
consciousness, even while such combinations can enhance body consciousness (in
this respect, the surrealism of music videos is the reverse of transcendental). The fantastical domain of popular songs in musicals is perhaps the most obvious example of
this separative function; song-and-dance numbers in musicals easily shift into a
"supradiegetic" register that is nothing if not surreal.[68]

[67] E. Ann Kaplan, *Rocking Around the Clock: Music Television, Postmodernism, and Consumer Culture* (New
York: Methuen, 1987).

[68] On the aggregative and surreal functioning of the song and dance number in film musicals, see Martin
Rubin, "Busby Berkeley and the Backstage Musical." in Steven Cohan, ed., *Hollywood Musical: The Film Reader*
(London: Routledge, 2002), 53–61, 60. On the concept of the supradiegetic (a fantastical extension of the con-
cepts diegetic and nondiegetic), see Rick Altman, *The American Film Musical* (Bloomington and Indianapolis:
Indiana University Press, 1987), 69. For Altman, the supradiegetic demarcates "a 'place' of transcendence where
time stands still, where contingent concerns are stripped away to reveal the essence of things" (ibid.).

Surrealist videos are, as I stated earlier, only peripherally included in this book. I do not claim that all music videos are surreal, although the work of Carol Vernallis demonstrates how the shorthand narrative techniques and montage-like approach to editing in videos produce end results that can be as radically disjunctive and densely sensorial as early experimental cinema.[69] Be that as it may, music videos commonly paraphrase the conventions of live performance, stage condensed narratives, or they simply package the star and their song in a way that is designed to promote the music. At the creative end of the spectrum, however, examples could be cited aplenty of directors and other collaborative parties who push the threshold by working in ways accurately described as surreal. Maureen Turim takes up this matter in relation to several of the more influential music video directors, including Jeff Stein, Spike Jonze, Chris Cunningham, and Michel Gondry.[70] Steering clear of the usual rhetoric of psychological depth and revolutionary intention surrounding the writing on historical surrealism, Turim argues that historical surrealism and postmodernist pop are "conjoin[ed] through their twin interests in performing a good joke."[71] This element of humor is something the majority of commentators on avant-garde surrealism seem to have missed entirely (perhaps because of anxieties about proving the artistic seriousness of their subject of research), but it is an essential starting point for any discussion of (neo)surrealism in pop. Turim is not the only writer who discusses on an affinity between recent popular artists and surrealist precursors; several (earlier) studies commented on the nature of this relationship.[72] Even when writers do not explicitly draw attention directly to expressive parallels, their analyses will often highlight solutions that seem to indicate an affinity with the tenets of historical surrealism. Stan Hawkins's research on performers like Björk, Annie Lennox, the Pet Shop Boys and Aphex Twin does precisely this.[73] My writing on surrealism in Peter Gabriel's music video "Sledgehammer" (dir. Stephen R. Johnson, Nick Park and the Brothers Quay) illustrates how techniques of stop animation and claymation closely resemble the approaches of noted surrealist ani-

[69] Carol Vernallis, "The Kindest Cut: Functions and Meanings of Music Video Editing," *Screen* 42/1 (Spring 2001): 21–48.

[70] Maureen Turim, "Art/Music/Video.com," in Roger Beebe and Jason Middleton, eds., *Medium Cool: Music Videos from Soundies to Cellphones* (Durham, NC: Duke University Press, 2007), 83–110.

[71] Ibid., 95.

[72] Authors who have explored the influence of surrealism in popular culture include Marcus Greil, *Lipstick Traces: A Secret History of the Twentieth Century* (London: Faber and Faber, 2001 [1989]); Jon Savage, *England's Dreaming: Anarchy, Sex Pistols, Punk Rock, and Beyond* (London: Faber and Faber, 2001 [1991]); and Bernard Gendron, *Between Montmartre and the Mudd Club: Popular Music and the Avant-Garde* (Chicago: University of Chicago Press, 2002).

[73] See Stan Hawkins, "Musical Excess and Postmodern Identity in Björk's 'It's Oh So Quiet,'" *Musiikin Suunta* 2 (1999): 43–54; *Settling the Pop Score: Pop Texts and Identity Politics* (Aldershot: Ashgate), 104–58; "Aphex Twin: Monstrous Hermaphrodites, Madness and the Strain of Independent Dance Music," in John Richardson and Stan Hawkins, eds. *Essays on Sound and Vision* (Helsinki: Helsinki University Press/ Yliopistopaino, 2007), 27–53.

mators like Jan Švankmajer, while bringing to mind popular forms such as the British-produced clay-animated series, *Wallace and Grummet*. The approach in the "Sledgehammer" video deconstructs some persistent myths surrounding popular performance, while directing attention toward auditory microrhythms that encourages listeners to hear the music differently. Without question, the artistic ambition of this conspicuously surrealist video paved the way for the commercial success of the song and the album.[74]

When it comes to combinations of popular music and surrealist visual imagery, there is something about the style that seems conducive to an aesthetic of incorporation or "borrowing." This can be seen as far back as Buñuel's first surrealist film, *Un chien andalou*, which was designed to include the "Liebestod" aria from Wagner's *Tristan und Isolde* (used to accompany a shot of a woman sucking the toe of a statue) and assorted tango melodies, among other musical resources. Classical music in this context was used primarily to parody the bourgeois values of the film's anticipated audience, and because the incorporated music comprised classical favorites, a case could be made that this was also the popular music of the time.[75] It is worth noting that early surrealist filmmakers drew eclectically from diverse musical styles, with little respect for conventional assumptions about high and low, to produce the desired audiovisual effects. The use of tango would have a long-lasting effect on the art-house genre, as I discuss in the next chapter. However, a case could be made that widely known and commodified musical styles best served the purposes of the surrealist aesthetic, as those are the forms most powerfully invested with sedimented cultural memories. Music, in this sense, functions in surrealist films much like found sonic objects: leftover cultural detritus to be incorporated in collage-like assemblages similar to surrealist photographers' use of existing photographs. Musical pieces function like iconic objects, rebounding against the context of the surrounding film in a way that is sure to create jolts of recognition, even while the experiences become unhinged from the shackles of narrative consciousness and attention is redirected toward the unfolding audiovisual Now.

This function, more than any other, is characteristic of the materials examined in this book. In nearly every chapter, the music analyzed resonates with echoes of earlier musical iterations, be they the Argentinian tango, vintage American country music (transformed by translation to Mandarin), strains of French impressionism (transformed through the iterative stylist devices of American postminimalism), Jamaican reggae or "British invasion" pop, as well as vintage R&B. These musical

---

[74] See John Richardson, "Plasticine Music: Surrealism in Peter Gabriel's 'Sledgehammer,'" in Michael Drewett, Sarah Hill and Kimi Kärki, eds. *Games Without Frontiers: Peter Gabriel From Genesis to Growing Up* (Farnham and Burlington: Ashgate, 2010), 195–210.

[75] See Priscilla Barlow, "Surreal Symphonies: L'Age d'or and the Discreet Charms of Classical Music," in Pamela Robertson and Arthur Knight, eds. *Soundtrack Available. Essays on Film and Popular Music* (Durham, NC: Duke University Press, 2001), 31–52.

styles teem with auditory specters.[76] But in the contexts in which they are found, they comment more effectively on the attitudes and styles of the present day than on previous eras. If there is a general affective tone to the popular audiovisual surreal, it is here that we should begin the search for it.

A useful light is cast on surrealist uses of music by looking closely at the research on popular music that takes as its subject musical styles that seem designed for repeated uses in different social contexts. Rose Rosengard Subotnik takes as her point of departure Theodor Adorno's disparaging comments about the Tin Pan Alley songwriting tradition, and she sets the record straight by asserting how music of this kind was designed for repeated usage (or reusage).[77] Straddling the high-low divide, Tin Pan Alley songwriters (dominated by Golden Age songwriters such as Jerome Kern, Irving Berlin, the Gershwin brothers, Cole Porter, and Rodgers and Hart) put a low premium on personal self-expression, which might be perceived in confessional popular songs since the 1960s. They produced musical objects that would allow users from diverse backgrounds to customize the songs according to different personal and dramatic circumstances. Whether composed according to similar principles or not, many of the musical "objects" investigated in this book evidence a similar predisposition for artifice and depersonalized subjectivity that Subotnik aligns with the Tin Pan Alley song, resulting in an aesthetic that encourages appropriative modes of consumption. Always more than mere repetitions, the uses of popular music that I investigate in this book signal a transformative sensibility that directs attention both to the surface details of the individual transformation and to the contexts in which the recycled forms make their appearances.

---

[76] For a discussion of the role of auditory spectres in bringing to life the deceased character of Laura Palmer in David Lynch's *Twin Peaks*, see John Richardson, "Laura and *Twin Peaks*: Postmodern Parody and the Musical Reconstruction of the Absent Femme Fatale," in Annette Davison and Erica Sheen, eds., *The Cinema of David Lynch: American Dreams, Nightmare Visions* (London: Wallflower Press, 2004), 77–92.

[77] Rose Rosengard Subotnik, "Shoddy Equipment for Living? Deconstructing the Tin Pan Alley Song," in Steve Baur, Raymond Knapp, and Jacqueline Warwick, eds., *Musicological Identities: Essays in Honor of Susan McClary* (Aldershot: Ashgate, 2008), 205–18.

3

Neosurrealist Tendencies in Recent Films: *Waking Life* and *Be Kind Rewind*

Reading Recent Cinema through the Optic of Surrealism

THEORETICAL ALIGNMENTS AND PREMISES

A strong current in recent cinema demonstrates concern with exploring dream-like inner landscapes, or mindscapes, and a tendency toward implausible characters, plotlines and combinations of objects in the world.[1] A closer consideration of the subject reveals the tendency is widespread, yet this is rarely reflected in the writing on new cinema. Surrealism seems like an obvious point of reference, although preconceptions about the concept and the historical movement can be misleading. Jameson famously described tendencies in postmodernist expressive culture as "surrealism without the unconscious."[2] While this description has some currency, this theorist does not explore with sufficient rigor the extent of the affinities that exist between historical and contemporary forms. Concentrating on sound-image relations in film and television, other writers have drawn attention to an irrational element within audiovisual texts that rises up as if from the unconscious to hijack the narrative away from plausible expectations.[3] While not directly addressing the irrational or the surreal, Robynn Stilwell's discussion of a "the fantastical gap between diegetic and nondiegetic" music touches on

---

[1] This chapter has benefited greatly from the critical comments and encouragement of Claudia Gorbman, Robynn Stilwell and Carol Vernallis.

[2] Fredric Jameson, *Postmodernism or The Cultural Logic of Late Capitalism* (Durham, NC: Duke University Press, 1991), 67.

[3] Kevin Donnelly, *The Spectre of Sound: Music in Film and Television* (London: BFI, 2005), 23; Susanna Välimäki, *Miten Sota Soi? Sotaelokuva, ääni ja musiikki* (Tampere: Tampere University Press, 2008), 253–66.

similar issues, in reference to what she calls the liminal region that lies between levels of narration.[4] The makers of film musicals have traditionally explored such terrain through the techniques of audio and visual dissolve (transitions from realism to fantasy mediated through song and dance; see chapter 4), but the same principle is increasingly found in other cinematic genres, often with darker narrative implications than in musicals.[5] As in musicals, movement between narrative levels in recent films maps a complex field of implied spatial relations that is rooted in perceptions of physical sounds in actual theaters (including the orchestra pit, which still existed in early cinemas adapted from theaters), but which extends beyond those real-world contexts into subjective and hypothetical territory. More than simple spatial mapping, audiovisual sounds resonate in the theater of the mind, where they invite complex identifications that bring into play the lived experiences and complex cultural and personal identities of individual members of the audience. Sound in audiovisual contexts, therefore, occupies a space of subjective response that because of the permeability of the mind allows it to move along a continuum from the dramatically plausible to the equally real but emotionally conditioned realm of subjective fantasy. To recognize this passage into the liminal for what it is, is to partake of pleasures that are distinctly surreal.

By the same token, an emphasis on auteurist approaches, taken to its logical conclusion, pushes film into a hypothetical or imaginary arena that is no longer governed by the usual expectations concerning verisimilitude.[6] Queerness (and the politics of queering) is another rubric that overlaps with epistemological concerns about the nature of reality and its fantastical extensions, which can become a focal

---

[4] See Robynn J. Stilwell, "The Fantastical Gap between Diegetic and Nondiegetic," in Daniel Goldmark, Lawrence Kramer, and Richard Leppert, eds., *Beyond the Soundtrack: Representing Music in Cinema* (Berkeley: University of California Press, 2007); Claudia Gorbman defines the three terms in accordance with Genette: "the diegetic (arising from the primary narration), the extradiegetic (narrative intrusion upon the diegesis, and which I shall henceforth call nondiegetic), and the metadiegetic (pertaining to narration by a secondary narrator)." *Unheard Melodies: Narrative Film Music* (Bloomington: Indiana University Press, 1987), 22. While I accept these definitions, I propose the addition of the term extranarrative to imply a level of narration that occupies an ambivalent position between narrated reality and the implied world outside of the artistic frame. In this respect it is evocative of the extrafilmic or everyday, although it is impossible in practice for it to escape its symbolic frame. Holbrook's "ambidiegetic," addressing the function of sung performances by characters in films, does not go far enough in this direction. See Morris Holbrook, "The Ambi-Diegesis of 'My Funny Valentine'," in Steve Lannin and Matthew Caley, *Pop Fiction: The Song in Cinema* (Bristol: Intellect, 2005), 48–49. Similarly, Altman's transcendent "supra-diegetic music" from film musicals goes as far as the fantastical but not beyond, which is something newer musicals and "independent" films routinely seek to do. Rick Altman, *The American Film Musical* (Bloomington: Indiana University Press, 1987), 70.

[5] Ibid., 74.

[6] Claudia Gorbman, "Auteur Music," in Goldmark, Kramer and Leppert, eds., *Beyond the Soundtrack*, 149–62, 159–61.

point for reimagining identities.[7] (I explore this aspect more fully in chapter 4.) Other writers have focused on the phenomenal and affective qualities of neosurrealist forms; the argument being that implausible character-plot alignments and fragmented narrative expositions direct attention toward more immediate concerns.[8] Each of the aforementioned viewpoints is relevant to the present discussion, which nevertheless concentrates on the somewhat different perspectives brought to the subject by ideas about surrealism.

As the reference to auteurist discourses and their overlap with surrealism might seem to suggest, there exists a close connection between surrealism and the avant-garde. The term neosurrealism in the title of the chapter is intended to align surrealist tendencies in recent films with what Peter Bürger called the neo-avant-garde.[9] There is, however, significant overlap between this term and the categories "postmodernism" and "post-avant-garde," each of these temporal modifiers ("neo" and "post") suggesting a revisionist attitude toward earlier avant-garde forms. Bürger was dismissive about the transformative potential of the neo-avant-garde (everything from Andy Warhol's pop art to minimalism, concept art and performance art); his objections revolved around the centrality of shock tactics in earlier avant-garde forms like Dada and surrealism. In his view, neo-avant-gardist attempts to produce shock were destined to become mere repetitions of earlier, more radical gestures, producing nothing more than objects intended for consumption by the art literati.[10] Hal Foster disputes this argument, claiming that the neo-avant-garde constituted a positionally effective anti-aesthetic that applied the lessons of Dada/surrealism and Russian Constructivism to the issues of its time relating to technology, the proliferation of audiovisual media and the like.[11] Foster revises Bürger's argument in a productive direction by turning attention toward the historical contingency of avant-garde forms. He nevertheless retains the idea of shock as the primary index of value in the avant-garde. This view can be contested. More than aspiring to shock audiences into a confrontation with "the real," exponents of pop art, minimalism and performance art (and I hold neosurrealist cinema to be a direct descendent of these forms) might have been commenting on its elusive nature by showing just

[7] Harry Benshoff and Sean Griffin, eds., *Queer Cinema: The Film Reader* (London and New York: Routledge, 2004), 61–62; Susanna Välimäki, "Musical Migration, Perverted Instruments and Cosmic Sounds: Queer Constructions in the Music and Sounds of Angels in America," in John Richardson and Stan Hawkins, eds., *Essays on Sound and Vision* (Helsinki: Helsinki University Press/Yliopistopaino, 2007), 177–220; Stan Hawkins, *The British Pop Dandy: Masculinity, Popular Music and Culture* (Farnham: Ashgate, 2009).

[8] See, e.g., Steven Shaviro, "Emotion Capture: Affect in Digital Film," *Projections* 1/2 (Winter 2007): 37–55; Carol Vernallis, "Music Video, Songs, Sound: Experience, Technique and Emotion in *Eternal Sunshine of the Spotless Mind*," *Screen* 49/3 (Autumn 2008): 277–97.

[9] Peter Bürger, *Theory of the Avant-Garde*, trans. Michael Shaw (Minneapolis: University of Minnesota Press, 1984).

[10] Ibid, 81.

[11] Hal Foster, "What's Neo about the Neo-Avant-Garde?" *October* 70 (Fall 1994): 5–32, 8.

how immersed we all are in consumer culture (and culture in general). Exploring the possibilities of the imagination in a discourse that is ironic and self-consciously constructed is arguably a better description of the new ethos—starting in the 1960s and extending to the present day—than one that concentrates exclusively on the capacity to shock.[12] If this is the case, then Bürger might have been right in one significant respect: the idea of shocking audiences is now secondary to other considerations. Why should this matter in the context of critical evaluations? Shock has the capacity to transform perceptions of the world, but it can cause diversions into ethical quagmires, or as Bürger claimed, simply lose its affective power due to its assimilation in dominant discourses.[13] The new film forms that are the subject of this chapter explore ambiguities that make audiences *wonder* (What is real and what is fiction? What is the nature of identity? What is the nature of the mind?) more than they jolt them out of habituated responses. For this reason, I consider these practices to be unashamedly neo- or even post-avant-garde, a result of a postmodernist (or post-postmodernist?) sensibility that draws increasingly indistinct lines between "popular" and "high" forms, overlaying avant-gardist intentions with vernacular ones in an effortless and nonjudgmental way, which would have been incomprehensible to first generation avant-gardists and high-modernist critics like Greenberg and Adorno.

Ambivalence is a keystone of the neosurrealist sensibility that is inseparable from the mutable and plural subject positions that have proliferated in postcolonial, gender-marginalized and other complex and cosmopolitan cultural formations (as discussed by Stuart Hall, Paul Gilroy and others). Such a positional and layered attitude toward identity and subjecthood is conducive to a sense of irony that does not denigrate and a relationship with lived experience that understands it, as the surrealists would have insisted, as embedded within the imaginative faculties rather than the other way round—as phenomenological as much as ontological. That is the basis for my readings of the new *audiovisual* cinema through the interpretive frame of writing on surrealism.

A central hypothesis of this chapter is that the influence of music video aesthetics on film has brought with it a greater tendency toward surreal strategies. Many of the

---

[12] In private correspondence, Robynn Stilwell reminded me that the fractured nature of discourse in recent audiovisual forms affords multiple points of entry for audiences, allowing us to take up "different identities along different axes." In this sense, "the slipperiness of representation may be a function— or may be an exposure—of our contingent existence." I am grateful to Robynn for articulating this point so eloquently in her comments on this chapter.

[13] The surrealists' refusal to take a stand against acts of violence in their attempts to undermine bourgeois morality has been a course of concern in some recent criticism. From a present-day standpoint the following statement in Breton's "Second Manifesto of Surrealism" reads as irretrievably irresponsible: "The simplest surrealist act consists of dashing down into the street, pistol in hand, and firing blindly, as fast as you can pull the trigger, into the crowd." André Breton, *Manifestoes of Surrealism*, transl. Richard Seaver and Helen Lane (Michigan: University of Michigan Press, 1972), 125.

films I review under the rubric of surrealism might be considered stretched, elabo-
rated, unpacked, or unfolded music videos. This brings its own set of challenges,
which I respond to in different ways in the two case studies offered in this chapter:
Richard Linklater's *Waking Life* and Michel Gondry's *Be Kind Rewind*. The path I
navigate in this chapter addresses this tendency: the remediation of music videos in
the full-length feature film, while touching on broader aesthetic and technological
factors that impinge upon current practices. These include the impact of digital
technologies and a tradition of surrealist expression in audiovisual media that
extends back several decades. A case will be made that the most successful directors
in these emerging practices are those that have learned to balance the concerns of
the present with lessons learned from the past.

BEYOND MUSIC VIDEOS

Aside from the general theme of neosurrealist aesthetics, this chapter is concerned
with identifying a line that can be shown to run from music video aesthetics to
recent films. Carol Vernallis addresses this question most directly in her discussion
of Michel Gondry's *Eternal Sunshine of the Spotless Mind* (2004).[14] Gondry, like
many other current film directors, received an apprenticeship of sorts by directing
music videos. Vernallis mentions the similar career paths of others: Jonas Åkerlund,
Michael Bay, David Fincher, Antoine Fuqua, Jonathan Glazer, Gary Gray, Michel
Gondry, Spike Jonze, Francis Lawrence, Marcus Nispel, Mark Pellington, Mark
Romanek and Hype Williams. The large number of directors with a background in
music videos (there are others, including Anton Corbijn, Joseph Kahn and, in
parallel to his career in film, Derek Jarman) constitutes a compelling case for
arguing how they have influenced new approaches to film, and Vernallis backs up
her hypothesis with convincing evidence from her close reading of the Gondry
film. Building her argument on the tendency of music video directors to "illuminate musical form,"[15] she contends that a new "intensified audiovisual aesthetics"
has found its way to film form, in which "everything becomes heightened, set off,
voluble."[16] The term intensified aesthetics is derived from David Bordwell's idea of
"intensified continuity," a concept he introduces to account for a tendency toward
the intensification of traditional narrative means in what he calls "post-classical
cinema," including such features as rapid editing (quantified with research on
average shot length, or ASL), bipolar extremes of lens length, closer framings in
dialogue scenes, and the use of free-ranging cameras.[17] Vernallis extends Bordwell's

[14] Vernallis, "Music Video, Songs, Sound."

[15] Ibid., 277; see also Andrew Goodwin, *Dancing in the Distraction Factory: Music Television and Popular Culture* (London: Routledge, 1993), 50–56.

[16] Vernallis, "Music Video, Songs, Sound," 278.

[17] See David Bordwell, "Intensified Continuity: Visual Style in Contemporary American Film," *Film Quarterly* 55/3 (2002):16–28, 16–21.

argument to include a range of additional audiovisual parameters, including "acting, lighting, performance, sound effects, [and] musical materials."[18] In essence, she contends that music video aesthetics accentuates an already existing tendency by adding musical structuring to the mix. Features like multiple motivic threads, unpredictable narrative structuring, open-endedness, hook-like repetition, rhythmic editing practices, and the layering of sound all contribute to an overriding musical sensibility.[19]

Two main points arise from Vernallis's analytical work that bear on the present discussion. The first is that Gondry employs a far greater density of audiovisual motivic threads, which he repeats, loops and transforms over the course of the film: more than thirty in comparison to the standard Hollywood number of five to seven. This attention to microlevel detail releases meanings unpredictably, in accordance with the priorities of surrealistic filmmaking.[20] The second is how sound and vision are often combined in unlikely configurations, becoming "untethered" or "pushed away from their sources," which opens the audiovisual text up to unconventional decodings in precisely the manner the surrealists promoted.[21] In a sense, the entire duration of the film becomes analogous to a surrealist "exquisite corpse" game, in which anything might be conjoined with anything, but in a symbolically evocative way rather than arbitrarily, as might have been theorized in the writing about postmodernism. The origins of a sound matter and exert an influence over audience interpretations of what they see and hear. An example from Vernallis's analysis is the combinations of sounds from an airport with a library scene, which produces a disturbing, alienating effect.[22]

Vernallis's theoretical apparatus works well in the context of her analysis of Gondry, and it is relatively unaffected by an aspect of technological determinism that creeps into Bordwell's work on this subject, in which formal changes are attributed primarily to the novel possibilities afforded by new media rather than the agency of directorial choice or other more complex sociocultural interactions.

Kay Dickinson has made a similar case concerning the infusion of a pop sensibility into film in an essay that discusses the proliferation of the so-called MTV aesthetic in recent films catering to "youth" taste cultures.[23] Dickinson argues that speed is a crucial factor in determining how the new films are encoded as young and exclusionary in relation to the dominant codes of older generations. Digressing from E. Anne Kaplan's ideas about subjective fragmentation in 1980s postmodernism, she argues that young people's understanding of the music-image nexus is

---

[18] Vernallis, "Music Video, Songs, Sound," 278.

[19] Ibid., 286–87.

[20] Ibid., 280–81.

[21] Ibid., 287.

[22] Ibid.

[23] Kay Dickinson, "Pop, Speed, Teenagers and the 'MTV Aesthetic,'" in Kay Dickinson, ed., *Movie Music. The Film Reader* (London: Routledge, 2003), 143–51.

shaped with reference to complex cultural formations.[24] In her view, youth films such as Baz Luhrmann's *Romeo + Juliet* (1996) cater to a teen sensibility that values musical energy, spontaneity, impatience, superficiality and speed as indices of an alternative but not necessarily fragmented subjectivity. In addition to the phenomenal presence of popular music, which resists integration into suturing narrative formations, this is conveyed through impatience with shot/reverse shot conventions, "rapid edits, often constituted from restless moving shots, zooms and swish pans of, at times, less than a second."[25] Dickinson's theory works well when applied to the genre of teen movie; teenagers do tend to appreciate fast music, fast recreational activities, fast food, and a quick turnover of everything from fashions to relationships. The value of Dickinson's formulation lies in its specificity, although the category "youth" becomes problematic as audiences age and MTV-styled editing practices become more firmly established than ever in the middlebrow and middle-aged mainstream.

Of course, many of the above tendencies can be related also to more sweeping changes in advanced capitalist, postindustrial society, as well as to the proliferation of what Anahid Kassabian calls the compiled popular soundtrack and the looser contract between the filmmaker and audiences that this transformation has occasioned.[26] Undoubtedly, commercial interests are also bound up with the renewed interest in popular soundtracks. However, I would join with Dickinson in cautioning that to attribute the new aesthetic look of recent films solely to economic factors is to oversimplify the complex nature of the social formations that surround them. Something is lost in Dickinson's account, however, insofar as she overlooks the affinity of music videos with earlier avant-garde cultural formations; a matter that Kaplan labored over in her groundbreaking work on music videos, but which the second generation of music videos research, inspired by Andrew Goodwin, seemed determined to dismantle.[27] The use of surrealist techniques may well not result in a cluster of empty signifiers, but it does destabilize semantic operations in directions that can be productive.

Film conventions are changing in other ways as well, not solely in response to the influence of music videos, but more as a wave of generational and "alternative" resistance to the perceived Hollywood mainstream. Jeffrey Sconce addresses a significant locus of change in his discussion of the "the new American 'smart' film."[28] It is not hard to perceive similarities between this aesthetic and that charted in the Nicholas

---

[24] See E. Anne Kaplan, *Rocking Around the Clock: Music Television, Postmodernism and Consumer Culture* (New York and London: Methuen, 1987).

[25] Ibid., 144.

[26] Anahid Kassabian, *Hearing Film: Tracking Identifications in Contemporary Hollywood Film Music* (New York and London: Routledge, 2001).

[27] See the chapter "MTV and the Avant Garde: The Emergence of a Postmodernist Anti-aesthetic?" in E. Anne Kaplan, *Rocking Around the Clock*, 33–48.

[28] Jeffrey Sconce, "Irony, Nihilism and the New American 'Smart' Film," *Screen* 43/4 (2002): 349–69, 342.

Rombes collection, *New Punk Cinema*.[29] Sconce discusses films directed by Quentin Tarantino, David Fincher, Todd Haynes, David Lynch, Spike Jonze, and Paul Thomas Anderson. Rombes makes reference to all of these directors and a significant number of Europeans, including Christopher Nolan, Alex Cox, Lars von Trier and Thomas Vinterberg. Perhaps this last group best encapsulates the "no bullshit," DIY ethos of punk, although there is significant overlap. Features common to both theoretical accounts include an emphasis on ironic address; nonlinear, "network" or other obscure narrative configurations; a "blank" or "dark" quality; the inclusion of random turns of fate; and a savviness with respect to coexisting cultural codes that reflects investment "in the politics of taste, consumerism and identity."[30] Not commented on at length in either of these accounts is the intimate relationship to the sounds, rhythms and moods of popular music in many of the directors' films.

A feature that distinguishes the American films in these discussions from their European counterparts is their "focus on the white middle-class family as a crucible of miscommunication and emotional dysfunction."[31] Sconce holds Todd Solondz's *Happiness* to be an exemplar of this tendency, and this film certainly demarcates a crisis in middle-class morality in contemporary North American life. This attitude toward the middle class has been popularized in studies on the American suburban dream by the British director Sam Mendez in *American Beauty* (1999) and *Revolution Road* (2008). In both films, the floating sonorities of Thomas Newman's music provide an apt auditory backdrop to the tone of the cinematography, the piano standing for a nostalgic sense of communal pleasure at the heart of white, middle-class familial life (the archetypal bourgeois piano), but in these soundtracks without teleological motivation and echoing ironically (while signifying uncannily) over stark emotional landscapes. Like the spatial expansiveness and haunting lack of resolution in the soundtracks, the visual identity of these films is characterized by liberal use of long shots and tableaux-like images of couples and familial groups thrown together awkwardly. The family in modern America has clearly changed, and this tendency as reported in recent audiovisual expression can be read as ironic commentary on right-wing calls for a return to "traditional family values." Similar aesthetic territory is explored in a number of HBO series produced in the United States, including *Six Feet Under* (2001–2005), *Angels in America* (2003), and *Hung* (2009–); and the Showtime series *Weeds* (2005–). All of these employ black humor directed at the seemingly anachronous image of the conventional American family. The first two feature soundtracks composed by Newman. The television series *House, M.D.* (2004–) explores similar audiovisual themes in its use of the surrealistically displaced piano as a nondiegetic atmospheric backdrop in countless episodes. Once again, the instrument signifies the leading character's uncanny removal

[29] Nicholas Rombes, ed., *New Punk Cinema* (Edinburgh: Edinburgh University Press, 2005).
[30] Sconce, "Irony, Nihilism," 358.
[31] Ibid.

from the supposed locus of communal well-being in the context of American cultural life, the family.

A distinct anti-Hollywood slant can be identified in many recent independent films, which err toward greater shot length at one end of the scale and extreme fragmentation at the other, both approaches articulating an oppositional attitude. In Europe, directors like Lars von Trier, Aki Kaurismäki, Wim Wenders and Derek Jarman are quite vociferous about their distaste for the Hollywood mainstream.[32] In Sconce's discussion of "the American smart film," this form of aesthetic positioning is achieved in formal terms by the use of long shots, static composition and sparse cutting.[33] But it is most powerfully conveyed in terms of mood: in an all-pervading sense of distance or "coolness" that stands in marked contrast to the dominant tone of warmth, "human" narrative contouring, and moral certitude of mainstream film.[34]

This coolness in tone, I argue, is found in soundtracks and is a feature of recent audiovisual forms on both sides of the Atlantic (and in world cinema more widely). One way in which it is conveyed is through an emphasis on repetitive sonic patterning as the driving force behind the visual narrative. In addition to the strident beats of popular music it is closely related to the tendency Susan McClary labels "minimaromantica" in her discussion of film scores by Philip Glass, Michael Nyman and Alexander Balanescu.[35] Danny Elfman's ironically tinged neo-Gothic soundtracks for the Tim Burton films, *Batman* (1989), *Edward Scissorhands* (1990), and *Mars Attacks!* (1996), evince a similar relentless and impersonal quality—an impression of mechanical rather than organic movement in time. Jon Brion's orchestral music for Paul Thomas Anderson's *Magnolia* (1999) and Hans Zimmer's for *Inception* (2010) function in much the same way, employing classical scoring means but invested with a kinetic pulse that hijacks narrative agency away from the actors, turning them into passengers on a runaway train. Common to both Elfman and Brion is a background in popular music that they bring to their encounter with the classical movie underscore. Anahid Kassabian picks up on this same iterative and nondevelopmental quality in her discussion of the science fiction genre, dubbing it "the sound of a new film form" and picking up on affinities to the experiences offered in other cultural forms, such as gaming and techno music.[36]

[32] Annette Davison has addressed this matter in her writing on European cinema, in *Hollywood Theory, Non-Hollywood Practice: Cinema Soundtracks in the 1980s and 1990s* (Aldershot: Ashgate, 2004), 70.

[33] Sconce, "Irony, Nihilism," 359.

[34] Ibid.

[35] Susan McClary, "Minima Romantica," in Goldmark, Kramer, and Leppert, eds., *Beyond the Soundtrack*, 48–65.

[36] Anahid Kassabian, "The Sound of a New Film Form," in Ian Inglis, ed., *Popular Music and Film* (London Wallflower, 2003), 91–101. On affinities between video game logic and changing ideas of filmic narrative, see also Thomas Elsaesser and Warren Buckland, *Studying Contemporary American Film: A Guide to Movie Analysis* (London: Arnold, 2002), 146–67.

As such, the idea of an "intelligent" approach to film is persuasive, just as phenomena like intelligent dance music (IDM) and periodicals with titles such as *Intelligent Life* and *The Word: Intelligent Life on Planet Rock* find a growing market-niche in an age when the avant-garde has increasingly infiltrated the popular vernacular. To the extent that intelligence presupposes an intelligent agent as producer, the concept is synonymous with a new emphasis on the *auteur* director. These days, more important to many filmgoers than the subject of a film or the presence of star actors is who directed the film: Lynch, Tarantino, Gondry or von Trier? The association of a film with an *auteur* director is widely held to be guarantor of quality or seriousness of intention. More specifically, it is an index of the values, attitude and atmosphere of a film—and even the style of music one is likely to encounter: Finnish Tango with Aki Kaurismäki; traditional jazz with Woody Allen; quirky rhythmic music composed for orchestra and sampled sounds with Tim Burton. A factor that distinguishes some of the newer auteurist films from their predecessors in the French new wave, for example, is the increasing prevalence in American films in particular of "multi-protagonist stories and episodic story structure."[37] Aside from expressing a dispassionate or "blank" disposition and evoking the parallel narrative structures of television dramas, this tendency might well go hand in hand with the increasing prominence of the auteur-director, the absence of any single leading character or character pair on which to pin identifications serving to highlight the agentic role of the director. Given the new prominence of the auteur-director in recent years, it is only a small move to include the director as an actor in the film, at the same time rendering its fictional world more self-conscious and opaque. This has been seen in films by Alex Cox (*Sid and Nancy,* 1986; *Straight to Hell,* 1987), Quentin Tarantino (*Reservoir Dogs,* 1992; *Pulp Fiction,* 1994; *Death Proof,* 2007), Sally Potter (*The Tango Lesson,* 1997), Richard Linklater (*Slacker,* 1991; *Waking Life* 2001), and David Lynch (*Twin Peaks* 1991–1992), and has an obvious precedent in films by Hitchcock and Godard. Annette Davison writes that an auteurist perspective on film allows attention to be focused on "deep structures" of meaning that extend beyond the bounds of the individual work, thereby spilling over the boundaries of the film as a sovereign work.[38] The presence of directors in the two films discussed in this chapter (Linklater as an actor; Gondry as a musician) certainly seems to indicate a certain open-endedness of conception, which encourages audiences with sufficient cultural capital to direct attention toward the extrafilmic in the filmic. In other words, it tells them that the boundaries of the form are permeable and a matter of convention; that new films have an emergent quality, to borrow Nicholas Cook's terminology; that they are performative assemblages.

For Claudia Gorbman, a taste for montage in the films of what she calls *mélomane* (or music loving) directors allows for richer experiences of the intertextual

---

[37] Sconce, "Irony, Nihilism," 362.

[38] Davison, *Hollywood Theory, Non-Hollywood Practice,* 77.

value of incorporated music.[39] In the essay "Auteur Music," Gorbman contends that directors like Quentin Tarantino, Jean-Luc Godard, Stanley Kubrick, Martin Scorsese, Spike Lee, Woody Allen, Alain Resnais, Sally Potter, Jim Jarmusch, Wim Wenders, Aki Kaurismäki and Tsai Ming-Liang imbue their films with a distinctive audiovisual imprint through their choices of music and the disjunctive relation of the soundtrack to moving images, as opposed to the techniques of previous generations, where a director would work closely with a single composer in search of more seamless audiovisual configurations (for example, Fellini-Rota, Hitchcock-Hermann, Leone-Morricone, Speilberg-Williams). Both of these approaches demarcate authorial style but Gorbman makes a convincing case that the approach of the *mélomane* director offers a culturally resonant model for directorial choices into the twenty-first century, in which the exalted status and commodification of the auteur-director takes second place to the choices they can be seen and heard to make—choices that resemble those many of us make in our daily lives, such as what music to play on our iPod or when entertaining. Culminating in a discussion of Tsai's *Dong* (*The Hole*, 1998), Gorbman identifies a "queer surrealist sensibility" in this director's neo-auteurist approach to the audiovisual contract, an assertion that implies that the same is true of other films constructed along similar aesthetic lines.[40] As Sheila Whiteley and Jennifer Rycenga insist, queering in popular forms implies a fluid and taboo-breaking outlook that extends beyond gender politics to destabilize fixed-identity categories across diverse arenas of expressive life.[41] This element of queering often coincides with surrealist strategies of displacement, the intention in both cases being to dislodge taken for granted perceptions, which in turn allows a looser leash on the imagination than is commonly taken in classically designed mainstream films. In cases of the auteur music lover, the ability to mix and match through techniques of montage and incorporation implies an intermediary presence that has the potential to upset existing orders.

A predilection for mixing can be recognized in how directors labeled as postmodernist have played with genre categories. The title of the iconic postmodernist film, *Pulp Fiction* (dir. Tarantino, 1994), points toward a preoccupation with genre mixing and the transformation of earlier genres into darker, uncanny versions of their former selves. The new compound genre of the self-reflective metamusical brings forward these tensions most directly. This will be the subject of the following chapter. For the present, suffice it to say that the element of exposure that is implicated as one genre category switches to the next opens up a space for negotiation between the filmmaker and audiences that obscures narrative transparency and, in

---

[39] See Claudia Gorbman, "Auteur Music," in Goldmark, Kramer, and Leppert, eds., *Beyond the Soundtrack*, 149–62, 151.

[40] Ibid., 160.

[41] Sheila Whiteley and Jennifer Rycenga, "Introduction," in *Queering the Popular Pitch* (New York and London: Routledge, 2006), xiv.

so doing, leaves signs of damage—a sense that everything is not as it should be. Depending on how convincing the build-up has been and how unexpected the shift, the passage away from realism is likely to occasion an element of shock resembling the convulsive effects (of the marvelous in the everyday) that preoccupied the surrealists. David Lynch's work is teeming with such gestures, applied with such precision and sensory power that even forewarning that something bizarre is likely to happen in a film cannot entirely prepare audiences for what they will experience. This can be seen in a key scene in the film *Mulholland Drive* (2001) where even explicit narrative forewarning that a singer is lip-synching seems insufficient to ward off the uncanny power of the gesture of separating the diegetic soundtrack from its corresponding images.[42]

The inclusion of music video sequences in films and television can produce analogous although usually milder disjunctive effects; such as the way actions are cut to the music in sections of Richard Kelly's *Donnie Darko* (2001). In a more subtle way, this has impinged on filmmaking at the "independent" and art-house end of the spectrum; see for example Claudia Gorbman's consideration of how the action is cut to the music in the opening sequence of Stanley Kubrick's *Eyes Wide Shut* (1999), imparting to the actors the semblance of puppets.[43] This tendency of cutting to the music can be traced at least partially to the so-called MTV aesthetic, although there are noteworthy antecedents, such as Fernand Léger's *Ballet mécanique* (1925, with music by George Antheil) and the entire genre of the Hollywood musical. The music video sequences in *Miami Vice* (1984), originally titled *MTV Cops*, are frequently cited in this regard; *Moonlighting* (1985–1989) and *Ally McBeal* (1997–2002) are other noteworthy examples.[44] Nowadays the technique is commonplace, being found in television dramas from *ER* (1994–2009) to *House M.D.* (2004–). The final episode in the final season of *Six Feet Under* (2001–2005) featured a video montage cut to the Sia song "Breathe Me," in which the future deaths of the series' leading characters are poignantly enacted.

More disjunctive and therefore more surreal than straightforward montage sequences is when characters are made to step out of the reality of their roles and react to nondiegetic music. One of the most compelling examples of this in recent cinema comes two hours and fifteen minutes into the film *Magnolia* (1999)—well past the "golden section" point of a film lasting more than three hours, when the viewer-listener is conditioned to expect no further surprises in a film's general mode

[42]   See Annette Davison, "Demystified, Remystified, and Seduced by Sirens," in John Richardson and Stan Hawkins, eds., *Essays on Sound and Vision* (Helsinki: Helsinki University Press/Yliopistopaino, 2007), 119–54, 132–34.

[43]   Claudia Gorbman, "Ears Wide Open: Kubrick's Music," in Phil Powrie and Robynn Stilwell, eds., *Changing Tunes: The Use of Pre-Existing Music in Film* (Aldershot: Ashgate, 2006), 3–18, 8.

[44]   See Julie Brown, "Ally McBeal's Postmodern Soundtrack," *Journal of the Royal Musical Association* 126/2 (2001), 275–303; and Robynn Stilwell, "It May Look Like a Living Room...: The Musical Number and the Sitcom," *Echo* 5/1 (spring 2003), paras. 1–74, 55.

of address.[45] At this point, just as audiences would expect the film to arrive at its denouement, the full cast of characters—who are embroiled in nine separate strands of a complex network narrative—join up with the nondiegetic voice of the singer-songwriter Aimee Mann to perform the song "Wise Up." The poignant nature of the moment is brought home in the melancholic mood of the song and its lyrics. The hook-line, "It's not going to stop" (until you wise up), is repeated in turn by several protagonists and comes to represent a kind of narrative aggregate or "mood barometer" of the film, while the lyrics correspond to plot details relating to individual characters. The relentless drive of Jon Brion's nondiegetic underscore leading up to this breach in the narrative fabric, and the dramatic tension it engenders, contributes greatly to the effectiveness of the montage sequence. More than an hour of scored music is heard prior to this moment in the film, while incorporated songs account for around twenty minutes of film time. Consequently, the greater part of the film is saturated with music, much of which is closely related to the film's fast-paced visual editing and seems to propel it onwards. The drama (but not the musical rhythm) is temporarily suspended in the music video sequence, whereafter the narrative takes on an increasing urgency, culminating in a biblical shower of frogs and the psychological meltdown of several characters. Over the top, doggedly grim and narratively overdetermined (because of the repetition of similar elements in the life stories of several characters), this is unquestionably one of the smarter and artier of the new American "smart films"—also with respect to its soundtrack.[46] This is, in part, because of the film's indebtedness to the affective mood of Aimee Mann's pre-existing songs, which the director readily admits. It is also because the director allows us to "see the music" and the directorial agency that put it there in the brief but telling intermission.

Genre mixing and nonrealist approaches are also prominent in what has been called the "new digital cinema."[47] Digital technology can obviously effect the aesthetics of cinema in costly and conspicuously high-tech ways, through uses of CGI technology and elevated production values. This has implications for surrealist aesthetics with increasingly unlikely visual spectacles becoming achievable with relative ease by the use of computer simulation and "blue-screen"

[45] A more detailed consideration of the use of Aimee Mann's music in *Magnolia* is found in Pauline Reay, *Music in Film: Soundtracks and Synergy* (London: Wallflower, 2004), 59–73.

[46] A similar, if inverse, sense of the uncanny is produced in director Sam Tyler-Wood's music video for Elton John's song "I Want Love" (2001). Here the star identity of Robert Downey Jr. impinges on the subject matter of the song when he lip-synchs to the vocals in place of the absent singer. What the audience knows about the actor and his highly publicized struggle with drug addiction is played out in an audiovisual narrative that vacillates between art and life. In addition to music videos, a conspicuously similar lip-synching sequence to that in *Magnolia* is found in series three, episode two of the HBO television series *Flight of the Concords* (2007–2009). Much like the *Magnolia* sequence, the characters join in with the nondiegetic song "Hurt Feelings," the lyrics each character sings apparently commenting on the plot as it relates to them.

[47] Lev Manovich, *The Language of New Media* (Cambridge, MA: MIT Press, 2001), 293–308; Holly Willis, *The New Digital Cinema: Reinventing the Moving Image* (London: Wallflower, 2005).

acting techniques. Much of the work produced in this way has, up until now, fallen into the category of "fantasy" or "science fiction," in so far as it constructs an internally consistent and plausible other world rather than drawing attention to the boundaries between reality and fiction. (The distinction is not always clear-cut, but it is worth making.) The rapid development of technologies such as photorealistic 3D computer animation and digital compositing, however, has brought about a substantial blurring of boundaries between animation and lens-based approaches.[48] At the opposite end of the scale is an emphasis on low-tech, low-budget solutions; this is typical of the Dogme 95 group in Denmark (most notably, Lars von Trier and Thomas Vinterberg), whose "vow of chastity" was meant to impose rigorous rules prescribing abstention from Hollywood's high-gloss aesthetics. Projects involving the extensive use of handheld cameras that result in a documentary or "home video" feel fall into this category as well, including the much-hyped *The Blair Witch Project* (dir. Daniel Myrick and Eduardo Sánchez, 1999) and, more recently, *Paranormal Activity* (dir. Oren Peli, 2007). The second case study of this chapter, on Gondry's *Be Kind Rewind*, can be regarded on one level as a metafilm about such user-oriented approaches. Surrealism is rare in such an aesthetic, which tends to lean heavily on perceptions of mimetic realism. Some such films do, however, bring to the fore an element of the surreal (or marvelous) in the everyday. Von Trier's *Breaking the Waves* (1996) and *Dancer in the Dark* (2000) both include elements whose surrealism is accentuated precisely because unlikely events are surrounded by a context of narrative and audiovisual banality.

Clearly "digital film" can be different things to different people and to align a style or movement directly with a given technology is questionable because of the different artistic ends they can be put to in different hands. Undoubtedly, though, new technologies—everything from mini-DV-cameras to Final Cut software—has changed how filmmakers work. At the entry point of the spectrum, editing software is more affordable than in the past, thereby enhancing the possibilities for low-tech or DIY approaches (an equivalent to lo-fi sound in music), which have at least a theoretical chance of crossing the threshold into mainstream distribution. YouTube and other forms of participatory distribution via the Internet are playing a part in this emerging nexus of creative possibilities. The documentary or archivist approach of such films and their occasional focus on absurdity in everyday life resembles the approaches of the surrealist writers Aragon and Breton. A different route toward surrealist expression is offered by the technological possibilities of digital animation technologies, a matter I reprise in my first case study, on Linklater's *Waking Life*.

Another instance of the new expressive avenues opened up by digital technologies is Peter Greenaway's use of multiple in-screen images and visual layering.[49]

---

[48] Manovich, *The Language of New Media*, 294–95.

[49] This tendency to divide up the screen was adumbrated in the early cinematic experiments of Vertov, which achieved similar end results with considerably more primitive technologies. Ibid., xv–xxxvi.

Combined with this director's pastiche-like borrowings from painterly forms and a ritualized sense of absurdity conveyed largely by musical and choreographic means, his art-house films, starting in the 1980s, represented a strong diversion away from the naturalistic mainstream. Michael Nyman, who provided the scores to many of Greenaway's most critically acclaimed films (including *The Draughtsman's Contract* [1982], *A Zed and Two Noughts* [1985], *Death in the Seine* [1988], *Drowning by Numbers* [1988], and *The Cook, the Thief, His Wife and Her Lover* [1989]), conceived of his approach to the soundtrack along the lines of music videos. Above all, Nyman's scores are characterized by their extensive use of pastiche incorporations from historical styles and by their powerful iterative quality. It is an approach to audiovisual structuring that was pioneered by Philip Glass, including his film collaborations with Godfrey Reggio: *Koyaanisqatsi: Life out of Balance* (1983), *Powaqqatsi: Life in Transformation* (1982) and *Naqoyqatsi: Life as War* (2002). An element of surrealism is invariably felt in such approaches, especially when the rhythmic structures of the soundtrack are allowed to disrupt the realistic depiction of time, through the use of slow motion, accelerated motion and time-lapse photography. Filmmakers in Hong Kong take advantage of such techniques extensively; for example, the spellbinding use of slow-motion images set to music in the films of Hong Kong director Wong Kar-Wai, such as *Chung Hing sam Iam* (*Chungking Express*, 1994), *Fa yeung nin wa* (*In the Mood for Love*, 2000), and *2046* (2004). Martial arts specialist John Woo's breakthrough film, *Hard Boiled* (*Lat sau san taam*, 1992) is a further example of the effective use of slow-motion sequences interspersed in the course of normal film action. Numerous instances of such approaches can be found in British and North American "postmodernist cinema," such as Oliver Stone's *Natural Born Killers* (1994), Danny Boyle's *Trainspotting* (1996) and *127 Hours* (2010), Guy Ritchie's *Lock, Stock and Two Smoking Barrels* (1988), Richard Kelly's *Donnie Darko* (2001) and Quentin Tarantino's *Death Proof* (2007). The technique of altering filming speed to convey a sense of the character's subjective orientation is fast becoming a conventional and therefore unnoticed feature in film and television. To the extent that this is the case, it can arguably no longer be considered a surrealist technique.

MAPPING THE AUDIOVISUAL SURREAL

While many of the above techniques impart a surrealist sensibility to audiovisual materials, surrealism often requires commitment to a specific set of stylistic and expressive principles that blur the boundaries between oppositions we have on several occasions rehearsed: art and life, waking life and sleep, life and the afterlife, consciousness and the unconscious, the physical and the metaphysical. Although numerous recent films have navigated this liminal territory, the fact that so few scholars comment on surrealist imagery reflects current critical priorities more than it does the nature of the materials. Recent years have seen a proliferation of different ways of theorizing the audiovisual in contemporary culture. Each of these has specific strengths and weaknesses. Neosurrealism is productive for how it cuts a (historicizing) swathe through existing categories, which tend to be fixated on the present day. In addition, the guiding principle in surrealist aesthetics of paradigmatic displacement suggests a willingness to reconstitute the past in strange and potentially liberating ways.

As discussed in chapter 2, Robert Ray called for the reestablishment of such a line of film theory alongside the dominant "scientific" and "classical" mode of interpreting cinema, as represented, for example, by the David Bordwell's influential approach.[50] Ray's realignment of scholarly writing on cinema along those principles envisaged by surrealist artists and filmmakers in the 1920s, overlaps closely with the concerns of the present study. Applied to a corpus encompassing everything from surrealism, Godard's French New Wave and contemporary remix music, Ray attends to those aspects of audiovisual expression that fall outside the reach of dominant rationalizing discourses. Specifically, he calls for the revolutionary moment in filmic expression to be extended in such a way that the ambiguities and surface-level specificities of audiovisual messages are understood to occupy a more central position. Thinking in similar terms to Susan Sontag in her influential essay "Against Interpretation," Ray argues for a perspective on the audiovisual that recognizes the sensory and the erotic. Ray applies this approach to the sounds of contemporary remix culture, as well as to contemporary film and photography, which offers some promise for research that is sensitive to surreal sounds as well as visions.

A primary mission of the current project is to elaborate on this conception of surreal audiovisuality with reference to the question of the neosurreal. Historical surrealism is merely a touchstone for the present discussion, although the writing on surrealism offers some useful pointers to those features worth attending to in present-day contexts. Two caveats should be kept in mind, however, when it comes to evaluating writing on surrealist film. First, this corpus of writing has very little to say about sound or audiovisuality (implying intermodal experience). Second, writing on film is often surprisingly blinkered when it comes to evaluating the broader cultural and artistic significance of the surrealist movement, especially the literary wing of surrealist thinking (Breton, Bataille, Aragon, and others), which had an important impact on early attempts to shape the movement. The influence of this body of thinking on several generations of theorists, from Benjamin to Barthes, was profound, and these perspectives inform many arguments and themes developed in these pages.

Ado Kyrou's *Le surréalisme au cinéma*, discussed in chapter 2, is an important document on cinematic surrealism, not least because of Kyrou's personal involvement in the movement as a filmmaker.[51] Nonscholarly in conception, his book

[50]   Robert B. Ray, *How a Film Theory Got Lost, and Other Mysteries of Cultural Studies* (Bloomington: Indiana University Press, 2001).

[51]   Ado Kyrou, *Le surréalisme au cinéma* (Paris: Éditions Ramsay, 1984. [1963]).

nevertheless offers some useful windows into the modes of thinking endorsed by artists in the French surrealist movement. Sections of Kyrou's work are summarized in the important English-language anthology *The Shadow & Its Shadow: Surrealist Writings on the Cinema*, which was edited and translated by Paul Hammond.[52] Again, the writings compiled in the volume are not so much academic reflections as documents evidencing how the surrealist practitioners thought. Thus, they constitute valuable secondary sources, revealing important information about discursive constructions of surrealism in its foundational stages.

Several of the more comprehensive discussions of surrealism in film begin (and often end) with some consideration of the canonical surrealist filmmaker, Luis Buñuel, especially his two early films, *Un Chien andalou* (1929) and *L'Âge d'Or* (1930).[53] Man Ray's short films (including *L'Etoile de Mer*, 1928), René Clair and Francis Picabia's *Entr'acte* (1924), Fernand Léger's *Ballet mécanique* (1925), and Germaine Dulac's *La Coquille et le clergyman* (based on a script by Antonin Artaud, 1928) are further earlier examples that are frequently mentioned in the literature. Some writers go back to the *trompe l'oeil* illusions of Georges Méliès and advance through German expressionism (Robert Wienne's *Das Cabinet des Dr. Caligari*, 1920; F. W. Murnau's *Nosferatu, eine Symphonie des Grauens*, 1922) to the French *Nouvelle Vague*, particularly the films of Alain Resnais (*Hiroshima Mon Amour*, 1959; *L'Année dernière à Marienbad*, 1961), and Jacques Rivette (such as *Céline et Julie vont en bateau* [1974]). Jean-Luc Godard's films are thought by some writers to be incompatible with surrealist aesthetics because of his Brechtian distrust of illusion, manifested in an emphasis on realistic *mise-en-scène* and the previously discussed *politique des auteurs*.[54] However, I contend that the auteurist propensities in his films could be understood as providing fertile soil for the emergence of surrealist principles. Enclaves of surrealist activity (proper) are generally held to survive to this day, through the activities of avant-garde exponents such as the Czech animator Jan Švankmajer and other work conducted under the umbrella of accredited surrealist groups (by this I mean those closely affiliated to Breton and/or his followers).[55]

Rigid definitions of surrealism based on the intentional affiliations of producers fail to accommodate the sort of "accidental" surrealist imagery that is frequently

---

[52] Paul Hammond, ed. and trans., *The Shadow & Its Shadow: Surrealist Writings on the Cinema* (San Francisco: City Lights Books, 2000).

[53] See J. H. Matthews, *Surrealism and Film* (Ann Arbor: University of Michigan Press, 1971); Michael Richardson, *Surrealism and Cinema* (Oxford: Berg, 2006); Wendy Everett, "Screen as Threshold: The Disorientating Topographies of Surrealist Film," *Screen* 39/2 (Summer 1998): 141–52; Phil Powrie, "Masculinity in The Shadow of the Slashed Eye: Surrealist Film Criticism at the Crossroads," *Screen* 39/2 (Summer 1998): 153–63; Ramona Fotiade, "The Untamed Eye: Surrealism and Film Theory," *Screen* 36/4 (Winter 1995): 394–407; Ramona Fotiade, "The Slit Eye, the Scorpion and the Sign of the Cross: Surrealist Film Theory and Practice Revisited," *Screen* 39/2 (Summer 1998): 394–407.

[54] Richardson, *Surrealism and Cinema*, 166.

[55] Ibid., 13–15.

found in popular genres, including the slapstick comedy of Charlie Chaplin and in film genres such as horror, musicals and romance.[56] Michael Richardson has done more than most commentators to flesh out the concept of the surreal film by flagging elements of surrealism in more recent cinema, even while his treatment of the subject remains rooted in a fairly conservative understanding of what constitutes surrealism in film. Among those that he lists as displaying surrealist proclivities include the Italian directors Michelangelo Antonioni, Frederico Fellini, Bernardo Bertolucci and the Taviani brothers; the Polish directors Wojciech Has and Krysztof Kieslowski; the Germans Werner Herzog and Wim Wenders; the Belgian André Delvaux; the Spaniards Carlos Saura, Victor Erice and Pedro Almodóvar; and the Japanese Nagisa Oshima, Kenji Mizoguchi, Hiroshi Teshingahara, and Hayao Miyazaki.[57] Richardson further identifies pockets of surrealism in countries including Iran, India, Hong Kong and Mali, but he remains strangely reticent on the issue of surrealism in recent Anglophone cinema and television—central to the present discussion.[58] Claudia Gorbman rightly considers the Taiwanese director Tsai Ming-Liang's approach to be surrealist. In addition, the films of the Chinese director Jia Zhangke (*San Xia Hao Red* [*Still Life*, 2006]; *Shijie* [*The World*, 2004]) reveal a strong surrealist impulse, even if this is conveyed (as often seems to be the case) through an aesthetic of intensified realism interspersed by convulsive breaks from a realist baseline.

The view advanced here is somewhat different from these earlier discussions. The blurring of the independent-studio divide (as commented on by Bordwell and others), among other factors, has made it increasingly difficult to distinguish between mainstream, art-house/independent and experimental cinematic forms. Remakes highlight a particular problem area. Critical opinion tends to favor the artistic original over the commodified copy and accords art-house status more readily. Significant surrealist remakes include Cameron Crowe's *Vanilla Sky* (2001), a literal copy of Alejandro Amenábar's markedly surrealist *Abre Los Ojos* (1997); Stephen Soderbergh's *Solaris* (2002), a remake of Andrei Tarkovsky's *Solyaris* (1972); and why not also Sergio Leone's *A Fistful of Dollars* (1967), which drew its inspiration from Akira Kurosawa's *Yojimbo* (1961). For producers, repackaging a proven product that stands out as artistically challenging is a potentially lucrative modus operandi. This is just one way in which the influence on recent American cinema of international art-house traditions is being felt: through strategies of incorporation. More indirect stylistic incorporations in the films of new generation directors are another, including the influence of Hong Kong and French cinema on Quentin Tarantino. I further contend that an influx of surrealist approaches is making its way into the "independent" mainstream by other paths, not least in the work

[56]   See Matthews, *Surrealism and Film*; Ado Kyrou, *Le Surréalism au cinema*, 3rd edition (Paris: Le Terrain Vague, 1985).

[57]   Richardson, *Surrealism and Cinema*, 168.

[58]   Ibid., 165–71.

of music video producers turned filmmakers, such as Spike Jonze (*Being John Malkovich,* 1999; *Adaptation,* 2002); Michel Gondry (*Eternal Sunshine of the Spotless Mind,* 2004; *The Science of Sleep,* 2006; *Be Kind Rewind,* 2008); and Jonathan Glazer (*Birth,* 2004).

An absurdist, surrealist or extended-realist British tradition spanning Ken Russell, Dennis Potter (the Anglophile American expatriate) Terry Gilliam, Derek Jarman, Sally Potter, Danny Boyle, not to mention aspects of surrealist absurdity in popular culture, from *Monty Python* to *The League of Gentlemen,* has paved a crooked path toward wider acceptance of surrealist expression.[59] Andrew Spicer traces a surrealist strain in British popular culture back "at least to the nonsense genre in the mid-Victorian period," which is "part of a rich fantasy tradition that had its origins in Gothic fiction and the Romantic poets."[60] Surrealism in the British tradition often takes the form of an eccentric nonconformity and irreverence, which can be recognized in genres such as the British horror film and the madcap comedy, in addition to the films of maverick auteur-directors. Auteur films by such directors as Michael Powell and Emeric Pressburger, Ken Russell and Derek Jarman are included in Spicer's evaluation of the British filmic surreal.[61] Not included are Nicolas Roeg, Peter Greenaway, and Danny Boyle, although a strong case could be made for their inclusion. Terry Gilliam is a prime case for inclusion, not least because of his collaborative role in the absurdist and frequently surreal Monty Python films, but more notably as auteur-director of the films *Brazil* (1985), *Twelve Monkeys* (1995), *Fear and Loathing in Las Vegas* (1998), *Tideland* (2005), and *The Imaginarium of Doctor Parnassus* (2009). Gilliam's work builds on an absurdist line in Anglo-American audiovisual culture spanning vaudeville, television comedy and contemporary film.

In the North American context, auteur-directors such as Stanley Kubrick (*A Clockwork Orange,* 1971; *The Shining,* 1980; *Eyes Wide Shut,* 1999), Francis Ford Coppola (*Apocalypse Now,* 1979), Martin Scorsese (*Taxi Driver,* 1976) and Robert Altman (*Nashville,* 1975; *Short Cuts,* 1993) have all in different ways pushed cinema away from mimetic realism for several decades, their example coaxing younger directors toward the ambiguous rewards and prestige status of the unfathomable.[62] Surrealist influences have probably been picked up from neighboring artistic

[59] See Kay Dickinson, *Off Key: When Film and Music Won't Work Together* (Oxford: Oxford University Press, 2008), 81–117; and Annette Davison, *Hollywood Theory, Non-Hollywood Practice,* 117–38.

[60] Andrew Spicer, "An Occasional Eccentricity: The Strange Course of Surrealism in British Cinema," in Graeme Harper and Rob Stone, eds., *The Unsilvered Screen: Surrealism on Film* (London: Wallflower Press, 2007), 102–14, 102.

[61] Ibid., 103.

[62] It should be recognized up front that surrealist discourse often reveals an investment in Bourdieu's problematic politics of distinction: it is a "difficult" discourse that requires a high level of competence from audiences, which can translate into a form of cultural capital. See Pierre Bourdieu, *Distinction: A Social Critique of the Judgement of Taste,* trans. Richard Nice (Cambridge, MA: Harvard University Press, 1984).

discourses as well: the influence of theater and performance art in particular are likely to have had an impact on film directors. Theater directors like Robert Wilson and Julie Taymor, and performance artists like Laurie Anderson and Meredith Monk have all favored nonrealist modes of presentation that build on a tradition of absurdist and anti-rationalist theater going back to Samuel Beckett and Antonin Artaud. In addition, the surrealist novel (an approach some have called "magical realism") is currently exerting a growing influence, with writers like Salman Rushdie, David Mitchell, and Haruki Murakami exploring the threshold between realistic writing and flights of the imagination.

The greatest impetus for change, however, is arguably through the realization that this is simply how the edgier films are being made these days. Many films mentioned in discussions of "new punk cinema," "the American smart film" and "new digital cinema" fall into this category, although a significant proportion do not. Dramatic rationales for a collective pull away from realism across the entire audiovisual field are diverse. Often the films I class as neosurrealist (or which alternate between heightened realist and surrealist styles) have a marked psychedelic feel, reflecting the desire to capture a druggy experience or some mode of altered consciousness. Ken Russell's *Altered States* (1980) is an important precursor in this respect. Danny Boyle's *Trainspotting* (1997) and *Shallow Grave* (1994), Terry Gilliam's *Fear and Loathing in Los Angeles* (1998), and Richard Linklater's *A Scanner Darkly* (2006) fall into this category. Others are concerned with metaphysical or indeterminately "spiritual" subject matter, a line that goes back to Kubrick's *2001: A Space Odyssey* (1968), as well as Andre Tarkovsky's *Solaris* (*Solyaris*, 1972) and *Mirror* (*Zerkalo*, 1975). Science fiction that borders on a surrealist sensibility includes Ridley Scott's *Bladerunner* (1982) and the Wachowski brothers' *Matrix* trilogy (*The Matrix*, 1999; *The Matrix Reloaded*, 2003; *The Matrix Revolutions*, 2003). To the extent that science fiction as a genre is concerned with "virtual reality," it falls squarely into the domain of the surreal. Genre expectations surrounding science fiction as a (heightened) realistic depiction of future lives work against its inclusion as surreal in the strictest sense of the term, however. These expectations and the restrictions they impose on directors undoubtedly have something to do with both Tarkovsky's and Kubrick's disaffection with the genre, even after both directors had produced what are widely lauded as seminal works in the science fiction genre.

Neosurrealist films can be many things: they can be reflexive (Resnais's *L'Année dernière à Marienbad*, 1961; Jonze's *Adaptation*, 2002), playfully deconstructive (Gondry's *Be Kind Rewind*, 2008; Anderson's *Magnolia*, 1999; Jim Jarmusch's *Broken Flowers*, 2005; Wes Anderson's *The Royal Tenenbaums*, 2001; Errol Morris's "performative documentaries" *The Thin Blue Line*, 1988; *and Mr. Death*, 1999), noncommittally metaphysical (Kelly's *Donnie Darko*, 2001; Lynch's *Twin Peaks*, 1991–1992), grotesque in a Bataillean way (Cronenberg's *Videodrome*, 1983; Lynch's *Eraserhead*, 1977; and *Blue Velvet*, 1986), or carnivalesque/burlesque (after Fellini; Lynch's fascination with giants and dwarfs; circus aesthetics; Luhrmann's *Moulin Rouge*, 2001).

Sometimes they can be all of these things at once. David Lynch is perhaps the most compelling example of a director who is able to draw on all of the above qualities.

Neosurrealist films do not shy away from big issues such as the nature of life, death, physical and/or metaphysical issues, memory, the darker side of humanity or the complex nature of identity.[63] As a downside they have a tendency toward earnestness, narrative obscurity and solipsism, although some are couched in a campy humor designed to deflect such perceptions (e.g, dir. Luc Besson, *The Fifth Element*, 1997). Some neosurrealist films are studies on memory, most notably Alain Resnais's (*Hiroshima Mon Amour*, 1959; *L'Année dernière à Marienbad*, 1961), Christopher Nolan's *Memento* (2000), Gondry's *Eternal Sunshine of the Spotless Mind* (2004) and Lynch's *Lost Highway* (1997). A preoccupation with dreams (or the subconscious) and the impression of suspended or alternative reality they evoke is a feature of many of the most obviously surrealist films. The term oneiric film has been coined to describe this approach. Akira Kurosawa's *Dreams* (1990) is an obvious example (incorporated in a scene of another such film, Linklater's *Waking Life*). An impression of suspended reality is conveyed in several of Kieslowski's films, including *The Double Life of Véronique* (1991) and *Trois couleurs: Bleu (1993)*. Lars von Trier's characters become caught up in dark or frivolous parallel worlds, most notable the female protagonists of the "Golden Hearts" trilogy: *Breaking the Waves* (1996), *The Idiots* (1998) and *Dancer in the Dark* (2000). Many of David Lynch's protagonists are uncertain whether what they are experiencing is imaginary or real (e.g, *Mulholland Drive*, 2001; *Inland Empire*, 2006).[64] Cronenberg's *Videodrome* (1982) is a critical reflection on a dreamlike, disempowered state imposed on individuals by contemporary consumer society, wherein lies a possible critical function of the oneiric film. Much like music videos such as Bowie's *Ashes to Ashes*, or the depictions of solipsistic "inner worlds" in films like Resnais's *L'Année dernière à Marienbad* and Rivette's *Céline et Julie vont en bateau,* the purpose seems to be to issue a kind of warning, an injunction on behalf of waking consciousness and human agency, even while the mesmerising power of the dreams (or the unconscious) is recognized as indispensible to the human condition. A compelling (political and personal) argument for neosurrealist forms is that they present us with a world so hermetically

---

[63] Todd Haynes's *I'm Not There* (2007), featuring multiple Bob Dylans played by male and female, adult and child, white and black actors is a radical example of the last category.

[64] Kelly's *Donnie Darko* (2001) is conspicuously Lynchian in this respect, although his approach might be considered a kind of "Lynch-lite": Lynch rendered more palatable for the lucrative teen demographic. The same could be said of *Kiss Kiss Bang Bang* (dir. Shane Black, 2005) in relation to Tarantino's *Pulp Fiction*. Such films offer a more accessible take on the aesthetics of independent filmmaking, with more obvious narrative signposting, less shock and an all-round lighter mood. As such they serve a valuable crossover function and point toward how the aesthetics of the independent or smart-film is permeating the mainstream. The impact of mainstream-indie crossovers is also evidenced in the box-office success of films like *Fargo* (dir. Joel Coen and Ethan Coen, 1996), *Lost in Translation* (dir. Sofia Coppola, 2003), *Little Miss Sunshine* (dir. Jonathan Dayton and Valerie Faris, 2006), and *Juno* (dir. Jason Reitman, 2007).

sealed, so seductive in its narrative pull, that it repels even while it entices—in a sense it sucks us in and spits us out. When we see characters in films by Lynch or Resnais asking themselves what is real and what imagined, when we encounter twist and turns in the plot that are not comfortably or credibly resolved, or genre-shifting crises in signification (localized moments of shock, which I prefer to think of as *wonder*; often indicated by uncomfortable diegetic-nondiegetic transitions), it prompts us to ask similar questions about experiences in our daily lives. In this respect there is a deconstructive or *reflective* agenda to oneiric films that alongside their close attention to sensory experience becomes one of their most distinctive (and redemptive) features. I will now turn to a film that seems to encapsulate many of the issues discussed above.

Richard Linklater's *Waking Life*—on Sensory and Didactic Cinema

VISUAL MICRORHYTHMS AND AUDIOVISUAL ARTIFICE

Arguably, the most striking feature of Richard Linklater's *Waking Life* is its shimmering visual quality. This is the first feature-length film produced exclusively by using rotoscoping, which requires the animator to trace the outlines of previously filmed images onto new film stock frame by frame, after which new colors and shading can be applied. The history of the technique extends back as far as Disney's *Snow White* (1937); its purpose to imbue animated films with a level of mimetic realism or detail that they do not ordinarily possess. Linklater charged animator Bob Sabiston with the job of developing a software-based approach to rotoscoping for the film, which would then be employed by a team of animators as the technical basis for their overdrawing of footage filmed predominantly with handheld digital cameras. The documentary style of *Waking Life* is strongly reminiscent of the same director's *Slacker* (1991). However, the rotoscoping technique transforms filmed materials markedly, while raising implicit questions about the nature of the audiovisual contract and the meanings it is equipped to convey.

Obviously evocative of children's cartoons, the film's adult mode of address nevertheless seems to indicate an uncanny sense of detachment from childhood experiences that cannot be regained, merely recalled. We see this most directly this in the opening moments of the film: a flashback to the protagonist's childhood. More than this, the imagery invokes elements of the music video aesthetic (for example, Aha's critically acclaimed "Take on Me" was produced using rotoscoping), while bringing to mind the pop-art feel of Andy Warhol's gaudily colored photo-silkscreen prints. An additional precursor is the avant-garde technique of painting directly onto film stock, developed by video artists like Stan Brakhage. Apparently at odds with all of the above is the style of the cinematography in *Waking Life*, which draws on radical techniques in transitions between scenes, but for the most part relies on the standard conventions of documentary filmmaking, including a predominance of headshots and the use of on-location diegetic sound. In this respect, the film conforms to realist audiovisual conventions, even though its visual look is far from being realistic. The subversive potential of animation is most tangibly experienced when the animators take license to stray from the primary directive of the filmed material to illustrate or to comment on spoken dialogue in their uses of animated imagery. This produces an element of visual counterpoint that resembles the uses made of foreground-background discrepancies in Aardman Animations films, such as *Wallace and Gromit*.[65] It is a technique that highlights Brechtian concerns about the distribution of agency among the constituent elements of the audiovisual text and in this way indicates a broadly critical and dialectical function.

Each character in *Waking Life* is furnished with a distinctive visual identity, a result of the mode of production, in which a separate character was assigned to each animator, some of them appearing nearly photographic while others are sketchy or impressionistic. Notwithstanding this stylistic diversity, the film has a uniform visual feel, which results both from the nature of the preexisting camerawork and the visual fingerprint left by the technique of rotoscoping. It is a fingerprint that addresses a specific interpretive community: one weaned on the audiovisual products and technologies of the MTV age. This is the same "smart audience" referred to earlier, which responds to the infectious pull of popular culture while also drawing on more refined audiovisual codes.

Rotoscoping produces images whose movement is alive with microvisual fuss and flurry, which in Michel Chion's words highlights "the swarming movement of photographic grain itself."[66] This grounds the turnover of images in the unfolding Now while foregrounding the intermediary role of the producers. An element of defamiliarization implicit in the approach matches the subject matter of the oneiric film. It therefore serves two distinct ends that are not contradictory: the technique is simultaneously immersive and estranging. Alienation as conveyed in the dark hews of early twentieth-century works of art does not, however, appear to be what the technique is about. David Hockney's iridescent color palette or the stylistic language of comic books are closer matches to the color scheme of this film, but inscribed with a sense of perpetual motion that that brings to mind the iterative beats and shifting timbral patterns of musical styles like minimalism or electronic

---

[65] For a discussion of how similar effects are produced in the Peter Gabriel video, "Sledgehammer," see John Richardson, "Plasticine Music: Surrealism in Peter Gabriel's 'Sledgehammer,'" in Michael Drewett, Sarah Hill and Kimi Kärki, eds., *Games Without Frontiers: Peter Gabriel From Genesis to Growing Up* (Farnham and Burlington: Ashgate, 2010), 195–210.

[66] Michel Chion, *Audio-Vision: Sound on Screen*, trans. Claudia Gorbman (New York: Columbia University Press, 1994), 16.

dance music. On a phenomenal level, this directs attention to the frames' passing, and therefore the temporality of the filmic media. It further prompts audiences to attend to the fact that *Waking Life* was assembled frame by frame, thereby indicating a bottom line of stasis, emptiness or death.[67] The film's wobbly appearance is therefore a marker both of its vitality and the fact that it is essentially *on life support*, the juxtaposition of life and death, past and present consciousness, and the liminal position it occupies between the two anticipating the narrative outcome of the film.

SYNOPSIS AND OVERVIEW

To talk about a synopsis in reference to this film is somewhat misleading. *Waking Life* does not have an obvious narrative structure, being a string of episodic interview fragments tied together more loosely than is customary in mainstream cinema. In this respect, the film might best be described using the analogy of a Deleuzian "body without organs," to the extent that the usual hierarchies of narrative form and their interdependencies are not present as you would expect in traditional film form. *Waking Life* does, nevertheless, have a structure of sorts and an implied narrative design. In short, the film's action track the adventures of its largely silent hero, a young man named Wiley Wiggins, who essentially plays a lucidly dreaming and imaginatively embellished version of himself. Wiggins spends the greater part of the film trying to work out his place in the grand scheme of things. He does this by consulting experts and lay people, from philosophers and poets to film directors. Most pressingly, he tries to ascertain whether he is asleep or awake, independent or controlled by external social or natural forces, and alive or dead. These questions and the surrounding atmosphere of mystery place the film quite firmly in the domain of surrealist expression. The plotline, such as it is, unfolds by means of a series of embedded dreams within dreams (or false awakenings), which in a pivotal scene coincides with the protagonist's visit to a cinema, thereby turning the Russian doll-like structure of his experiences into something the viewer can relate to directly, through the embedded image of a film within a film. Loosely speaking, the beginning, middle, and end sections are characterized by positive affect and what might, in a limited sense, be considered reliable narrators (people in the real world who offer helpful advice). Both the middle and end sections, however, are preceded by more confused encounters, which occasion existential concern on the part of the protagonist. These are characterized by a predominance of negative effect. Examples include encounters with a prisoner consumed by hate, a self-destructive man who splashes himself with gasoline before setting himself on fire, and a shoot-out between two proselytizers of permissive U.S. gun laws, culminating in the death of both. Both the

---

[67] See Laura Mulvey, *Death 24x a Second: Stillness and the Moving Image* (London; Reaktion Books, 2006).

beginning and end sections of the film feature cameo appearances by the director, as a passenger in the backseat of a car and as a man playing a pinball machine. Preceding both of these encounters are live musical performances filmed in documentary fashion. Central to the design of the film is that the individual scenes do not fit together by means of traditional cause-and-effect linearity. Instead the protagonist dreams his way from one apparently random encounter to the next, the dreamscape being provided by Glover Gill's atmospheric music and animated images of the boy drifting skywards. Despite the film's seemingly random structure, a sense of order can be perceived in the layout of its scenes, which frames the intentions of the author-director. This authorial presence is visible at the film's beginning and end, in Linklater's cameos, as well as being implied through the reflexive technique of the film within a film, a meditation on the film theories of André Bazin, which happens at about its golden-section point. The distinctive audiovisual style, moreover, points toward an auteurist appreciation of directorial agency. *Waking Life* is a dense and complicated tapestry of filmic materials, comprising a cornucopia of significant details, including allusions to the director's own earlier films (explicitly, *Slacker*, 1991; and *Before Sunrise*, 1995); the films of other directors (e.g., Kurosawa's *Dreams*, 1990); quotations from scholars (e.g., Guy Debord, Benedict Anderson, and Robert C. Solomon, a former philosophy professor of Linklater's); and numerous other indicators of its status as an "intelligent film." Any analytical consideration must therefore be selective. Mine focuses on audiovisuality and the nexus of issues surrounding neosurrealism. There is a psychedelic, spacey or new-agey atmosphere to certain scenes—an approach that is well served by the animated means of production, which become more evident in Linklater's subsequent rotoscoped film, *A Scanner Darkly* (2006).[68] This is expressed in the director's willingness to give even the most outrageous ideas an airing, and his attention to matters of extended or altered consciousness. As such it speaks to the open-mindedness of the film's director and is consistent with his surrealist outlook.

EXISTENTIAL BEGINNINGS AND ENDINGS: HAPTICITY AND SECONDNESS

The opening moments of *Waking Life* depict a flashback to childhood that takes place in the mind of the film's unnamed protagonist: a kind of silent everyman, who because of his passive stance easily substitutes for the audience. Indeed, he is often seated in a cinema like the assumed audience. A young girl (the director's daughter, Lorelei) pulls back the leaf of a paper puzzle and reads to the boy: "Dream is destiny." The girl's enigmatic linguistic cue cedes to the first musical

---

[68] These are not the only Linklater films that dealt with drug-related experiences. In an early film, *Dazed and Confused* (1993), this subject matter is dealt with directly.

cue of the film, in which dreamy arpeggio figures played softly on the piano outline a haunting sonority: a thirdless minor sixth with added ninth. This tonally ambiguous chord rises in its second instance to incorporate the missing minor third of the tonic triad (A minor min6). The initially missing minor third serves as a signifier of absence, by dint of the fact that an uncanny void is found where the primary determinant of musical affectivity ought to be, conveying a cool or depersonalized agency that is typical of the film's atmosphere. (We will encounter this sonority in later chapters, primarily in chapter 7). Here it imparts to the images a retrospective quality, since music of this type does not belong to childhood. It represents a form of emotional conditioning that interprets childhood through the lens of melancholic adult experience; just as the animated imagery is redolent of childhood while simultaneously intimating a more knowing contemporaneous consciousness.

The sense of mystery conveyed by the opening chords is strengthened when a haunting *bandoneón* joins almost imperceptibly on an extended high fifth, only to descend stepwise to the irresolute and depersonalized added second. The manner in which the dissonant minor sixth rubs against the adjacent fifth and the resonant piano articulation both produce a mood of pensive displacement. Nostalgic and ethnically marked, the presence of the bandoneón (as a messenger of absence) reinforces a pervasive sense of the uncanny.[69] The boy looks up to see a shooting star in the darkened sky, his vision accompanied by rumbling signifiers of an existential sublime, which evidently plays a part in propelling the young protagonist skyward. Levitation, we will learn, is a sign that he is dreaming and is confirmed by a shot of a youth dozing on a train. This was evidently a flashback in the older boy's head; a flashback that leaves a great deal unexplained. A move to the subdominant function (A thirdless D minor sixth with added ninth) brings a small injection of romantic pathos through the addition of a degree of chromaticism, which situates the soundtrack along a borderline between sophisticated nuevo-tango and the post-Romantic chamber orchestra.

A fade to black and its sonic counterpart silence bring a shift in narrative levels. An onscreen chamber orchestra resumes the interrupted music ("Mi Otra Mitad de Naranja"), but now played at a faster tempo, modulating around a pivot chord of F7 and with a strident nuevo-tango rhythm (see Figure 3.1.). A cascade of laughter from members of a string quartet offers a snapshot of feminine *jouissance* in a sonic context of heightened realism. Documentary realism is conveyed above all by small auditory details such as the sound of a dropped pencil and the way the instruments become louder as the camera approaches them (indicating realist

[69] See, for example, Powrie's discussion of the French accordion as a signifier of melancholic retrospection. Phil Powrie, "The Fabulous Destiny of the Accordion in French Cinema," in Powrie and Stilwell, eds., *Changing Tunes*, 137–51, 148.

"point of audition" camera work). The music of this scene is characterized by a marked tactile feel, which is brought home by the corporeality of the musicians' relationship to their instruments. The use of "extended" performance techniques in the scoring further accentuates this aspect, as the string players bow behind the bridges of their instruments (*dietro il ponticello*) to produce a scraping, percussive

Figure 3.1   (continued)

Figure 3.1 (continued)　Rehearsal scene from *Waking Life*, "Mi Otra Mitad de Naranja." Music by Glover Gill. Copyright Beethoven's Bust (ASCAP).

sound, which causes them to laugh.[70] The (male) double bass player employs rockabilly-styled "slap" techniques. Verbal instructions from the *bandoneón* player, band leader and composer, Glover Gill, "rock-out" to the bass player, "dig in" to the string quartet, highlight the informal mood of what is evidently a band rehearsal. A

[70] Note that grating tone is accentuated in the musical score by references to the use of sandpaper as a percussive instrument.

similar visceral quality is imparted through the cinematography, both in terms of the animated blurriness of the images, which brings about a sensory bifurcation between visual flatness and depth, and because of the nature of camerawork, where the jerky handheld feel of the footage and abrupt swish-pans synchronized to musical transitions imply both embodied movement and connotations of MTV-styled cool. This mode of cinematography is rooted in video art, but when seen in the context of an energetic musical performance, it is intuitively understood as a generational marker that invokes music video aesthetics.[71]

All of this signals a crossing of narrative levels from the diegetic underscore to the "nondiegetic" or implied extrafilmic "beyond" occupied by the director and musicians. Shots of the musicians rehearsing strongly recall similar scenes in Godard's *Prénom: Carmen* (1984), not only because of an element of diegetic-nondiegetic ambiguity as one scene transitions to the next, but also because of the use of handheld cameras, close-ups of hands, ambient sounds, and the use of pizzicato, which produces a markedly percussive and corporeal feel. The animated visual style nevertheless remains constant throughout, reminding us of the fictive or performatively real nature of *all cinema* (even documentary cinema). Comments by the composer seem to reflect on the aesthetic of the film beyond the soundtrack: "I want it to sound rich and maybe slightly wavy due to being slightly out of tune"; and "I think that it should be slightly detached" (3:41). According to Glover Gill, who spoke them, these comments were unscripted and were taken from of an actual rehearsal filmed by Linklater and his team. In the context in which they are placed at the start of the film, however, they take on a more profound significance, reflecting back on the film's visual aesthetic: "richness" could apply equally to the color scheme of the film; "waviness" brings to mind the unstable qualities of the digitally "detuned" rotoscoped forms.[72] Detachment and distance are qualities that might be applied to other aspects of the film as well, such as the use of collage and self-reflexive techniques. Distancing does not necessarily imply a strict Brechtian understanding of the term; however, it could equally refer to the foregrounding of aesthetic surfaces over content, as implied in a monologue by a car-boat captain, who the protagonist meets immediately after the rehearsal scene. Aesthetics understood as something fluid is foremost in these comments: "You wanna keep things on an even keel," he proclaims. "You wanna go with the flow. The sea refuses no river. The idea is to remain in a state of constant departure while always arriving." We reprise this aquatic sensibility in the following chapter; for the present, suffice it to say these comments communicate something essential about the aesthetic workings of the

---

[71] For a detailed discussion of visual haptics and erotics in video art, see Laura Marks, "Video Haptics and Erotics," *Screen* 39/4 (Winter 1998): 331–48.

[72] Personal correspondence with Glover Gill (February 15, 2009): "The initial rehearsal was just that: A real rehearsal of two new pieces we were reading while the crew filmed—no script, though Wiley [Wiley Wiggins, the actor] was on location just in case Rick [Richard Linklater] wanted him."

film. It seems no accident that this monologue is granted such a prominent position in the film. Both music and images bob around through much of its duration like so much flotsam and jetsam. These comments seem to reveal an element of intentionality concerning these effects.

This dual focus between narrative detachment and sensory involvement is placed in a technological rubric when the music once again segues from a documentary (and diegetic extrafictional) to a conventional nondiegetic function, as attention turns toward the image of a youth on a train. The driving force of the music synchronizes with the movement of the engine and wheels of the train in the process of mutual attribution Chion calls synchresis. This depersonalized, because mechanical, use of music is easily related to the revisionist approaches to classical underscoring found in numerous recent films, including those of Michael Nyman, Philip Glass, Jon Brion and Danny Elfman. The diegetic sound of screeching brakes, heard as the train and its accompanying nondiegetic music come to a halt, points in this direction, hinting that an element of trauma might be enfolded within the action (consider the ominous undertones of a composition like Steve Reich's *Different Trains*).[73] Even while the music prominently employs Modernist instrumental techniques, the rigid affective qualities of the tango provides a conduit for musical sounds that are never quite as human, expressive or *musical* as mainstream audiences are comfortable hearing. In this way the music, much like the animated images, comes to occupy a liminal position between waking life and the inanimate (or posthuman) world that lies beyond.

This kind of tango is a ubiquitous presence in the soundtrack. Most of this music was performed by the Tosca Tango Orchestra, an ensemble from Linklater's home town of Austin, Texas, directed by the composer, Glover Gill, who plays himself in the film (the heavily tattooed bandoneón player mentioned previously). The choice of tango music for the soundtrack is easy to understand. Because of its stringent formal qualities, the dance has an impersonal quality that complements the corresponding depersonalized images. In its ballroom forms in particular, the tango's abrupt head snaps, staccato footwork and sharp interlocking kicks desubjectify the body in a way that corresponds to Linklater's cool approach to the images—but still implying a highly disciplined and *disciplining* form of passion. The cultural history of the dance invokes a popular, occasionally vulgar, line spanning its origins as an Argentinian folk dance, cross-cultural appropriation in the glitzy and camped up world of ballroom dancing, a somewhat elevated renaissance in nuevo tango, as well as localized hybrids around the world, such as the Finnish tango. The use of the tango is evocative of Ástor Piazzolla's refined approach to the style, but conjoining with both popular expression and experimentalist aesthetics, the latter of which comes out in the attention given to the more abrasive and embodied aspects of the dance.

---

[73] For an important essay on the dysphoric connotations of repetitive music when combined with concrete sounds and textual allusions to the holocaust, see Naomi Cumming's "The Horrors of Identification: Reich's *Different Trains*," *Perspectives of New Music* 35/1 (1997): 129–52.

Passionate yet detached, mechanical yet human, coarse yet refined, in contemporary contexts the tango is easily perceived as a form of intelligent dirty dancing. Gill's musical score reflects the hybrid lineage of the dance, which allows the composer to incorporate high modernist expressive techniques while nevertheless calling on the musicians to "rock-out."

The boundary-crossing qualities of tango music have secured for it a position in the art-house and auteur film niche across the years, including Buñuel's *Un Chien andalou* (1929), Bertolucci's *Ultimo tango a Parigi* (*Last Tango in Paris*), Sally Potter's *The Tango Lesson* (1997), several Aki Kaurismäki films (e.g., *Tulitikkutehtaan tyttö*, *The Match Factory Girl*, 1990; and *Mies vailla menneisyyttä*, *The Man Without a Past*, 2002), and Terry Gilliam's *Twelve Monkeys* (1995) and *The Imaginarium of Doctor Parnassus* (2009).[74] A camp sense of anachronism allows the dance to occupy an ambiguous position between expression and reflection that resembles the use of other recuperated Latin dance form in cinema: for example, the Bolero in Almodóvar's films.[75] The dance's hyperbolic drama and climactic passion make it the ideal musical form to situate in proximity to the final dramatic turn of a film, a function it serves in *Last Tango in Paris*. Linklater may well have been thinking of Bertolucci when he set the decisive scene of his film in a tango club, with the young protagonist an intoxicated spectator to a song and dance spectacle; not intoxicated from alcohol as Brando was, but from a surplus of sensory stimuli and an abundance of (literally) floating signifiers, the corporeal feel of the music and the kinaesthetic qualities of the dancing and energetic camerawork giving rise to an element of Eisensteinian attraction.

Preceding the tango dance that initiates the ending of the film, Linklater offers a meditation on aging, at first in a resigned mood, but visually rendered with an enriched and impressionistic palette of colors—albeit with a detached, painting-by-numbers feel. Here the protagonist ambles through a garden populated by elderly artists, one of whom presents him with a portrait; all the while this is accompanied by melancholic piano arpeggios and a floating clarinet (*Balade* 3; 1:18:25). A visual cut finds Wiggins in darkness, situated in a concrete underpass in downtown Austin where he is surrounded by traffic noise. A passing stranger utters the line, "Kierkegarde's last words were 'sweep me up'"—one of numerous apparently random encounters in the film, which in this instance indicates that the film is approaching its own narrative dissolution. As the boy nears a nightclub, he and we perceive the muted tones of a tango orchestra drifting into the night. The sounds become clearer in tone and louder as he enters the building, where the tango ensemble from the opening scene performs to a small group of dancers. Evidently

[74] For commentary on the Finnish tango in Kaurismäki's films, see Erkki Pekkilä, "Tango, twist ja Tšaikovski: Musiikki Aki Kaurismäen elokuvassa Tulitikkutehtaan tyttö," *Musiikki* 3 (2005): 45–65.

[75] See Vanessa Knights, "Queer Pleasures: The Bolero, Camp and Almodóvar," in Powrie and Stilwell, eds., *Changing Tunes*, 91–104.

this is a sign that we have come full circle and are now approaching the film's liminal or extranarrative plane once again. This is signaled in the physical *feel* of the music and the kinaesthetic qualities of the dancing and camera movement.

The combination of sound and image in this scene implies a heightened affective orientation that Gilles Deleuze has addressed in his writing on film. Especially germane to the present discussion are his comments about Bresson's *Pickpocket* (1959), where he relates how the haptic qualities of visual imagery are reinforced through shots of hands and feet connecting with objects in the world. This encourages cross-modal awareness of objects: awareness not just of their ocular qualities but how they are recalled from earlier experiences of physical contact.[76] Laura Marks refers to this mode of perception as "haptic visuality," a term that is employed to explain how the impression of touch can be conveyed through visual images; as if the perceiver could touch the screen with her eyes.[77] Add to this, the impact of sound as probably the most effective vehicle for conveying embodiment, and the sense of the heightened physicality is further accentuated. In Chion's writing, certain sounds convey a sense of physical involvement more effectively than others: namely, those that imply a sense of physical resistance to outside agentic forces. These he refers to as "materializing sound indices." More precisely, a sound of this type

> directs our attention to the physical nature of its source, to whatever it is that is blowing, scraping, rubbing—the indices of resistance of the real, reminding us that a voice does not issue from the pure throat of an angel but from a body, that a violin's sound comes not from the air but from horsehair rubbing against taut catgut.[78]

Chion's formulation comes conspicuously close to the quality of "secondness" as it is expounded in Peircian semiotics. Secondness designates an existential connection with matter in the world that implies emotive responses to perceived struggle. As such, secondness contains elements of the more immediate category of experience C.S. Peirce calls firstness, which I return to later. It is distinct from this category, however, in the attention the perceiving subject directs toward a physical encounter with an object other than the self. Peirce describes secondness

---

[76] Gilles Deleuze, *Cinema 2: The Time-Image*, trans. Hugh Tomlinson and Robert Galeta (London: Continuum, 1989), 12. See also Marks, "Video haptics," 337.

[77] See Laura Marks, *The Skin of Film: Intercultural Cinema, Embodiment and the Senses* (Durham, NC: Duke University Press, 2000), xi and 164. See also Thomas Elsaesser and Malte Hagener, *Film Theory: An Introduction through the Senses* (New York and London: Routledge, 2000), 124–25. A phenomenological argument for the primacy of sensual impact registered through the cinematic image is made in relation to the Jane Campion film *The Piano*, in the chapter "What My Fingers Knew," in Vivian Sobchack, *Carnal Thoughts: Embodiment and Moving Image Culture* (Berkeley: University of California Press, 2004), 53–84, 64–65.

[78] Michel Chion, *Film, A Sound Art*, trans. Claudia Gorbman (New York: Columbia University Press, 2009), 244–45.

as conveying the "rough and tumble of life" and implying a sense of "bumping up against hard fact." That seems like an apt description of the kind of experience that is related in this scene.[79]

This modality is strongly activated in the sections in which musicians and dancers are depicted onscreen, where their music and physical movements are heard. Peircian secondness overlaps with the Deleuzian affection-image as it relates to perceptions of tactile contact. This can be seen in the use of extreme close-ups in this sequence—a staple surrealist technique. Such shots bring home the material nature of the filmed reality while dehumanizing it (surrealistically) through an implied element of aesthetic separation—the separation that the cinematic frame implies in relation to a larger totality. Such objects exert an affective pull for two reasons: because of the level of intimacy they afford through proximity with another human being, but also because of an element of astonishment or wonder at how the "human" image has been uncannily transformed.[80]

In *Waking Life*, the affect-image is actualized through close attention to the detail of physical execution as the camera tracks the movement of musicians' hands across fingerboards and keyboards, but also in the movement of the dancers' hands and legs. The effect is more pronounced because of the way the music is composed. This can be heard in the penultimate scene of the film, where an extended passage of pizzicato playing features prominently early in the musical composition. This locks the spectator-auditor into an engagement with the physical qualities of the performance and an element of resistance as the body comes into contact with an external object (*El Cholulo*; 1:19:45). In orchestral film scoring, pizzicato is often used as an index of light-footed stealth and agility, attributes that are played on in the way the camera follows the dancing action, the subtle glide of a foot becoming invested with attributes of coquettish evasion, while kicks, shuffles and stamps are made to appear more nimble than they probably are. The appearance of the dancers' movements (what Deleuze would call "opsigns": a contraction of optical signs) is accented in much the same way aurally through the presence of environmental sounds: feet stomping, clicking and scraping on the parquet floor (Deleuze would call these "sonsigns": sonic signs). As the music accelerates, energetic left-hand piano runs suggest a push toward bodily participation (Deleuze's opsigns and sonsigns uniting to become "tactisigns," or tactile signs).[81]

[79] See Charles Sanders Peirce, *The Collected Papers, Vol. 1: Principles of Philosophy* (1931), online resource, available at http://www.textlog.de/charles_s_peirce.html, retrieved December 1, 2010.

[80] Gilles Deleuze, *Cinema 1: The Movement-Image*, trans. Hugh Tomlinson and Barbara Habberjam (London: Continuum, 1986), 97–104. Several critics have perceived an aspect of symbolic violence in surrealist artists' readiness to fragment the human body. Such acts might be perceived as misogynistic to the extent that representations of women are frequently on the receiving end of such treatment (e.g., Bellmer's dolls). Others have pointed out, however, that masochistic impulses infuse such representations, even while they portray the fragmentation of female bodies. See Hal Foster, *Compulsive Beauty* (Cambridge, MA: MIT Press, 1993), 122; Phil Powrie, "Masculinity in the Shadow of the Slashed Eye," 163.

[81] Gilles Deleuze, *Cinema 2*, 12.

This impels the young man to rise to his feet and to approach a stairway that will take him to a final human encounter, this time with the director of the film—not quite a stairway to heaven but the next best thing: the film's liminal and "extranarrative" plane.

Compressed into this scene is a densely packed erotics of sound, movement and tactility that imparts a heady sense of intensified experience, even while the visual dimension is seen through the distancing gauze of the animated medium, as manifested in the increasingly restless oscillations of animated fragments. As the protagonist approaches (narrative) death and the film its conclusion, entire sections of the *mise-en-scène* detach themselves from the structures of which they are a part: the front of the piano bobs around, paving stones wobble, the façade of a house shifts from side to side, eyes become detached from faces. The music too shifts on its axis, becoming more microtonal. In fact, it is as if the use of string glissandos corresponds directly with the protagonist's inability to remain on terra firma. We see this in the final moments of the film, when Wiggins becomes airborne once again in a scene that mirrors the opening sequence. Similar music carries him now on a more unsettled wave, modulating through several key centers in rumbling tones as an existential torrent of diegetic wind and low-register tremor sweeps him toward apparent oblivion (1:29:57; *Balade 4*, part 2).

In scenes such as this, we are made to see *and to feel* both music and images. Preceding the boy's final levitation, the encounter with Linkater himself becomes a narrative turning point (1:22:07). After listening to an extended monologue from the director, the character begins to wonder if he is dead. A car might have collided with him in an early scene; he awoke in bed immediately prior to the impending impact. So this would make narrative sense. Linklater implores the young man to "Wake up!" Advice he appears to heed as he is again transported back to his bed. However, this proves to be yet another in a series of the film's false awakenings.

HOLY MOMENTS, FIRSTNESS AND SURREALIST SENSIBILITY

The scenes elucidated previously are among the most evocative in the film. Otherwise it can be considered a loosely compiled portfolio, or filmic scrapbook, of readings on sleep, dreams and altered consciousness. In his choice of interviews, Linklater provides a running commentary on the aesthetic of the film. A novelist tells us, "There's no story, it's just people, gestures, moments, bits of rapture, fleeting emotions." In fact, this is one of the most remarkable aspects of this film; something that sets it apart as tangibly as its distinctive visual appearance: *Waking Life* provides a conceptual apparatus for its own interpretation in comments included in the documentary footage. In a sense this renders criticism obsolete; the director adopts the positions of both producer and critic. All that remains for the viewer-listener is to accept or to contest the interpretive rubric offered by the director.

This is most evident in what might be considered the centerpiece, an interview with filmmaker Caveh Zahedi which spells out this director's endorsement of Bazinian integral realism as a guiding aesthetic principle (52:30). The idea of realism apropos of this film might seem odd if we understand the term as implying a purely mimetic and indexical relationship to filmed action (as Zahedi puts it, "reality is reproduced" in film), since the animations obviously announce their own artifice. The argument is more convincing in this context if realism is understood to imply attention to the spectator-auditor's lived reality including *cinematic* reality. Realism, it should not be forgotten, can be different things to different people. For Kracauer it requires the fragmented nature of the cinematic image to be understood as a concrete articulation of alienated social structures see page 286. In other writing on cinema it has been understood differently. Zahedi's view conflates two separate ideas of the real: that the filmed image directly reflects an external reality and that it produces its own reality.

Zahedi in this scene makes a case for what he considers to be "holy moments" (after Bazin's spiritualist inclinations): those aspects of cinematic experience when attention is concentrated exclusively on the unfolding Now—a form of immersion in which perception and affective response override discursive consciousness. Cinematically, this is a moment of considerable visual eloquence, as the speaking heads of the two speakers gradually transform into cumulous clouds—an exquisite rendering of Now-consciousness that vividly captures the sublime nature of Zahedi's vision. This is precisely the mode of consciousness espoused in several of the theories of surrealism reviewed in chapter 2: a revelatory mode of perception that surrealist "objects" occasioned either through interruptions or rhetorical interventions or by attunement to emerging consciousness (as is thought to happen in automatic writing). The surrealists understood such experiences to be fleeting, however, which is why they advised spectators to leave the theater whenever the discursivity of the film secured too tight a hold over the imagination. In a sense, Linklater does something similar whenever his protagonist is wrenched out of one dream situation and jettisoned into the next. The protagonist, to the extent that he is passive (a listener more than a speaker), easily comes to stand in for the cinematic viewer of the film in this regard. (In the "holy moments" scene, he is explicitly represented in this way.)

Commenting on this how this scene works as a theorization for the film's aesthetic, Steven Shaviro writes:

> *Waking Life* presents a series of moods or "holy moments" that are ephemeral, free-floating and disjunct. Each scene is a separate intensity, a pure present with no relation to what comes before or after ... *Waking life* offers us a beautiful sense that digitally generated images and sounds are perfectly real, and adequately grounded in and of themselves, regardless of any questions as to what they might represent.[82]

---

[82] Ibid., 9.

All of this is true, and to a significant extent those scenes I have reviewed so far lend support to such an understanding. Moreover, an element of realism in the classical sense is implied in the way the images and *sounds* have been recorded— the documentary approach to recording sounds. More importantly though, and this is what Shaviro seems to be getting at, the cinematic reality possesses its own gravitational pull that to some extent obviates the need for more conventional decoding strategies. It is hard, though, to refrain from taking a position similar to that of Zahedi's interlocutor in the scene, the poet David Jewell, when he notes how difficult it is to detach the "holy moment" of unfolding experience (comprising perception and feeling alone) from everything else that is going on at the same time. What is implied here is a form of phenomenological bracketing that comes close to religious experience in its meditative aspirations. In terms of Peircian semiotics, the affective nature of such bracketed perceptions falls under the category of firstness, which suggests a "predominan[ce of] feeling, as distinct from objective perception, will, and thought."[83] In Peircian understanding, the three qualities of firstness, secondness and thirdness (discursive understanding) are enfolded within one another at all times, with each quality rising to the surface in different measure at a different moment. This understanding is implicit in both Jewell's and Zahedi's comments in this scene, although Zahedi seems to aspire to the quality of firstness in an unusually determined way, while aligning this orientation with the aspirations of Bazinian integral realism. Jewell seems to realize the idealistic direction of Zahedi's commentary when he interjects, "Everything is layers, isn't it? There's the holy moment and then there's the awareness of trying to have the holy moment...I was in and out of the holy moment, looking at you. But you can't have a holy...you're unique in that way, Caveh."

The truth is that while films of this type might be said to offer a vehicle for approaching "the holy grail" of Peircian firstness, this is ultimately down to the perceiver and depends upon dynamic interplay between all three modalities, requiring discursive as well as affective layers of understanding.

For certain, the film elevates its own intrinsic reality in such a way that it comes to matter little what is real and what is fake, a view that in fact comes closer to surrealism's phenomenological understanding of existence than it does Bazin's ontological one. (This view is articulated in his discussions of techniques such as the extended single-camera shot and uses of depth of field camerawork, both of which avoid upsetting what Deleuze calls the time-image.) Aside from Bazin's realism, ideas akin to those found in writing on surrealism are found in several of the film's interviews, especially ideas that comment on the phenomenal equivalence of dream experience and waking life. A few minutes prior to the discussion of Bazin, the protagonist finds himself in a large room where several figures are waiting to talk with

---

[83] In Charles Sanders Peirce, *The Collected Papers of Charles Sanders Peirce*, vol. 1, Charles Hartshorne and Paul Weiss, eds. (Cambridge, MA: Harvard University Press, 1931–1935), 302.

him—a kind of cinematic "chat room." One of these comments: "To the functional system of neural activity that creates our world, there is no difference between dreaming a perception and action and, actually, the waking perception and action." In this way the entire lifespan is equated with the phenomenal status of dreams, an attitude that is repeated elsewhere in the film. Another character continues: "The trick," he tells us, is "to combine waking rational realities with the infinite possibilities of dreams. Because if you do that you can do anything." (00:39:00) This comes conspicuously close to assumptions articulated in Breton's writing on surrealism. In the 1924 "First Manifesto of Surrealism," for example, he declares: "I believe in the future resolution of these two states, dreams and reality, which are seemingly so contradictory, into a kind of absolute reality, a *surreality*, if one may so speak."[84] All of this suggests that the film might be understood as surrealist as much as it is realist in a Bazinian sense; keeping in mind earlier arguments about the interdependency of the two categories (see chapter 2, pages 39–41). There can be no denying that the spectator is pushed into confronting filmic reality, nor that the emphasis on recorded documentary footage in the sound recording grounds experiences in everyday phenomenal experience. In other ways, though, it encourages a discursive, even intellectual attitude, implying recognition of Peirce's categories of secondness and thirdness: the thick symbolic actuality of discourse spinning through reality.

DIDACTIC INTENTION AND THE SPOKEN WORD: A PREDOMINANCE OF THIRDNESS

Aside from those aspects just discussed, *Waking Life* is an unusually vococentric film. Constantly shifting from one walk-on character's monologue to the next, the different takes on reality offered in the film in fact meld together to form a fairly cogent didactic message. How much room this leaves for a pensive attitude on the part of audiences is open to debate. Much of the film seems to stimulate in a one-way fashion, which is reflected in how opinion is divided on the Rotten Tomatoes *Waking Life* website. While some contributors applaud the film as innovative and stylistically *sui generis*, others are not so impressed, comparing the experience to being "trapped in a painting filled with philosophy students" and chastising the director for his "mind-numbing...wall of words." I would disagree with these evaluations to the extent that Glover Gill's score, when present, supplies an intoxicating adjunct to the animated images. Moreover, the visual look of the film is strangely compelling and the points of view presented intellectually stimulating. *Waking Life* does, however, seem to lack both the sustained dreamlike atmosphere and the interpretive ambiguity of classic oneiric films like Resnais's *Last Year at Marienbad*, Kubrick's *Eyes Wide Shut* or Kurosawa's *Dreams* (1990) (incorporated in one of the scenes). It offers different pleasures, requiring an

---

[84] Breton, *Manifestoes of Surrealism*, 14.

impassive attitude on the part of the listener that mirrors the interpersonal positioning of the film's protagonist. Shaviro rightly contrasts this with the more
angst-ridden sexual charge found in surrealist films, noting how Wiggins offers a
more compliant model of masculinity in this regard.[85] The point is well made. If
Waking Life is to be understood in reference to surrealism, then it should be viewed
as articulating an emerging neosurrealist sensibility based on present-day tastes
and attitudes rather than those of the past. Wiggins does not strive for control (in
fact, narrative control is *denied* him) and he is therefore an atypical (male) hero.
He listens and in this way becomes a model for receptive (or submissive?) audience behavior. But what of Linklater himself—who is the final speaker of the film,
and therefore the last to don the mentor's cap—in the penultimate scene? The
impression is of a director overflowing with things to say about his philosophy of
art and life. So much so, he might be accused of inadvertently blocking less direct
didactic pathways.

In this respect, an element of Peircian thirdness might be said to override the more
poetic sensibility that is transmitted in the scenes that have been the main subject of
consideration in this section of the book. Thirdness in Peirce's theoretical model
encompasses the entire symbolic apparatus, which plays a fundamental role in shaping and mediating human experiences. Containing a further embedded triadic framework, comprising the sign, the object, and the interpretant, none of which are
especially relevant to the present discussion, the key function of thirdness according
to Peircian semiotics is to mediate between the two aspects of experience discussed
earlier: firstness and secondness. This interdependency is a central premise of the
Peircian view, whose significance cannot be overstated. From this it follows that any
given audiovisual presentation can be categorized according the prominence it
assigns to each of these categories and that this emphasis is constantly in flux. Such is
the case with *Waking Life*, which pays close attention to matters of firstness and secondness, while nevertheless signposting these qualities in a dramatization that over-
spills with informational "content." If measured in time, I would hazard a guess that
this category might even make up the greater part of the film, something that could
certainly not be said of the films of Tsai Ming-Liang or Aki Kaurismäki, which contain very little speech. Sally Potter's *Yes*, discussed in the next section, is also heavy on
the spoken word, but it differs from *Waking Life* by being made up entirely of poetic
verse, which affords easier mobility between Peirce's categories.

In the penultimate chapter of this book, I offer a consideration of the value of
cinematic silence as opening up a space for the emergence of what Laura Mulvey
(after Bellour) calls the "pensive spectator" in relation to moments of temporal
suspension in cinema.[86] Silence, or the suspension of linguistic narrativity, similarly

[85]   Shaviro, "Emotion Capture," 8.

[86]   See Laura Mulvey, *Death 24x a Second: Stillness and the Moving Image* (London; Reaktion Books, 2006),
181–96.

allows for the emergence of what I call "pensive listening." As the surrealists maintained, even the most conventional film contains moments of disruptive potential. *Waking Life* contains a greater number of such moments than the average mainstream film. Is it a cinema of the senses? In some respects, it is. Mostly it is a cinematic experiment, whose success or failure should be measured not in terms of its influence on mainstream practices, but as a highly personal artistic statement shaped in large measure by its auteur-director and his chosen collaborators. Glover Gill's musical "voice" is among the most compelling to be heard in *Waking Life*. It imbues the film with a mystical tone that conditions its negotiations between the affective states of remembered childhood (which is aligned with firstness) and unfolding adulthood (which is more closely aligned with secondness and thirdness). The gap Linklater and Gill open up between those modalities is arguably what makes the film so compelling.

Waking Life brings into the spotlight a problem directors working at the margins of the mainstream in the digital age seem to be grappling with each in different ways: how to sustain interest across the temporal expanse of the feature-length film (since this is the format they have chosen) in light of their greater attention to audiovisual flow (implying repetition), narrative fragmentation, microrhythmic and microvisual detail, surrealist juxtapositions and so forth; features that are found in much of the post-music-video era cinema. Such are the rewards and the risks of working with emerging audiovisual forms—the risk of failure or partial success, of course, being something that adds to the excitement of any creative enterprise (a characteristic of the avant-garde). In the absence of conventional narrative structures, one way to deal with temporal expanse of the feature film is to fill it with episodic fragments of spoken-word content. This can be highly effective in a film whose message, about dream consciousness and elusive childhood experiences, is conveyed with such remarkable originality. Michel Gondry is another director who has confronted these issues with some consistency and who has developed an audiovisual style that is instantly recognizable.

Michel Gondry's *Be Kind Rewind*—On Readymades, Childhood Dreams and the Legacy of Music Videos

BACKGROUND AND SYNOPSIS

Michel Gondry's *Be Kind Rewind* (2008) is to *Eternal Sunshine of the Spotless Mind* as Linklater's *School of Rock* (2003) is to *Waking Life*: an apparent concession to the consumption-driven Hollywood dream machine, or perhaps an attempt to branch out beyond expectations that surround the studio-funded "independent" film. Coincidentally, both *Be Kind Rewind* and *School of Rock* share the same leading actor, Jack Black, known for his upbeat personality and madcap juvenile antics. Cute, unapologetically mainstream and imbued with a slapstick sense of fun, *Be Kind Rewind* nevertheless benefits from a subtle post-avant-garde *esprit* that belies its feel good (Inc.?) billing (see chapter 6). In a different way to Linklater's film, *Be Kind Rewind* can be understood as commentary on the emerging aesthetics of digital film; not in this case because of its conspicuous use of new technologies but in how it historicizes them by parodying them with low-tech means.

A synopsis might read as follows: In an absurd act of misguided political activism, Jerry (Jack Black) breaks into a small power plant he thinks is responsible for brainwashing the neighborhood in downtown Passaic, New Jersey. While scaling a fence to enter the plant he is electrocuted and becomes implausibly (read: surrealistically) magnetized. This magnetism is exploited for all its comic worth as objects attach themselves to him and he to them, including a fence and a lamppost. By urinating luminous toxic waste, Jerry is apparently rid of his ailment, but not before he has accidentally erased every VHS-video in the rental store where his friend Mike (Mos Def) works as an assistant. An interest in outmoded analog technology goes to the heart of the film's narrative construction and its cinematic style. The video rental company, owned by the elderly Elroy Fletcher (Danny Glover), is situated in a rundown, ethnically mixed quarter of town. The entire building where the shop is located is soon to be demolished in order to make way for a high-end property development. Jerry and Mike set about solving the more immediate problem of the erased tapes by transforming them into their own low-tech remakes, or "swedes"; so named because the protagonists claim to be shipping the films from Sweden. Shot in single takes and using only the crudest of DIY special effects, the remakes quickly became popular among a growing clientele because of their personal style and offbeat humor. Seeing this as a path out of his financial difficulties, the initially skeptical proprietor goes along with the plan, which nevertheless disintegrates as film industry representatives turn up to destroy the sweded videos on the grounds of copyright infringement. As a gesture of commitment toward their ill-fated project, the filmmakers join forces to produce one last film, a film within a film (as in the dramatic turning point in *Waking Life*) that is constructed around the character of jazz pianist Fats Waller. Waller as depicted in the film is a simulacrum of the real singer made up by the store's proprietor as a ploy to save his building from demolition. *Be Kind Rewind* ends with a screening of the obviously fictitious biopic, intended only for the occupants of the shop and their friends, but a crowd gathered on the street outside is able to view the film in reverse projection. The impromptu screening brings about an unexpected moment of communitas between the filmmakers, the local community and the waiting demolition crew.

"NOTHING FROM NOTHING": USES AND PLEASURES
OF OUTMODED OBJECTS

Be Kind Rewind is surreal in a more subtle way than many of the films discussed so far because of the relationship demarcated in the film between the constantly advancing modern world (as represented by DVD technology and the architectural development that will replace the shop) and the outmoded culture surrounding the Passaic community (an actual community in New Jersey drawn upon as a resource when making the film). In the film's fictive world, this obviously impoverished community is still in the process of making the transition from VHS to DVD technology, so when the time comes to produce their own videos, an antiquated VHS video camera is the only available option. Gondry claims to have come up with the idea for *Be Kind Rewind* three years earlier, when filming *Eternal Sunshine of the Spotless Mind.* While visiting a car repair shop in Passaic, he overheard workers from a nearby junkyard complaining that the neighboring power plant was causing them headaches and nausea. Gondry was so taken with the spirit of the community and the junkyard-power plant plotline that he resolved to make a film on the subject.[87] These urban spaces are crucial to the design of the film. The building's condemned tenements and outmoded shops have much in common with the condemned Parisian *Passage de l'Opéra* arcade, which formed the hub of Louis Aragon's surrealist aesthetic as set forth in the book *Le Payson de Paris.* This is a theme Walter Benjamin would explore in considerable detail in his extensive montage study, *Passagenwerk.* The Parisian urban spaces recounted in these books were similarly condemned, and they were inhabited by a colorful and economically disadvantaged people who had little choice but to make do with the leftover material objects and discarded spaces of the official culture. The aesthetic premises of Parisian surrealism and Gondry's film therefore have something in common.

An additional urban space is the junkyard, where many of the sweded films were made and where props used in the making of the films appear to have been found. Jerry's outfit for the Robocop character, for example, is a composite of car parts. The junkyard in the film functions in much the same way as did the *Marché aux Puces* flea market in Paris for surrealists like Breton, Éluard and Aragon, who would scout there for outmoded objects. The appreciation and repurposing of such objects was a core principle of historical surrealism that seems to have got lost in popular accounts of the movement. Gondry invokes this set of historical

---

[87] Gondry's sympathy with the shopkeepers of Passaic has a background. His father was the proprietor of a shop selling musical instruments. In the booklet to the Directors Series DVD, he comments on how he grew up in a mall. Arguably this left an imprint on his artistic approach, particularly his deconstructive understanding of consumerism as implying processes of recycling and re-enchantment.

practices in the way his protagonists make the best of what is at hand.[88] Jerry and Mike recuperate something of value in the discarded objects that surround them, many of which define their lowly socioeconomic status. And their investment of these found objects with an uncanny afterlife speaks to an ambivalent relationship to the dominant audiovisual culture, a form of double consciousness that takes pleasure in the products of the Hollywood dream machine, just as it does in more cerebral cinema, such as Kubrick's *2001: A Space Odyssey*. Neither high nor low are valorized in this view, but seen as contributing equally to the social construction of a popular consciousness that has fallen out of vogue—ultimately as someone else's take on reality that can be woven together with the material circumstances of current life in order to make (non)sense out of it. This flattening of conventional binary structures is a distinctive trait of much surrealism and camp aesthetics as well.

Benjamin's encounter with French surrealism in his essay, *Surrealism: The Last Snapshot of the European Intelligentsia*, offers perhaps the most productive theoretical prop to the present discussion. He dwells in particular on the uses made by the surrealists of outmoded forms, arguing that by resurrecting the "immense forces of atmosphere" in them "to the point of explosion," their emancipatory energies might be brought to bear on the present.[89] These include "the first factory buildings, the earliest photos...the dresses of five years ago, [and] fashionable restaurants when the vogue has begun to ebb from them."[90] Like Breton and Aragon before him, Benjamin advocated an aesthetic of montage, in fact going so far as to structure his scholarly writing in the manner of surrealist novel, as a series of incorporations of past and present texts interwoven with scant critical commentary. The affective direction of the surrealists' attachment to the outmoded was not Romantic melancholy over the passing of time, but a way of allowing objects from the past to reflect back on the present in a dialectic that would transform both, uncovering them "for purposes of resistance through re-enchantment."[91] For the surrealists, the outmoded object carries traces of the hands it passed through, the utopian aspirations of its designers, as well as signs of how it was used, and the degree of damage it suffered. If remnants from the past bestow an affective residue that carries into the future, then the same is true of new ideas: the fashions and innovations of the present day

---

[88] Surrealism comes up in many contexts in reference to Gondry's work. In an episode of the BBC1 documentary *Imagine*... devoted to new forms of surrealism ("It's the Surreal Thing," 2007), Gondry figured prominently. The website for the show features a drawing by Gondry and Jean-Paule Gaude produced in the style of the surrealist game "exquisite corpse." See http://www.bbc.co.uk/imagine/article/exquisite_corpse.shtml, retrieved 5 March 2009.

[89] Walter Benjamin, *Reflections*, Peter Demetz, ed., trans., Edmund Jephcott (New York: Schocken, 1978), 182.

[90] Ibid., 181.

[91] Ibid., 166.

will one day lose their sparkle, seeming quaint, ghostly and ideologically marked. As Foster notes, the mobilization of such awareness in new artistic production is not without political implications:

> To invoke such outmoded forms is to advance a two-fold immanent critique of high capitalist culture...On the one hand, the capitalist outmoded relativizes bourgeois culture, denies its pretense to the natural and the eternal, opens it up to its own history, indeed its own historicity...On the other hand, the capitalist outmoded challenges this culture with its own forfeited dreams, tests it against its own compromised values of political emancipation, technological progress, cultural access, and the like.[92]

Foster is quick to point out that Benjamin's "revolutionary nihilism" is not as nihilistic as it might at first appear; the sense of loss or "destitution" afforded by the outmoded object cultivates a breathless awareness of the present as emerging from but not indentured to the past. Benjamin's comments concerning the topical nature of fashion bear this out most directly: although expressive of the values of capitalism, when viewed dialectically such objects can facilitate leaps "into the open air of history" that are potentially transformative.[93]

The relevance of the uncanny to this nexus of ideas is not difficult to fathom. Adorno does not refer explicitly to the uncanny in his writing, but the main direction of his argument reveals an affinity with Freud's line of thinking while adumbrating theories of postmodernism (see chapter 2, page 33).[94] The primary tension that surrealism articulates in Adorno's account is bound up with schizophrenia and abstraction, features of (post)modern society at large, while artists' taste for "making compositions from what is out of date" reveals a preoccupation with "*nature morte.*"[95] Anxieties surrounding these concepts become more concrete and troubling when it comes to the representation of human form: "Breasts that have been cut off, mannequin's legs in silk stockings." Detached from the organic and human contexts that would ordinarily breathe life in them, such objects take on an uncanny aspect that speaks to "the violence that prohibition has done to the objects of desire."[96] Adorno compares the effect with "the changes that occur in the pornographic image at the moment at which the voyeur receives gratification."[97] The description is illuminating

[92] Foster, *Compulsive Beauty*, 162.

[93] Walter Benjamin, *Illuminations: Essays and Reflections*, trans. Harry Zohn (New York: Schoken, 1968), 261.

[94] Theodor Adorno, "Looking Back on Surrealism" (1954), in *Notes to Literature*, vol. 1, trans. Shierry Weber Nicholson (New York: Columbia University Press, 1991), 86–90.

[95] Ibid., 89.

[96] Ibid., 90.

[97] Ibid., 89.

both in terms of what it reveals about the dominant affective tone of historical surrealism and, perhaps unwittingly, about sexual politics at the time. Notably, both Adorno and Freud presuppose a male heterosexual subject bent on scopophilic modes of consumption. On balance, Adorno comes down in favor of surrealist aesthetics, which allows the Marxist idea of the "commodity fetish" to be recognized as such, and he appears to mourn its decline in the postwar years as an opportunity for reflexive consciousness lost. Undoubtedly he would not have approved of the strain of neosurrealism in popular culture examined in the chapter; its complicity with commercial interests and mass cultural appeal most likely rendering it inherently suspicious, but this shall not be our primary concern here.[98]

The Adornian view of surrealism is most apparent in a film like Tsai Ming-Liang's *The Wayward Cloud* (discussed in the next chapter), not least because of its focus on the abstracted representations of the body found in pornography; or in Paul Thomas Anderson's *Boogie Nights* (1997), in which the director employs glitzy, lush, and ultimately "tasteless" disco music to comment on the decline of 1970s pornography industry—becoming an allegory for the decline of North American urban life.[99] *Be Kind Rewind* shares with *Boogie Nights* a similar sense of loss concentrated around the ethnically segregated centers of North American cities.[100] But whereas Anderson seems determined to cast the musical culture of previous decades as irretrievably tacky or kitsch, Gondry's approach is more concerned with allowing these retrieved objects to resonate with current cultural formations in a way that is more restorative and bound up with the surrealists' attention to childhood experiences and an element of camp aesthetic conditioning (for more on this aspect of camp, see the next chapter). In this respect, the soundtrack probably comes closer to Woody Allen's use of traditional jazz to comment faux-naïvely and with unrelenting "good faith" on contemporary urban experience than it does with Anderson's relentlessly

---

[98] Adorno's comments highlight an aspect of the subject that warrant further commentary; namely, the role of women in the movement. Male surrealist artists have been criticized for their representations of women, which tend to idealize them as muses (Dalí's numerous portraits of Gala), to reduce them to irrational manifestations of the unconscious (Breton's Nadja), or to inflict symbolic violence on them. This criticism is justified, but should be balanced against the recognition that some women participated actively in the movement, including Remedios Varo, Frida Kahlo, Leonora Carrington, Meret Oppenheim, Leonor Fini, Toyen, and Dorothea Tanning. Typical of women's work in the idiom is a more self-reflective attitude toward representations of the human body (not least that of the artist herself). The legacy of these approaches can be recognized in the self-representational photography of Cindy Sherman and Tracey Emin's installation art. Both of these artists can be understood as developing themes that first emerged in Dada/surrealism.

[99] See Adam Krims, *Music and Urban Geography* (New York and London: Routledge, 2007), 61–87.

[100] Krims lists films that comment on this change in urban experience as including *Falling Down* (1993), *Sugar Hill* (1994), and *Clockers* (1995). Ibid., 76. Those that take a less gritty approach he calls "fantasy/denial" films. Given these two alternatives, *Be Kind Rewind* would probably fall into the latter category, although I am convinced it offers a more nuanced perspective on these issues than the dichotomy of brutal realism versus cozy fantasy permits.

smart(ing) and disenchanted approach.[101] Like Allen before him, Gondry is an amateur musician (a drummer) whose appreciation of past styles shines through even when he performs music with a distinct indie or new wave feel. His outmoded music is not presented nostalgically or with derisory irony, but as a source of unlikely resonances to be tapped and channeled according to present-day priorities.

There is nothing stylistically pure in the soundtrack of *Be Kind Rewind*. Like the reconstituted films that are the main focus of the plot, the dominant strategy in the soundtrack is that of pastiche. One moment the nondiegetic soundtrack is evocative of 1970s blaxploitation films, with a funky afro-beat, wah-wah guitar, bongos and chilled wind section, as the proprietor of the store spies on a rival business through binoculars; the next it is exaggeratedly suspenseful in the mode of Bernard Hermann, featuring this composer's trademark combinations of tremolo, dissonant chords, chromaticism, and loud brass stingers.[102] The latter of these cues begins when a dissatisfied customer confronts Mike over an erased tape (00:20:57; on the soundtrack, "Little Mickey"). Reminiscent of the acrophobia shots in *Vertigo*, a loud brass stinger is timed to the moment when the fuzzy image of the erased video first appears on a television screen, obviously overplaying the drama. The scene builds in rhythmic intensity as Mike frantically rummages through other videos, culminating in an extended dissonant chord and an echoing cry as he views a second erased tape. Thus, even Jean-Michel Bernard's nondiegetic underscore does not transparently convey the characters' emotions but these experiences are perceived through a distancing aesthetic of incorporation. Elsewhere in the film, howling, bleeping and crackling sounds fill the diegetic (?) soundtrack, while further sonic markers of weird science are conveyed in nondiegetic music that evokes 1950s science fiction B-movies. These aspects are especially prominent in Black's slapstick scenes involving magnetization (00:24:00; 00:18:26; in the CD, "Microwaves" and "I'm Bill"), an approach that resembles Danny Elfman's heavily ironic score for the film *Mars Attacks*. Extracts from a number of other soundtracks are found in parts of the film, including the theme to *Ghostbusters*, Jerry and Mike's first sweded film (00:29:38). Other sweded films feature pastiche music composed by Bernard, including nondiegetic music to the sweded remake of *Rush Hour 2* (dir. Brett Ratner, 2001). This music parodies the clichés of action movies as well as borrowing Orientalist traits from Lalo Schifrin's original score ("Chinese Bamboo"; 00:37:04).

[101] The "method acting" feel of much of *Be Kind Rewind* also comes close to that of Allen's films, most probably because of the sketchy nature of the script. Björk has compared Gondry to Allen, not for any of the above reasons but because of his neurotic personality (interview in *The Work of Director Michel Gondry*, Directors Label DVD).

[102] Bruce Graham, "Bernard Herrmann: Film Music and Narrative," (PhD dissertation, University of Michigan, 1985); John Richardson, "'Black and White' Music: Dialogue, Dysphoric Coding and the Death Drive in the Music of Bernard Herrmann, The Beatles, Stevie Wonder and Coolio," Yrjö Heinonen, et al, eds. *Beatlestudies 1: Songwriting, Recording, and Style Change* (Jyväskylä: University Press of Jyväskylä, 1998), 161–82.

Much of the remaining music pertains to the historical figure of Fats Waller, including original recordings and cover versions of songs like "Your Feets Too Big," "Swing Low Sweet Chariot," "I Ain't Got Nobody" and "Ain't Misbehavin'."

A further category is incorporated R&B styled music and soul music from the 1960s and 1970s. Like many an auteur-director before him, Gondry selected and organized all of the music in the film, as well as performing as a drummer on at least three tracks rendered in this style. On the track "I Ain't Got Nobody," he performed on drums together with vintage Memphis soul combo Booker T. & the MG's. Of note is that this group plays a cameo role in the film, where they join the store's proprietor to reminisce about the good old days while listening to a scratchy old Fats Waller record (00:18:42). In the context of the film's plot (not the only level on which their inclusion might be understood), the musicians play entrepreneurs who have made their fortune by designing a new adaptation of a stainless steel hose attachment brush. The theme of creating something new by reworking existing objects seems to be abiding message of the film, as indicated in the title of another nondiegetic song, Billy Preston's "Nothing from Nothing." In this way the director challenges Romantic assumptions about creativity. In Gondry's view, creativity arises only from dialogical engagement with the creative activities of forebears. This attitude can be recognized in the older generation's interest in Waller, which is heard alongside their own music (performed by Booker T. & the MG's). Consequently, each generation in the film becomes guardian and entrusted interpreter-arranger of the creative produce of the preceding generation, which becomes suffused with personal meaning because it is the music of their childhood. Cultural values are thus transmitted from one generation to the next, but transformed with each pair of hands they pass through. Gondry's musical activities fit this picture. Throughout the film, the director-drummer performs his parts cleanly in recordings that stand out as "versions" of existing music. Even when the director performs with his own contemporary-styled band (Oui Oui's "Ma Maison"), the music is indebted to vintage R&B. Rather than making fun of the style in a way that would detract from the originals, the naïve sound of much of this music indicates that the musicians are making fun of (if anything or anyone) themselves. What is conveyed is a reparative more than an overtly critical orientation (a matter I return to in the next chapter). Of course, by playing with outmoded styles in this way, an implicit critique is suggested concerning the turnover of goods in the current world order. But more than this, the essence of Gondry's approach is found in his appreciation of experiences so obvious they are often overlooked. As in *Waking Life*, this can be related to a desire to retrieve something of the self that was forfeited in the passage from childhood to adulthood.

Gondry's approach to visualizing music implies a childlike receptiveness to freshly perceived experience, new ways of understanding objects, as he plays with frames of references (visual and cultural) in a way that encourages audiences to see the world with new eyes (and to hear with new ears). In the DVD collection of Gondry's music video work (2003), the director confesses to having "been twelve forever." It is easy to find support to this statement in both his music videos and films, which has led some critics to dismiss his work as puerile. There are at least two reasons for questioning such a view: First, childhood experiences have a power and immediacy that is abdicated by most people later in life. Several schools of psychology have argued that childhood is the repository for our affective understanding of the world into adult life. Second, misunderstandings and unlikely connections (even mistakes) belong to the domain of childhood experience, and it is through mistakes and incongruous combinations that we learn. In his characteristic broken English (almost a parody of a French accent), Gondry explains his approach to creative activity: "You see an object, and that makes you think of another one, and those two objects together is [sic] an idea." This comes remarkably close to Breton's and Barthes's formulations concerning the nature of the surreal object, which highlights the importance of the metaphorical axis of language and the idea of syntagmatic substitutability (see chapter 2, 36–38).[103]

CHILDHOOD IMAGES AND RE-ENCHANTMENT

Gondry's fascination with childhood is something the surrealists would surely have recognized. Recalling the earlier discussion of the uncanny, altered and *unheimlich* (unhomely) perceptions of objects held to be comforting in childhood were central in Freud's theorization. This view of childhood object resonates with Gondry's fascination with oversized teddy bears (in the Björk video "Human Behaviour"), doll houses (in both *La science des rêves* and *Be Kind Rewind*, Figure 3.2.), toy cars (Jerry's car is a life-sized parody of a toy), cardboard cutouts and the like. Childhood and creative play for thinkers of the surreal disposition from Baudelaire and Breton to Benjamin is not something that can be lost, but a resource to be drawn on throughout adulthood requiring nothing more than a shift in consciousness.[104] The attitude is noticeably different than the classical theorizations on postmodernism, which speak of "lost innocence" (Eco was among the first to declare such a stance). This is the standard postmodernist

---

[103]   See Roland Barthes, "The Metaphor of the Eye," trans., J. A. Underwood, in Georges Bataille, *Story of the Eye*, by Lord Auch [pseudonym] (London and New York: Penguin, 1982), 120–25.

[104]   Benjamin was less interested in toys as material objects than the open-ended possibilities of play. For both Baudelaire and Benjamin, however, the realization that toys are not real marks the beginning of adult melancholy. Gondry plays with the subtext of trauma in adults' relationship with toys in the way he exploits their uncanny potential to seem animated. Walter Benjamin. "The Cultural History of Toys," in *Walter Benjamin: Selected Writings, Volume 2, part 1, 1927–1930* (Cambridge: Belknap Press, 2005), 114; Charles Baudelaire, *The Painter of Modern Life and Other Essays*, trans. Jonathan Mayne (London: Phaidon 1995), 198–204. Baudelaire's appreciation of toys is distinctly surrealist: "Is not the whole of life to be found there in miniature—and far more highly coloured, sparkling and polished than real life?" Ibid., 199.

Figure 3.2 Deconstructing the universal omniscient camera. Gondry's life-sized doll house resembles the surrealists' fascination with childhood. "Sweded" film montage in *Be Kind Rewind*.

and post-punk attitude starting from the 1970s and arguably culminating in the reflexive "smart film." Gondry, however, rarely exhibits such tendencies. Disenchantment does play a part in this film, but Gondry's response is recuperative more than it is deconstructive, involving a positive more than a negative affective charge. What has already passed does not need to be taken apart as such, but objects from the past can be held in relief against the present in such a way that the energies they have accrued over time (their ghosts) are permitted to speak.[105] As touched on previously, Benjamin considered this mode of existence a historicizing jump into open air, which might sound like a contradiction in terms but makes better sense if "historicizing" is understood to imply perceiving more than retrieving the past. In other words, it implies a dialectical engagement between the past and the present that opens up a discursive space where the imagination can to take flight.[106]

---

[105] Gondry's approach is somewhat reminiscent of Derrida's concept of "hauntology." See Jacques Derrida, *Specters of Marx* (New York and London: Routledge, 1993). Without going into the details of Derrida's argument in reference to the legacy of Marx, the mode of apprehension he described when discussing the ghosts of Marxist philosophy in contemporary experience has something in common with the attitudes of the surrealists when it comes to outmoded fashions. Most of all, this conceptual cluster is characterized by an interest in the uncanny, indicated conceptually in Derrida's word play on ontology (implying presence) and the verb to haunt (implying absence). A significant difference is that while Derrida paints a disaffected picture of the world as damaged even before the old became old, Gondry at least points toward the possibility of recuperative action, if only by means of naïve repurposing.

[106] Benjamin, *Illuminations*, 261.

In some ways, *Be Kind Rewind* seems like a concession to the film industry on Gondry's part. Both *Eternal Sunshine of the Spotless Mind* and its Francophone follow up, *La science des rêves* (*The Science of Sleep*, 2006) suggest a bold and uncompromising aesthetic vision. Both were oneiric films that employed advanced techniques to portray dreamlike mindscapes, including rapid and disjunctive editing, the use of handheld cameras to produce an unstable and kinesthetic feel, and unconventional narrative formations, all of which direct attention toward the sensory qualities of the medium.[107] The narrative pretext for the first film was a futuristic medical procedure that erased the contents of the two protagonists' memories; the second a downhill slide toward madness brought upon by the protagonist's inability to differentiate waking life from dreams.[108]

In strong contrast to these two earlier films, *Be Kind Rewind* relies heavily on classical camerawork, extended shots filmed with fixed cameras, crane shots used to establish *mise-en-scène*, and a substantial amount of videography employing vintage technologies like VHS video cameras (resulting in a "soft" analog feel). Because of its eclectic and self-consciously dated style, the film might be understood as constituting an implicit critique of teleological views about advancing cinematic technologies. CGI technology is employed in Hollywood mainly to provide a heightened sense of realism, or hyperrealism, as can be seen in the impressive special effects in Peter Jackson's remake of *King King* (2005). In contrast to this, Gondry's alter-ego filmmakers use a rudimentary depth of field illusion to make Jerry-in-monkey-suit appear almost (*although not really*) capable of holding a female actress in the palm of his hand. This effect is closer in spirit to the unintentionally campy and markedly surreal stop-animation effect used to produce the original RKO-produced monster (*King Kong*, 1933) than it is its digitally enhanced successor (see Figure 3.3.). In a similar vein, the famous revolving corridor scene from *2001: A Space Odyssey* (Stanley Kubrick, 1968), a special effects landmark of its time, is satirized in miniature by connecting a camera to a small revolving tube (see Figure 3.4.). This makes it appear almost (*but not really*) as if a motionless actor is negotiating a 360 degree loop. Sound effects are similarly deconstructed as a woman hits a punching bag with a baseball bat while cartoon-like boxers slug it out in the ring.

These mock-ups of classic films have been strung together in a way that accentuates the protagonists' resourcefulness, and by proxy Gondry's, just as the sweded films demystify canonical cinematic achievements. Otherwise the film is filled to the brim with ludicrous miniature models, cardboard cutout cars, and the entire

---

[107] Shaviro, "Emotion Capture"; Vernallis, "Music Video, Songs, Sound."

[108] In addition to Gondry's influence, the critical and box-office success of *Eternal Sunshine* can be attributed to the major studio resources at the director's disposal: the presence of a strong screenplay written by Charlie Kaufman (writer of such other neosurrealist screenplays as *Being John Malkovich* [1999], *Adaptation* [2002], and *Synecdoche, New York* [2007]), Jon Brion's music, the work of a large team of sound effects specialists, the contributions of two major Hollywood stars (Jim Carrey and Kate Winslet), and an element of coherence the star text bestows upon what is an otherwise fragmentary film.

Figure 3.3 Parodying *King Kong*, with the help of a rudimentary depth of field illusion and props from the junkyard. "Sweded" film montage in *Be Kind Rewind*.

Figure 3.4 Corridor scene from Kubrick's *2001: A Space Odyssey* deconstructed. "Sweded" film montage in *Be Kind Rewind*.

side of a house converted into a cutaway doll house (see Figure 3.2.), a technique that parodies cinema's omniscient camera (seen, for example, in the famous upstairs-downstairs shot in *Top Hat* [1935], where the camera moves unhindered through the floor of a building; more on this in the following chapter). *Be Kind Rewind* revels in illusionist manipulations of *mise-en-scène* and unexpected interpolations in frames of visual reference, which allows us to see originals as never before. There is undeniably something childlike in all of this, which could be criticized on the ground that fooling around in this way implies relinquishing responsibility. The film infantilizes the actors as agents in a way that could be seen as problematic, especially when it comes to the representation of disenfranchised ethnic groups.[109] Rather than simply infantilizing these parties, however, Gondry ends up doing it to everybody, not least himself, through the playfulness of his directorial agency. All of this reverses some common assumptions about the nature of creative activity, which the film argues requires the suspension of adult preconceptions.

A METAFILMIC ENDING

The film's apotheosis comes with the screening of the Fats Waller short film, sections of which have been previewed throughout the course of Gondry's longer film. This is the first opportunity members of the Passaic community, fictional and real (since many locals were employed as extras), have to come together to celebrate their filmmaking achievements, even while demolition workers standby to dismantle the buildings where the fictional characters live and work. Just as fictionally these sections of the film celebrate participatory approaches to filmmaking, so in real life the producers of Be Kind Rewind have set up a YouTube channel, which includes provisions for uploading user-made sweded films.[110] In this way the film connects with the participatory spirit of the digital age, although the skeptic might argue that this is simply a canny synergetic marketing strategy.

In audiovisual terms, the closing scene is one of the film's most striking. Here Gondry plays with the boundaries between diegetic and nondiegetic sounds by muting the former for extended periods, with the exception of the soundtrack of the Waller metafilm, which continues in lieu of the soundtrack proper (1:27:50). In this way audience immersion is conveyed, but the technique is not without more reflective dimensions. This element surfaces as audience reactions fade sporadically *and audibly* into the soundtrack mix, the sudden juxtaposition of immersive and realistic sounds highlighting the constructedness of the situation. Narrative ambiguity in the background music of the metafilm is an additional factor adding to the reflexivity of the scene. As shots of a four-handed Fats Waller lookalike appear on the screen (a second pair of hands belongs to someone obviously seated below the instrument), the piano music the audience has heard from the beginning of the scene almost syncs up with the rhythm of the hands, making its narrative function resemble source music (in reference to the film-within-a-film) more than the nondiegetic function it has served up until this point. The ambiguous status of the music

---

[109] See Hawkins for a discussion of similar issues in relation to the occasionally infantilized persona adopted by Björk; most notable in videos by Jonze and Gondry. Stan Hawkins, "Musical Excess and Postmodern Identity in Björk's Video 'It's Oh So Quiet,'" *Musikin Suunta* 2 (1999): 43–54.

[110] At the time of this writing, the *Be Kind Rewind* pages can be found on YouTube, http://www.youtube.com/user/bekindrewind, retrieved December 1, 2010.

in fact transports it to an *extranarrative* and liminal plane similar to that discussed in connection with the films *Magnolia* and *Waking Life*. This strategy directs attention toward the image of Gondry as *auteur* and the film as a construction as much as it signifies the transcendence of characters in the plot.

The scene risks descending into Hollywood schmultz as the door to the video store opens to reveal a sizeable gathering on the street, including members of the local community and the demolition crew. However, a stereotyped "happy ending" is avoided. After an initial shower of diegetic laughter from the crowd, all diegetic sound is once again muted, the wistful but warm tones of Jean-Michel Bernard's piano music take over, later to be joined by strings. More than encouraging a sentimental interpretation of the images, the music invests them with a subtle melancholic quality, even undertones of traumatic loss, as dialogue and other human sounds are submerged beneath the nostalgic tones of piano and accompanying orchestra. As the past intrudes on the present day in the vaguely bluesy mood of the sonorous but spatially empty piano voicing, the present day is consigned to the past—it is silenced. This draws attention to what all film does by invoking the modus operandi of an archaic form: silent film. It signifies above all that the reality depicted, registered on the filmic medium, took place in the past. In other words, it is no longer part of the present-day phenomenal world. The removal of diegetic sound confirms this status.[111] In *Be Kind Rewind*, the scar that the absence of diegetic sound brought into audibility should not be considered *shock* in the sense of the term in historical surrealists' writings (in my evaluation, more a sense of *wonder*: implying both semantic indeterminacy, or ambiguity, and astonishment), but something close to that meaning does impinge on the dramatization of the final scene. Most of all, the removal of diegetic sound draws attention to the transitory nature of the images. Might these too disappear? We know that the building will soon be demolished. What then?

A further rationale for why the final scene might be perceived as representing a moment of deconstructive rupture is due to the spectral status of acousmatic nondiegetic sounds. Why are they there in the first place and to who do they belong? Michel Chion has plumbed this subjective territory with the greatest persistence in his writing on the uncanny affects of the disembodied voice.[112] Kevin Donnelly considers such nondiegetic incursions to be manifestations of the unconscious welling up to overflow across the narrative territory of the film.[113] An element of

---

[111] The same technique of silencing the diegetic soundtrack has been employed in films depicting the trauma of war, to convey the isolation and numbness (actual or subjective loss of hearing) of those who have suffered from shell shock. A battle scene in Akira Kurosawa's *Ran* (1985) employs this technique to poignant effect. Sally Potter uses the same technique in the deathbed scene of *Yes* for the same reason. See the discussion in chapter 4.

[112] Michel Chion, *The Voice in Cinema*, trans. Claudia Gorbman (New York: Columbia University Press, 1999), 17–30.

[113] Kevin Donnelly, *The Spectre of Sound*, 23.

irrationality that results from the forceful interpolation of an exterior element within the narrative world of the film is easily understood in terms of Freud's conception of the unconscious. More immediately, though, this exterior world is also the extranarrative world of the director *and* the musicians—an aspect that is visibly registered on two occasions in *Waking Life*. An "extrafilmic" dimension is underlined in the complete removal of diegetic sound. In effect, this leaves audio-viewers stranded halfway between filmic and extrafilmic planes of reality. It leaves the fictive (and real) local people of Passaic stranded as well. It seems that they face an uphill battle ahead if they are to successfully navigate the detritus of urban decay that conditions the affective tone of their lives; notwithstanding a backdrop of mass media saturation, corporate interference and governmental indifference. By turning inwards toward the wellspring of the imagination, it is suggested, a path might just be navigated out of this darkness. Needless to say, this models how we as audio-viewers might come to terms with similar conditions; how we might learn to make the best of things in an imperfect world by seeking to re-enchant the cultural detritus we have inherited.

A Short Music Video Coda

In terms of its script and artistic scope *Be Kind Rewind* is no classic, but it is a lot of fun. The approach it delineates points toward a subtle form of critique that is neither preachy nor condescending. Both of the case studies considered in this chapter demonstrate, in different ways, the extent to which music video aesthetics impinge on film. In the final scene of *Be Kind Rewind*, Gondry reverts to what he knows best: by removing the diegetic soundtrack he turns the film into something resembling a music video. Efforts so far to translate (or remediate) the music video aesthetic into film have been hit and miss: Robynn Stilwell touches on the crux of the problem when she describes a subset of the new generation directors starting from Robert Altman as "songwriters trying to write symphonies."[114] *Eternal Sunshine* succeeded not because it discarded narrative altogether, although some writers have lauded Gondry's attention to the musicality of the image in that film, but because of the way narrative is retained but treated in a novel way. Arguably, those directors who tackled narrative structuring imaginatively in music videos have had the greatest artistic successes in film. Gondry learned many of his tricks, as wells as his taste for surrealist imagery, when directing videos for his band, Oui Oui—creative work that attracted the attention of the equally surreal musician and multimedia artist Björk. It might have been Gondry's appreciation of the surreal and the readymade that appealed to Björk, as well as his fascination with childhood, since these are qualities shared by both artists. It is, above all, in this

---

[114] Personal correspondence with Robynn Stilwell.

creative partnership that Gondry would forge a style that would also define his approach to full-length feature films.

Music videos like Björk and Gondry's "Army of Me" spotlight some distinctive features of Gondry's directorial style in germinal form. The phat bass line and driving electronic sounds of the music find visual counterparts in an oversized sci-fi truck the singer commandeers in the song's opening verse. Viewed retrospectively, this vehicle closely resembles Jerry's customized car in *Be Kind Rewind*. As the verse of the song progresses, cyborg butterflies fly off the radiator grill in a visual flurry that complements the fluttering and shimmering sounds of a synthesizer. In the chorus, shearing metallic whooshes slice downward as the visual imagery becomes further divorced from reality. The surreal is implied as revolutions of the truck's oversized wheels fail to correlate with the vehicle's forward motion. Brass hits sync with impatient horn blasts as the driver makes her way toward a less than amiable gorilla dentist.

Upon escaping from the sadistic gorilla, the video's protagonist passes through a barren industrial wasteland, on her way to a pristine postindustrial museum filled with painterly modernist art: everything from abstract impressionism to Mondrian-like geometric studies. Her goal is to release an incarcerated male companion, who has been transformed into a freeze-dried museum exhibit. Believing the institutionalization of the artist to be a fate worse than death, she explodes the museum, whereupon the letters "SEUM" fall, leaving only the legend "MUM." Ambiguous semantically, the word signifies both a secret that cannot be told and a return to nondifferentiated (maternal) subjectivity—something that eludes the symbolic twists, turns and evasions of institutional art theories. Miraculously, Björk's companion survives the blast. Like a gender-bending sleeping beauty, he awakens to join the singer when fleeing the post-apocalyptic wreckage of the building. This happens to the accompaniment of searing electronic sounds. Having succeeded in dismantling the barriers between "art and life" in true avant-gardist style, through a surrealist explosion (see Benjamin quotation on page 95), the couple are free to pursue their more innocent take on reality and its upended forms. In this and other audiovisual forms, Gondry has done his fair share of symbolic detonation. His artistic sensibility connects creative work with everyday life, but more striking, it draws attention to just how surreal everyday experiences can be. The new museum, or "mum," for those who choose to perceive the world in this way, is not a real or even a virtual museum, but rather the phenomenal theater of the mind.

4

Neosurrealist Metamusicals, Flow and Camp Aesthetics: *Yes* and *The Wayward Cloud*

Contextualizing Metamusicals

ON INTERMEDIALITY, AFFECT, AND CAMP PERFORMATIVITY

If music videos conditioned the conventions of recent cinema more than is commonly assumed, a parallel tradition exists that was from the outset closely related to the modus operandi of music videos: the film musical.[1] This chapter explores by means of two case studies a significant direction in recent auteurist filmmaking that draws on a wide array of genres, including, most centrally, the film musical, but also the audiovisual codes of music videos, experimental films, amateur filmmaking and even hardcore pornography. At the center of this investigation are two recent films that reference while subverting the conventions of the film musical: Sally Potter's *Yes* (2004) and Tsai Ming-Liang's *The Wayward Cloud* (2005). These films demarcate not only the resurrection of the musical as a genre, which has been strongly indicated along more overtly popular fronts (*Moulin Rouge*, 2001; *Chicago*, 2002; *De-Lovely*, 2004; *Sweeney Todd*, 2007; *Mamma Mia*, 2008), but a shift in the entire dynamic of the form that adumbrates a more thoroughgoing realignment of critical priorities.[2] The guiding questions behind this chapter include: Precisely what shapes do these realignments take in the films

---

[1] I express my deepest gratitude to Caryl Flinn and Stan Hawkins for their detailed and insightful comments on this chapter. In the same breath, I would like also to thank Carol Vernallis and Miguel Mera for critical comments that helped me to find an orientation for this part of the study.

[2] For a discussion of the transformation of the musical across popular culture, illustrated by means of a case study on *The Sound of Music*, see Caryl Flinn, "The Mutating Musical," in Claudia Gorbman, John Richardson and Carol Vernallis, eds., *The Oxford Handbook of New Audiovisual Aesthetics* (New York: Oxford University Press, 2012).

that are the subject of this discussion? To what extent can they be interpreted as commentary on changing aesthetic and cultural priorities? Further, to what extent does an understanding of neosurrealist aesthetics help to illuminate both of the above questions, as well as shed light on the aesthetic and affective tones of the films?

Continuing in the direction of the book so far, I concentrate on those forms and styles that articulate a broadly neosurrealist agenda. And since the subject of the chapter is musicals or closely related forms, it goes without saying that the aesthetics of popular music is seldom far away. Several assumptions underlie the readings undertaken in the remainder of this chapter. First, that musicals are an inherently intermedial and therefore an "impure" (with no derogatory connotations implied) audiovisual form. Second, a lineage of gendered assumptions exists that is attached to ideas about film musicals and is part and parcel of what they are all about. It is ignored at the writer's peril. This lineage includes a surreal sense of queerness resulting from the transformation of transparent and realist modes of representation in the musical number. Camp aesthetics is an important part of this, and several recent studies have shown how influences exerted by sexual minorities have informed an ostensibly mainstream set of conventions. Third, the types of musicals addressed here are at one remove experientially from those with which audiences of my generation grew up. I employ the term *metamusicals* in the same sense as terms like "metatheory" or "metalinguistics," as denoting a mode of address that is reflective on the conditions that gave rise to the form itself. In other words, the forms discussed are demonstrably musicals, independent films, television shows or music videos that are *about* musicals more than simply being *musicals*. In this respect, this chapter continues the former one, where both of the case studies examined pivotal film-within-a-film scenes, in which audio-viewers are encouraged to reflect on their position as audio-viewers by witnessing others in the same position onscreen. In this way, both *Waking Life* and *Be Kind Rewind* took on an obvious metafilmic dimension. They did this also more subtly, however, through the inclusion of rhetorical markers of authorial style, other forms of narrative multilayeredness (such as the inclusion of extranarrative actors and musicians), and through a mode of de-centering occasioned by stylistic hybridity. The same is true of the metamusicals in this chapter. The first of these points is, undoubtedly, key when it comes to the subgenre of the neosurrealist metamusical. Authorial agency is presupposed in the tradition of independent and art-house filmmaking and, for many audio-viewers, this aspect defines the audiovisual identity of films, as well as the interpretative expectations audiences bring to their encounter with them.[3]

---

[3] On the significance of *auteur* politics in contemporary independent film, see Annette Davison, *Hollywood Theory, Non-Hollywood Practice: Cinema Soundtracks in the 1980s and 1990s* (Aldershot: Ashgate, 2004).

It is hard to fully appreciate film musicals without understanding that they are intrinsically intermedial. By this I mean that even the earliest films of this type were concerned with relating to cinematic audiences a set of conventions that had originated in live stage performances—of prefilmic forms such as vaudeville, cabaret and so on. The early backstage musicals of Busby Berkeley (e.g., *42nd Street*, 1933; *Footlight Parade*, 1933) are perhaps the most obvious examples of this intermediality. This aspect permeates each of the different subgenres of the musical in varying degrees, and it is exaggerated almost to the breaking point in the subgenre that is the primary focus of this chapter: neosurrealist metamusicals. Theory on intermediality and remediation was reviewed in the introduction, so there is no need to rehash definitions of those terms in this context (chapter 1, pages 7–8). Here intermediality implies a transportation of some existing and established form of expression into new or alien territory; a recontextualization that is understood to be transformative. I employ this idea because of how it addresses the performative and technological contexts of the current digital age and the cultural transformations such contexts imply. Both of these aspects come strongly to the fore in Chapple and Kattenbelt's discussion of intermediality, which elevates "the incorporation of digital technologies and the presence of other media within the theatrical and performance space."[4] These writers further list a cluster of concepts related to this performance dynamic, including "blurring of generic boundaries, crossover or hybrid performances, intertextuality, intermediality, hypermediality, and a self-conscious reflexivity that displays the devices of performance in performance."[5] The last of these categories, performative self-reflexivity, as conveyed through intermedial and cross-generic acts of translation is crucial to understanding the governing aesthetic assumptions behind the films discussed in this chapter.

Intermediality in film musicals has been commented on in passing in some of the existing writing on the subject, insofar as it has tracked changing conventions from stage musicals to the screen (and back again).[6] What the intermedial history of film musicals brings to light is, above all, an element of continuity with traditional values dating from the prefilmic forms to which musicals, especially "backstage musicals," in varying degrees allude. Musicals hark back to these values, even if they do not always successfully embody them. Some of the most influential writing on the genre made the case that this is a highly conventionalized expressive form that supports a correlative cultural apparatus relating to such deleterious categories as utopian escapism, prescribed gender identities, and unequal labor relations. Richard Dyer has paid particular attention to the utopian function of musicals by showing how

[4] Freda Chapple and Chiel Kattenbelt, eds., *Intermediality in Theatre and Performance* (Amsterdam: Rodopi, 2007), 11.

[5] Ibid.

[6] See, for example, the chapter "Non-Filmic Sources to Filmic Sources During the Studio Era," in Jane Feuer, *The Hollywood Musical* (London: Macmillan Press, 1982), 94–102.

they articulate a sensibility embodying the categories of energy, abundance, intensity, transparency and community.[7] To articulate these qualities at a historical time when they were in short supply (the golden age of musicals in the first half of the twentieth century) was to offer a model of *how it feels* to live differently and thereby to temporarily escape from the constraints and drudgery of daily life (in the light of recession, war, economic deprivation and so forth). This model was both deeply nostalgic, in its assumption of a better time existing in the past rather than the present or future, and colored by the prejudices of its era relating to relations between the sexes, among other things.[8]

Musicals today do not signify in the same way as they once did; they do not or could not *feel the same* since feelings are structured differently in different historical contexts. Nor have the aesthetic and performative practices associated with the film musical solidified completely, since musicals continue to be performed on the stage. As such, they remain a point of reference for some filmed media performances. Moreover, as live performances of popular music become increasingly theatrical and economically necessary to artists (because of decreased revenue from recorded media), modes of expression familiar from musicals have found new outlets in popular culture and these are spilling over onto other expressive spheres. In the digital age, there is ample evidence of cross-contamination among forms that is bringing about substantial changes in modes of production and aesthetic understanding. These different forms and media have a profound impact on musicals, be they mainstream or more critically orientated, such as those that are the focus of the present study.

The audiovisual performances examined in this chapter constitute a second reworking, or remediation, of the aesthetic of musicals that is differentiated from the first (from stage performance to cinematic) by the manner in which transitions between forms are signposted. Theories of performativity are easily brought to bear on questions of expressive transformation and have constituted, in different ways, much of the recent writing on intermediality. Since gender performance goes to heart of the definition of musicals as a form, it follows that theories of gender performativity might also have some relevance. This is true also of the emerging forms discussed here, which are revisionist and therefore express a special interest in highlighting the nature of conventional gender formations. By performativity, I refer to the idea of identity (gendered and otherwise) as nonfoundational and inflected through the very acts that prompt its recognition. Such performances create "gender trouble," as Judith Butler expressed it some years ago, stemming from "repeated stylization of the body, a set of repeated acts with a highly rigid regulatory frame that congeal over time to produce the appearance of substance, of a natural sort of

---

[7] Richard Dyer, "Entertainment and Utopia," in Rick Altman, ed., *Genre: The Musical* (New York: Routledge, 1981), 175–89.

[8] Ibid.

being."[9] Gender perfomativity, when visible as such, denaturalizes those gender for-mations that we take for granted and which we would ordinarily interiorize without a second thought. It is the "second thought" which demarcates difference.

The view of performativity adopted here owes as much to the writing of Eve Kosofsky Sedgwick as it does to Butler or the large number of theorists who have grappled with this issue since *Gender Trouble* first appeared in print. Referring back to the writing of J.L. Austin and Jacques Derrida (particularly his idea of "iterabil-ity," discussed in chapter 1, pages 23–24), Andrew Parker and Sedgwick note that writing on peformativity in linguistics and philosophy has always attended to the aberrant or queer nature of performative acts.[10] Enactments of such aberration sep-arate performances from their points of reference, thereby allowing the complex nature of citational activity to be disclosed.[11] In more recent writing, Sedgwick attends less to the function of exposing essentialism in performative acts and more to the effects they produce in terms of embodied experience and affect.[12] To a con-siderable extent, my discussion follows this imperative. This will be undertaken by attending as much to the sensory, pleasurable and unpleasurable qualities of sounds and images in the audiovisual performances that are the subject of these investiga-tive pursuits, as to the ways in which they reveal the normative structures that pre-ceded them and which they pervert.

Gender is not all that is at stake in discussions of performativity. Amy Herzog argues, in a discussion drawing on Gilles Deleuze's understanding of repetition and difference, that the structural and cultural repetitions found in the popular song in recent musicals can be understood as repetitions stacked atop existing repetitions.[13] This second level of repetition recontextualizes culturally conservative originals, turning them into something far more radical. Second-order repetitions of this kind permit songs of the same to be perceived as dreams of difference, the relatively con-servative ideological baggage of the traditional film musical to become something other than its former self.[14] My approach is especially close to Herzog's in the discussion of Tsai Ming-Liang's *The Wayward Cloud*, when this director employs song-forms that can be recognized as obvious repetitions of earlier forms in which ideological meanings were established long before the film was produced. Performativity works differently in Sally Potter's *Yes*, where the iterative qualities of the musical discourse itself function more subtly in correspondence with other

[9] Judith Butler, *Gender Trouble* (London and New York; Routledge 1990), 43–44.

[10] Eve Kosofsky Sedwick and Andrew Parker, "Introduction: Performativity and Performance," in their *Performativity and Performance* (New York: Routledge, 1995), 1–18, 2.

[11] Ibid.

[12] Eve Kosofsky Sedgwick, *Touching Feeling: Affect, Pedagogy, Performativity* (Durham, NC: Duke University Press, 2003), 17.

[13] Amy Herzog, *Dreams of Difference, Songs of the Same* (Minneapolis: University of Minnesota Press, 2010), 2–3.

[14] Ibid., 38.

aspects of the soundtrack to recondition expectations about how music should sound and feel. The referential quality of the music is more implicit in this case, the affectivity of the sounds more predominant, but performativity is nevertheless a salient angle from which to view the subject when understood through the mediation of camp aesthetics. In the writing on new media, performativity is implicit in the notion of hypermediality, which denotes an awareness of inter-referencing between media that distracts from representational layers of meaning. Perceiving performances *as* performances can imply a reflexive attitude that has its roots in the aesthetic goals of the historical avant-garde (although this might not be the case for all audio-viewers). Given that this is an expressive form with roots in popular culture, but which nevertheless occupies an ambivalent space between consumption and critique, neo-avant-garde and neosurrealist are more fitting designations.[15]

Embedded in the film musical are notions of camp queerness that are either latently or more manifestly to be found across the genre. Since the earliest days of the musical film, and its stage counterpart on Broadway, the form courted a significant gay following among both audiences and those involved in putting on productions.[16] Even prior to this, the drag style of Mae West set a precedent for camping it up on stage and screen in song-and-dance numbers that has carried through to the present day.[17] Some recent studies argue that a specific, if heavily encoded, agenda of camp expression underlies the entire corpus of film musicals produced in the MGM-Freed production unit. This is no accident and can be attributed to the presence of an influential gay contingent on the production staff of the studio.[18] The fact that this studio's films were produced for mainstream consumption belies the fact that they have always also catered to more marginal constituencies. As Steven Cohan maintains, "Camp strategies for achieving ironic distance from the normative have always exploited the slippery space between a 'posture' and an 'imposture,' between 'resembling' and 'dissembling'—in one way or another, camp signaled the queer eye for a straight gaze."[19] For this reason musicals are commonly stereotyped in television sit-coms and casual conversation as a "gay form"; not entirely without justification. This is epitomized in the acting style of a star like Judy Garland, whose performances

---

[15] Chappl and Kattenbelt, eds., *Intermediality*, 11–12. Peter Bürger, *Theory of the Avant-Garde*, trans. Michael Shaw (Minneapolis: University of Minnesota Press, 1984), 81; Hal Foster, "What's Neo about the Neo-Avant-Garde?" *October* 70 (Fall 1994): 5–32, 8.

[16] See D.A. Miller, *Place for Us: Essays on the Broadway Musical* (Cambridge, MA: Harvard University Press, 1998); also George Chauncey, *Gender, Urban Culture, and the Making of the Gay Male World 1890–1940* (New York: Basic Books, 1994).

[17] See Pamela Robertson, *Guilty Pleasures: Feminist Camp from Mae West to Madonna* (Durham, NC: Duke University Press, 1996).

[18] Matthew Tinkom, *Working Like a Homosexual: Camp, Capital, Cinema* (Durham, NC: Duke University Press, 2002); Steven Cohan, *Incongruous Entertainment: Camp, Cultural Value, and the MGM Musical* (Durham, NC: Duke University Press, 2005).

[19] Cohan, *Incongruous Entertainment*, 1.

signify authenticity on the level of content, but wrapped in a performative style that conveys a level of theatricalized irony to those disposed to see it.[20] I will return to this matter in chapter 5 (when considering syncing practices involving the film *The Wizard of Oz*), but for the present purposes it is important to recognize this subterranean expressive potential in the form and style of the film musical and to acknowledge it as a resource to be tapped for those with the inclination to do so. This bears on the question of why Sally Potter and Tsai Ming-Liang employed the codes of film musicals (or something resembling them) in the first place when making their films, both of which might be considered subversive of mainstream forms in different ways. To the extent that constructions of gender and sexuality are strongly implicated in the subject matter of both films, what they have to say in this regard might be related in some way to agendas already encoded in the form. The fact that I call these meta-musicals (films about the aesthetic of musicals) does not imply that they should be understood as simply commenting ironically on musicals; an equally plausible understanding is that they comment through the inherent expressive properties of musical form even while they are signifying difference from that form. It is not a question of *either* uncritical identification *or* critical irony when it comes to the engagement of these forms with film musicals; the relationship is more finely nuanced and mediated through affective consciousness.

If camp is a form of expression distinctive to musicals as a form, the above discussion begs the question, what is camp and how are we to understand its subversive effects?[21] (If indeed it is to be understood as subversive.) Most academic discussions refer back at some point to Susan Sontag's pathbreaking collection of observations contained in the essay, "Notes on 'Camp'" (written in 1964).[22] Attending to the origins of the sensibility in gay communities, Sontag commented how camp was not restricted to its originating gay constituencies but had a wider currency in emerging aesthetic sensibilities. If that was true then, it has been increasingly true since the advent of 1970s glam rock, 1980s androgyny, and 1990s metrosexuality. All of these have stirred up the gender-identity pot to such an extent that any attempt to align gender identities in an uncomplicated way with the reproductive functions of men and women is starting to look increasingly absurd. Adopting a queer studies perspective on the subject, Fabio Cleto contends that camp in the current cultural landscape should be understood as a "queer discursive

---

[20] Ibid., 102.

[21] For definitions and discussions of camp in popular music, see Freya Jarman-Ivens, "Notes on Musical Camp," in *The Ashgate Research Companion to Popular Musicology* (Farnham: Ashgate, 2009), 189–203; the chapter "Singing the Body Fantastic: Corporality and the Voice," in *The British Pop Dandy: Masculinity, Popular Music and Culture* (Farnham: Ashgate, 2009), 121–51; and John Richardson, "Intertextuality and Pop Camp Identity Politics in Finland: The Crash's Music Video 'Still Alive,'" *Popular Musicology Online* 2 (2006). Internet source, www.popular-musicology-online.com/issues/02/richardson-01.html, retrieved December 4, 2010.

[22] Susan Sontag, "Notes on 'Camp,'" reprinted in Fabio Cleto, ed., *Camp: Queer Aesthetics and the Performing Subject. A Reader* (Edinburgh: Edinburgh University Press, 1999), 53–65.

architecture" which "can't be tamed into homosexual property."[23] (Of course, to wrest camp away from its close affiliation with homosexual subjectivity is to divest it of much its critical force; therein lies a significant problem that should not be skirted over.) The power of camp for this writer inheres precisely in the middle ground it occupies between conventionality and its perversion. In constant danger of being misrecognized or simply overlooked, its subversive power inheres in precisely this quality: its refusal to be pinned down to the bedrock of conventional meanings. For these purposes, I take the position that camp does not exist only in the eye of the beholder, although Sontag held this to be the highest form of pleasure associated with camp.[24] Instead, I understand it to be a quality that can be intentionally encoded in aesthetic forms, although the line between encoding and decoding is admittedly, at times, a fine one.[25] Fundamental to camp is an artistic disposition that highlights such qualities as aestheticism, irony, and theatricality.[26] More than this, the performative aspect of camp expression implies a citational relationship to conventional forms that Sontag was the first to acknowledge in academic writing. Note 31 of Sontag's "Notes on 'Camp'" has special relevance to the discussions undertaken in this and the previous chapter. It is easy to perceive a relationship to the incorporational priorities of surrealism in her observation that "many of the objects prized by Camp are old-fashioned, out-of-date, *démodé*."[27] She continues:

> It's not a love of the old as such. It's simply that the process of aging or deterioration provides the necessary detachment—or arouses a necessary sympathy. When the theme is important, and contemporary, the failure of a work of art may make us indignant. Time can change that. Time liberates the work of art from moral relevance, delivering it over to the Camp... Another effect: time contracts the sphere of banality. (Banality

[23] Fabio Cleto, "Introduction: Queering the Camp," in *Camp: Queer Aesthetics and the Performing Subject*, 1–42, 33.

[24] Flinn is one of several writers to challenge Sontag's view that the more refined forms of camp cannot be knowing. See Caryl Flinn, "Restaging History with Fantasy: Body, Camp, and Sound in the Films of Treut, Ottinger, and von Praunheim," in *New German Cinema: Music, History, and the Matter of Style* (Berkeley: University of California Press, 2004), 173–230, 176.

[25] Kay Dickinson's recent study of film and music that "won't work together" largely addresses a camp sensibility that requires neither subversive intent nor an understanding of camp aesthetics on the part of producers to achieve its effects. Dickinson nevertheless chooses not to pursue the contestable pleasures of camp interpretations, preferring to concentrate on how economic conditions have impacted on mainstream interpretations. See Kay Dickinson, *Off-Key: When Film and Music Won't Work Together* (New York and Oxford: Oxford University Press, 2008), 14.

[26] These attributes are foremost in Babuscio's consideration of camp in cinema. See Jack Babuscio, "The Cinema of Camp (*AKA* Camp and the Gay Sensibility)," in Fabio Cleto, ed., *Camp: Queer Aesthetics and the Performing Subject*, 117–35.

[27] Sontag, "Notes on 'Camp,'" 60.

is, strictly speaking, always a category of the contemporary.) What was banal can, with the passage of time, become fantastic.[28]

Whether fantastic or marvelous, the incongruity of outmoded forms in present-day contexts signals an aspect of dislocation leading to aestheticization that is equally at home (while being distinctly "unhomely," *unheimlich*) when viewed through the aesthetic lenses of both camp and surrealism. For the same reasons as surrealist uses of outmoded objects signal an underlying critical orientation, the same might be said of camp. Among the definitions of camp offered in the existing research, Andrew Ross has paid the most concentrated attention to this aspect of the sensibility, arguing how camp is related to modes of productions from the recent past that are now in decline.[29] The element of denaturalization that this understanding occasions cannot but also reflect back onto present-day sensibilities and modes of production.[30] With this in mind, I argue that the pleasure of camp aesthetics in recent cinema is closely related to the historical surrealists' appreciation of outmoded objects. Both *Yes* and *Wayward Cloud* make conspicuous reference to modes of expression that are conspicuous because of their anachronism. When rapidly changing modes of expression of capitalism are subjected to a form of imminent critique, concurrent gender formations are easily dragged into the semiotic crossfire, especially when addressing a cultural form that is already saturated with gendered assumptions. This is the case for the two films discussed in this chapter. The material articulations of outmoded gender roles are as viable as any other "objects" for camp re-enchantment.

Arguably the resurrection of musicals in the present era can be understood as both a symptom of and a causative factor behind the turn toward a new sensory cinema, a mode of consumption that is related also to the turn toward digital culture. But musicals being an "unrealistic" and "anachronistic" cultural form have needed to adapt to the spirit of the times by adopting a more savvy identity in order to satisfy audience demands for artistic forms that are on some level "credible." The middle years of the twentieth century saw a gradual falling out of favor in the mainstream of musical sensibility, even if some aspects of it were retained in children's films, youth films, and musical biopics. Concurrent with an increasing recognition in recent years of the currency of film musicals among sexual minorities, there has occurred a new tendency: the co-opting of the subversive potential of musicals by auteur-directors with a view to critiquing

---

[28] Ibid.

[29] Andrew Ross, "Uses of Camp," in Cleto, ed., *Camp: Queer Aesthetics and the Performing Subject*, 308–29, 312.

[30] Flinn has explored this issue further by attending to the problem of the female body in decline as a privileged site of camp appreciation. See Caryl Flinn, "The Deaths of Camp," in Cleto, ed., *Camp: Queer Aesthetics and the Performing Subject*, 433–57.

mainstream culture (consumerist, middle class, "straight," Western). The theatrical performativity of the musical is the main reason it is able to occupy this ambivalent position: of the mainstream yet apparently able to reflect critically (on) mainstream values. Herzog reads the subversive power of the form in terms of Bergson's concept of fabulation, which denotes a mode of affective resistance that steers clear of the "major" forms of the dominant culture, preferring instead a kind of myth-building function that aims to construct new assemblages and to demarcate new territories.[31] A different way of looking at is this, and the one I expound here, is to view the deployment of musical numbers as disrupting narrative sequentiality in a manner that resembles the surrealists' idea of the marvelous, the performativity of the musical number or elevated (read: surreal) musical expression bringing about a rupture in the continuity of dominant discourses that has the power to emancipate the imaginative faculties.

The musical's attention to affective response is a big part of what makes it camp. Sometimes categorized as spectacle and at others in terms of Eisenstein's notion of a cinema of attractions, another way of thinking of the pleasures of recent musicals is in terms similar to those discussed in the previous chapter: as demarcating a mode of address that evokes a cinema of the senses.[32] Sensory saturation and camp irony are both prominent in the films to be discussed. These facets elevate structures of experience that audiences have long understood to be politically resistant and affectively queer. Circling in more closely on the dominant affective modalities of the films presented below, strategies of perpetual flow and formal interruption set the audiovisual agenda. These give rise to specific moods and responses that deflect attention away from the obvious meanings of mainstream narrative cinema. Flow, on the one hand, and interruption, on the other, both hold attention within an affective and visceral register. This is a response, no doubt, to the possibilities of digital sound.[33] But more than this, it is a reaction to the audiovisual mainstream and an aspect of logocentrism that remains the norm in the commercial sphere, even in an age when avant-gardist strategies are proliferating like wildfire among popular discourses.

---

[31] Herzog, *Dreams of Difference*, 33.

[32] See Sergei Eisenstein's "The Montage of Attractions: An Essay," in *The Film Sense* (London: Faber and Faber, 1943), 166–68. Eisenstein relates the concept of attraction to classic avant-gardist strategies of "shock" and "aggression." Fundamentally, though, the concept is identified with a form of "free montage" that is tied to onscreen action as much as it is to film editing. Eisenstein recognized above all the attractions of theatrical performance as setting the standard for cinematic innovations. Attraction is to be found "chiefly in music-hall and circus, which invariably (substantially speaking) puts on a good show—from the spectator's viewpoint." Ibid., 168. See also Tom Gunning, "The Cinema of Attraction: Early Film, Its Spectator, and the Avant-Garde." in Robert Stam and Toby Miller, eds., *Film and Theory: An Anthology* (London: Blackwell, 2000), 229–35.

[33] See Michel Chion, *Film, A Sound Art*, trans. Claudia Gorbman (New York: Columbia University Press, 2003), 117–45.

FROM SELF-REFLECTIVE MUSICALS TO NEOSURREAL METAMUSICALS

Yes and *The Wayward Cloud* can both loosely be classed as self-reflective film musicals. Jane Feuer's article, "The Self-Reflective Musical and the Myth of Entertainment," provides a benchmark for theorization on this subject as it relates to older films.[34] Feuer's primary concern is with early backstage musicals and the commentary provided on the birth of the genre in the MGM musicals, *The Barkleys of Broadway* (1949), *Singin' in the Rain* (1952) and *The Bandwagon* (1953). Although Feuer addresses an antiquated repertory, her theorization nevertheless provides a useful starting point for the present discussion. In her theorization, self-reflexive musicals such as those listed above imply an oscillation between two primary strategies: those of demystification and remythicization.[35] In each of the above films, the artifice of earlier musicals is unveiled through attention to the mechanical aspects of staging and audiovisual artifice. An example is the famous closing scene in *Singin' in the Rain* (1952), where the leading lady in a film within a film, Lina Lamont (Jean Hagen), is shown in a promotional "live performance" to be lip-synching. The fakery of this act becomes apparent when a curtain opens to reveal the real singer, Kathy Seldon (Debbie Reynolds), who in the actual production of *Singin' in the Rain* lip-synched her singing performances. In contrast to the demystifying function when it comes to earlier practices, therefore, the musicals in Feuer's discussion are remarkably unreflexive about their own means of production.

Feuer goes on to list three processes of mythification found in what she calls self-reflective musical: the myth of spontaneity, which suggests that elaborate performances emerge seamlessly out of everyday life; the myth of integration, which suggests that the musical is a "folk art" arising directly out of congenial collective activities; and the myth of audience, which implies a participatory spirit through shots of reacting audiences, which is a far cry from the alienated consumption practices actually propagated by the film industry.[36] As Feuer contends, musicals are a form of entertainment produced for mass consumption that repeat and therefore mythify conservative and utopian attitudes about gender, consumerism, creativity and the like. They are ideological products full of deceptions. In revealing only the deceptions of other producers, the makers of the self-reflective musicals, in her view, abstain from a significant moral responsibility. Thus the musicals of this period function differently from the self-reflexive avant-garde films of Godard, for example,

[34] Jane Feuer, "The Self-Reflective Musical and the Myth of Entertainment," in Steven Cohan, ed., *Hollywood Musicals: The Film Reader* (London and New York: Routledge, 2002), 31–40; See also Jane Feuer, *The Hollywood Musical* (London: Macmillan Press, 1982), 102–110.

[35] Feuer, "The Self-Reflective Musical and the Myth of Entertainment," Cohan, ed., *Hollywood Musicals*, 32.

[36] Ibid., 32–38.

which interrogate their own narrativity in a manner that has widely been understood to be deconstructive.[37] In might even be argued that they are not self-reflective at all, although an interpretation of musicals through camp aesthetics is bound to complicate any such assertions. This is arguably the main weakness of Feuer's argument: that it does not attend sufficiently to the full range of pleasures afforded to different audience groups.

The writing on more recent films is more useful to the aims of the present discussion insofar as it identifies a new self-conscious sensibility in the work of auteur-directors like David Lynch and Tsai Ming-Liang, in whose films the codes of film musicals are simultaneously deployed and dismantled.[38] Noteworthy is the attention these directors give to the audiovisual assembly of the soundtrack in lip-synching practices, which, as Rick Altman's pathbreaking work has shown, is integral to the processes of mythification by which the genre is defined. Altman's theorization of "audio dissolve" and "video dissolve" in particular sheds important light on how the transition from diegetic realism to supradiegetic fantasy is negotiated in the genre. Requiring a tripartite passage from the everyday realism of speech, toward song and finally dance, the musical moments of the classical film musical stage a release from societal constraints that is through and through utopian. In auditory terms the soundtrack thus fashioned enters the fantastical domain of the supradiegetic. Necessitating temporal suspension and spatial displacement, the techniques of audio and visual dissolve signal the primary objective of musicals: to facilitate escape from oppressive social and personal circumstances through the seductive power of the song-and-dance number. By "leaving normal day-to-day causality behind," Altman writes, "the music creates a utopian space in which all singers and dancers achieve a unity unimaginable in the now superseded world of temporal, psychological causality."[39]

Due to its implausibility, the musical fell out of favor in the heyday of youth films and social realism. However, the genre's apparent otherness in relation to the mainstream realist drama of contemporary Hollywood has made it a favorite among auteur-directors looking to hold a mirror to the entertainment industry. This can be seen and heard in the films of David Lynch, particularly his use of obviously artificial lip-synching practices in *Wild at Heart* (1990) and *Mulholland Drive* (2001), which effectively short-circuits the conventions of naturalistic sound editing while shifting attention toward what Chion calls the audiovisual contract. Paul Thomas Anderson's use of implausible lip-synching in *Magnolia* (1999), discussed in the previous chapter, is a further example of this trend among so-called indie directors.

[37] Ibid., 39.

[38] See Herzog, *Dreams of Difference, Songs of the Same*, 33–38; Annette Davison, "Demystified, Remystified, and Seduced by Sirens," in John Richardson and Stan Hawkins, eds., *Essays on Sound and Vision* (Helsinki: Helsinki University Press/Yliopistopaino, 2007), 119–54.

[39] Rick Altman, *The American Film Musical* (London: BFI, 1989), 69.

Self-conscious audiovisual synchronization combined with some notion of what I call audiovisual flow is among the dominant features of the films discussed in this chapter.

More obviously than Lynch, both Sally Potter and Tsai Ming-Liang are indebted to Dennis Potter's engagement with the film musical, an approach that can be seen in his television dramas starting in the 1970s. The genre-crossing television series *Pennies from Heaven* (1978), *The Singing Detective* (1986), and *Lipstick on Your Collar* (1993) combined realistic drama with staged song-and-dance performances mimed to scratchy vintage recordings in a way that proved to be highly influential. Surrealism plays a part in these stagings as characters drift into inner fantasy worlds to escape from the pain and degradation of their ordinary lives. The resulting displacement of genre expectations creates a darkly humorous and self-reflexive atmosphere that dovetailed with many of the assumptions found in postmodernist audiovisuals forms. Viewed in light of the audiovisual tradition of film musicals, Potter's approach is most obviously indebted to those musicals that used dream sequences as a pretext for staging elaborate and markedly surrealist song-and-dance numbers. MGM's *An American in Paris* (1951), featuring Gene Kelly and Leslie Caron in the leading roles, is a prime example of such a musical.[40] The suspension of everyday logic in dream sequences, not just in musicals but in films in general, including the genres of *film noir* and children's cartoons, is easily related to Freudian ideas about dream consciousness and its supposed ability to resolve problems in conscious life. The surrealist dimensions of dream logic are most apparent in cases where recognized surrealist artists have collaborated with filmmakers, such as Salvador Dalí's dream sequences for the Hitchcock film *Spellbound* (1945) and Disney's *Destino* (2003[1945]). Recent examples have been concerned as much with how dreams create confusion in protagonists' daily lives as how they help to resolve problems and clarify understanding. Much of Dennis Potter's work falls into this category. Michel Gondry's *La science des rêves* (*The Science of Sleep*, 2006) is one such film; Lars von Trier's *Dancer in the Dark* is possibly another (2000). Tsai Ming-Liang's musical numbers can be understood as dream sequences, although often they provide oblique commentary on surrounding narrative events (more than offering solutions to problems). Musical numbers as dream sequences allow for abrupt transitions between realist and surrealist expressive levels, while audio and video dissolve between these levels is not ordinarily required since, in such cases, there is a dramatic pretext for the occurrence of the implausible: the dream.

Neosurrealist musical numbers are an increasingly popular mode of address among television producers and filmmakers from remarkably different backgrounds. Articulating a passionately felt distrust of Hollywood-styled naturalism, directors like Lars von Trier (*Dancer in the Dark*, 2000), Alain Resnais (*On connaît la chanson* [*Same Old Song*], 1997), Neil Hardwick (*Jos Rakastat* [*If You Love*], 2010), Sally

---

[40] For more on dream sequences in musicals, see Feuer, *The Hollywood Musical*, 73–76.

Potter and Tsai Ming-Liang have all worked in an idiom indebted to Dennis Potter, while nevertheless attending to local aesthetic and cultural priorities in the subject matter of their films. In fact, the reflexive musical seems to have a unique capacity to pry open a critical divide between local and transnational circumstances. The appeal of this style to independent filmmakers can be explained in part by the obvious otherness of the audiovisual codes, which self-evidently come from nowhere but Hollywood while appearing to come from nowhere at all (being totally transcendent, expressing Eisenstein's montage of attraction, the spectacular display of undiluted affect). It is this positioning that allows metamusicals to critique dominant codes. Perhaps the easiest way to distinguish neosurrealist metamusicals from earlier forms is by attending to their stylistic hybridity, by which I mean that the codes of the film musical are re-presented as contingent and therefore open to re-imagining, insofar as they appear *and sound* alongside competing codes (chiefly those of avant-garde filmmaking, but also neighboring genres such as music video and hardcore porn). The two films discussed below address this nexus of issues in strikingly different ways. Not marketed as a film musical, Sally Potter's *Yes* nevertheless employs remarkably similar expressive means.

The Affirmative Pleasures of Sally Potter's *Yes*

DRAMATIC PREMISES AND NARRATIVE STRUCTURE

Written and produced in the aftermath of the September 11, 2001 terrorist attacks, Sally Potter's *Yes* (2004) approaches the ensuing atmosphere of distrust between the Arabic world and the Anglophone West by mapping this opposition onto the protagonists of the film: She (played by Joan Allen), an Irish-American microbiologist trapped in a loveless marriage with a British politician; and He (Simon Abkarian), a Lebanese surgeon now working as a chef in London, who fled his homeland after watching a patient shot dead by soldiers claiming to fight for his freedom. The allegorical positioning of the main romantic pair is reflected in their names, She and He; generic labels that to some extent obstruct the classical identificatory mechanisms of Hollywood feature films. In mapping the primary gender opposition against a series of secondary social oppositions, the film holds true to the classic design of the film musical. The central opposition can further be understood as Shakespearean (*Romeo and Juliet, West Side Story*), which complements the linguistic tone of the film, including its extensive use of poetic meter. The plot is generic as well. She becomes estranged from her husband, Anthony (Sam Neill), following his affair. She meets him (He) at a banquet and the two embark upon a passionate affair. Conflicts in religion and global politics gradually impinge on their relationship after He becomes subject to anti-Islamic taunting at work and is sacked after reacting aggressively in self-defense. The situation culminates in his return to his homeland, while She is inspired by the death of her Irish Auntie to return to the site of this woman's finest hour, as a revolutionary fighting for the Cuban cause. Reconciliation is effected in the final scene as He joins her in a Savanna hotel room. While the broader strokes of the plot might seem archetypal, various subplots and peripheral characters complicate the narrative design. These include the teenaged goddaughter, the inappropriately named Grace (Stephanie Leonidas), who the husband comes close to hitting on, and who the wife indulges with a shopping trip. Less conventional is the housecleaner (Shirley Henderson), whose role resembles the chorus in Greek drama, commenting on the actions in direct address to the camera while ostensibly occupying a position within the diegesis. This character's attention to the material consequences of the protagonists' lives, at the microlevel of germs and material traces (condoms and bed bugs), forms an apt complement to the soundtrack and the cinematography, which similarly attends to sensory detail on a moment-by-moment basis. As well as resembling the direct address of the Greek chorus, this mode of address resembles that of singers, or "lip-synchers," in other surrealist metamusicals, such as those of Dennis Potter, who also address the camera directly when breaking away from standard narrative form.

As implied above, the narrative structure of *Yes* is deceptively simple. More than the linear, cause-and-effect structure of classic narrative films, Potter's film conforms loosely to what Rick Altman calls the dual-focus narrative of the Hollywood film music. The actions of the two protagonists are compared and contrasted in parallel sequences: She is rich, He is poor; She has servants, He belongs to a service profession; She is a Scientist (a secular rationalist, despite her Catholic background), he is Muslim and works creatively with food. These conflicts are resolved in the course of the film as he returns to his former profession as a doctor and she drops the ordered appurtenances of her profession to travel to Ireland and to Cuba. As in the design of the classical film musical, music in the broadest sense (an abstract pulse, a rhythmic beat more than discursive musical content) provides the primary means of mediating conflicts in the primary romantic relationship, and by extension in suggesting a resolution to the global issues that are the subtext of the film. The music can do this for two reasons: much of it suggests formal and affective continuity, a kind of gravitational pull, which nevertheless remains strangely detached from the conflicting positions of the narrative. In other words, the different elements of the soundtrack have to them a uniform quality, even though they are pooled from divergent sources: classical and popular music, Western and "Worldbeat" styles. In this way they become an apt intermediary for negotiating cultural conflict, embodying difference but taking on a distinct deterritorialized and impersonal quality as a means to accomplish this end.

The soundtrack of *Yes* is jam-packed with music, most of which I have categorized in Table 4.1, according to musical type as well as narrative and affective function. The clearest narrative functionality in the soundtrack is predictably to be

Table 4.1 **Dramatic Functions and Affective Roles of Musical Styles in Sally Potter's *Yes***

Musical style or genre	Title, composer and performer	Dramatic/affective work in the film
1. Main theme music	Philip Glass, "Paru River," performed by Uakti	Bonds the various styles of rhythmic music in the soundtrack. Connotes a dreamlike shift in consciousness, desire pulling the characters onwards (11:10; 34:20; 54:10; 1:15:00; 1:15:00)
2. Incorporated classical music. Various narrative contexts	Frédéric Chopin, Waltz in C sharp minor, Op. 64 No. 2, performed by Dimitri Alexeev	Provides an air of refinement in the banquet scene (4:00)
	Johannes Brahms, Waltz in A flat major, Op. 39 No.5, performed by Katia and Marielle Labèque	Chef's confrontation with kitchen workers. Ironic and anempathetic function (46:39). Housecleaner's existential musings about dirt and meaninglessness of the universe (1:16:15).
	Sergei Rachmaninoff, piano concerto no. 2 in C minor Op. 18, 1st movement	Builds dramatic tension during lovers' conflict (42:55).
3. Contemporary classical music	Erik Satie, Gnossienne, No. 1, arranged and performed by Claude Chalhoub	Establishes a sensuous mood in a love scene. Exoticism is eroticized in the "Worldbeat" sound of the Lebanese arrangement. The beat music further suggests life-flow (27:00).
	Kronos Quartet, "12/12," composed by Café Tacubar, arranged by Osvaldo Golijov	The collage aesthetic of concrete music complements the kinetic style of the visual editing and an aspect of surrealism in the visual Cuba montage (1:24:15).

(continued)

Table 4.1 **Continued**

Musical style or genre	Title, composer and performer	Dramatic/affective work in the film
4. Latin American popular music	"Iguazu," composed and performed by Gustavo Santaolalla	Similar to Glass's theme, flowing desire with a South American feel. Rhythmic bubbling as couple lies on bed; contemplative and exotic mood (14:53).
	"El Carretero," composed by Guillermo Portables, performed by Gonzalo Grau	South American mood music to accompany her in Cuba; Armenian duduk is the solo instrument—referential of him and how he has transformed her (1:20:00).
5. Middle Eastern popular music	"Norketsou Bar," performed by Winds of Passion (Trad.)	He dances for her in seductive Middle Eastern style (39:54).
	"Yeghishi Bar," performed and composed by Yeghish Manoukian	Contextualizes his journey to Lebanon. Used diegetically with shot of a woman dancing (1:22:00).
6. Electric Blues	"Ten Long Years," composed by B.B. King and J. Bihari; performed by B.B. King and Eric Clapton	Parody of tortured masculinity, used when Anthony (the husband) gets drunk and plays air guitar. Also found at the end of her appropriation of (male?) sexual agency following exhibitionist sex scene with Him in restaurant. Visual cut to Anthony and more conventional alignment (1:50; 36:45; 48:45).

7. Mood music by Sally Potter, Fred Frith, Tom Waits and Kathleen Brennan	"Run," composed by Sally Potter and Fred Frith; performed by Fred Frith	Fast rhythmic sounds synched with arty fence shots (31:10). Closing credits music (1.31:00).
	"Pink Shoes," performed and composed by Sally Potter and Fred Frith	Fast electronic beat and electric guitar for She and goddaughter, Grace, when shopping for shoes. The music parodies the "retail" sounds of commercial pop (40:48).
	"Sweet," composed by Sally Potter, performed by Thomas Bloch and Fred Frith	Used nondiegetically in bedroom scene of lovers. Ambient synth pad with high microtonal sounds (like whale song) and electric guitar. Played in the absence of diegetic sounds, signifying a now blissful interiority (1:28:14).
	"Fawn," composed by Tom Waits and Kathleen Brennan; arranged by Sally Potter and Fred Frith; performed by Thomas Bloch and Fred Frith	Accompanies moody slow-motion sequence of the two lovers at the end. Lyrical and airy, the melody resembles and dissembles an Irish folk song (1:29:00).

found in uses of classical music to indicate refinement or to build dramatic tension; uses of world music to designate ethnic identity and geographical location; and the use of electric blues to denote stereotypical male sexual strutting combined with angst. While the remainder of the soundtrack does to some extent exploit the narrative connotations of existing styles, this function is secondary on the whole to an element of blanket affective conditioning that I discuss further. Despite an impression of heterogeneity, therefore, there is an underlying uniformity to Potters conception of the film.

THEORIZING AUDIOVISUAL FLOW

As Table 4.1 demonstrates, Potter's film is awash with music; not solely because of the amount and prominence of the soundtrack music, but because of the musicality of the spoken dialogue and, intermodally, as a result of the film's visual style, which might also be said to possess musical qualities. Indeed, words like "awash" and "flow" seem particularly apt when discussing this film, which might have something to do with directorial intention. It seems that Potter specifically sought out music with a mellifluous mood to complement her ideas about fluidity and affective flow in the film's larger audiovisual design. "[T]he language of the film is intended to flow," she has commented, "like a cinematic stream of consciousness."[41] The director discusses dialogue in the film in very similar terms. "In the screenplay," she comments, "the verse is like a river running through the film as we delve into the characters' thought-streams and back out into their speech."[42] Flow, then, is understood to transect music, spoken language (exterior and interior), and cinematography in a manner that is integral to the stream-of-consciousness design of the film. This speaks to a conception of becoming or emerging subjectivity that the soundtrack is largely responsible for conveying.

In scholarly writing, flow has been addressed in several ways. Gilles Deleuze and Félix Gauttari's idea of flows of desire has been one of the most influential in recent theory. Flow in this sense can be channeled or blocked depending on whether one connects with the world in terms of static things or as a dynamic process of unfolding experience.[43] Looked at in these terms, *Yes* might be considered an assemblage, a configuration of discrete parts or fragments that in different circumstances can take on different effects. Becoming is the process of transformation engendered when these individual elements migrate across new contexts. A constant pulse is found across all of the disparate elements of the soundtrack,

---

[41] http://www.yesthemovie.co.uk/soundtrack.HTM?articleType=Content.SOUNDTRACK,retrieved February 15, 2010.

[42] http://www.futuremovies.co.uk/filmmaking.asp?ID=131, retrieved February 15, 2010.

[43] For example, Gilles Deleuze and Félix Gauttari, *A Thousand Plateaus: Capitalism and Schizophrenia* (London: Continuum, 1987).

and similar musical refrains are heard at various junctures in the film's unfolding structure. This use of similar musical figures in different contexts allows the audio-viewer to track the passage of sound from one audiovisual setting to the next—from one territory to another—in a continual flow of becoming. This process of unfolding thereby becomes not secondary or merely stylistic; rather, it is definitive of the "meanings" that might be attributed to the film. Potter seems to take considerable pleasure in such processes of flow and contextual transformation between one state and the next. Her use of music reveals a playful appreciation of how sounds can be defined and redefined contextually. In this way too the protagonists of her films are constantly transforming, at least the more interesting ones. He and She both undergo significant personal transformations that are reflected (even produced) audiovisually, while the husband remains in a more static condition from the beginning to the end of the film, both in terms of the film's narrative trajectory and audiovisually.

Flow is not always understood in such ameliorative terms. Raymond Williams writes of it as a distraction from everyday temporality that leads toward a myopic, media-centered view of life.[44] Arising out of the repetitive nature of television programming, flow in this sense represents a structure of feeling designed to lure consumers into an uncritical relationship to dominant capitalist forces. The key elements of flow according to Williams are the containment of contrasting elements within a seductive sequential structure characterized by speed, variety and miscellaneity.[45] Flow is regarded as undesirable mainly because of how it prevents individual elements in television programming from being perceived as discrete and meaningful, while elevating the commercial function of advertising to a status equal to that of serious content such as news programming.[46] Williams's argument concerning the repetitions of the culture industry is broadly analogous to that advanced by Adorno concerning the repetitive structures of popular music. In both theorizations a deleterious hidden agenda is identified in popular forms, which distracts consumers from recognizing their position of subservience in the capitalist world order. Pursuing a more Benjaminian line of thinking, however, the distracting properties of these forms might be deployed to critical ends by attending to the secondary auratic properties of reproduced forms; their mediated physicality as an element to be enjoyed in its own right. Arguably this is the case in much of the new media art and filmmaking. The types of flow afforded in the emerging forms discussed in this book can be understood as articulating the structures of contemporary society while simultaneously offering a means of reflecting on them. Along these lines, Manuel Castells writes of experience in the information age as being

[44] Raymond Williams, *Television: Technology and Cultural Form* (London and New York: Routledge, 1974).

[45] Ibid., 107.

[46] Ibid., 118–20.

shaped in accordance with spaces of flows rather than spaces of places.[47] This could be understood as a radical extension of the tendencies Williams began to conceptualize in his work on television and with implications he could not have foreseen. If this is the case, performative articulations of flow restage while illuminating the dominant structures of current life, even while their unfolding character suggests a mode of becoming that is more dynamic.

A third understanding of flow is offered in Mihaly Csikszentmihaly's theorization of peak psychological experiences. Flow for this writer arises in connection with a sense of immersion in the task at hand leading to experiences of elevated consciousness.[48] The condition requires activity that is sufficiently challenging to push the participant out of her comfort zone, but never so difficult that it will cause frustration. Settling into a task for which the participant has been trained, she is able to transcend her ordinary abilities as a sense of automatism takes hold that characterizes the condition of flow. What is sought in this respect resembles the condition of automatism involved in creative activities, such as writing and drawing, which the surrealists often espoused. It implies an attitude of letting go; giving in to interior or exterior impulses in a manner that eschews the usual blocks and critical diversions. Two further aspects concerning the subjective experience of flow are relevant with respect to the concerns of the present discussion: loss of self-consciousness and an impression of transformed time—seeming to be either suspended or extended.[49] Flow theory was developed to explain the experiences of actors/performers rather than perceivers/audiences—it is a phenomenological category. However, an argument could be made that certain sorts of events encourage or afford perceptions of flow in audiences more successfully than others. The audiovisual design of *Yes* is arguably designed to evince responses along these lines. Characters in the film seem to be swept along in its audiovisual tide, which is available also to audio-viewers, to such an extent that they lose themselves (or are lost) *as characters*: in other words, the musicality of film helps them to step outside of their historical/chronological/named selves and respond more interactively with the rhythms and intensities of their audiovisual environment. At several junctures in the film, moreover, the audiovisual flow of the music suggests the suspension of narrative time. Such perceptions can be transmitted to the audio-viewer: on the first occasion when I watched the film, it seemed far

---

[47] Castells refers to "flows of capital, flows of information, flows of organizations interaction, flows of images, sounds, and symbols" as the organizing forces within contemporary experience. Manuel Castells, *The Rise of the Network Society: The Information Age: Economy, Society and Culture*, vol. 1 (Oxford: Blackwell, 1996), 442. The space of flows is "the material organization of time-sharing social practices that work through flows" (ibid.). By flows he is referring to "purposeful, repetitive, programmable sequences of exchange between physically disjointed positions held by social actors in the economic, political and symbolic structures of society" (ibid.).

[48] Mihaly Csikszentmihaly, *Flow* (London: Rider, 2002).

[49] Ibid., 62–67.

shorter than its actual duration. Others I have discussed the film with report similar experiences.[50]

In addition to the above definitions, flow has been discussed in relation to questions of musical rhythm, groove or beat. Timothy Hughes employs flow as an analytical category in his discussion of the music of Stevie Wonder. Flow for Hughes is a quality produced as a result of the repetition of musical materials in a dynamic relation between perceptions of sameness and the realization of qualitative differences as time unfolds. Of note here is how Wonder creates a general sense of whirring, unabating flow not just with the use of one musical element, but by means of the dynamic interaction of musical elements found simultaneously across several different levels, referring not only to questions of rhythm and meter but "to the principles that underlie *all* music."[51] By extending this definition to include all elements of the multiplanar soundtrack, we approach a definition of auditory flow that has considerable resonance with the approach taken to sound in this film. Flow in this understanding can result from repetition and difference in one musical element; but it can also be the result of compound musical patterning, engendering what Hughes calls "a flow of flows."[52]

The term *flow* belongs to vernacular discussions of popular styles and is widely employed in reference to styles of rap vocalization.[53] In Hughes's analysis it implies a sense of forward motion that is attributable to the patterns of cognition and recognition that govern our understanding of repetitive musical styles. A repeated musical element is never the same as that which preceded it since it is caught up in a play of expectations about whether the music will repeat again or transform into something different. In this way, processes of repetition and transformation keep perceivers guessing. Hughes suggests that a strong kinship to physical motion is implied in relation to flow because of a similar deployment of mental processes, involving attention to where we came from, where we are, and where we are going.[54]

Embodied motion is, of course, very much a part of the performance and reception of rhythmic styles of music. When we walk or dance, it requires both a complex embodied and multidimensional set of rhythmically distributed actions, producing a correlative sense of motion in time and space. If we do this to the accompaniment of

[50] I have argued elsewhere that experimental filmmakers strive for a sense of immersion through techniques of audiovisual flow. See John Richardson, "Transforming Everyday Life: Analytical Perspectives on Experimental Film Soundtracks," in John Richardson and Stan Hawkins, eds., *Essays on Sound and Vision* (Helsinki: Helsinki University Press/Yliopistopaino, 2007), 88–116.

[51] Timothy S. Hughes, "Groove and Flow: Six Analytical Essays on the Music of Stevie Wonder," (PhD dissertation, University of Washington, 2003), 6.

[52] Ibid., 18.

[53] Concerning the concept of flow in rapping, see Adam Krims, *Rap Music and the Poetics of Identity* (Cambridge: Cambridge University Press, 2000), 48–49.

[54] Ibid., 17.

music or in order to produce music, then the music becomes an extension of these activities or the other way round. Sexual activity is certainly an important factor conditioning the configurations of desire that are musically produced in several scenes of this film. The repetitive actions involved in such activities imply a similar sense of motion, both temporal and physical. Flow then is very much an embodied and affective, as well as being a cognitive and psychological, domain of experience. On a more discursive level, flow is a means of representing patterns of desire and of signifying camp sensibility (achieved through the use of excessive or accentuated repetition, for example). In *Yes*, the latter effect is achieved by the sonic pulse of the film invoking musical conventions new and old, and with a mode of vocal phrasing cast in a conspicuously anachronous mold. This imparts to the sonic surfaces a distinct surrealist flavor, not only because sounds in the film resemble the forms of emerging consciousness—a sought after quality in surrealist automatic writing—but because this type of elevated discourse plays no part in everyday communication. People in the real world do not converse in this way, although the feelings communicated through the characters' actions resemble those we encounter in ordinary life. Because of its implied and phenomenal corporeality, sound in *Yes* is conspicuously of this world while nevertheless connecting with external discursive formations and forms of temporal patterning in a manner that seems extremely implausible.

GLASS'S "PARU RIVER"—A SUBTERRANEAN STREAM OF SOUND

The cyclical patterning of Philip Glass's "Paru River" is, as Potter's comments imply, a subterranean stream of sound uniting several of the films narrative tributaries:

> When writing a film script I often find myself playing a piece of music again and again. Something in the piece guides me to where I am trying to go; or echoes a quality in the subject matter or its emerging form. In the case of *YES* the piece was "Paru River," composed by Philip Glass and played by the Brazilian group Uakti. As this screenplay is written in verse it may have been the insistence of the rhythms in "Paru River" that resonated so strongly, or perhaps the reason lies in its name; for the language of the film is intended to flow, also, like a cinematic stream of consciousness.[55]

Glass's music comprises shifting modal harmonies and a constant babbling undercurrent of percussive sound produced with the marimbas of the Brazilian group

---

[55] http://www.yesthemovie.co.uk/soundtrack.HTM?articleType=Content.SOUNDTRACK, retrieved February 15, 2010.

Uakti. Built around three four-measure patterns strung out in ritornello loops, the main theme changes little with each instance that is heard in the course of the film. In the first pattern, the bass outlines the minimal movement of a descending minor second, falling again to the fifth degree of the scale, which then pumps energetically and hocket-like against the root. In this way, the pattern becomes a kind a shorthand chaconne. All the while, the constant pitter-patter of the marimba's upper voice moves upward by a minor second, striving toward a goal and yet relinquishing with each repetition. A minor-to-major sideways shift in pattern two (from the tonic E flat minor to E flat major) and back again imparts a queer, shape-shifting quality to the musical refrains. In the third pattern, a pseudo-modulation to the subdominant (A flat minor) heightens the intensity of the music, while parallel movement in the top and bottom voices outlines a modally inflected upward trajectory to the major chord built on the minor sixth degree (E major), and onward a step higher to G flat major (the "flat" or Aeolian 7th degree), followed again by alternating bass movement between the root and the fifth, suggesting but not confirming the dominant tonal function. The effect, with each change of pattern, is like shifting to a higher gear when driving a car—even while the speed and direction of the musical phrases remains constant. To accentuate this impression of growth within stasis, the music expands in range as it passes from pattern one to pattern three. Typically for Glass, the harmonic movement in all three patterns owes much to the canny use of neighboring tones, shifting triadic harmonies that defy categorization along conventional harmonic lines, and the apparent interchangeability of major and minor, voice leading taking priority here over the requirement of "common-language" functional tonality. Flow is suggested by the omnipresence of similar musical motifs in changing harmonic contexts and by the constant rhythmic beat. Onomatopoeia might partly explain why the music sounds "liquid." The soft percussive sounds of the performers' struck idiophones could be though to mimic the constant drip-dropping of a fast-leaking tap onto a hollow object.

Glass's theme betokens a transformation of the utopian language of the Romantic orchestral idiom into a contemporary "posthuman" context in which affectivity replaces pathos. Recontextualized by their inclusion in a rigid framework of three mechanically repeating patterns and pulsating microrhythmic textures, conventional signifiers of transcendence (the minor to major shift) and lament (the descending bass figure) come to be apprehended as participating in a Benjaminian leap "into the open air of history," such as that which was undertaken by surrealist writers and collectors of outmoded objects.[56] As I have written elsewhere, there is something camp about the way Glass evokes the signifying mechanisms of Romantic orchestral music while nevertheless divesting them of their power to move the

---

[56] Walter Benjamin, *Illuminations: Essays and Reflections*, trans. Harry Zohn (New York: Schoken, 1968), 261.

listener towards pathos.[57] It is an approach that works to "re-enchant" objects from the musical past by activating their latent affective potential rather than commenting on them with ironic derision or disenchantment.

If a surrealist camp sensibility can be recognized in Glass's musical language, it is either present or has been added in the arrangement to other music used in soundtrack. An example is Erik Satie's mystical and exotic sounding "Gnossienne No. 1," which matches the mood of sensual discovery in the love scene where it is played (27:00). Satie is a composer who was present at the birth of the Dada/surrealist movement and whose repetitive approach anticipated the direction musical minimalism was to take several decades later.[58] Because of this affinity, Satie's music integrates seamlessly with other music in the soundtrack. Claude Chalhoub's pulsating Arabian-colored arrangement retrieves exotic layers of meaning that were only latent in the composer's original piano orchestration (for example, in the use of ornamental grace notes and the prominent use of the tritone, b^1, in the melody). Syncopated percussive figures establish a bubbling undercurrent comparable to that which is produced by the marimbas in Glass's music, while the microtonal inflections and drones of the violin arrangement in the A section tease out the exoticism of the composed music, which in turn reflects on his (i.e., He) Middle-Eastern identity and the hybridity of the compound identity the two lovers will assume during the course of the film. Most affecting and beguiling in this piece is an aspect of faux naïveté that creeps up as if from below as a result of a twice descending minor-second figure in the B section, which is heard in the context of a simple root-position plagal cadence: B flat minor to F minor. Grace note ornamentations serve the precise purpose of investing the musical articulation with effeminate grace. The musical figures in question present us with the epitome of musical pathos (the dysphorically encoded minor third) while embedding it within a repetitive context of contemplative simplicity that causes us to question the meaning of what we know—thus the element of mystery connoted in the word Gnostic. The tone of the music in its audiovisual context is one of teasing eroticism combined with an element of childlike play and mystical discovery. However, an aspect of camp pleasure can be perceived in the adoption of a musical language that is outmoded and deliberately oversimplified in the first place. This aspect was present in Satie's original work, a suggestion of humorous playfulness resulting from an excess of repetition, which allows the music to take on a self-reflective quality.

The music is initially heard in a moment of postcoital reverie and with the camera's gaze substituting for hers (and, by proxy, the director's) by focusing on his

---

[57] See John Richardson, *Singing Archaeology. Philip Glass's* Akhnaten (Hanover, NH and London: Wesleyan University Press and University Press of New England, 1999), 200.

[58] Erik Satie is often associated with Dada/surrealism, most directly because of his music for René Clair's surrealist film *Entr'act* (1924). Guillaume Apollinaire is usually credited with the first use of the term surrealism in reference to Jean Cocteau's ballet *Parade*, which featured stage designs by Pablo Picasso and music by Satie.

muscular male physique. The exotic attributes of the violin's elaboration of Satie's theme are called upon to construct him as an object of desire, while his work in the kitchen (he is cooking) places him in an androgynous zone, a result of his effeminate attention to detail when cooking, not to mention a blue apron he wears that could easily substitute for a skirt. Conventional roles are inverted, by her assuming the stereotypically "masculine" role of the voyeur, while apparently passing judgment on his adopted profession as a cook.[59] When this happens, the music become dissonant in Chalhoub's improvised elaborations and it is eventually abruptly silenced, leaving only the rhythms of his now indignant speech intermixed with suddenly louder existential traffic noise filtering in from outside. This is one of many queer moments in a film that seems determined to ask questions about conventional gender positions. Her androgynous appearance and behavior throughout the film is an important aspect of the characterization, although androgyny is not so much in evidence as it is in Potter's earlier film, *Orlando* (1992).

Otherwise the soundtrack flows freely from one musical style to another, incorporating abrupt stylistic jumps, yet all the time infused with a constant rhythmic pull that Potter describes as communicating "yearning." This yearning quality can be attributed to a combination of factors that depend upon audiovisual context. In general, there is an emphasis on the meditative qualities of "quiet" acoustic sounds combined with tonal procedures that either pull at the heartstrings (in the case of Romantic music), engage the body (in the case of dance beats), or signify quasi-Romantic longing infused with "posthuman" depersonalized subjectivity (Glass). Whenever the dialogue implies the slightest whiff of desire (desire that pushes characters to reveal themselves, often physically, or which engenders change), this musical undercurrent is likely to surface, as we see in several cases of the "Paru River" theme, but also in much of the remainder of the nondiegetic soundtrack. Yet the yearning the music communicates is not a type that signifies Romantic-styled longing for a lost utopia. Two factors prevent this from happening: First, the music is conditioned, for the most part, by the citational and affected discourses of camp; second, the repetitive musical texture has an emergent quality that is positively inflected.

The overall musical character of the film is best addressed through what Altman and his co-authors call the relational and multiplanar nature of film soundtracks. Put differently, the full complexity of audiovisual meanings produced in the soundtrack can only by recognized by attending to each of its auditory components and

---

[59] I am not suggesting that the cinematic gaze be understood as intrinsically male, as has sometimes been said of Mulvey's initial theorization. See Laura Mulvey, "Visual Pleasure and Narrative Cinema," *Screen* 16/3 (1975): 6–18. Female directors like Sally Potter and Jane Campion have long challenged the ascriptive conditioning of conventional mainstream representations in their independent films. My understanding of the female protagonist's position as somehow "masculine" and/or queerly androgynous arises from the compound effect of the scene, not least of which is his gender-indeterminate behavior. Even in mainstream contexts, the field of interpretation is open to contesting interpretations as recent theory has stressed.

their interrelationships: sound effects, music, and dialogue.[60] Chion's concept of "audiovisual phrasing" might similarly be invoked to explain how the temporal content of the soundtrack is integrated with the visual structures of the film. For Chion, audiovisual phrasing sculpts the temporal progression of the film in such a way that everyday and linear temporalities are transposed into musical ones. He describes this type of phrasing as a way to "arrest temporal flow in favor of a kind of editing that is non-linear and kaleidoscopic."[61] Phrasing in soundtrack music is therefore integral to phrasing in dialogue and visuals. It is part of a connected whole or assemblage, not an independent structural entity. In other words, the musical and linguistic structures might be said to hijack conventional narrative organization, substituting narrative and semantic continuity with rhythmic and sensory continuity. The audiovisual character of Yes is dominated by this different notion of audiovisual flow.

SPEAKING IN VERSE OR BREAKING INTO SONG?

Although not strictly speaking a musical, Potter's film shares with its historical antecedents a congenital musicality. For much of its duration, the audiovisual discourse occupies the mid-point of Altman's audio dissolve, threatening to drift into outright musical fantasy or to return with a jolt to everyday banality, but acceding to neither of these alternatives. Characters speak in the rhythms of Shakespearian iambic pentameter, as if about to break into song, but never quite get there. In this respect, Yes resembles film adaptations of Shakespearean drama, such as Kenneth Branagh's (Much Ado About Nothing, 1993, Love's Labour's Lost, 2000, and As You Like It, 2006) and Baz Luhrmann's (Romeo+Juliet, 1996).[62] Like the last of these films in particular, Yes is shot in the intensified contemporary style we recognize from music videos, and the characters seem to be of our time, and yet, the spoken language is archaic. Potter's Orlando (1992) represents a similar stylistic doubleness: set in various historical periods but recognizably modern, not least because of the flowing stream of consciousness script that draws on the original book by Virginia Woolf.

The film has a smart, educated and even upper-class tone due to its literary style, which simultaneously locks it into an aestheticized mode of addresses that converges with camp sensibility. This encoding is ambiguous, however. Potter speaks of being inspired by rhythms of rap and the kind of street talk in which every other

---

[60] See Rick Altman with McGraw Jones and Sonia Tatroe, "Inventing the Cinema Soundtrack: Hollywood's Multiplane Sound System," in James Buhler, Caryl Flinn, and David Neumeyer, eds., *Music and Cinema* (Hanover, NH: Wesleyan University Press, 2000), 339–59.

[61] Chion, *Film, A Sound Art*, 263.

[62] The film of adaptation of *Kiss Me Kate* (George Sidney, 1953) is an early example. A backstage musical, this film features long extracts of performances of Shakespeare's *Taming of the Shrew*, which are also recited in iambic pentameter.

Figure 4.1 Exhibitionist love scene in *Yes*. Philip Glass's "Paru River" accompanies his whispered "sweet nothings." Abrupt transition to guitar solo of B.B. King and Eric Clapton's "Ten Long Years" signals the moment of climax.

word is modified by an expletive.[63] This rhythm and flow of rap can be heard especially when the kitchen worker Whizzer argues with He: "I've had it with this fucking God and shit. There ain't no paradise, this fucking crap is it. This country's full of wankers in sheets; asylum fucking seekers on our streets. And taking all our fucking jobs. Arab wanks!" Similar language is heard from the protagonists, however, when He whispers sweet—and unapologetically dirty—nothings into her ear while attending to her manually under the table: "What can I give you lady you, lady luck? What other words and names? I'll fuck/You as a mistress, as a queen; I'll worship you with words obscene/And ugly all the more to show/How I adore you; bring you low/With language from the gutter; Hear me now, I'll gently mutter/Things into your ear; flowing streams/Of words from fantasies and dreams/You've never confessed to anyone. SHE Yes—please!/Yes—say it all!" Encapsulating Bahktin's lower bodily stratum and the destabilizing potential of marketplace speech ("Billingsgate"), the power of the latter utterance is arguably as emancipatory and reparative in its illocutionary force as the former is injurious (see Figure 4.1.).

As tangibly as it references both high and low linguistic registers, the rhythmical regularity of dialogue spoken in verse is reminiscent of the rhythmic phrasing that precedes diversions into song in musicals. Nevertheless, the full degree of transportation toward the transcendental that is implied in the supradiegetic song-and-dance numbers of musicals is never achieved in *Yes*. The nondiegetic music of *Yes* loosely resembles the speech rhythms of the (diegetic) dialogue but it never fully converges with characters' *singing voices* as one would expect to happen in film musicals. Rather, it vacillates between these two modalities. This complementary but not entirely synchronic relationship can be heard in an early scene when She and He walk in a park accompanied by the cascading cadences of Glass's "Paru River." Here the phrasing of the poetic dialogue seems to interlock serendipitously with the underlying musical structures.

HE: (Verbal anacrusis) We have cherries,
        (Pattern 2, "Paru River") plums, and peaches
        And the queen of all, the tree that reaches
        For the sun to fill its seed with gold
        The yellow fruit
        (pause for musical cadence)
        (Pattern 2, "Paru River," 2nd repetition) the apricot. The old
        And wisest say this fruit will keep them young ... *He leans towards her*
        And you can taste her secret with your tongue
        (pause for musical cadence).
        Their eyes meet, briefly, and then she turns away.
SHE: *(Pattern 3, "Paru River")* Potato is our apricot. We bake
        We boil, we mash, we fry; and we make
        A flour of it for dumplings in our stew
        Or bread or scones or pancakes ...
        (pause following cadence)
        (Pattern 3, "Paru River," 2nd repetition) The famine haunts us still, you see
HE: *(Last measure of pattern 3, verbal anacrusis)* We too are haunted by our
        dead, it seems
        (Pattern 1, "Paru River") They speak to us in riddles in our dreams;
        So many killed. They ask the question—why?
        Did we have to die?
        (Over cadence, pause for 1st measure of pattern 1 repetition)
SHE: Look ... shall we think of something sad?
        This conversation's far too light
HE: That's bad ... Yes. Absolutely. You are right.
        (cadence of "Paru River", pattern 1 repetition)
        They smile at each other, fleetingly. And then she touches him lightly, consolingly, on the arm.

As can be seen from the screenplay extract (with notes I have added about the accompanying music), the reversion to the higher-register third pattern of "Paru River" coincides with her lines, while the music reverts back to the home key of E minor and lower-register marimba patterning prompted by his response. Moreover, on several occasions the lovers seem to pause or to bring their dialogue to a close in approximate synchronization with musical cadences. The synchronization is far from precise but a dialogical exchange between the two soundtrack elements—audiovisual phasing that traverses the multiplanar soundtrack—does seem to be indicated.

As important as synchronous exchange between coexisting soundtrack elements is diachronous exchange between elements presented one at a time. An example can be found immediately following the park scene. "Paru River" fades out as they enter her flat and begin to make love. This becomes a cross-fade as He starts to sing a passage of Middle-Eastern music just as Glass's music is disappearing from audibility—intriguingly, both are in the same key, E flat. The couple then exchange lines in iambic pentameter, the musicality of the spoken verse taking over from nondiegetic soundtrack music. At the end of their exchange a new musical cue is introduced, again strongly rhythmic but now in the closely related key of F minor. The track is "Iguazu," composed and performed by the South American artist Gustavo. It is based on a tremolo drone of the pitch classes F and C, alternating with pungent excursions to the tritone (B), and minor third (A flat). Although the performer is South American, the filmic context makes the music sound geographically indeterminate. Exotic, effervescent and meditative, it could signify the Middle East or it could equally represent a utopian deterritorialized zone—a kind of no man's land—where the couple goes in order to find common ground. This music too eventually cedes to dialogue that is initially introduced over it in loose synchronization, cadences in the music once again seeming to interlock freely with speech rhythms. In this way, flow in the dialogue does not work as an isolated element of the soundtrack, but instead overflows from one element of the multiplanar soundtrack to the next, both synchronously and diachronically, in a form of audiovisual phrasing in which each part is recognized as an element within a constantly changing larger assemblage.

At risk of becoming something arty and intractable, Potter's approach to the dialogue in fact works remarkably well because of the looseness of the implementation, which privileges the affective content of the acting over formal qualities. The rhymes seeded into the dialogue seem therefore more like accidental convergences than resulting from a rigidly implemented formal design. However, this element of freeform in the midst of underlying strophic repetitivity required careful planning.

> I had learnt from the five-minute film [A short film based around the car park scene that had inspired *Yes*] that the actors delivered the verse best, paradoxically, when they ignored it; when they spoke concentrating on the meaning, rather than the rhymes, as if the text was just a heightened form of ordinary speech. (For this reason many viewers of the film don't really notice its rhymes or its metre.)[64]

---

[64] www.futuremovies.co.uk/filmmaking.asp?ID=131, retrieved February 16, 2010.

The technique engenders above all a sense of suspended time, with the characters occupying the nonlinear and cyclical temporalities of the music rather than the strict linearity of everyday time. It is an approach that transports the audio-viewer toward the liminal zone between reality and fiction, the metrical division of the dialogue serving to obscure the identificatory mechanisms of Hollywood films from the classical era, just as the characters' names (He, She, Auntie and so on) point toward the distanced mode of address of allegory and of camp expression. In practical dramatic terms this allows the actors to step outside of the action and reflect on the events they are experiencing, a move that would not be possible in the context of naturalistic realism. An example of this technique in Altman's subgenre of the folk musical can be found when the father in *Fiddler on the Roof* withdraws spatially and, by implication, temporally from the action to comment on events in direct address to the camera and, tellingly his God (while the characters of which he speaks become static and silent).[65] A similar sense of temporal suspension is produced here. In both Auntie's hospital scene and one of the first scenes of conflict between him and her at his apartment, the "Paru River" theme is used to accompany interior monologues that transport characters away from their immediate surroundings, leaving other characters who occupy those spaces in a state of silence and temporal suspension (this is indicated visually on some occasions, by means of blurry slow-motion cinematography). In *Yes*, however, temporal diversions are seamlessly integrated with the metrical time of the spoken verse, which allows actors to stray away from linear time without breaching the extended temporal flow of the film's narrative. In other words, the use of rhythms spanning both nondiegetic music and diegetic dialogue allows for a more flexible experience of time, in which internal reverie is distinguished from external (diegetic) dialogue primarily by subtle means such as the silencing of other diegetic sounds and the absence of lip movement.

Commenting on the role of music in suspending normal (and normative?) filmic temporality, Chion writes how

> the sound film...retains from the silents a marvelous mechanism for stopping, expanding, and contracting time: music. Often heard while synch sound is temporarily absent (and helping to "fill the gaps"), music provides the sound film a respite from the infernal rule of successivity; it allows a flexible temporality, and elasticity, the capacity to condense a year, to draw out a second, to linger over a fleeting summer before replanting us on the terra firma of real time.[66]

[65] Rick Altman, *The American Film Musical* (London: BFI, 1989), 273.
[66] Chion, *Film, A Sound Art*, 264.

This aspect of detachment from everyday time and the ubiquitous presence of music are factors that tip the balance toward a flowing sensibility that is remarkably similar to that which Csikszentmihaly discusses in relation to the experience of psychological flow. The film might, therefore, be said to articulate a representation of psychological flow that transects each element of the multiplanar soundtrack. It further transports the characters into a detemporalized zone that resembles the dream sequences of early film musicals and films. This ability of characters to slip in and out of interior experience without skipping a beat pushes the entire experience of the film into a mode of expression familiar from surrealism. While there is a psychological and affective realism to parts of the film, the majority of the scenes are enacted in a way that could not happen in everyday life and reflect back allegorically on our perceptions of everyday lived reality. At the same time, the focus on the flowing qualities of the medium function similarly to a film like *Waking Life*, in which the audio-viewer is seldom permitted to forget filmic reality.

BEYOND THE SOUNDTRACK: RAPTURE AND RUPTURE IN SILENCE AND SOUND

The dominant approach in the soundtrack is unquestionably the almost constant dialogical exchange between soundtrack music and recited verse. But this takes place within audiovisual contexts that reinforce the presence of flow in the soundtrack at the same time as they seem to indicate an existential beyond, an audiovisual Other, which might be understood in terms of Derrida's concept of spacing. Because of the presence of this musicalized discourse, different forms of silence, where they do appear, take on an exaggerated significance. The combination of acoustical sounds (the greater part of the soundtrack comprises acoustic instruments) and sparse arrangements is one way of highlighting the gaps between sounds and thereby invoking a broad ecological awareness. A second is the use of what Gorbman calls nondiegetic silence, which in fact implies nothing more than muting of the diegetic soundtrack. The film features several scenes with interior monologues in which this happens, each time with an affective impact that Potter considers to be illustrative of personal trauma.

> Quite a lot of the shots are mute, with just the inner voice of the character speaking. During the Auntie sequence, for example, you see Joan walking but you can't hear her feet, you just hear her Auntie's voice. It seemed to me that was something of an equivalent to what happens in your mind in a crisis situation or in a state of great emotional trauma or loss. Your world closes down and the irrelevant sounds disappear. You don't hear your footsteps, you just hear what is important at that moment. It's a kind of emergency state of stream of consciousness and

> I tried to find an equivalent in the sound world of the film, and the music
> was a part of that.

This sense of interior sound or music (and external silence) as representing
trauma is an increasingly common trope in art-house films. A battle scene in
Kurosawa's *Ran* (1985) accompanied by tragic orchestral music in the style of
Mahler is a frequently cited example.[67] This approach has spilled over onto some
mainstream films, for example, in the final scene of Gondry's *Be Kind Rewind*
(admittedly, produced by an auteur-director). Potter herself discusses the use of
this technique in the scene where the elderly Irish Auntie reminisces on her
deathbed about her experiences helping the Cuban revolutionary cause. As her
(She) monologue gives way to the Auntie's interior monologue, all other diegetic
sounds are momentarily silenced. At the same time the camerawork becomes
blurry, temporally suspended (by the use of slow motion) and skewed, indicating
the more subjective attitude of the speaker. Nondiegetic silence is broken
abruptly when the Auntie chooses to communicate with the outside world by
speaking the words "in Cuba" and "Castro." When this happens, She comes into
focus in now more conventional camerawork. The Auntie's dreamscape in this
way gives way to the female protagonist's more realistic perspective. When the
interior monologue resumes, Glass's ebullient "Paru River" insinuates itself
under the dying woman's words. Before long, nondiegetic music takes over and
the interior monologue in turn is silenced. Eventually the music will synch up
randomly with flashing Christmas tree lights in the hospital corridor, reflected
onto the window in front of the protagonist in a moment pure audiovisual poetry.
A kind of audio dissolve is therefore constantly negotiated in how the elements
intersect in the soundtrack, although dissolve from realism to fantasy is never
"consummated" in the transcendental act of song and dance as the audiovisual
norms of Hollywood demand. Instead there is a constant give and take of dialogue ceding to silence ceding to music—a technique that imparts a miraculous
(or marvelous, to invoke surrealist vocabulary) mood to the moments of convergence that occur along the way.

A further factor that contributes to audiovisual flow is Potter's constant
attention to the "musicality" of the filmic medium. The director imports her staple
techniques from experimental film by playing with the textures and in-built
rhythms of visual materials: the dynamic motion of the camera, the disjointed
effect of individual frames in slow-motion shots, conspicuous uses of zoom, dol-
lying, focus and other techniques. Throughout the film, Potter gives considerable
attention to visual microrhythms, which vie with simultaneously presented

---

[67] In a currently unpublished article draft, "Takemitsu's Composed Space in Kurosawa's *Ran*," Miguel
Mera considers the use of music and silence in this film as correlating with ideas from Zen Buddhism about
space and emptiness.

auditory rhythms and microrhythms for sensory dominance, converging and diverging in apparently random configurations. Reminiscent of the techniques of writers like James Joyce (*Ulysses*) and Virginia Woolf (especially *Mrs. Dalloway*), the presence of sonic and visual rhythms provides a mode of rhythmic structuring analogous to the constant flow of words on the page in stream-of-consciousness writing, which is both visual and, through the invocation of sensory memory, also auditory. It is therefore crossmodal: auditory on an implicit level; evocative of a musicality that traverses both visual and linguistic registers of reader experience. In much the same way, little distinction is made in *Yes* between the interior voices of characters, their external voices and other sounds in the diegetic world. Barthes's "grain of the voice" is here divided across the senses including the interior worlds of characters, as in his original conception. Style as such—the *jouissance* of the readerly text—could thus be considered to occupy the foreground of the reader's attention. An example of such crossmodality is found in *Yes* when She and a female friend jog together in a fenced recreational area. Again the musical ground for the scene is a pulsating tremolo figure, this time taken from the track "Run" (composed by Sally Potter and Fred Frith). The musical microrhythms here strain against the corresponding visual rhythms of the camera as it traverses the geometrical patterns of the fencing. In the music, the droning tremolo sound provides a grainy foreground texture, while the combination of camera movement and the spatial organization of the fencing serve a similar function visually. Both elements are juxtaposed against middle-ground subject matter: visually, the filmed actors; auditively, the harmonic and thematic movement of the music. One level is mechanical and depersonalized, almost primal in its phenomenal "thereness," the other gently elegiac and bound up with visual and musical narrative. Like so much of the film, there is give and take between rhythmical patterns of the dialogue and those in the nondiegetic music. Audiovisual flow exerts a continuous undertow. Matters are complicated, however, by the introduction of distracting environmental sounds, in this case a siren, which seems to engender tension while pushing the characters toward interior monologue.

The presence of audiovisual flow in *Yes* is perhaps most conspicuous when it is interrupted. At several points in the film lines of dialogue that are especially loaded occasion a sudden cessation of the auditory flow. These occur as natural punctuations in the rhythmic continuity of the film, however, almost like temporary pauses in an ongoing compositional process. One such moment was described previously, in connection to the cue comprising Satie's "Gnossiennes No. 1." Elements of audiovisual confusion or overdetermination through missynching occur more rarely, and these generally coincide with moments of conflict, as when the lovers argue. Environmental noises, such as the sound of the siren in the example given above, the sound of traffic in the car park where the main conflict between the couple takes place (the original five-minute short), and the ubiquitous sound of mobile phone ringtones, are further elements that engender auditory and narrative confusion.

These discomfiting sounds impinge on the consciousness of the protagonists with a force that is experienced as existential.

SEXUAL HEALING, REPARATION AND LOVE

As John Berger notes in a personal response to *Yes*, included with the published screenplay, there is nothing puritanical about this film.[68] The clearest evidence of this is in a scene reminiscent of Meg Ryan's fake orgasm in the romantic comedy *When Harry Met Sally*. Potter's scene, however, depicts actual exhibitionist sex in a restaurant, not its simulation. Cinematography, music and dialogue capture how it feels for her to be swept away in wave of affect, the trickling tones of "Paru River" interlocking with whispered "sweet nothings" (for the more conventionally predisposed, verbal filth), blurry slow-motion images, and jerky handheld camera movement. Climax when it comes precipitates the guitar cries of B.B. King's Lucille, appropriated from her husband in a symbolic gesture of sexual empowerment and agency (see Figures 4.1. and 4.2.). Undoubtedly the steamiest scene in the film, all of this is achieved in a way that is suggestive more than explicit, since the hand movements that occasion her rapture are all the time concealed under the restaurant table. The power of the scene instead comes from the qualities and poetics of the spoken word, from an appreciation of situation, and the kinetic and sensory nature of audiovisual language.

Conspicuous in this scene is an element of audiovisual queering that seems to be closely aligned with Potter's priorities in the film. By queering, I am not referring to a moment portraying homosexual desire and thereby displacing the heteronormative assumptions of mainstream cinema (a matter that is addressed in much of the writing on "queer cinema"). I am referring instead to a concern to denaturalize conventional gender positions through a range of strategies that have concerned those working in the field of queer studies over the past couple of decades. While we are accustomed to thinking of such transgressions as occurring in the context of homosexual performative traditions, this need not necessarily be the case. Potter's "queering" does not call into question the heterosexual sexual orientations of her protagonists, but it does undermine the power basis of the gender coding upon which social constructions of heterosexuality have conventionally been premised. Music in this instance is the means by which an effect of queering is achieved. While the first part of the scene unfolded to the accompaniment of Glass's "Paru River," climax is signified with the use of strongly masculinized musical discourse, the "crying" sound of B.B. King's guitar in a song and musical style that has conventionally been deployed to signify a strutting masculinity. The scene depicting her euphoric pleasure continues for some time before the visuals cut to a shot of the husband in the next scene, thus confirming the more conventional masculine agenda of the

---

[68] Sally Potter, Yes, *Screenplay and Notes by Sally Potter* (New York: Newmarket Press, 2005), xiii.

Figure 4.2 The politician husband plays air guitar in *Yes*: musical onanism and a representation of strutting masculinity. "Ten Long Years" performed by B.B. King and Eric Clapton.

music. But its presence already in the preceding restaurant scene pushes our understanding of the depicted sexual pleasure in a transgendered direction—implying her usurpation of what was formerly his sexual agency. Although implying transgendered displacement, on another level this moment of epiphany seems apt, since the guitar cry falls more comfortably within a soprano vocal register, which would ordinarily be considered female more than male. Add to this the fact that King is known to give his guitars a female name (Lucille), then the encoding of the wailing guitar as her surrogate voice begins to make sense. Rather than *being* King, in both senses of the word, as the husband seems to wish, she is allowing herself to *be done* by King (and implicitly *to be* King as well). By fitting herself into her husband's masculine narrative in a role that she was never intended to occupy, she is simultaneously excluding him from the role he has authored for himself.

Representations of sexual desire in this film are not without their problems, including the husband's questionable pursuit of the teenaged goddaughter. For much of its duration, however, there is something reparative about depictions of heterosexual desire and bodily pleasure, which counteracts the atmosphere of distrust that pervaded in much of the academic research and critical artistic production of the 1990s (see Figure 4.3.). The film would seem to demarcate a move away from what Eve Kosofsky Sedgwick (drawing on Paul Ricoeur's writing on "the hermeneutics of suspicion") has dubbed "paranoid reading" strategies, an orientation that has been much in evidence in academic work and artistic production in the twentieth century.[69] In the chapter of her book *Touching Feeling: Affect, Pedagogy,*

---

[69] Sedgwick, *Touching Feeling*, 124.

Figure 4.3 Audiovisual poetry and gender balance in *Yes*. Heterosexual love depicted in a reparative light.

Performativity entitled "Paranoid reading and reparative reading, or you're so paranoid, you probably think this essay is about you," Sedgwick distinguishes between these two reading strategies, arguing that a more prominent position be accorded to the latter in critical writing. The suspicious scholar (modeled after such figureheads as Freud, Marx, and Nietzsche) takes it as her duty to reveal through interpretative inquiry the hidden mechanisms that give rise to the multifarious forms of oppression current criticism has been concerned with tracking.[70] This approach has given rise to valuable research findings over the years, although Sedgwick contends that it has also lead to an imbalance in which our view of the world is conditioned primarily by negative affect. In response, Sedgwick calls for the recognition of reparative approaches, which require closer attention to what she calls positive affects, by which she means those feelings that seem to pave the way toward encounters with the world that are more about pleasure, the "merely aesthetic," and the ameliorative.[71]

Paranoia in Sedgwick's account implies a "strong" theoretical alignment, which wields considerable power to expose or demystify practices that are perceived to be harmful. Reparative reading, in contrasts, implies a "weak" theoretical positioning, where we attend more closely to distinct actions, their responses and local consequences. In Sedgwick's view, the most valuable scholarly work contains elements of both of these positions. Reparation for Sedgwick and the psychologist Melanie

[70] For another perspective on the reparative-paranoid dichotomy, see Suzanne Cusick, "Musicology, Torture, Repair," in *Radical Musicology* 3 (2008), available: http://www.radical-musicology.org.uk/2008/Cusick.htm#_edn6, retrieved December 5, 2010.

[71] Sedgwick, *Touching Feeling*, 144.

Klein, from whose theories she draws, is fundamentally about processes analogous to love.[72] In this respect, reparation becomes a strategy of resistance that is affirmative and empathetic as much as it is critical; campy in a way that does not negate; smart without smarting. I visited this cluster of ideas in chapter 1, principally in reference to methodological implications: weak theory is aligned more closely with phenomenology and strategies of close reading, strong theory with hermeneutics and the determination to apply explanatory theories to situations that seem to demand interpretation; weak theory is concerned with affect, strong theory with semiotics and representation.

The principle relevance of the above theoretical apparatus in terms of the present discussion is how it helps Sedgwick to modify her idea of the concept of performativity in relation to Butler's early definition, the primary directive of which is to expose and demystify existing social structures through staged mimesis. Without putting this idea entirely to rest (since performativity in a Butlerian sense is of considerable value to the second case study presented here), Sedgwick introduces two ideas in her discussion of weak theory and reparative positioning that bear directly on the subject of the present analysis. Firstly, the idea that reparative reading is reconstitutive, that it resolves to take fragments or part-objects and reorganize them in a way that points toward a future that is not as fragmented and traumatic as the past. This has considerable resonance with the aesthetics of neosurrealism as I have discussed it in this chapter.[73] The binding rhythmic flow of Sally Potter's film cuts such a unifying swathe through circumstances that are heavily weighted with negative affect. In this way Potter deploys the local, the affective and the compassionate in opposition to a troubled past that was bereft of these qualities. This deployment overlaps with the aspect of surrealist sensibility that Benjamin called re-enchantment; the ability to weave something of value out of something devalued. A second idea that has special relevance here is Sedgwick's retheorization of camp aesthetics in light of her theory of reparation. In contrast to the dominant readings of camp as parodic, mocking and demystifying, Sedgwick chooses to attend to the frequently overlooked additive and accretive attributes of the sensibility. In her words:

> To view camp as, among other things, the communal, historically dense exploration of a variety of reparative practices is to do better justice to many of the defining elements of classic camp performance: the startling, juicy displays of excess erudition, for example; the passionate, often hilarious antiquarianism, the prodigal production of alternative historiographies; the "over"-attachment to fragmentary, marginal, waste or leftover products; the rich, highly interruptive affective variety; the irrepressible fascination with ventriloquistic experimentation; the

---

[72]   Ibid., 128.
[73]   Ibid., 146.

disorientating juxtapositions of present with past, and popular with high culture.[74]

Many of these qualities could be purpose-made descriptions of Potter's approach to sound and images in *Yes*, the title of which points toward the currency of a reparative attitude in the darkest of times. Isn't this the same quality of optimism that we have come to understand in discussions of historical film musicals to be a symptom of an escapist mindset when viewed through a paranoid optic? In terms of gender politics, there is nothing particularly queer or subversive about the somewhat flowery and romantic trajectory offered in the plotline to this film (comprising attraction between the heterosexual romantic pair, conflict, and resolution of conflict). The film's audiovisual style, however, taps into a quality of camp surrealism that is all about realigning priorities by bringing life into closer contact with art. *Yes* critiques normative power structures, for the most part, in immanent and affirmative ways. Above all, the film depicts a reflexive (because sur-realistically portrayed) and *reflecting* female protagonist whose primary relationship with her lover becomes an example of how to resolve conflict through compassionate application and personal transformation. In this respect, the musical, if that is what it is, is seen as a retrievable and ultimately a redemptive mode of expression rather than a vehicle for social escapism and heteronormative prescription. This can largely be attributed to the use of audiovisual flow as a conduit for the passions of all the leading characters, which allows them to dream beyond themselves and their circumstances. It leads each of them toward a mode of becoming that unleashes the radical potential of the musical, even while it resists the full extent of fantastical excursion for which the musical is known, lingering instead in a liminal zone between language and song, narrative time and musical time, fantasy and reality. It repeats existing formations (in both music and spoken dialogue) but in the context of a temporality in which repetition always implies the expectation of change.

Parodying Porn, Recamping the Musical: Tsai Ming-Liang's *The Wayward Cloud*

DRAMATIC PREMISES AND NARRATIVE STRUCTURE

Tsai Ming-Liang's *The Wayward Cloud* (*Tian bian yi duo yun*, 1995) approaches the reflexive musical from a different angle. Rather than holding a magnifying glass to practices of audio dissolve as Sally Potter does in *Yes*, the Taiwanese

[74] Ibid., 150.

Figure 4.4 Opening scene of *The Wayward Cloud*. The watermelon as surrealist-absurdist yonic symbol.

director makes a point of failing to gloss over the transitions between what might be considered hyperrealist and surrealist musical sections of the film. Tsai's musical numbers stand out as constructed and campy, whereas the remainder of the film takes place in almost total silence. Throughout the film, the escapist impulse of the Hollywood musical is strongly parodied, much as it is in Dennis Potter's television dramas. The plot tells of a period of drought in Taiwan, during which the female protagonist spends much of her time scavenging for water containers and watermelons become a fetishized commodity. A central motif of the film is how metaphorical slippage interferes with conventional meanings, constructing an alternative circuit of desire in which the fruit substitutes for objects of sexual desire both male and female (see Figures 4.4 and 4.5). Substitution along a metaphorical axis is a classic surrealist technique, as Roland Barthes noted in his writing on Georges Bataille's short novel *Story of the Eye*.[75] Bataille's surrealism is otherwise tangibly present in the film, much of which deconstructs the vulgar materiality of sex as it is depicted in hardcore porn by means of parodic excess.

The marketing of *Wayward Cloud* describes it as "high comedy, high-camp musical numbers and a vast amount of hardcore porn."[76] In fact, there is little (if any) hardcore in the film; only what looks like (but might not be) simulated sex, most of which serves a clear deconstructive function, being either too bizarre or too gro-

[75] Roland Barthes, "The Metaphor of the Eye," trans. J. A. Underwood, in Georges Bataille, *Story of the Eye*, by Lord Auch [pseudonym] (London and New York: Penguin, 1982), 119–27.

[76] Quotation from Peter Bradshaw of *The Guardian*, in *The Wayward Cloud*, Press Release (London: Axiom Films, 2007).

Figure 4.5 Opening scene of *The Wayward Cloud*. The watermelon as surrealist-absurdist phallic symbol.

tesque to titillate.[77] In an interview included as a DVD extra with the British release of the film, Tsai states that he wished for it to be marketed as pornography and in this way to have the greatest impact on unsuspecting audiences.[78] His position as a recognized art house director, however, makes such perceptions unlikely. More in keeping with the critical and online reception of the film is the director's description of it as a type of anti-pornography. The interruption of the film's deadpan drama and unglamorous sex with five camped up musical numbers certainly works toward this end. A sixth song without an accompanying visual performance is heard over the closing credits. The first four songs are of local origin, but written in styles that ape imported Western songs (from Tin Pan Alley to jazz and blues torch). The last two are Cantonese adaptations of Western popular songs (in country-folk style), which has a demonstrable impact on how the songs signify in the film: notably, these songs are heard immediately before and after the final twist in the film's plot, when the characters are most alienated. Music of foreign origin is an obvious way of representing this psychological alienation sonically. (The use of music in the film is illustrated in Table 4.2.) Two of the songs are recording by the Chinese film actress Grace Chang. This provides an element of authorial continuity with a later film, *The Hole* (*Dong*, 1998), which would comprise solely lip-synched musical numbers performed to this artist's recordings.

Structurally, the film rehearses the same upstairs-downstairs positioning as one sees in classic Hollywood musicals, of which *Top Hat* is perhaps the paradigmatic

---

[77]   This assertion is based on Tsai's comments in interviews and official press releases, which fail to draw a clear line between reality and fiction when discussing the use of actors in the film.

[78]   Tsai Ming-Liang, dir., *The Wayward Cloud* (London: Axiom Films, 2004).

example (1935, featuring Ginger Rogers and Fred Astaire). It is an opposition that would be repeated in *The Hole*. In *Wayward Cloud* it is played out through the actions of the leading male, Hsiao-Kang (Lee Kang-Sheng), who works upstairs as an adult movie actor; and the leading female, Shiang-chyi (Chen Shiang-Chyi), who lives downstairs and works as a tour guide at the National Palace Museum in Taipei. The spatial distance between the two is reiterated throughout the film and represents an underlying source of tension in their relationship, but it also signifies a mode of attraction that is founded on the recognition of difference. We see this positioning knowingly parodied in several scenes: as the couple play cat and mouse while ascending a stairwell; she is always one flight below as he ascends. The trope is repeated as the pair relaxes in her living room: him lying under a kitchen table, her seated on a chair above. She will eventual slide down to occupy his space, causing him to slide down further into a supine position. The scene implies a gendered inversion of the dominant order of the film and therefore serves a subtle transgressive and queering function: she is on top and vertical, he is supine (see Figure 4.6.). Elsewhere in the film, he occupies the conventional "masculine" position: he is physically "on top."[79] The scene is drawn out over an extended amount of quotidian time, with no dialogue and very little else in the way of sounds to interfere with sensory impact of the moment. It is only when he drifts off to sleep that the silence is rudely interrupted by one of the most elaborate musical sequences in the film. As happens in several of the other musical sequences, the musical dream sequence is apparently inspired by the actions that immediately precede it, although it is not closely connected to these actions. Only after he has drifted off to sleep (implying the depiction of dream consciousness) is a silence that is ubiquitous throughout the remainder of the film interrupted by one of its most extravagant musical sequences. Just as the love scene had begun with a spatially implied act of gender inversion, so his dream is one of gender inversion through cross-dressing. The song, "What a Date!" (sung and performed by Hong Chong), sounds like a Taiwanese version of "The Laughing Policeman" and is set to something resembling a Tin Pan Alley tune. The performance finds the male protagonist dressed in drag and participating in a localized and, in this way, also queer adaptation of dance sequences from *Les Parapluies de Cherbourg* (*The Umbrellas of Cherbourg*, 1964).

[79] I should stress that I consider the positions of "top" and "bottom" to be purely conventional and available to both sexes as well as to parties in same sex relationships. While these categories undoubtedly reflect historical imbalances between the sexes, here they are employed performatively in order to challenge such conventions. In music research, Suzanne Cusick has theorized the dynamic of musical performance in similar terms from the standpoint of lesbian listeners. See Suzanne Cusick, "On a Lesbian Relationship with Music: A Serious Effort Not to Think Straight," in Philip Brett, Elizabeth Wood and Gary Thomas, *Queering the Pitch: the New Gay and Lesbian Musicology* (New York: Routledge, 1994), 67–83, 74–78. On the constructed nature of camping it up when performing unequal gender relations and practices of camp masquerade in butch-femme lesbian relationships, see Sue Ellen Case, "Toward a Butch-Femme Aesthetic," in Cleto, ed., *Camp: Queer Aesthetics and the Performing Subject*, 185–99.

Table 4.2   **Tsai Ming-Liang's *The Wayward Cloud*: List of Musical Cues**

Musical numbers and timecode	*Information on music and style*	*Visual dramatization*
1. 00:20.50 	"Ban Ge Yue Liang" ("The Half-Moon"): Artist: Hung Chong; Writer: Jiang Yun; Composer: Xi Hua Style: 1950s styled mandopop (Mandarin popular music) with lush film music arrangement	While languishing in a rooftop water tank, he turns into a sequined sea monster. His androgynous appearance anticipates his musical appearance in the song "What a Date!"
2. 00:34:45 	"Ai De Kai Shi" ("Everlasting Love"): Artist: Yao Li; Writer/Composer: Wang Shu Yeh Style: 1950s mandopop with film music arrangement	She pays ironic homage to statue of a communist leader together with a camped up troupe of dancers. The dancers' flirtatious actions are exaggerated and they are surrounded by oversized flowers.
3. 00:45:25 	"Tong Qin Xin" ("To Keep My Heart True"): Artist: Grace Chang; Writer: Li Jun Qing; Composer: Ryoichi Hattori Style: plaintive torch song in blues jazz style	After being subjected to the obligatory facial "money shot," the actor playing the Japanese porn actress contemplates staying true to her heart (although her soul is dead). She is pursued by a surly group of men.

(continued)

Musical numbers and timecode	Information on music and style	Visual dramatization
4. 00:57:30 	"Qi Miao De Yue Hui" ("What a Date!"): Artist: Hung Chong; Writer: Hung Chong; Composer: Nicholas Dickman Style: Tin Pan Alley styled comedy song	Musical spectacular based on the gender inversion of the two stars during a date. The Japanese actress arrives, not in drag, and the two "women" vie for the travesty actress's attention.
5. 01:11:00 	"Jin Xin Deng" ("Be Patient!" originally "Sixteen Tons"): Artist: Chang Lu; Writer: Si Tu Ming; Composer: Merle Travis Style: workingman's country-folk ballad	His musical fantasy offers advice on how best to achieve an erection, enacted with the help of JP Gaultier-styled dancers and an anthropomorphic phallus. The lyrics of the original song are here given a perverse twist.
6. 01:46:17 	"Tian Bian Yi Duo Yun" ("The Wayward Cloud" originally "The Wayward Wind"): Artist: Bai Guang; Writers/ Composers: Stanley R. Lebowsky & Herbert Newman Style: country ballad	The song comments on the film's denouement, in which the male porn star achieves transcendence through sexual climax. The cue reflects ironically on an earlier use of the song as a love theme. Fade to black and titles

Discrepancies from the filmic precursor include umbrellas themed after watermelons and the incorporation of a local Taipei landmark as the *mise-en-scène*. The female protagonist appears in drag as well, although this option appears to be unavailable to the actress playing the Japanese porn star, who vies with the transvestite actor for the travesti singer's amorous attentions. The musical number is an enactment of the lyrics, which tells of a gender-bending date where the actors find out their true sexual identities only as they are about to part company.

> Oh what fun we had that day
> The time just slipped away
> We danced and had a walk
> And sat down for a talk
> But when I see it's time to go
> Oh, what a fearful blow
> She wasn't Chen, her name was Hsiao
> And she thought I was Zhao

The male protagonist's dream of gendered queering is thus identified as one of the most viable in the film, which elsewhere problematizes intergender relations. This is an unusually spectacular musical number for Tsai, filmed in and around a beautiful historical building bordering a river in Taipei. Nevertheless, the clumsy acting, inept dancing and missynched singing reveal the drama to be every bit as artificial as the character's cross-gendered apparel and the feigned bonhomie of their laughter (which is obviously that of a prerecorded singer). Even while the

Figure 4.6 The spatial coding of courtly love in *The Wayward Cloud*. Here the dominant positioning of the film is inverted: her head out of shot (dehumanizing her), and he is supine (and feminized).

scene portrays nonconventional gendered relations, its staging resolutely eschews the sleight of hand by which the binary gender positioning is naturalized in the classic film musical. No traces of visual or audio dissolve are to be found here. The transition is abrupt and unapologetic: one minute the male protagonist sleeps, the next we cut to a location that although spectacular may well signify touristy banality to Taiwanese viewers. It therefore falls short of the ordinary require-ments for exotic fantasy or folk believability in the film musical. It is an obvious camp setup.

The anachronous nature of the musical recording fits this agenda perfectly. A corny old joke song in a major key with a bouncy tempo, catchy eighth-note ana-cruses, and not-missing-a-half beat vocal delivery, its primary mission appears to be to sell a joke that wears thin already in the telling. An obvious example of a devalued object, it is not the joke of the original song that is likely to amuse audiences so much as the abrupt transition into a musical number, the way the characters succeed *and fail* in fitting themselves into the song, and the sheer color and frivolity of the audiovisual spectacle. Indeed, the song is not necessarily even funny in light of the more serious and contemplative atmosphere of the surrounding narrative. Its humor is forced; designed to make you sit up in your seat and attend to what the characters are dreaming.

WATER AND LOVE

Exchanges between the romantic male-female duo stand in stark contrast to the sex scenes between the leading male and his porn star opposite number, Yang Kuei-Mei, which are marked either by their crassness or their absurdity. Cooking is a privileged locus of humor and erotic frisson between the romantic pair. Smoking and drinking are eroticized as well, both corporeal pleasures that permit a certain amount of semiotic slippage into a sexualized zone. Water is the trans-formative element that characterizes their relationship, just as it is largely missing from the experiences of the Japanese porn actress. Significantly, the water supply is exhausted during the shower scene of a porn film, necessitating the absurd solu-tion of the (filmed) film crew emptying a can of murky river water onto the actors during shooting. Later the woman from downstairs attempts to revive the porn actress with a bottle of water when she finds her unconscious in a lift, evidently hoping it will bring about a positive transformation.

Water divides the women also in architectural space. This can be seen when they walk on opposite banks of an urban canal, with the romantic lead falling into line behind the actress as the paths converge on a concrete bridge. Characteristically, the scene is drawn out over an extended period of time. Both women carry sunshades (umbrellas), thereby encouraging comparisons between the two. The romantic lead is scruffily dressed and moves awkwardly yet somehow endearingly; the porn actress is an apparent paragon of refined femininity, dressed in fashionable clothes and dragging a suitcase on rollers behind her—indicating mobility and some degree of affluence; not enough, however, for her to afford a taxi. These are the material accoutrements her job evidently permits her to enjoy, which contrasts with the more meager circumstances of the romantic lead. Apart from these objects, there would seem to be little to envy in the actress's life. Any attempts by her to connect with the world on a more human plane are spurned, as when she approaches her male co-star with compassion following a scene where he fails to achieve an erection. Rather than helping the two to connect, these events lead directly to another fantastical diversion on the part of the protagonist in one of the more outrageous musical numbers of the film.

In this number he plays an anthropomorphized phallus surrounding by a troupe of dancing girls decked out in Gaultier-styled bikini tops draped with giant condoms. The music is a Chinese version of the familiar Merle Travis song "Sixteen Tons," but perverted from its original function as a workingman's anthem to address the salience of concentration as an aid to male potency. It is not hard to understand why Tsai would wish to subvert the meanings of the Chinese translation. Sung by the silky-toned chanteuse Chang Lu, who rose to public acclaim as a popular Shanghai diva in the war years, a great deal is lost in translation as the embittered lyrics, syncopated vocals and dissonant guitar work of the Merle Travis original are flattened to turn the song into a seductive call to follow the party line and in this way achieve transcendence within the body politic. Sung in a minor key throughout (the original is in E minor; the translation in B minor), the verse of the song descends in a laborious string of runs while the singer enumerates his grievances. The pinnacle of the original song occurs as the singer complains he will not qualify for admittance to heaven because he has sold his soul to the company ("Saint Peter, don't you call me 'cause I can't go. I owe my soul to the company store"). This line hits an emotive high E (e^2) on the word "owe," before descending through dark chord tones to a low B (b) for the final crushing admittance of defeat. In the Chinese translation, the lyric of this line is, "For happiness you need to strive," thus turning the suffering of the individual into something necessary for the greater good of the people. Thus, the Chinese worker achieves a level of transcendence that was denied his North American comrade in what was originally a protest song. Tsai clearly does not have the body politic in mind when he camps up Chang Lu's version of the song (lip-synched by the Japanese porn actress) through the actions of the female dancers and an oversized male phallus, which fill the lyrics to the brim with lewd sexual innuendo. Here Tsai counters the transcendental body politic with the corporeal human body, as he does also in the second musical number, "Ai De Kai Shi" ("Everlasting Love"), where a group of female dancers overact their devotion to a statue of a communist leader in moves that border on the lascivious, adorned in costumes that epitomize stagey female camp while surrounded by oversized yonic flowers.

The performance of the Chinese translation of "Sixteen Tons" is preceded by the stairwell scene (mentioned before) where the leading male drops a water container onto the safety net between floors of the apartment building in order to frighten off his romantic opposite number (and possibly to conceal the nature of his work). The water trickles away, symbolizing his apparent barrenness in the scene that follows. Water or its scarcity is an omnipresent theme across Tsai's cinematic output, including his landmark films *The River* (1997) and *The Hole* (1998). The director has described his characters as plants that are short of water, this physical thirst standing in for something equally fundamental that they crave: "Water for me is love, that's what they lack. They are never particularly well adjusted because they lack something. That something is love, which is represented by water...".[80] The dream of an abundance of water (and therefore also love) is seen in the very first musical interlude. Here the male protagonist (Lee Kang-Sheng) is found languishing in a rooftop water tank. As he sinks into reverie he is transformed into a sequined sea monster. The transformation is less than miraculous, however, as the location loses little of its squalor even when the tank is encircled by rows of theatrical fairy lights. The character's costume is conspicuous also due to its tacky staginess. The music, too, is conspicuous for two reasons: First, the presence of the musical sound jolts the audio-viewer awake because of the relative absence of sound in the preceding scenes; and second, because of its anachronism to the film's temporal world due to the sentimental style and low fidelity of the crackly vintage recordings. This scene, and the following one, evidence the binary characteristics of the dual-focus narrative, which can be seen as a bubble forms in the faucet of the female protagonist's bathroom—a result of his rooftop bathing. This connection established through water will carry through the remainder of the film, most notably in the cooking scene that precedes their most intimate encounter—culminating in the cross-dressing musical number. Different to the dual focus narrative of conventional narratives is the portrayal of the gender attributes of the sympathetic female lead, which are anything but stereotyped in the majority of the film: she is either de-sexed or looks androgynous. This look is reflected in the gender identity of the leading man, primarily in the musical numbers, as can be seen in the rooftop tank number where his movements are lithely "feminine." Otherwise his gender is defined by a "masculine" desire for transcendence, which the film critiques on several levels (in song lyrics, in the existence of the musical numbers, and in actions in the realistic sections of the film).

PERFORMING PORNOGRAPHY

In stark contrast to these romantic exchanges are two scenes noteworthy for how they displace and parody the sounds of the sex. In the first, the film's opening scene, a watermelon is placed in front of the porn actress's genitals, thereby

---

[80] Danièle Rivière, "Scouting," interview with Tsai Ming-Liang, in Jean Pierre Rehm, Olivier Joyard and Danièle Rivière, eds., *Tsai Ming-Liang* (Paris: Editions Dis Voir, 1999), 79, 118.

allowing the man to displace his manual attentions onto the fruit. Ludicrously, the woman continues to behave vocally as if she were the object of his manual attention—sighing and gasping as if there were no tomorrow (see Figure 4.4.). Combined with this are ridiculous squelching noises produced by his actions on the watermelon, which highlight the absurdity of sound effects in the genre and draw attention to the conventional nature of the audiovisual contract—Chion's synchresis (the process by which sound effects are naturalized through synchronization). The mirror image of this scene comes in the film's final moments. Here the now unconscious actress (presumably from a drug overdose, or perhaps from dehydration, an analogy for her unloved condition) is made to complete the film by being physically placed by the film crew in a series of sex positions. The male actress tries to go about his business as if this were business as usual—which of course it is, her pleasure and agency counting for little in the sexual economy of the porn industry. Of course, she does not respond audibly to his actions, which seriously undermines an important premise of the hardcore genre: perceptions of female pleasure—however phony and exaggerated they might be.[81] Sounds and silence (or muting) both in their own way deconstruct the premises of the genre, at the same time pushing the film in a markedly surreal direction—paradigmatic substitution being one of the fundamental techniques of surrealist aesthetics. We see this most clearly when the male actor, with a watermelon on his head, services his partner, an image worthy of Dalí or Magritte. (Figure 4.5.)

That the genre of the porn film is transformed to evince responses that are comparable both to the audiovisual strategies of the film musical and to those of surrealism is not as out of left field as it might seem. Linda Williams noted that the audiovisual priorities of hardcore porn are remarkably close to those of film musical, which can be explained by the use of overdubbing in both genres. Affective intensity through simulated intimacy trumps realism in the semiotic norms of the hardcore genre; much like the film musical, which produces utopian spaceless spaces through the use of exaggeratedly intimate sounds that (literally) have no place in the diegesis. Williams even goes so far as to state, "the hard-core feature film *is* a kind of musical, with sexual number taking the place of musical number."[82] Hence "the (surreal) effect of a great many post-dubbed sex scenes, as well as of the dialogue sequences of the more cheaply made hard-core features. When the lip movements of the performer do not match the sounds that come from those lips, the hard-won illusions of suture are rendered null and void."[83] We thus return to a

---

[81] Linda Williams has noted that the "articulate and inarticulate sounds of pleasure that dominate in aural hardcore are primarily the cries of women. Though male moans and cries are heard as well, they are never as loud or dramatic." Linda Williams, *Hardcore: Power, Pleasure, and the "Frenzy of the Visible"* (Berkeley: University of California Press, 1989), 123.

[82] Ibid., 124.

[83] Ibid.

central premise of the reflexive musical discussed at this chapter's beginning. Lip-synching is prominent in both of the incorporated genres of Tsai's film. The function of the reflexive musical is to draw our attention to this fact through knowing acts of displacement or exposure; as in the final scene, when the female protagonist aurally simulates (or experiences?) the orgasm her unconscious counterpart is unable to achieve. *The Wayward Cloud* applies the lessons learned from the reflexive musical also to the genre of hardcore porn, which it subverts by placing the two audiovisual genres in close proximity to each other (thereby allowing them to reflect onto one another). It does this by juxtaposing the two forms, but also by imposing on them a type of auditory realism that both genres have long since relinquished. The sex scenes are a little bit too realistic for contemporary tastes, in a debased Bataillean way, just as they are in some of the sex scenes found in Lars von Trier's *The Idiots* (1998), Paul Thomas Anderson's *Boogie Nights* (1997), or Michael Haneke's *La Pianiste* (2001). The musical scenes, on the other hand, are surrounded by an audio-visual realism that serves to highlight their exaggerated artificiality.

COURTLY LOVE AND EXISTENTIAL DIFFERENCE

If the porn actors' relationship is about crude (because it is loveless) physical contact, contact of this kind is largely missing from the activities of the actor and his romantic opposite. Theirs is a form of "courtly love," which suggests an unbridgeable difference in the face of the other's alterity, an idea that closely matches the ideas of Emmanuel Levinas concerning infinity and exteriority. At stake in Levinas's formulation is "desire without satisfaction which... understands... the remoteness, the alterity, and exteriority of the other."[84] Rather than attempt to assimilate the other as a means of completing the interior self, the Levinasian idea of interpersonal relations extols acceptance of the exteriority of the other, their absolute difference, which implies the metaphysical extension of the self—since the other cannot conceivably be integrated within the self. This, or so the argument goes, ensures that a modicum of mutual respect is maintained between lover and loved through the recognition of phenom-enal difference. It is a romantic positioning that produces a certain erotic *frisson*, which Tsai's scenes without question capitalize on. It does, however, engender a somewhat autistic view of interpersonal relations. We can see this as the couple keep one another at a distance throughout the duration of the film (see Figure 4.6). In fact, it is a positioning that extends beyond Levinas to historical tropes of romance in the West; beyond even the dual focus narrative musicals that Tsai's film parodies. It is found in a myriad of romantic archetypes, from Shakespeare's plays (*Romeo and Juliet*) to Rapunzel in her castle tower; not to mention medieval troubadour ballads and the romantic serenade—which in general requires the idealized positioning of the female on a balcony or some similar pedestal.

[84] Emmanuel Levinas, *Totality and Infinity* (Dordrecht: Kluwer Academic Publishers, 1991), 34.

Slavoj Žižek addresses the persistence of the idea of courtly love in his article, "From Courtly Love to *The Crying Game.*"[85] Drawing on Lacan's psychoanalytical theories, Žižek notes how this subjective construction is essentially founded on narcissism. The female love object is exalted by the male admirer to such an extent that she is divested of human substance, indicating a radical Otherness that has more to do with the fantasies and projections of the perceiver than the attributes of a real person.[86] In this view, the woman in courtly love is perceived as something uncanny, depersonalized, mechanical and even cruel (the extreme being a dominatrix figure). Communication with the exalted lady thus conceived requires an exaggerated level of courtesy and etiquette on the part of the male suitor, strategies that ensure that the object of romantic affection will remain forever out of his reach.[87] So far so harmless, and even fun in the context of performative role play, but problems arise to the extent that the symbolic value of the woman thus perceived turns her into a vehicle for male transcendence more than an experiencing subject in her own right. The investment here is one of libidinal intensification, since an obstacle placed in the path of a desire is sure to strengthen the wish to attain it.[88] Obstacles are necessary in this understanding to maintain the illusion that without them the object would be "instantly accessible." The narrative trajectory therefore moves from the premise of denying another person's (phenomenal) Otherness to the consequence of constructing a sublimated Other that remains forever out of reach and thereby usurps the position of the original idealized person.[89]

Žižek discusses these constructions in relation to several films, but it is noteworthy that he begins with a discussion of surrealist director Luis Buñuel's *Cet obscur objet du désir* (*That Obscure Object of Desire*, 1977), a film that encapsulates, probably better than any other, the principles of sublimation and intensified desire that are at the center of courtly interpersonal relations. Surrealist film has invested in this libidinal economy probably more than any other filmic style. It is therefore unsurprising to find that another more contemporary surrealist, David Lynch, is prominent in his discussion as well.[90] Žižek unfortunately misses an element of

---

[85] Slavoj Žižek, "From Courtly Love to *The Crying Game,*" *New Left Review* 1/202 (November/December, 1993): 95–108.

[86] Ibid., 96.

[87] Ibid., 97.

[88] Ibid., 100.

[89] Ibid., 101.

[90] I have addressed the element of projection involved in Agent Dale Cooper's obsession for the deceased schoolgirl, Laura Palmer, in Lynch's *Twin Peaks* elsewhere. See John Richardson, "Laura and Twin Peaks: Postmodern Parody and the Musical Reconstruction of he Absent Femme Fatale," in Annette Davison and Erica Sheen, eds., *The Cinema of David Lynch: American Dreams, Nightmare Visions* (London: Wallflower Press, 2004), 77–92. In this interpretation, I argued that Palmer is aligned in the series both visually and sonically with the film noir *femme fatale*, a type of characterization that Žižek holds to be representative of "courtly love."

performative queering in the plotline of *The Crying Game* (Neil Jordan) when he argues that the male protagonist is apparently blinded because of his courtly infatuation to a transvestite to such an extent that he is willing to relinquish his initial heterosexual inclinations.[91] Another way of interpreting the film is that the protagonist was simply more polymorphous in his desires than at first he was willing to admit to himself. The film would seem to be open to alternative readings, although it is possible that Žižek's interpretation is a fair interpretation of authorial intentions (which are not, of course, a determining factor when it comes to justifying interpretations).

Žižek's understanding of courtly love is an excellent match when it comes to interpreting *The Wayward Cloud*. In Tsai's film, however, the conventional position of the female in courtly love as situated on a pedestal is often inverted. Expressing an unwelcome desire for intimacy, the female protagonist attempts to close the Levinasian gap demarcating absolute alterity on several occasions, when she follows him up the stairwell always one floor behind, and when she slips down to his level beneath the table. However, we generally see a corresponding countermove on his part toward transcendence and away from intimacy, as he rises to the top floor of the building or sinks into personal reverie—implying transcendence through interiority and utopian escape. One passionate encounter between the couple in a video storeroom finds her falling to her knees following a passionate embrace, only to realize immediately after that her voluntary action has resulted in a loss of intimacy. Only does this positioning begin to break down close to the end of the film, as the couple evidently become more intimate in a meaningful interpersonal sense while dancing playfully on a bridge in a tight embrace. This intimacy does not last for long, however, following the discovery of the unconscious porn star in an elevator and the ensuing final scene.

As previously stated, this is a bizarre sort of courtly love; a relationship in which the difference of the other is not compromised, their personal space is rarely invaded, but in which there is little sense of bridging the interpersonal divide (it seems fitting that when this does happen momentarily, it happens on a bridge). The relationship is respectful, modern and decidedly East Asian in its affective style. Aside from a few touching scenes in the middle of the film, principally when they are cooking together, their relationship remains strangely sterile to the end of the film. The fragility of this positioning is exposed in the denouement, when his move toward transcendence seems to require her debasement, as the terms of the secondary male-female opposition (the porn actors) are transferred onto the primary opposition of the leading romantic pair. When he transfers his physical attention from the (unconscious) porn actress to the leading lady, at the moment of climax, the spell of their relationship is broken and she is made to occupy the impassive position of the actress, her arms flopping powerlessly to her side after providing him with release

---

[91] Žižek, "From Courtly Love to *The Crying Game*," 105–07.

through the act of fellatio. This is one of the few times she is physically inactive in the film, which makes the dramatic impact of the scene all the more striking. Significantly his head remains out of shot, in the clouds. Her face pressed tightly against his groin, a single tear falls across her quivering cheek. The scene is filmed is extreme close-up and is drawn out over an extended period of time (around 90 seconds).

Reflecting on both the metafilmic dimensions of the film and the importance of an extended temporal frame of reference, Tsai comments:

> The reason for my making *The Wayward Cloud* was to show the basic nature of sex through this film. You made love with bright light and recording devices present, and sex was just work, nothing else...The whole process is ridiculous. But the audience of *The Wayward Cloud* would feel very disturbed. Because instead of porn they were watching the shooting of porn. They'd see a porn film in it, but also the entire camera crew. And the duration is very long. They cannot control the playing speed in a cinema. You can only sit and watch. Therefore it is almost anti-pornography. Yes, it is an anti-pornography film.[92]

Played out in the scene described earlier is perhaps the main cautionary message of the film: how the modes of consciousness we experience from mass media become templates for our actions in ordinary life. This scene is similar in its direction to Luce Irigaray's powerful critique of Levinas's idea of transcendence. For Irigaray, the female-encoded Other that remains eternally out of reach in Levinasian ethics is destined to remain in darkness with no recourse to pleasures of the flesh (*volupté*), including the loving caress. Her primary purpose would appear to be to sustain his desire, his *jouissance*. This attitude of transcendence when contemplating a remote and unattainable Other (an uptown girl) appears to be available primarily to the classic male subject.[93] Through such encounters the Levinasian subject approaches the essence of his being, which is found in the experience of infinity, a mode of experience that smacks of the Romantic idea of the sublime (as Žižek's references to sublimation in courtly love also confirm). Much like constructions of the sublime, which I return to in the next chapter, the Levinasian lover (as Other) lacks physical substance. As Irigaray writes, Levinas

> knows nothing of communion in pleasure...The distance is always maintained with the other in the experience of love. The other is "close" to him in "duality." This autistic, egological, solitary love does not correspond to the shared outpouring, to the loss of boundaries which takes

---

[92]   Interview in Tsai Ming-Liang, dir., *The Wayward Cloud* (London: Axiom Films, 2004).

[93]   Luce Irigaray, "Questions to Emmanuel Levinas: On the Divinity of Love," trans. Margaret Whitford in *Re-Reading Levinas* (London: Athlone Press, 1991), 109–18.

place for both lovers when they cross the boundaries of the skin into the mucous membranes of the body, leaving the circle which encloses my solitude to meet in a shared space, a shared breath, abandoning the *relatively dry* and precise outlines of each body's solid exterior to enter a *fluid universe* where the perception of being two persons…becomes indistinct, and above all, acceding to another energy, neither that of the one nor that of the other, but an energy produced together as a result of the irreducible difference of sex. [Emphasis mine.][94]

Irigaray's critique of Levinas succeeds in pinpointing precisely why it is that there is so little real eroticism in Tsai's films. A poetic yet strained sort of erotic frisson is found in the scenes depicting romantic attachment, but it is contained within a Levinasian design that charts the course of a desire that is always deferred. The thirst Tsai's characters feel can never be quenched. This is perhaps the main difference between Tsai's film and Potter's; in the case of the latter, the fluidity of sexual connection is more obviously reparative and results from relinquishment of dualistic thinking. Tsai's characters achieve this level of intimacy mostly when cooking.

A Levinasian understanding of the final scene is reinforced by the lyrics of the final song, which tell of the hero's detachment from worldly concerns. The song that gave the film its title is again an adapted Western tune: Stan Lebowsky and Herb Newman's country classic, "The Wayward Wind." Originally a hit for Cogi Grant, in later years it has been interpreted by countless country and folk artists (including Patsy Cline and Neil Young). The female protagonist sings a short extract of this song's melody wordlessly in an elevator following her first amorous encounter with the man from upstairs (00:41:45). In this context its use is naïve and affecting: it illustrates her heartfelt contentment, which turns out to be short lived. Later it is given a quite different spin when arranged for a small group of jazz musicians and performed by a leading Chinese torch singer of the postwar period. The Mandarin cover version draws attention to the dynamic between local and global politics that has such a tangible impact on the characters' desires and aspirations—from their taste in hardcore porn to stereotyped ideas about gender identity. We see the latter in images of the Westernized flight attendant, whose feminine grace and mobility are attributes the Japanese porn actress in particular seems to aspire to. A cardboard cutout of two flight attendants is included in the final shot of the film (when this song is heard for the second time), which contrasts ironically with the act of passive fellatio performed by the boyish and physically awkward leading lady. The use of country music and its removal from the historical contexts in which the original song and its East Asian copy were produced accentuates the campiness of the audio-visual bond. Something has been lost in translation, just as the characters are lost in

[94] Ibid., 111.

their dreams of cultural mobility (in a Westerly direction). The music helps to draw our attention to this fact.

Apart from embodying the politics of cultural appropriation, "The Wayward Cloud" is a song about (male) transcendence. As the female vocalist tells us:

> A wayward cloud, lonesome and proud,
> slipping through my hand. To a far-off land.
> My heartless love, drifting high above,
> like a wayward cloud. With no earthly bound.

Unlike "Sixteen Tons," where the meaning of the translated song was willfully misinterpreted in the Chinese translation and whose meaning is playfully perverted again in Tsai's audiovisual incorporation, Chinese actress Bai Guang's mandarin interpretation of "The Wayward Wind" is close in both sound and semantic meaning to Cogi Grant's country hit. This is essentially a torch song about a male lover who is prone to wander. The original hit song features affectations of the "Wild West" that we would expect to hear in the country and western genre, most audibly in the clattering "wagon wheels" rhythm (something resembling a bolero) and the Disney-style mimetic wind sounds, produced by a female choir singing wordlessly with occasional "gusts" of portamento. Other aspects of the arrangements are similar. The Cogi Grant arrangement sounds like country music usually does in folk musicals: a big arrangement for big country, featuring orchestral strings, horns, harp, and jazz combo. The Bai Guang song is more modest in the resources it employs, comprising only a small jazz combo of accordion, lead guitar and rhythm guitar. The two songs are in the same key (B major) and in the same relaxed tempo. The singing style is similar, an engaging torch style in which the lonesome and winsome singer pines for her itinerant lover. Bai possesses a rich low register, reaching up to more nasal tones as she pushes to the top of her range. All of this lends the music a warm and comforting quality. The singer will wait patiently, we are led to believe, while her lover ventures off to pursue his destiny, a free spirit untroubled by worldly concerns. As these descriptions convey, Bai Guang's Mandarin version of "The Wayward Cloud" is closely modeled on Cogi Grant's "The Wayward Wind." So much so that it represents an idealization not only of compliant and empathetic femininity, but also, implicitly, of the West. We can see this in the image of the two female flight attendants, which reminds us of the Western origins of the song. Like the singer of the song, the glamorous flight attendants are only too happy to service their itinerant passengers. Meanwhile the real female protagonist drops her arms in despair as his head remains in the clouds.

We have seen the male protagonist in this light on several occasions in the film: staring at painted clouds, emitting muffled sex noises while she gazes upwards toward his apartment, and at the end of the film, with his head out-of-shot while she is debased through the act of fellatio. Here we might perceive the secret meaning of the conventional upstairs-downstairs positioning in the musical (and that of courtly love in general). As the song lyrics and dramatic content of the film imply, what is conveyed is above all *his* transcendence. She remains grounded in corporeal life; his very groundlessness appears to be the deciding factor in the couple's inability to connect. In a tangible sense, his elevated position keeps her down.

Afterthoughts, on Metamusicals and Other Matters

REFLECTIONS ON TIME, CAMP AESTHETICS AND POLITICS IN *YES* AND *THE WAYWARD CLOUD*

How do the musical sequences fit into the design of Tsai's film? And why are they there? They are, primarily, responses to the drudgery of daily life, whether digging up keys from a recently surfaced road, dragging an unconscious body through endless corridors, or hauling watermelons from one location to another. Everything in Tsai's world seems to require a concentration of manual labor. Importantly, mobile agents such as water and elevators provide the impetus for moments of becoming through flow experiences. Transcendence, when it does arrive, is audiovisually staged, with all of the glitz and glamour of Hollywood standing out in stark relief against the still visible quotidian world. In other words, the production numbers are never quite lavish enough to outshine the material circumstance that give rise to them. The antiquated production values of the songs and their translation from English reinforce this artificiality, showing us how the transcendent parallel worlds that are glimpsed in the protagonists' dreams are impossible to achieve. Transcendence, therefore, is ultimately something to be mistrusted, be it the utopian dreams of the pornographic imagination or the seductive dreams of (Western) commodity culture.

The closest the characters come to actual transcendence is through corporeal involvement in the free-flow of their physical actions, which allows them to step outside of the constraints of social time and enter a mode of fluid becoming. Similarly to *Yes*, the characters seem caught up in the unfolding materiality of everyday life. In *Wayward Cloud*, however, this is achieved in the soundtrack more through an appreciation of silence than it is through the use of rhythmic sounds. Importantly, extended everyday temporality deconstructs the teleological imperative of hardcore porn culminating in the inevitable money shot. It is after one such scene, culminating in a facial money shot (ejaculation to the face) that one of the five musical diversions occurs (Grace Chang's plaintive and bluesy torch song, "To Keep My Heart True"). Here the actress is made to look as unattractive as possible; her make-up is smeared, her false lashes visibly peel away, and the lighting is stark. In this way the performativity of genre is made visible, just as the musical sequence

that follows, including its musical suspension of time, illustrates that we were witnessing all along a staged number of a different kind—both the hardcore number
and the musical number imply falsity and temporal suspension. Here the moment
of visible transcendence is shown to be the one-sided pleasure that it is, while the
extended temporarily that wraps the two related sequences, musical number and
porn "number," destabilizes the teleological economy that they draw on for their
effects. The protracted hyperrealism of Tsai's soundtrack in combination with the
film's slow-cooked visual style serves this function more generally. But this modality
needs a foil in order to achieve these effects, which is where the musical number
comes in.

Music and the musicality of dialogue are deployed differently in *Yes*, as a means
of challenging the verisimilitude of classical narrative procedures and to allow flexible passage between externally and internally experienced time. Potter fundamentally makes a case for the phenomenology of the filmic experience as something
mimetic to other flow experiences. In some respects her stream-of-consciousness
approach resembles the surrealists' interest in automatism, as well as their frequent
espousal of the mind-expanding properties of dream consciousness. Tsai's characters similarly move as if in a dream, albeit a physically demanding and temporally
extended one. Their experiences are primarily sensory and they seem unable to par-
ticipate in discursive forms of consciousness. This twilight existence allows Tsai's
characters to slip with apparent ease between dream consciousness and waking life.
In this respect they are undoubtedly intended to resemble us all in an age of mass-
media saturation and blurring cultural identities. How should we find our edges
(culturally and personally) in a global age if not by means of a form of phenomenological bracketing that risks being even more restrictive than the mode of consciousness it is intended to replace? The choice would seem to be between schizophrenia
(sonically, shizophonia) and autism; a middle path of sorts perhaps lying somewhere between the two.

Camp is undoubtedly relevant in both of these cases—each in different ways.
Both deal with erotic subject matter, either with a critical or more ameliorative slant.
Equally important though is a kind of audiovisual eroticism that Susan Sontag was
among the first expound (in the essay "Against Interpretation"), and which can be
related to the aesthetics of camp. Camp comes through as well in the very acts of
intermedial transliteration by which the musical as a genre is defined and which the
reflexive metamusical brings into even sharper focus. Camp has a political component and both of these films home in on the subversive potential of camp strategies,
although not always in obvious and deconstructive ways. Depictions of Anthony in
Yes and of the conventions of hardcore pornography and film musicals in *The
Wayward Cloud* speak to a strong deconstructive agenda, but the primary mode of
expression in both films is arguably more affirmative. This comes closer to Sedgwick's
understanding of camp as caught up in the pleasures of action and affect than
implying an inherently distrustful mode of address.

Neither of these films deconstructs sexual erotics entirely; instead they posit alternative models of the erotic than those that have dominated the Western imagination. Both films see water as a potent transformative agent; something fluid, replenishing and implying movement away from fixed positions or subjectivities. Water is apparently everywhere in *Yes*; in *Wayward Cloud* it is a scarcer commodity. In both films it is equivalent to love. Both films oppose what they perceive to be the waterless state of anti-love. In *Yes*, the state of loveless dehydration is to be found in the atmosphere of mutual distrust and the elevated threat of reactionary violence that characterizes politics in the years following the attacks of September 11, 2001. In *Wayward Cloud*, it is a cluster of ideas that stem from the dominant representations of audiovisual culture in the West (and beyond) and how these impact on the popular imagination. Both films argue for a reassessment of cultural priorities and both provide (audio)visions of what these new priorities might look like, sound like, and *feel* like. How one might feel differently in a global and digital age amid growing international tensions and confusion about cultural identity is perhaps the dominant message or *question* of both films. This is conveyed through audiovisual idiolects that articulate different ways of attending to experience, and by implication that suggest affirmative measures toward different ways of negotiating interpersonal relations.

Both camp and surrealist aesthetics are implied above all in how existing musical materials are handled like found objects: not objects to be derided (although Tsai's approach sometimes comes close to this function), but rather as vehicles for re-enchantment through transformative recontextualization. A pertinent question is whether the songs heard in Tsai's metamusicals are nothing but worthless commodities. Does such music yield only hallucinatory pleasures, having little relevance to contemporary life? Those of us working in popular musicology have long been familiar with Adorno's arguments along these lines concerning popular songs composed in the Tin Pan Alley style. Instead of dismissing such songs as formulaic (likewise those discussed in this chapter), I would prefer to think of them as carefully crafted and willfully open-ended; imbued with qualities of humane beauty, optimism or cathartic drama, and because of their relatively depersonalized nature, encouraging multiple points of entry for interpreters. This might be why music of this kind has been recycled in this and other contexts, not merely as kitsch designed to occasion derisory laughter. This points to a more reparative way of understanding cultural "borrowing" than theories in popular music studies have offered in the past. Rose Rosengard Subotnik's eloquent defense of Tin Pan Alley songs is worth mentioning in this regard.[95] Her reading of the Tin Pan Alley songwriting tradition, which informs and overlaps with the conclusions I have arrived at in this chapter,

---

[95]   Rose Rosengard Subotnik, "Shoddy Equipment for Living? Deconstructing the Tin Pan Alley Song," in Steven Baur, Raymond Knapp and Jacqueline Warwick, eds., *Musicological Identities: Essays in Honor of Susan McClary* (Aldershot: Ashgate, 2008), 205–18.

reverses several priorities that have been articulated in critical readings of "standard" popular songs in the past. Subotnik appreciates these forms above all for their adaptability to a wide range of performance contexts, while recognizing the value of artifice over authenticity, craftsmanship over expressiveness, when it comes to giving audiences narrative positions they can fit their lives into. This perspective on the subject offers a path toward appreciating both of these films in terms of a surrealist sensibility that partakes also of those (reparative) qualities of camp performativity that Sedgwick values so highly. Repetition with a performative difference would seem to be a primary motivation behind both of these films; performativity as a means of keeping audiences on their toes, while furnishing the audiovisual spectacle with an added level of sparkle.

FURTHER REFLECTIONS ON INTERMEDIALITY: ANOTHER MUSIC VIDEO CODA

A central assumption of this chapter is that neosurrealist metamusicals tap a potential for subversion that is present in the musical forms from which they draw their inspiration. Both *Yes* and *The Wayward Cloud* unlock the camp potential of musical numbers from a reflexive distance. Closely related to this, they expose the intermediality of film musicals, either by refusing to gloss over the points of rupture that mark transitions between everyday and fantastical audiovisual registers, or by setting up camp in the liminal zone between these two registers. Both films attend more closely to female experience and agency than is the norm in Hollywood filmmaking. They do this while focusing on the musicality of ordinary life, rather than its transcendence, in new hybrid formations that incorporate incongruous discourses. As discussed earlier, Dennis Potter was an important forerunner in this regard. Auteur filmmakers have been quick to exploit this new savvy mode of expression, followed in rapid succession by producers at the bolder end of television drama, including *Hill Street Blues* producer Steven Bochco's spectacular TV flop, *Cop Rock* (1990).[96] Since then there have been numerous safer, because they are shorter, excursions into the modus operandi of musicals in episodes of *ER*, *Buffy the Vampire Slayer*, *Chicago Hope*, and *The Simpsons*. *Glee* represents perhaps the most persistent venture into the territory of the backstage musical in recent television.

Postmodernist musical extravaganzas like Baz Lurhmann's *Moulin Rouge* and independent/art-house offerings like Lars von Trier's musical-melodrama *Dancer in the Dark* both illustrate in different ways just how closely bound the new musical aesthetic is to the aesthetic precepts of music videos. The former incorporates and reworks songs by recognized popular artists (from Sting to Madonna and Kylie Minogue), while the latter includes the Icelandic singer Björk as its female

---

[96] See George Plasketes, "Cop Rock Revisited: Unsung Series and Musical Hinge in Cross-Genre Evolution," *Journal of Popular Film and Television* 32/2 (2004): 64–73.

protagonist. Because of how the star text spills over individual performances, Björk's acting in this film is strongly reminiscent of her appearances in a number of widely known, critically acclaimed, and markedly surrealist music videos (including those of directors like Michel Gondry and Spike Jonze), one of whom was discussed in the previous chapter. Björk's music videos and her work as an actress in *Dancer* become interreferential to a considerable extent because of the music video, "It's Oh So Quiet" (dir. Spike Jonze).[97] Videos including Michael Jackson's "Thriller" (1982), Madonna's "Material Girl" (1985) and Britney Spears' "Baby One More Time" (1998) have from the birth of the form been strongly indebted to song-and-dance numbers in musicals.[98] That much is clear. Jonze's video ups the ante in a manner resembling the work of auteur-directors like Tsai and Potter because of his use of a dark irony that requires the transitions between "real life" and musical number to be playfully juxtaposed. Intriguing about "It's Oh So Quiet" is how the whispered verse sections are filmed in slow motion, much as Tsai's cinematography takes place over an extended timeframe and the musicality of the dialogue in *Yes* also distorts narrative time. In this way the shouted musical sections of the song reflect back on ordinary or "lived" reality in a manner that denaturalizes the banal—turning it, more than the fantasy of musical spectacle, into something surreal. Playing with time is central to Jonze's video approach, as we witness when characters launch into song and dance while the filming makes gradual transitions from slow motion to "real-time" cinematic techniques. The adjustment is made at the level of the exposure length in a manner that is conspicuous to the eye. The end result is that the fantasy of the musical number seen in the glitzy big band choruses is tangibly more realistic than the dreamlike extended temporality of the sequences taking place in a shopping mall. Of course, the entire video is accompanied by song, which is hardly a natural state of affairs. Further parallels might be made between Tsai's *The Wayward Cloud* and Jonze's video. Both allude to Jacques Demi's *Les Parapluies de Cherbourg* (1964), most obviously through the actors' use of umbrellas as dancing props. All of this underlines the intermediality of the forms, which as I have argued in the introduction demarcates a shift toward a performative mode of address.

To conclude this chapter, it seems fitting to ask to what extent the films I discussed can be read as implicitly critiquing the traditional film musical. It is not inconsequential that both Tsai and Potter, in different ways, articulate an attitude that is highly critical of global consumerism and its consequences. Tsai commented in an interview: "In this age of consumerism, is there anything that can't be sold for profit?"[99] Along similar lines, the Auntie in *Yes* pointedly asks what use is there in "a

---

[97] For an insightful, close reading of this video, see Stan Hawkins, "Musical Excess and Postmodern Identity in Björk's 'It's Oh So Quiet,'" *Musiikin Suunta* 2 (1999): 43–54.

[98] For more on this affinity, see John Mundy, *Popular Music on Screen: From Hollywood Musical to Music Video* (Manchester: Manchester University Press, 1999).

[99] Quotation in *The Wayward Cloud*, Press Release (London: Axiom Films, 2007).

life spent longing for things you don't need!" The musical number, if anything, is a form that illustrates what it takes to sell a tune. These are the repetitions that the musical as a form is saturated with; undoubtedly they are those of Adorno's "culture industry," although they are always more than this. Both of these films juxtapose the utopian and placeless (but nevertheless Western, North American) contexts of classic film musicals with sonic and visual elements that accentuate local identities. In *Wayward Cloud*, the songs are all from somewhere else, or they could have been, even while they are performed and mimed by local people in less than glamorous circumstances. *Yes* similarly subverts identities by means of its ambiguous play on auditory accents and styles that defy easy categorization (rap, Shakespearean verse, local speech dialects and musical styles).

Despite the conclusions I have arrived at in the course of my investigation, I will refrain from categorizing reflexive metamusicals as "critical" or reparative in a straightforward way. The strangeness of the new reflexive musical is always disclosed through audiovisual and narrative details and by specific and variable contexts of production and reception. There are no hard and fast rules as to what such musicals mean. A common thread, however, is their marginal positioning with respect to mainstream discourses. Neosurrealist metamusicals define themselves as spatially and temporally other. They tend to assert local identity and presentness in one way or another, whether knowingly or inadvertently. This is not always uncomplicated, however. An example is the work of the Finnish music video director, Tommi Pietiläinen, who produced a number of videos for the Finnish indie band The Crash. Of particular relevance to the present discussion is a music video that I have analyzed in detail elsewhere.[100] The video for the song "Still Alive" is obviously influenced by Jonze's work for Björk.[101] Mimicking the visual style of the vintage television series *Hill Street Blues*, the song's verses and chorus are divided in accordance with narrative and musical sections in an identical fashion to "It's Oh So Quiet." The action similarly relies upon visual dissolve as a means of smoothing over the transitions between dramatic action and dance: fight moves become dance moves, dancers fall into synch with the singer as he walks rhythmically down a staircase. The primary difference from musicals, of course, is that song is present throughout the video; although music of one form or another is ubiquitous in *Yes*, and the suspended temporal flow of *The Wayward Cloud* suggests something other than conventional narrative time. In this respect, both this music video and Jonze's have a close affinity to the films I have been discussing. Local identity in the Finnish video is mainly implicit. Teemu Brunila, the singer-songwriter of The Crash, self-identifies primarily with British indie bands, sings in English in a campy style resembling Pet Shop Boys singer Neil Tenant, and makes few intentional references to his

---

[100]   Richardson, "Intertextuality and Pop Camp Identity Politics in Finland."

[101]   At the time of this writing, the video can be viewed on YouTube, at http://www.youtube.com/, retrieved May 18, 2011.

homeland in his music. Rather than asserting local identity directly (which is complicated in his case because he belongs to the country's Swedish-speaking minority),
The Crash's music video seems to be about bringing diverse codes of camp (from
British camp rock to film musicals) into incongruous contact with one another. This
attitude confronts the conformity of local mainstream culture (which has traditionally required assimilation among minority populations) more than expressing resistance toward some "external" cultural entity (be it consumerism or Western
dominance). Most pressingly, the campiness of the video operates on a more subtle
aesthetic plane that is strongly affirmative in its valence. The same is true of the films
discussed in this chapter. Their principal mode of address is richly affirmative and
unapologetically camp.

5

Rescoring the Moving Image: *La Belle et la Bête*, Mashups and (Mis)syncing

> The acceptability of various solutions depends on our tolerance of
> strange collisions, emotional mixtures we didn't expect ever to see.
> Perhaps post-modernism is a good rehearsal for this.
> —Brian Eno, *A Year with Swollen Appendices: Brian Eno's Diary*

On Composition and Recombination

Addressing performances of cinematic opera and the Internet phenomenon of
syncing, the instances examined in this chapter are not a world apart from the
musicalized discourses of neosurrealist films and reflexive metamusicals, dealt
with previously. Of particular interest are combinatory forms where an existing
audiovisual text is taken as the primary source material for new audiovisual configurations. Often this will imply silencing an existing soundtrack so that a new
one can be inserted in its place. Akin to practices of montage in the historical
avant-garde, but also to vernacular practices of remix and "versioning" that have
been in cultural ascendancy since the 1980s, this aesthetic orientation has found
fertile soil in the flow spaces and participatory discourses of the Internet.[1]

Some of the most striking examples of such forms are music videos that have
either been "mashed up," either by editing the sounds and music of two videos
together, or by replacing much of the original video's soundtrack with a new and
incongruous version of the original song. Some of the most striking examples of the

---

[1] Parts of this chapter are based on earlier work. Much of the first section was written for a keynote presen-
tation at The First International Conference on Music and Minimalism, organized by Pwyll ap Siôn at the
University of Bangor, in August 2007. An earlier version of later sections of the paper can be found in John
Richardson, "Resisting the Sublime: Loose Synchronisation in *La Belle et la Bête* and *The Dark Side of Oz*," in
Steven Baur, Raymond Knapp and Jacqueline Warwick, eds., *Musicological Identities: Essays in Honour of Susan
McClary* (Aldershot: Ashgate, 2008), 135–48. The chapter has benefitted from the input of numerous scholars,
including (but not limited to) Carol Vernallis, Annette Davison, Susanna Välimäki, Anne Sivuoja and the
editors of *Musicological Identities*.

latter are death-metal arrangements of Britney Spears songs, which seem to take an ambivalent pleasure in the originals even while despoiling them.[2] The irony is heightened in such cases because of the turbulent turn Spears's career took in recent years. Supposedly countering pop fakery with rock authenticity, in fact, the two forms reflect on each other in more complicated and troubling ways, not least of which is by revealing the artifice that has always existed in constructions of heavy rock and the brutal truths that lie under the sheen of girly pop. When it comes to the countless remixes, mashups and parodies of Spears's "Toxic" found on the Internet, the effectiveness of the "copies" has to be premised in some measure on the striking and multivalent nature of the original audiovisual work.[3]

Along similar lines, recent years have seen a renewed interest in live performances of silent films: First, soundtracks recuperated through recordings or performances of original scores matched to restored films; and second, the composition of new soundtracks to existing films. My central concern is the latter category. Electronica forerunner Giorgio Moroder's soundtrack to Fritz Lang's *Metropolis* (1927 [1985]) in is an early example. In the same genre are the Pet Shop Boys' performances of Sergei Eisenstein's classic of early montage aesthetics, *Battleship Potemkin* (1925), performed with the Dresdner Sinfoniker (2004). Canonical avant-garde and art-house films are prime candidates for such reworkings, particular those that converge uncannily with present-day artistic sensibilities (such as the "cut-up" style of music video aesthetics). It helps, moreover, if the status of incorporated film is firmly established because this reflects favorably on perceptions of the contemporary artist in the form of garnered cultural capital. Dziga Vertov's *Man With A Movie Camera* (1929) has been a magnet for musical reworkings, including those of the Alloy Orchestra (1996), the Cinematic Orchestra (2000), and Michael Nyman (2002). Crucially, the last two of these have been performed live, which reveals an important tenet of the aesthetic: the assertion of "now-ness," through the visible presence of the musicians and the composer/author, in contrast to the temporally marked "then-ness" of the incorporated materials. Changes in recording and restoration technologies are an essential precondition for the proliferation of works of this type. Advances in digital technology permit the restoration of films in the first place, which makes screening them afresh a more viable proposition. Furthermore, the DVD format permits multiple soundtracks to be included on a single release. It is largely due to digital developments, therefore, that

---

[2] MTV's mashup of Britney Spears's "Toxic" and Linkin Park's "Faint" was one of the first such mashups. Available at www.youtube.com/watch?v=Lcuq4K5jNRM. Metal covers of Britney songs featuring the original videos include, I Set My Friends On Fire's version of "Toxic": www.youtube.com/watch?v=U33FfCP2qPI; and Children of Bodom's version of "Oops, I Did It Again": http://www.youtube.com/watch?v=D1sguF2D1UAan dfeature=related. All retrieved on December 10, 2010.

[3] For a detailed analysis of "Toxic," see Stan Hawkins and John Richardson, "Remodeling Britney Spears: Matters of Intoxication and Mediation," in *Popular Music and Society* 30/5 (2007): 605–29.

multiple and reversioned soundtrack recordings have come into their own. This is the same technology that allows the reinstatement of "lost soundtracks" as DVD bonus materials and YouTube extracts, for example, Bernard Hermann's diegetic underscore for Hitchcock's *Torn Curtain* (1966) and Alex North's for Kubrick's *2001: A Space Odyssey* (1968).

There can be no mistaking the historical impulse that motivates such activities, even when it is apparent that the new version consciously inscribes historical distance as much as it seeks to bridge the gap between the present day and the past. In a similar spirit, and immediately following the success of the screen-opera discussed later, Philip Glass would add a nondiegetic underscore performed by the Kronos Quartet to Tod Browning's early talkie classic, *Dracula* (1931)—a film that originally contained very little music.[4] The acceptability of such pastimes is largely to be judged on the level of skill demonstrated in reworking an original or, more fundamentally, how unassailable the original is held to be in the first place. Implicit in such acts of appropriation is the assumption that even canonical works are never so complete that they cannot be subjected to readerly reimaginings. If nothing else, these instances chart a sea change in the status of what were formerly considered to be inviolate works, which reflects a changing dynamic in the relationship between current artists and their antecedents.[5]

The cases considered below raise similar issues. The primary focus of this chapter is to chart aesthetic responses to Philip Glass's cinematic opera, *La Belle et la Bête*, and the Internet-mediated phenomenon of "syncing" as expressed in the cinematic-progressive rock mashup *The Dark Side of Oz*. These two examples are linked through a mode of appreciation distinctive to recent aesthetics that foregrounds the remediation of existing materials, an approach Susan McClary calls "Reveling in the Rubble," but which also invokes the mode of engagement registered in surrealist responses to outmoded objects, which Adorno refers to as "the world rubble of surrealism."[6] This implies a revised notion of "com-position" (literally, putting together) in which the idea of music making as a dialogic activity emerges. By directing attention toward these artists' engagement with recognized forms, McClary argues that they are "both self-conscious and unapologetic about the

---

[4] For a detailed analysis of this film, see Tristian Evans, "This is (not) a Soundtrack: Dracula the Movie or Music Drama?" in his *Towards a Theory of Multimedia Integration in Post-Minimal Music* (PhD dissertation, University of Bangor, 2010), 200–39.

[5] On the changing nature of the work concept and its relation to the assumptions of Romantic aesthetics, see Lydia Goehr, *The Imaginary Museum of Musical Works: An Essay in the Philosophy of Music* (Oxford: Oxford University Press, 1994), 176–204. See also contributions to the anthology, Michael Talbot, ed., *The Musical Work: Reality or Invention* (Liverpool: Liverpool University Press, 2000).

[6] Susan McClary, *Conventional Wisdom: The Content of Musical Form* (Berkeley: University of California Press, 2000), 141. See also Theodor Adorno, "Looking Back on Surrealism" (1954), in *Notes to Literature*, vol. 1, trans. Shierry Weber Nicholson (New York: Columbia University Press, 1991), 86–90, 87.

constructedness of their music and images."[7] In line with a Benjaminian view of montage, this permits the emergence of a form of historicity in which differences between the present and the past are elevated reflexively by acts of contextual displacement. The examples discussed below are further united by their time of composition, the mid-1990s, while both involve the transformation of materials that are several decades older. Above all, the examples discussed here evidence the strained relationship between music and images in recent audiovisual forms, which is inseparable from the cultural, economic and technological landscape of the digital age. In such circumstances, cultural artifacts become information as much as art, which has profound repercussions for our understanding of what it is acceptable to *do* with these objects.[8]

An aleatory sensibility infuses these examples, with an approach to synchronizing media that is loose and occasional rather than narratively close-knit and causally continuous characterizing audiovisual relations. Such a sensibility brings to mind a line of avant-garde performance that has traditionally challenged the binary opposition of art and life: what Andreas Huyssen calls the "Duchamp-Cage-Warhol axis."[9] Of particular interest is how unlikely artistic juxtapositions that are temporally marked impact on questions of affect and agency, and how both of these considerations extend into lived experience in the present day.

Convergence and Divergence in Glass's *La Belle et la Bête*

At some point during his work on the acclaimed portrait opera trilogy (*Einstein on the Beach*, 1975–76; *Satyagraha* 1981; *Akhnaten*, 1983–84), Philip Glass stopped being an avant-garde composer. This is an oversimplification, but it is supported by the consensus of critical opinion. Of course, not all of us see this as an unfortunate turn of events. How many times can you listen to *Music in the Shape of a Square* (1967)—an example of what Keith Potter has called "prehistoric minimalism"—without hankering for greener musical pastures?[10] The remainder of the 1980s would see Glass donning more traditional musical caps, from symphonist to composer of mainstream Hollywood scores, not always, in the opinion of critics, successfully. A relative high point of this trajectory came

---

[7] McClary, *Conventional Wisdom*, 153.

[8] See Catherine Moore, "Work and Recordings: The Impact of Commercialisation and Digitalisation," in Talbot, ed., *The Musical Work*, 88–109.

[9] Andreas Huyssen, *After the Great Divide: Modernism, Mass Culture, Postmodernism* (Bloomington: Indiana University Press, 1986), 188.

[10] Keith Potter, "1976 and All That: Minimalism and Post-Minimalism, Analysis and Listening Strategies" (Presentation at the First International Conference on Minimalist Music, Bangor, Wales). Available at http://minimalismsociety.org/wp-content/uploads/2010/07/Keith-Potter.pdf, retrieved May 20, 2011.

in the early 1990s with the New York Metropolitan Opera's commissioning of *The Voyage* (1992), a grand opera recognized as such even by traditionalists. The scale and artistic ambition of this production could be seen as an attempt on Glass's part to rise to the challenge of contemporaries: most notably, John Adams, whose *Nixon in China* (1985–1987) and *Death of Klinghoffer* (1991) combined the techniques and textures of minimalism with expressive means rooted in operatic tradition. For Adams almost any musical procedure was admissible, and in *The Voyage* this was increasingly the case for Glass. But in courting traditionalists so successfully, Glass arguably consigned his avant-garde persona to the past. This was the view of Steve Reich, whose first collaborative foray in musical multimedia, *The Cave* (1992), sought to take up the gauntlet laid down by Glass in the seminal *Einstein*; pointedly, not a recent compositions but one he had composed a decade and a half earlier. When it came to Glass's next major dramatic undertaking, a wish to reclaim some of his former kudos in the domain of experimental theater could well have been a motivating factor, paired with a desire to work once again on a more intimate scale with the musicians of his own ensemble.

Much of Glass's creative energies in the 1990s would be channeled into composing and performing a second opera trilogy, in this case based on the work of French film director Jean Cocteau. Its first installment, *Orphée* (1993) is a traditional operatic adaptation of the film of the same name; its third, *Les Enfants Terribles* (1996), a combined chamber opera and ballet based on the Cocteau play. It is the second, however, that stands out as the most radical in terms of its mode of audiovisual presentation, and which will serve as the fulcrum for the present discussion. *La Belle et la Bête* (*Beauty and the Beast*, 1994) was composed for the Philip Glass ensemble and is characterized by the direct incorporation of the original film. This has led some writers to surmise that the composer treated his source materials like a silent film, which is true but only up to a point. In *La Belle*, Glass took the significant first step of silencing the existing soundtrack. The superimposition of live operatic voices synchronized with the voices of actors in the film, and a newly composed score, defines the modus operandi of performances, in which the relationship between "new" and "borrowed" materials is far from straightforward.

LEITMOTIF AND REVERIE: THE MUSICAL LANGUAGE OF *LA BELLE ET LA BÊTE*

The music of *La Belle et la Bête* is in many ways the culmination of Glass's postminimalist style filtered through a Francophile sensibility. As such, it does not represent a radical departure from his other recent works, in which a French influence might also be perceived. Glass attributes this influence to mentors such as Nadia Boulanger and Darius Milhaud, former member of Cocteau's Les Six group. Delving back further in time, Debussy's music echoes in phrases of *La Belle*, and the setting of lyrics in the opera in the French of the original film makes it tempting to draw comparisons between this opera and *Pelléas et Mélisande*. An obvious affinity exists between Glass's music and that of the French tradition, particularly the use of harmony, where an attraction to ambiguous tonality, parallel movement, and minimalist clarity of expression could be said to inform both styles. In *La Belle*, this convergence would extend to melody, through the use of the whole-tone scale, among other means. In interviews, Glass has downplayed the extent of the influence, pointing out that his approach does not sound like a pastiche of French music. He has a point, although the Cocteau operas are an obvious homage to an historical, and perhaps mythical, Paris of the composer's youth. It seems ironic in this light that Glass chose to silence music composed by Georges Auric, another member of the Les Six group, when beginning work on *La Belle*.

So what is it that is Glassian about *La Belle*? Most obviously, *rhythm*: the characteristic, perhaps manneristic, minimalist pulse and compound rhythms of his post-*Einstein* music; relentless arpeggios strung out in shape-shifting hemiola patterns across extended passages of time. No less important is *process*: less rigorously applied here than in the formative days of the style, but nevertheless a significant means by which the composer cuts a path from one musical event to the next. This can be heard in scenes of *La Belle* when a gradual increase in density is required, including the scenes leading up to the father's first encounter with Beast and the music depicting his experiences in Beast's castle. Arguably, though, the most distinctive feature of Glass's postminimalist style is found in his use of harmony, and it is noteworthy that it is a harmonic "problem" and its melodic extension that the composer considers to be the central musical "argument" of the opera. As we shall see, this argument is inseparable from a corresponding dramatic rationale. In Glass's conception, all three Cocteau operas function on one level as allegories for the creative act. According to this allegorical function, the father's passage into Beast's magical kingdom represents the artist's transformation of quotidian base materials into elements of artistic expression. The opposition of these two realms, therefore, the everyday and the magically (sur)real, is fundamental to Glass's conception of the opera.

Tonally, the first appearance of Beast is constructed as a significant moment of irruption in the opera's narrative fabric. Its opening scene is a jaunty rhythmic introduction to Beauty's ugly sisters in the key of B flat major with modulations to A major and occasional quirky sequential runs. This action is interrupted by more plaintive moments, in F minor, featuring Beauty and her human love interest, Avenant. But the initial light-hearted music sets the tone for much of the opening of the film. The levity does not last long, however. As Beauty's father approaches Beast's kingdom, the music has modulated again to F minor, signaled by a swelling elegiac leitmotif associated with quests (into the unknown), separation (anxiety),

Figure 5.1 Leitmotif associated with quests (into the unknown), separation (anxiety), and travel (usually by horse). *La Belle et la Bête.* An Opera by Philip Glass. Based on the scenario by Jean Cocteau © 1994 Dunvagen Music Publishers Inc. Used by permission.

and travel (usually by horse). Here Glass draws on traditional musical semantics in his evocation of what Raymond Monelle calls the noble horse topic in the long-short subdivision of the measure (see Figure 5.1.).[11] This music relinquishes, however, as the father enters the enchanted chateau, but it resumes and builds in intensity as he prepares to leave the chateau grounds. It is here that he stumbles across a slaughtered deer, associated indexically with its killer, the Beast. Shots of the animal are synchronized with a sudden reversion to E major (see Figure 5.2.). Later the same chord is heard as Beast introduces himself by name, thus cementing the audio-visual bond between this sonority and this character. Situated on the leading note, this chord towers threateningly over the tonic, F minor, just as the upward tilt of the camera when Beast appears in shot shows him towering physically over the father. A close-up of a rose, associated in the film with Beauty (the character and the quality), precipitates a sudden drop to C major, tonally distant to E major but still the dominant triad in F minor. Ties to the minor tonic are discarded, however, as the music swings emphatically between E major and C major, whose tonal disparity is underlined by marked differences in register and rhythm. Eventually, C major cedes to an agonizing C augmented triad, sustained over four bars, as Beauty's father plucks the rose. Glass raises the dramatic stakes here by his clever use of register, the musical range expanding to encompass extreme highs and lows. The dissonant chord remains unresolved as a somber pedal on C summons the opera's feral protagonist. This passage could almost have been taken from a Bernard Herrmann score, with its unresolved dissonances, extremes of register, and the juxtaposition of tonally remote chords. It is particularly evocative of the famous forward zoom-reverse tracking shot in *Vertigo* and its accompanying bitonal "stingers." In *La Belle*, the passage functions as a presentation of irreconcilable forces (Beauty and the Beast, the mundane and the magical), a kind of impossible musical object, although Glass's handling of the harmony and his avoidance of conventional tonal markers makes the reconciliation of these opposing forces easier than it might otherwise have been.

When broken down into its constituent notes, the augmented triad outlines the beginnings of the whole-tone scale, a favorite among the French impressionists

---

[11] Raymond Monelle, *The Sense of Music: Semiotic Essays* (Princeton, NJ: Princeton University Press, 2000), 45–65.

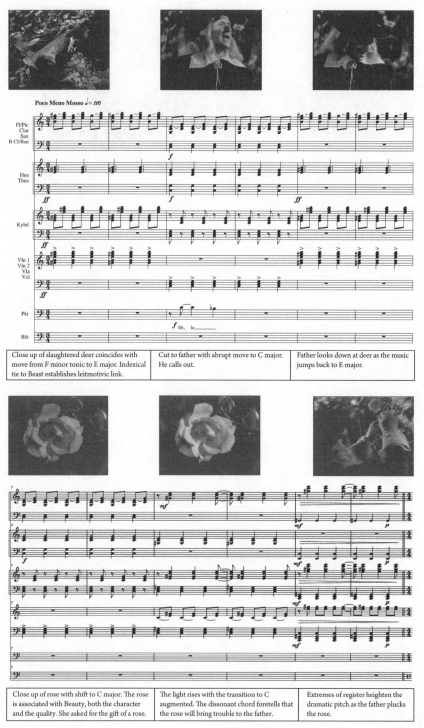

Close up of slaughtered deer coincides with move from F minor tonic to E major. Indexical tie to Beast establishes leitmotivic link.

Cut to father with abrupt move to C major. He calls out.

Father looks down at deer as the music jumps back to E major.

Close up of rose with shift to C major. The rose is associated with Beauty, both the character and the quality. She asked for the gift of a rose.

The light rises with the transition to C augmented. The dissonant chord foretells that the rose will bring trouble to the father.

Extremes of register heighten the dramatic pitch as the father plucks the rose.

Figure 5.2

(*continued*)

Figure 5.2 (continued) Use of leitmotifs in The Beast's Domain, *La Belle et la Bête*. An Opera by Philip Glass. Based on the scenario by Jean Cocteau © 1994 Dunvagen Music Publishers Inc. Used by permission.

Figure 5.3 In the Beast's Domain: Beast's "laughing" leitmotif. The Baroque *catabasis* (or *descencus*) topic: a conventional signifier of servitude and humility. *La Belle et la Bête.* An Opera by Philip Glass. Based on the scenario by Jean Cocteau © 1994 Dunvagen Music Publishers Inc. Used by permission.

precisely because of how it allowed them to skate across distantly related keys. In Glass's hands it likewise becomes a way of reconciling remote tonal centers; in the remainder of the scene, the whole-tone scale becomes the dominant tonal element, as descending hexachords prompt changes in the corresponding harmony, from C major to E major and B♭ major. This material is transformed into what Glass calls a "laughing motif," as whole-tone runs parse out into accented bass clarinet eighth notes (see Figure 5.3.). The alignment of Beast's mocking

Poco Meno Mosso ♩ = *116*

Figure 5.4 In the Beast's Domain: introductory passage. Simple additive pattern based on the whole-tone scale. *La Belle et la Bête.* An Opera by Philip Glass. Based on the scenario by Jean Cocteau © 1994 Dunvagen Music Publishers Inc. Used by permission.

agency is justified dramatically, since the passage in question is immediately preceded by his proposition that the father should exchange a daughter for the stolen rose to spare his life (00:24:36). The motif connoting Beast's mocking laughter continues to resound as the scene drives onward toward its endpoint, passing though the depths of the orchestra in contiguous hexachord streams, culminating in shuddering trombones. Here, too, an awareness of topic theory informs Glass's approach, as the relentless downward drive of the music invokes the Baroque topic of *catabasis* (or *descencus*), a signifier of servitude and humility, but above all connoting a passage toward misery or death.[12]

Glass's use of the whole-tone scale as a signifier of magic and reverie is not, of course, distinctive to this composer but goes back at least to impressionism, whence it has been plundered for inclusion in numerous film scores. Its dreamlike qualities are most audibly exploited in two scenes depicting the interior of the chateau. In these iconic scenes (mimicked in Disney's *Beauty and the Beast*, 1991, and in the surreal television serial *Angels in America*, 2003), first Beauty's father, then the protagonist herself are welcomed to the chateau by a host of anthropomorphized household objects. The accompanying music is characterized by elements of the whole-tone scale superimposed over an interval of a minor third (f–a♭. What I hear as a synthesized marimba/bell sound (marked in the score as a harp) iterates an oscillating cluster of pitches derived from the whole-tone scale (a♭–b♭–c), initially in short additive rhythmic configurations, and then as the ground to a series of variations (see Figure 5.4.). Within the context of four-bar frame, the music undergoes a series of subtle rhythmic and textural transformations. Cannily, Glass invests the actions of this scene with a sense of mechanized agency (implying an absence of human agency), through the use of additive rhythms and block additive processes, thus importing that the house is in control rather than the father. The house and its music casts a spell on this character, as

---

[12] See Dietrich Bartel, *Musica Poetica: Musical-Rhetorical Figures in German Baroque Music* (Lincoln: University of Nebraska Press, 1997), 214–15.

ascending whole-tone phrases extend and grow in strength, and a tangled web of crisscrossing melodic threads imports a growing sense of disorientation. The music seems oblivious to the father's actions, as it fails to react to two obvious sync points: when he jumps physically, in reaction to the appearance of a severed hand and to a carved lion's head on his chair that roars. The choice of instrumentation reflects an intoxicating and markedly impressionistic atmosphere, through the use of the saxophone and flute, while low woodwinds and flanged clock chimes establish an appropriately ominous mood.

While by no means every dramatic detail is reflected in the score, a leitmotivic approach to key visual cues ensures a sustained engagement with the plot as it is conveyed in the film and its libretto. A concern with symbolism pervades Cocteau's film, and Glass responds to this with his own take on the film's iconography, in which the Beast's signs of power are equated with the necessary assets of an artist: the rose with beauty, the glove with nobility, the key with technique, the mirror with artistic vocation (or "passage"), and the horse with strength and perseverance. The opera's leitmotivic construction does not prosaically underline this compositional ground plan, but there is some overlap, and moods and relationships in the film are consistently inflected in corresponding musical themes. In this way, for example, we learn that Beast and his charismatic doubles, Avenant and Prince Ardent (all played by Jean Marais), are united by their love of beauty, since the opera's main love theme is heard in the presence of all these characters (when Beast carries the sleeping Beauty to her bed, in the scene "Avenant's Passion," and in the final scene of the film, "The Transformation") (see Figure 5.5.). Significantly, we learn this in music even before it is revealed in the visual action.

Figure 5.5 Belle Travels to the Chateau: Beast's love theme (RM 40 Score 00:34:41). *La Belle et la Bête*. An Opera by Philip Glass. Based on the scenario by Jean Cocteau © 1994 Dunvagen Music Publishers Inc. Used by permission.

LOOSE SYNCHRONIZATION AND AUDIOVISUAL COUNTERPOINT

The discussion so far has treated Glass's *La Belle* as if it were any other dramatic composition. Any consideration of the opera as an audiovisual performance, however, reveals that it is not. Especially unsettling in live performances of *La Belle* is the simultaneous presence of live singers and cinematic actors—the former usurping the latter insofar as their presence points to the authentic source of the voice. Working against this impression, however, are the physical scale of the projected actors, their movements on the screen in contrast with the relatively static live singers, and the fact that the singers' voices are mediated by a public address system, thus making the visual sources of sounds difficult to ascertain in purely auditory terms. Consequently a gap opens between simultaneously unfolding performances: musical and cinematic, live and recorded, contemporary and historical. This is physically indicated as well in how performers are situated ambiguously between the projected film and the nonperformative domain of the audience (which *is* performative in the broader Butlerian sense of the word). The following comment seems to indicate a Brechtian rationale for this performative doubleness:

> There are moments when Beauty is on the screen and our Beauty is looking up at her, and I could almost cry. Then there's the scene where the Beast is dying and our Beast is singing, and the two of them together make you realize that this is a music-theatre experience, not just a film.[13]

These comments speak against audiovisual unity, which is reflected also in the manner in which the media are synchronized. Audiences in Northern Europe and America typically have low tolerance for loose synchronization. Instances that diverge from the norm of tight synchronization are perceived as either unacceptably poor quality or in some way challenging the norms of mainstream cinema. An example of the latter is the approach of spaghetti-Western director Sergio Leone, in which slightly dissynchronous overdubbing of the actors' voices is employed as a kind of distancing effect.[14] The same could be said of Glass's approach in *La Belle*, although here the looseness of the synchronization points to the composer's engagement with an existing historical artifact and its audiovisual remediation.

---

[13] Glass quoted in Jonathan Cott, "A Conversation with Philip Glass on *La Belle et la Bête*," CD booklet in Philip Glass, *La Belle et la Bête* (Nonesuch Records, 7559-79347-2, 1995), 12–21, 20.

[14] See James Buhler, "Analytical and Interpretive Approaches to Film Music (II): Analysing Interaction of Music and Film," in Kevin Donnelly, ed., *Film Music: Critical Approaches* (Edinburgh: Edinburgh University Press, 2001), 39–61, 46–7.

In keeping with conventional views of synchronization, writing on *La Belle* has tended to regard the absence of tight synchronization in the opera as a design flaw, albeit a tolerable one. In a *New York Times* review, Edward Rothstein writes that, "the lip-synching never quite works and it never quite matters."[15] Tellingly, at the end of the review he remarks, "For all its flaws, I hope to hear it again."[16] The scholar Jeongwon Joe similarly has little to say about the affective repercussions of loose audiovisual synchronization, except to note that ensuring "reasonable synchronization" was a "technical problem" for the composer.[17] This it certainly was, as the following quotation confirms:

> I took the film and put a time code on it, timed every line in it, wrote down the libretto… I timed every word, I placed it mathematically in the score… and then when I was done, [musical director] Michael Riesman and I recorded it and put it up against the film and discovered it wasn't accurate enough. So we began using computers to move the vocal line around until it synched with the lips, and then I had to rewrite the music to achieve a better synchronization with the film.[18]

To reduce the question of synchronization to a mere technical consideration, however, belies the central role that this aspect has occupied in the reception of the opera. Like many attending a performance of *La Belle* at London's Barbican theater, I was initially taken aback by how the voices of the singers seemed to move randomly in and out of sync with the projected images of corresponding actors, converging "serendipitously" after extended periods of divergence. Alongside Glass's trademark musical style, synchronization was pushed to the forefront of the audio-viewers' experiences.[19] Consequently, *La Belle* would seem to be as much about the relationship between the media as it is about musical and dramatic "content," entailing a dialogue between the composer, performers and preexisting source materials. Following Marshall McLuhan, there is a tangible sense in which the medium is made to be the message, although this assertion begs the question: what are the messages of the medium? In searching for answers to this question, it is helpful to turn to discourse on audiovisual "counterpoint" in cinema.

[15] Edward Rothstein, "Not Quite an Opera Transforms a Film," *New York Times*, December 9, 1994, C5.

[16] Ibid.

[17] Jeongwon Joe, "The Cinematic Body in the Operatic Theater: Philip Glass's *La Belle et la Bête*," in Jeongwon Joe and Rose Theresa, eds., *Between Opera and Cinema* (New York and London: Routledge, 2002), 59–73, 59.

[18] Glass quoted in Cott, "A Conversation," 19–20.

[19] For more on the cultural study of Glass's musical language, see John Richardson, *Singing Archaeology: Philip Glass's* Akhnaten (Hanover, NH: Wesleyan University Press, 1999), 53–89; and McClary, *Conventional Wisdom,* 142–45.

Dissynchronous audiovisual relations in *La Belle* might be considered an atypical example of "audiovisual counterpoint," insofar as sound and vision are perceived to be divergent. It is noteworthy that Glass uses this very term to describe the relationship between live performers and the recorded film. His usage invokes a line of theorizing that extends back at least as far as Eisenstein, Alexandrov and Pudovkin in cinema, and Brecht in theater.[20] Adorno and Eisler explain a sociological rationale for audiovisual divergence in cinema thus:

> The alienation of the media from each other reflects a society alienated from itself, men whose functions are severed from each other even within each individual. Therefore the aesthetic divergence of the media is potentially a legitimate means of expression, not merely a regrettable deficiency that has to be concealed as well as possible.[21]

Alienation between media is homologous, therefore, with social alienation and becomes a form of reflection on this condition. Given these writers' taste for counterpoint, one might expect that the principle of "accidental synchronization," championed notably by Cocteau, would be to their liking; yet this does not appear to be the case.[22] In *Music for the Films*, Adorno and Eisler resist this notion as representing a "synaesthesic" sensibility in which the qualities of one media are viewed as being arbitrarily transferred to the other, resulting in "the magic of moods, semi-darkness, and intoxication."[23] This is consistent with other aspects of Adornian thought. Notably, when it came to John Cage's "aleatory" music, he could not countenance a style whose "material laws...seem to preclude the subjective intervention of the composer."[24] Centered romantic subjectivity loomed large in Adorno's vision of avant-garde resistance, and any relinquishment of agency—such as that undertaken by Cocteau and arguably also Glass—was likely to be viewed with the utmost suspicion.

Here, as in previous chapters, the value of a Benjaminian perspective is apparent. Performances that are audiovisually split, in the manner of *La Belle*, would seem to encapsulate Benjamin's ideal of shifting subject positions, in this case determined not by shifting camera angles but by the historical perspective implied in the use of

[20] See, for example S.M. Eisenstein, V.I. Pudovkin, and G.V. Aexandrov, "A Statement," in Elisabeth Weis and John Belton, eds., *Film Sound: Theory and Practice* (New York: Columbia University Press, 1985), 83–85; and V.I. Pudovkin, "Asynchronism as a Principle of Sound Film," in Weis and Belton, eds., *Film Sound,* 86–91.

[21] Theodor Adorno and Hanns Eisler, *Composing for the Films* (London: Athlone Press, 1994 [1947]), 74.

[22] See Jean Cocteau, *Beauty and the Beast: Diary of a Film,* trans., Ronald Duncan (New York: Dover, 1972), 128.

[23] Adorno and Eisler, *Composing for the Films,* 72.

[24] Adorno, Theodor W., *Quasi una Fantasia,* trans., Rodney Livingston (London: Verso, 1992 [1963]), 268.

an incorporated visual text.[25] Undoubtedly Glass's opera conforms to an aesthetic of montage and audiovisual counterpoint, which is implied primarily through the looseness of the audiovisual contract. This is most striking in live performances, where the physical presence of the musicians onstage alongside their cinematic doubles makes constructivist readings almost unavoidable.[26] But the process of dialogue implied in the relationship is not entirely neutral or "equal"; it has a historical dimension, which I consider later.

CONVERGING BODIES

Just how the dialectic of convergence and divergence works in *La Belle* is best illustrated with the help of an example. A conspicuous moment of convergence occurs when Beast begins to win Beauty's affections while promenading with her through the grounds of his castle (DVD, 0:49:00; score, 0:48:11). The protagonists' hands lock for the first time as they descend a flight of stairs in step with each other and the music. Close synchronization brings to mind Steiner's classic "mickey mousing" technique as well as the dance sequences of Hollywood musicals. A rising anacrusis at the beginning of the section accompanies the upward movement of the couple's hands, the peak of this gesture occurring on an accented first beat. As the melody drops in stepwise motion, an outward zoom brings the couple's lower torsos into frame and eventually their legs, just in time to capture footsteps falling on accented third beats as they continue their ceremonious descent (see Figure 5.6.).

This theme, which like Beast's love theme becomes emblematic of the central character pairing and their unlikely emotional bond, is repeated in the later parts of the film, signaling the closest interlocking of audiovisual materials in the opera and, not coincidentally, some of its most kinetic imagery. In Glass's words, this is "music [the couple] goes places together with" (CD booklet). This is confirmed in several scenes, including a passionate encounter toward the end of the film where Beauty returns in haste from her bedroom in the "real world" to a parallel room in the castle in order to rescue a dying Beast (1:22:10). As the heroine speeds through the castle grounds, halting in time with musical cadences and hailing her companion in closely synched physical and musical gestures, "light-footed" triplet figures in the upper register seem to propel her partially concealed feet (1:23:55). Here the music

[25]   Walter Benjamin, "The Work of Art in the Age of Mechanical Reproduction," in Hannah Arendt, ed., Harry Zohn trans., *Illuminations: Essays and Reflections* (New York: Schocken, 1968), 217–51, 228.

[26]   In the DVD adaptation of the opera, in contrast, the singers' bodies are invisible, making it easier for spectators to reconstitute an "integrated performance" by melding sounds to visual actions utilizing what Chion calls synchresis. Michel Chion, *Audio-Vision: Sound on Screen* (New York: Columbia University Press, 1994), 63–55.

Figure 5.6 Audiovisual convergence in Promenade in the Garden, *La Belle et la Bête*. An Opera by Philip Glass. Based on the scenario by Jean Cocteau © 1994 Dunvagen Music Publishers Inc. Used by permission.

temporalizes the visual action, providing a greater sense of temporal animation as well as implying movement that is not represented onscreen.[27]

The iambic rhythms of Glass's majestic waltz combine with the couple's stately demeanor to transform these events into the dramatic pinnacles of the opera. Resembling the use of Waltz No. 2 from Shostakovich's Jazz Suite in Stanley Kubrick's *Eyes Wide Shut* (1999), or a neo-Gothic Danny Elfman film score, a sense

[27] Chion, *Audio-Vision*, 13–16.

of Old World grandeur and gravitas is projected onto the visuals by music that is not without humor.[28] Some residue of the "material and cultural wealth of imperial Vienna" continues to inform the reception of such music, reinforced through the couple's formal attire and their closely synchronized bodily gestures.[29] This aspect is further accentuated through close-ups of Cocteau's symbol of artistic nobility, the Beast's glove, and a long shot of the chateau's ornate arcades.

Matching up better than the original score with the decadent splendor of the *mise-en-scène*, there is nevertheless something uncanny, something not quite right about this take on the subject matter. Undoubtedly, this has something to do with the recognition of a historical lineage that spans practices of ironic distancing across Russian neo-classicism and postmodernist artistic practices. Not lost on composers of both eras is the mechanical aspect of the waltz, something Teresa Magdanz has researched in an important article, "The Waltz: Technology's Muse."[30] Magdanz shows how the subjectivities afforded by the waltz have been conditioned throughout its history by a close relationship to technologies of musical production and consumption, from early uses in barrel organs to fairground rides and, more recently, Kubrick's revolving spaceships. In her wide-ranging historical exposition, the revolving motion of dancers finds parallels in the revolutions of the organ-grinders wheel, which were intended to coincide with a single bar of waltz-time; the weightless thrill of a merry-go-round; and the interlocking wheels of machinery that brought about the industrial revolution (during the height of the waltz's popularity). In this way, the dance became a "human response to the dynamics of mechanical-cum-*human* motion,"[31] and a means of "dream[ing] through the machine."[32] It is in this weightless and elegant fashion, that Cocteau's couple "travel together"; much like the lifeless characters on a merry-go-round whose actions simulate but do not quite conform to our expectations of natural acts.

The dreamlike and mechanical qualities of the scene are accentuated through aspects of Glass's compositional style, not least his characteristic mechanical handling of rhythmic texture (he has described the technique as "wheels-within-wheels") combined with the use of synthetic sound textures. Key to the design of this composition, though, is the fact that the click-track that propels the music is all the time synchronized with another piece of machinery, the film projector—a relationship the viewer-auditor must on some level confront, due to the simultaneous

---

[28]   Gorbman has examined the significance of such Old World music in Kubrick's *Eyes Wide Shut*: Claudia Gorbman, "Ears Wide Open: Kubrick's Music," in Phil Powrie and Robyn Stilwell, eds., *Changing Tunes: The Use of Pre-existing Music in Film* (Aldershot: Ashgate, 2006), 3–18, 7.

[29]   Lawrence Kramer, *Musical Meaning: Toward a Critical History* (Berkeley: University of California Press, 2002), 227.

[30]   Teresa Magdanz, "The Waltz: Technology's Muse," *Journal of Popular Music Studies* 18/3 (December 2006): 251–81.

[31]   Ibid., 275.   [32]   Ibid., 252.

presence of singers and their cinematic doubles, who become little more than ventriloquists dummies—and the looseness of the synchronization, particularly evident when the characters sing.

DIVERGENT VOICES

An aesthetic of divergence is visibly inscribed, therefore, in Glass's writing from the voice. A striking example is found immediately following the stairway descent. Here Beauty allows Beast to drink from her hands, a mark of the couple's growing intimacy. A dialogue ensues between Beauty and her feral captor, filmed as a shot/reverse shot sequence in extreme close-up and with a softening filter on the lens. "Doesn't it revolt you to serve me water with your hands?" ("C'la ne vous répugne pas? De me donne à boire?"), Beast asks his companion in near-perfect synchronization; to which she responds in tender tones, "No, Beast. It gives me pleasure. I would never wish to cause you pain." ("Non, la Bête, c'la me plaît. Je ne voudrais jamais vous causer la moindre peine.") Only the initial sentence of this dialogue is synchronized naturalistically, however. In the original film, Beauty lingers over her words, lowering her eyes demurely and pausing for effect before the final admission of attachment. Singing Beauty, in contrast, presses on in a steady stream of eighth notes, meeting up with her cinematic double only at the final syllable. The audiovisual result is almost an entire measure of live singing during which the corresponding actor's lips remain resolutely sealed. It is possible, of course, to regard this ebb and flow of close and loose synchronization as an accidental outcome of the composer's less than perfect approach to synchronizing the two media. But to hold this view is to disregard the teasing reciprocity of sound and vision—the disruptive force of ventriloquist's dummies that have minds of their own.

Glass speaks of a new "authority" in his writing for the voice in *La Belle*.[33] By this he means the relationship between melody and harmony, resulting in a floating quality in the melodic line, a sense of nonattachment, which can be recognized also in earlier operatic works by the same composer, such as *Satyagraha*. But in *La Belle* the authority accorded to the voice is greater. This can, of course, be attributed in traditional fashion to the composer's choice of notes and their rhythmic setting. But it is also bound up with the technological design of the opera and with an aleatory element that infuses the compositional work. Semantically significant vocal phrases are synchronized, where possible, to beats, and clever advantage is taken of backs turned to the camera, shadowy lighting and long shots. Often, though, the positioning of phrases in musical time cannot be comfortably anchored to corresponding images, leaving two choices: disregard the timing of dialogue in the film, thereby

---

[33] Glass quoted in Cott, "A Conversation," 18.

accentuating the gap between singer and actor; or allow the temporal flow of the film—if you like, the *film's* authority (in an auteurist reading, Cocteau's authority)—to determine how the vocal part is synchronized to the musical accompaniment. Throughout the opera, voices swing between these poles, sometimes interlocking seamlessly with visual time—resulting in more of a randomized musical feel—sometimes adhering to the temporal requirements of the musical accompaniment, even if this is at the expense of audiovisual unity.

This element of compromise inscribes a sense of distance—spatial and temporal—between the contemporary singers and their acting counterparts, which can be thought of as reinforcing an awareness of dialogue between present-day performers and actors in the film. This visibly and audibly indicated Bakhtinian polyglossia (or many-voicedness), and the tensions engendered in performances between the present day and the past (recall that the cinematic voices are silenced), might explain why Glass calls the opera an unintentional "deconstructed version of the movie."[34] More than deconstructing Cocteau's original, the presence and telling absence of other "voices" challenges traditional ideas concerning the nature of creative activity—as issuing unmediated from a single composer/author, and remaining a static, inviolable entity across time. Seen and heard this way, *La Belle* becomes an exercise in audiovisual dialogue whose constructivist ethos spotlights the performative while drawing attention to new forms of alienation (namely, the posthuman) that characterize experiences of temporality in the digital age.

Much of what has been discussed here evidences how Glass imbues his music with a sense of mechanized agency that parallels the relentless action of the film projector (for us, the DVD player). Such a concerted avoidance of the natural suggests a subjective orientation that, while mindful of the perils of relinquishing control, takes a new kind of pleasure—saturated with anxiety—in the very recognition of this condition. Much has been written about this aspect of postminimalist music, including Naomi Cumming's important work on Steve Reich.[35] Minimalism's engagement with the mechanized muse undoubtedly extends back to the origins of the style and to the processes favored by Riley, Reich and others in their work with tape loops and beyond. Recent postminimalist practice continues to offer listeners a way to dream through machinery—dreams that are not always comforting. These dreams are offered in response to those of early generations, incorporated here in the form of musical representations of sublime grandeur and ceremonial pomp, which they to some extent dismantle.

This might be interpreted as an extension of a project Lyotard outlined in his early writing on the postmodern sublime, where what he calls "the unpresentable" is encoded in strategies of textual incorporation rather than expressive content—

[34] Ibid., 20.
[35] Naomi Cumming, "The Horrors of Identification: Reich's *Different Trains,*" *Perspectives of New Music* 35/1 (1997): 121–52.

with the caveat that the style has now progressed beyond its earlier aversion to content; it is how the content is *presented* that is now paramount.[36] For Lyotard, the sublime, as expressed in early postmodernist forms, was bound up with an undercurrent of indeterminism and emptiness that resides within the unfolding encounter with the art object. The anxiety experienced by the listener concerning what might happen next (the fact that *nothing* might happen), goes to the heart of this theorist's conception of the sublime, which has its origin in a Burkean understanding of the term.[37] Specifically, Burke's idea of privation, which subsumes such categories as vacuity, darkness, solitude and silence, occupies a privileged position in Lyotard's epistemological apparatus.[38] But privation in the context of discussions of the sublime implies only the threat of loss—loss of experience, loss of an object, and ultimately loss of subjectivity. The loss itself never actually happens, which imparts to experiences an ambivalent tension between our imaginative power to call up the unfathomable and an affective response of relief when it fails to actualize: an intoxicating cocktail of pleasure and pain.[39] It is this anxiety and the intensification of experience it brings about that goes to the heart of experiences of false synchronic relations in *La Belle*. Performances teeter on the brink of disintegration (literally, they threaten to split in two), which heightens the *relief* of pulling through and surviving an encounter with the void—and with a deftness of compositional hand that only amplifies the sense of relief.[40]

All of this emphasis on dehumanization and relinquishment of subjectivity might sound glum, but, fortunately, Glass's music doesn't. This is largely thanks to his writing for the voice, not least Beauty's quicksilver soprano, a significant humanizing element, whose function in relation to the surrounding musical milieu is social through and through, not least because of the singer's physical embodiment in live performances. Throughout the opera, Beauty lives up to her name, negotiating the underlying musical terrain in a captivating series of trickles and turns, all the while steadfastly resisting the temptation to fall into line with the rhythmic imperative (the tyranny?) of the musical accompaniment. More important, she keeps her distance when it comes to rhythms whose origins are further removed in time. Weaving a narrative web of social divergence and euphoric convergence, the opera thereby subverts the teleological imperative of existing forms by binding them to the humanely mechanized flow of the unfolding present.

---

[36] Jean-François Lyotard, *The Postmodern Condition: A Report on Knowledge*, trans. Geoff Bennington and Brian Massumi (Minneapolis: University of Minnesota Press, 1984), 81.

[37] Jean-François Lyotard, "The Sublime and the Avant-Garde," in Thomas Docherty, ed., *Postmodernism: A Reader* (New York: Columbia University Press, 1993), 244–56, 246. On the postmodernist sublime, see also Philip Shaw, *The Sublime*, The New Critical Idiom series (Abingdon and New York: Routledge, 2006), 115–30.

[38] See Edmund Burke, *A Philosophical Inquiry into the Origin of our Ideas of the Sublime and the Beautiful* (London: Routledge and Kegan Paul, 1958), 71.

[39] See also Shaw, *The Sublime*, 53–55.   [40] Ibid., 251.

The Dark Side of Oz: Syncing as Reading Against the Grain

More extreme, perhaps, than Glass's reworking of Cocteau's film are instances where two or more landmark texts of popular culture are singled out by composers/compositors and made, by virtue of their proximity, to comment on each other. Parodic displacement of this kind has been ubiquitous for some years in the hip hop culture of scratching and remix. Some of this has carried over into the audiovisual sphere in MTV's *Mash* series, where not only musical recordings but also the accompanying music videos are mashed up, often to the greatest effect when the resulting combinations can be recognized as incongruous and somehow transformational. A parallel phenomenon is the Internet-mediated practice of "syncing" classic movies with classic rock albums to produce new audiovisual conglomerations. The paradigmatic instance of this was first reported on the user-group "alt.music.pink-floyd" in the mid-1990s and involved the synchronization of Pink Floyd's *Dark Side of the Moon* (1976) with the MGM children's film classic, *The Wizard of Oz* (dir. Victor Fleming, 1939). Subsequently, the phenomenon has expanded to include numerous other combinations of popular music and film, receiving substantial coverage on radio and television and stimulating a significant amount of—often impassioned—debate; including, in this instance, rebuttals from *Dark Side of the Moon* producer, Alan Parsons, and Pink Floyd band member, David Gilmore: "Thirty years later you get *The Wizard of Oz* coming along to stun you. Someone once showed me how that worked, or didn't work. How did I feel? *Weary*."[41]

Subsuming "syncing" practices under the category of "urban myth," cultural theorists Lee Barron and Ian Inglis endeavor to explain *Dark Side of Oz*, as it has come to be known by some enthusiasts, by drawing on an assortment of recent theory, including media theorist Manuel Castells's notion of "the network society."[42] Above all, their discussion redirects attention toward practices of "misreading" associated with syncing practices, which are construed as a means for fans to achieve self-empowerment. The categories they assign practitioners—the believer, the cynic, the entertainer and the expert—cover a range of plausible motivations for the propagation of these "urban myths." The theory works well in some cases (when false knowledge is clearly propagated) and the theoretical models these writers employ match the subject well. In this case, however, the designation urban myth nevertheless implies some level of misguidedness on the part of the users (or synchronizers), who are driven more by a desire for "self-aggrandizement, group membership and

---

[41]   Gilmore quoted in John Harris, *The Dark Side of the Moon: The Making of the Pink Floyd Masterpiece* (Fourth Estate: London, 2005), 7.

[42]   Lee Barron and Ian Inglis, "'We're Not in Kansas Any More': Music, Myth and Narrative Structure on *The Dark Side of the Moon*," in Reising, ed., *The Legacy of Pink Floyd's Dark Side of the Moon*, 56–66.

socio-cultural status...than they are by the spirit of objective enquiry."[43] Some of those who promote syncing (sometimes referred to by the Jungian designation "synchronicity") are without question misguided, especially those who promote dubious conspiracy theories or indulge in new-agey metaphysical speculation. It is possible to understand syncing differently, however, by examining how the *Dark Side of Oz* works (and does not work) audiovisually and by taking into account different strategies of consumption and *prosumption* that the audiovisual form affords.[44] Viewed in this way, the "mashing up" of *Wizard* and *Dark Side* might for certain users have as much to do with myth-busting as myth-making. To provide substance to this assertion, it is necessary to take a brief analytical diversion.

UNPACKING THE DARK SIDE

The mode of synchronization that has received the most widespread endorsement requires that Pink Floyd's CD be started concomitantly with the third roar of the MGM lion immediately prior to the title sequence of *Wizard*. If this is done correctly with an NTSC copy of the film,[45] the audio-viewer can expect to perceive a number of striking coincidences. Some websites list more than a hundred of these and require the album to be run three times in succession. Most accounts agree, however, that the most convincing sync-points occur during the album's first hearing and are relatively small in number, if significant qualitatively.

An obvious sync-point occurs only three minutes into the film when Dorothy falls into a pigpen after balancing on a farmyard fence. This cinematic action coincides with Gilmore's emotive line, "balanced on the biggest wave, you race toward an early grave." With Dorothy wallowing in mud, the music segues into the techno-styled "On the Run," which matches the frenetic pace of the visuals as a farmhand rushes to rescue the young woman, played by the effervescent Judy Garland, only to be troubled by his heart ("race toward an early grave"). In an uncanny transformation, the same actor appears later in the film as the Tin Man, a character who does

---

[43] Ibid., 64.

[44] The term "prosumption" implies a move toward production among consumers in the digital age. See George Ritzer and Nathan Jurgenson, "Production, Consumption, Prosumption: The Nature of the Capitalism in the Age of the Digital 'Prosumer,'" *Journal of Consumer Culture* 10/1 (1994): 13–36.

[45] NTSC (National Television System Committee) is the standard television system in North America and several other countries. PAL (Phase Alternative Line) is a common convention in many other countries, including most of Europe. PAL films adapted from U.S.-produced feature films are generally made to run 4 percent faster due to the different frame-per-second rates of the two conventions (24 frames-per-second for NTSC films; 25 frames-per-second for PAL film). This can have a significant impact on how film soundtracks sound, changing the pitch and duration of both music and speech. Consequently, any attempts to synchronize films in a consistent way with external sound sources when switching between the two conventions will often run into difficulties (similarly playing along with performed music will often require tuning down). This lesson was learnt the hard way during my first attempts to lecture on this subject apropos of both case studies presented in this chapter.

not possess a heart. This realization is ironically commented on at the end of the album, where Dorothy and the Scarecrow appear to be listening to heartbeats emanating from the Tin Man's chest.

In place of the iconic song "Somewhere Over the Rainbow," the Pink Floyd soundtrack is characterized by strongly anempathetic audiovisual relations in the ensuing action. The throbbing sound of a VCS3 synthesizer playing automated arpeggios at breakneck speed, Gilmore's Doppler-effect simulations on electric guitar, the concrete sounds of running footsteps, and airplanes in flight all suggest a dystopic vision of postindustrial life. Here we find aural confirmation of Marx's bleak vision of the machine as servicing belligerent capitalist forces, causing a wave of disenchantment to engulf all aspects of modern life. This sonic vision provides an unnerving counterpoint to black and white, preindustrial, agrarian life as portrayed on the screen. While both scenarios suggest an underlying current of discontent, the surrogate soundtrack consistently undermines Dorothy's utopian dream of escape, seeming to offer cynical commentary on such misplaced optimism. This is most evident following this character's vertiginous tornado-borne flight, when she descends to the colorful world of Oz, transformed by Pink Floyd into a sneering parody of the Adornian culture industry by the addition of sounds from cash registers that precede the track "Money."

Because of the affective transformations brought about by the addition of the Pink Floyd soundtrack (and the subtraction of the original soundtrack), Dorothy in *Dark Side of Oz* takes on a decidedly more incredulous and world-wise persona than in the original film; a dark understudy of sorts who could be compared with the fallible Dorothy substitute in David Lynch's *Wild at Heart*. Technological alienation, and the unseen forces of capitalism that drive it, is posited as the primary agent of this transformation, in which the terrifying power of Nature is framed by the unflagging rhythms of Floyd's pulsating synthesizer and an automated cash-register loop. Thus the self-contained or "autopoietic" agency of the machine, as theorized by Deleuze and Gauttari, can be seen as harnessing the limitless power of Nature in a transformation of libidinal energy that is nothing if it is not sublime.[46] It is tempting to classify invocations of the sublime in this instance as belonging not only to postmodernism, but also to the digital age, given the fact that *Dark Side of Oz* is now available on (illegal) premixed DVDs. Vincent Mosco has coined the term the "digital sublime" to account for a wide range of phenomena belonging to the current era, from the dot.com bubble burst to the World Trade Center terrorist attacks.[47] An affinity with turntablism should be noted, however, in early accounts of syncing, which relied solely on uses of analog technologies: VHS videos and long-playing vinyl records. This matters

[46]   See Gilles Deleuze and Félix Guattari, *Anti-Oedipus: Capitalism and Schizophrenia*, trans. Robert Hurley, Mark Seem, and Helen Lane (Minneapolis: University of Minnesota Press, 1983); Gilles Deleuze and Félix Guattari, *A Thousand Plateaus: Capitalism and Schizophrenia*, trans. Brian Massumi (Minneapolis: University of Minnesota Press, 1986).

[47]   Vincent Mosco, *The Digital Sublime: Myth, Power, and Cyberspace* (Cambridge, MA: MIT Press, 2004).

because an element of anti-teleological retro-play might be perceived in how outmoded technologies were used in early instances of syncing. These two imperfect technologies were clearly never intended to be combined, just as the same could be said of the original audiovisual artifacts. The element of skill involved in the act of syncing, combined with a degree of pleasure to be gleaned from the idea that the technologies might be resisting the agency of the synchronizer, contribute to the unique pleasures of syncing in its original (predigital) manifestations.

Technology is also commented on explicitly in the content of these two forms. Images of technological dystopia feature prominently in *Dark Side* and can be found in other Pink Floyd music, including, most notably, the song "Welcome to the Machine" (1975). As Joseph Auner has commented, "these representations operate within an essentially modernist teleology."[48] It is older technologies, therefore, such as the sound of an FM radio on the track "Wish You Were Here," that are marked, while the transparency of contemporary recording technology goes unquestioned.[49] Things are more complicated in *Wizard*. Here preindustrial agrarian life is depicted in black and white, while the tainted utopia of Oz is filmed in state of the art Technicolor. Colored film is ostensibly the unmarked (or natural) form, but an argument could be supported that the reverse is the case, since the saturated colors of Oz today seem exaggerated or hyperreal, thereby drawing attention to its artifice. In this respect, modernity is revealed as reveling in artifice, while the technology that produced this parallel reality is called into question through the actions of the elusive Wizard, who turns out to be nothing more than an elderly man concealed behind machine-generated simulacra.

Of course, it is in the visibly artificial domain of Oz that Dorothy comes into her own, something we understand the second we notice how her perceptions of Kansas have changed when she awakens from her dream. Those who subscribe to revisionist ideas about cultural identity have seized upon this aspect with enthusiasm. Salman Rushdie, for example, argues that the film holds a strong appeal to expatriates who harbor ambivalent feelings toward their "homeland."[50] As Rushdie's own magical-realist writing attests, it is the power of fantasy, of the imagination, that is foremost in helping expatriate escapees to realize their dreams. Distance allows the homeland to be seen with different eyes, as happens when the fantasy world of Oz is made to reflect back on Pink Floyd's rock masterpiece and vice versa.

FROM THE SUBLIME TO THE COUNTER-SUBLIME

As I indicated earlier, the narratives of *Wizard* and *Dark Side of the Moon* are both inhabited by the romantic trope of the sublime. This is reflected in the album's

---

[48] Joseph Auner, "Making Old Machines Speak: Images of Technology in Recent Music," *Echo* 2/2 (2000): 32 pars, February 13, 2004, http://www.humnet.ucla.edu/echo, para. 7, retrieved December 10, 2010.

[49] Ibid., para. 11.

[50] See Salman Rushdie, *The Wizard of Oz*, BFI Film Classics (London: BFI, 1992), 9–23.

title, which posits the moon's dark side as a repository for human responses to the unknown, the unexplored, the uninhabitable, death, the insane and the unfathomably large. All of these qualities are conventional markers of the sublime as expounded by Burke and Kant. The tornado scene of *Wizard* exemplifies the romantic sublime in its depiction of Nature's awe-inspiring power. Through Clare Torry's ecstatic vocalese on "Great Gig in the Sky," synced in *Dark Side of Oz* with this scene, the sublime power of Nature is marked in a conventional way as "feminine" in a stirring of the passions that is intoxicatingly powerful.[51] The technocratic Wizard attempts to harness some of this power in the film's penultimate scene, its apparent purpose being to comment on the folly of human pretenses to divine power. The Wizard's technologically enhanced power is no match for the natural and transcendental forces that transported Dorothy to Oz in the first place.

A familiar theme already in the 1930s, when *The Wizard of Oz* was produced, a preoccupation with the technological sublime was taking an even stronger hold over the popular imagination by the 1970s, when *Dark Side of the Moon* was recorded, as human achievements were seen by a growing number of commentators as rivaling transcendental forces.[52] During the course of the twentieth century, opinions have been split down the middle between a techno-optimism that hailed every advance in technology as a revelation and a techno-pessimism that saw each new technological implementation as bringing with it new levels of estrangement from an Edenic garden (see chapter 7 for more on utopian constructions of the pretechnological).[53] Echoes of the latter attitude are summoned in Baudrillard's neo-Platonic vision of a ubiquitous virtual reality, or simulacrum, produced under the deleterious thrall of digital technologies, which have infiltrated every facet of modern life (discussed more fully in chapter 6). Pink Floyd's technological dystopia might be seen in a similar light, as arising from a convergence of discourses that understood the impact of technology in largely pessimistic terms: as an instrument of malevolent industrial forces that block human self-realization through the effacement of individual agency. *Dark Side of Oz* is more than the sum of its parts, however. Because of the fragmented nature of the audiovisual discourse in this compound form and the subjective damage that is implied through the loss of the original soundtrack (see chapters 3 and 4 on the traumatic effects of diegetic silencing in *Be Kind Rewind* and *Yes*), a new set of considerations is projected onto the first, raising the possibility of understanding syncing as a metapractice demanding interpretation on its own terms.

---

[51] See Sheila Whiteley, "Prismatic Passion: The Enigma of 'The Great Gig in the Sky,'" in Reising, ed., *The Legacy of Pink Floyd's Dark Side of the Moon*, 143–57.

[52] See Leo Marx, *The Machine in the Garden: Technology and the Pastoral Ideal in America* (Oxford: Oxford University Press, 1964); David Nye, *American Technological Sublime* (Cambridge, MA: MIT Press, 1994); Vincent Mosco, *The Digital Sublime: Myth, Power, and Cyberspace* (Cambridge, MA: MIT Press, 2004).

[53] Merritt Roe Smith and Leo Marx, *Does Technology Drive History? The Dilemma of Technological Determinism* (Cambridge, MA: MIT Press, 1994).

The combination of the two synchronized forms would not work to the extent that it does if they did not have something in common in the first place. Resemblances between the two on a narrative level go beyond the superficial. Barron and Inglis touch on this when they draw attention to similarities between the constructions of "home" in the two forms, as well as depictions of the "alien" domains of Oz and the moon.[54] An even tighter affective bond might be suggested by the thematics of the sublime, augmented in both instances to subsume contemporary technologies. In this respect the two forms evoke similar "structures of feeling," a designation that implies more than formal resemblance. Add to this Chion's idea of synchresis, which turns temporal coincidences into acts of semiotic exchange, and convergences between the two forms become either less or more remarkable, depending on the point of view of the beholder.

Neither of the two forms emerges unscathed, however, from their encounter. The very act of syncing steals agency away from the original artists, relocating it either in the intentions of users or in the technology itself, thereby imparting to it an eerie, uncanny quality. In *Dark Side of Oz* like Glass's *La Belle*, a mechanical process is initiated that once started cannot be stopped. In the former, the exclusive use of prerecorded materials makes the transfer of agency to spectators more likely, since they are responsible for initially synchronizing the two media, and they are encouraged by the loose character of the audiovisual contract to employ "active" interpretive strategies when searching for possible sync-points. Once the playback has been initiated, however, very little control is exerted over the artistic "end product." In a sense, control is relinquished, handed over to the reproductive machinery. It is here that one might speak of a technological counter-sublime—in the relentless unfolding of the parallel narratives, which continues on its course even when links between the two are at their most tenuous.[55] And the "miraculous" moments of convergence that punctuate performances seem to suggest that there is purpose as well as method to this technologically mediated madness. Precisely where this purpose lies, however, is difficult to ascertain—agency in such circumstance becomes unstable, even demonic (hence the preponderance of conspiracy theories surrounding the phenomenon).

In different ways, both of the cases discussed in this chapter can be understood in light of Harold Bloom's concepts of "anxiety of influence" and "daemonization," according to which artistic incorporation is viewed as a means for the poet to enfold and neutralize an existing notion of the sublime. "Turning against the precursor's

[54] Barron and Inglis, "We're Not in Kansas," 65.

[55] This formulation overlaps with Jameson's idea of the technological sublime in postmodernism, which focuses on the transfer of agency to machines. Fredric Jameson, *Postmodernism or The Cultural Logic of Late Capitalism* (Durham, NC: Duke University Press, 1991), 34–35. Birringer instructively discusses the technological sublime in postmodern theater; and Chapman in relation to drum'n'bass music (2004). Johannes Birringer, *Theatre, Theory, Postmodernism* (Bloomington: Indiana University Press, 1993). Fink has theorized what he calls the "media sublime" in relation to the repetitive musical structures of minimalist music. Robert Fink, *Repeating Ourselves: American Minimal Music as Cultural Practice* (Berkeley: University of California Press, 2005), 120–66.

Sublime," Bloom writes, "the newly strong poet undergoes *daemonization*, a Counter-Sublime whose function suggests the precursor's relative weakness."[56] Blooms theorization implies an aspect of resistance across generations that can be recognized in greater or lesser measure in both of the above instances. Not all aspects of Bloom's theorization match the examples I provide, however. The idea of incorporated material being "equivalent to repressed material in the mental life of the individual"[57] makes sense when it comes to canonical masterworks of poetry and music in Romanticism and Modernism. In these, critics have argued that the identity of the precursor is effaced. This is not the case in the examples I discuss, including Glass's engagement with Cocteau, which is suggestive of a citational attitude in which homage and indebtedness to precursors are openly acknowledged. The suppression of the original soundtrack could, however, be seen to serve a more traditional (Oedipal) function, effectively silencing the original film and thereby consigning it to the past. In this way, and in the gaps and discontinuities caused by imperfectly realized synchronization in performances, these new compound works adhere to the logic of Lyotard's postmodernist (counter) sublime—a sublime that is humanly instructed but technologically driven. Both *La Belle* and *Dark Side of Oz*, therefore, can be understood as forms of reading (and in a limited sense, *writing*) against the grain, although Glass's deconstruction of Cocteau's film is certainly not derisory, while the attribution of critical intent to those who sync *Dark Side* with *Wizard* depends largely on whose story one chooses to listens to.

"THE SUN IS ECLIPSED BY THE MOON"— SUBVERSION AND THE MISPRISM OF LAUGHTER

Los Angeles circa 1995 is the likely birthplace of the syncing phenomenon, if posts on the Pink Floyd user-group and one of the earliest popular websites on the subject are accurate.[58] Whether myth or fact, the idea of Tinseltown as a speculative point of origin seems apt.[59] If there is to be a geographical point of origin for

---

[56] Harold Bloom, *The Anxiety of Influence: A Theory of Poetry* (London: Oxford University Press, 1973). Musicological writing that has utilized Bloom's theory includes: Joseph Straus, "The 'Anxiety of Influence' in Twentieth-Century Music," *The Journal of Musicology* 9/4 (1991): 430–47; Marcia Citron, *Gender and the Musical Canon* (Cambridge: Cambridge University Press, 1993), 430–47; Lloyd Whitesell, "Men with a Past: Music and the 'Anxiety of Influence,'" *Nineteenth-Century Music* 18/2 (1994): 152–67; Raymond Knapp, "Brahms and the Anxiety of Allusion," *Journal of Musicological Research* 18 (1998): 1–30; and Richardson, *Singing Archaeology. Philip Glass's Akhnaten*, 188–99.

[57] Freud cited in Bloom, *The Anxiety of Influence*, 109.

[58] See Charles Savage, "The Dark Side of the Rainbow Website," August 1, 1995, http://members.aol.com/rbsavage/floydwizard.html, retrieved October 25, 2006.

[59] It seems apt for me personally also because my first exposure to *Dark Side of Oz* was when conducting postdoctoral research in the Department of Musicology at UCLA in 1996. My colleague Jim Westby was the first person to draw my attention to the subject.

syncing, then what better location than a city whose identity changes fundamentally from block to block.[60] More pertinent still, it is a location that has become synonymous with all the glitz and glamour of the Hollywood dream machine. Tempting though this line of thinking might be, Barron and Inglis are undoubtedly justified in considering this to be a phenomenon of the Internet and "the network society." The distinctive combination of intensified yet privative experience conveyed in *Dark Side of Oz* certainly resonates with modes of subjectivity distinctive to the information age, in which an element of semantic indeterminacy is to be expected.

Does the dawn of the information age, then, signal the demise of interpretive communities? Or is identity these days constructed more flexibly, involving looser and more voluntary affiliations that are established individually in the context of nonlocalized spaces of flows? This looser frame of reference brings to mind the surrealists' attitude toward found objects, especially the possibilities such objects afforded for re-enchantment when viewed with an aestheticizing eye. Such an attitude might be considered willful misreading; not syncing but *mis*-syncing. Even so it presupposes alignments that might be shared intersubjectively in the context of the virtual communities and social networks of the digital age. The forms we discussed seem idiomatic to such contexts, designed for multiple decodings that reflect the taste cultures of disparate and layered constituencies.

When considering affiliations that are unbound by conventional assumptions concerning place and community, it matters a great deal that there exists a long and colorful history of misreading when it comes to both of these texts. A significant "coincidence" in the reception of *Wizard* and *Dark Side of the Moon* is the prominent position both have occupied in drug "countercultures." Undoubtedly this has something to do with the "trippy" and "surreal" nature of both of the existing texts and with the fact that both contain allusions, direct or indirect, to narcotic experiences.[61] This could be a factor behind why they ended up being synced together in the first place. Another rationale for appropriative "misreadings" warrants serious consideration: the immense popularity of the film among sexual minorities. The plot of *Wizard* has an obvious appeal to such constituencies, dealing as it does with issues of escape and self-realization. In addition, the film's saturated Technicolor hues and effervescent cast of characters, everything from a dancing troupe of midgets to the Wicked Witch of the West, betrays a camp sensibility that research has attributed to a significant gay presence on the MGM-Freed roster of employees.[62]

[60] See, for example, George Lipsitz, "Cruising Around the Historical Bloc: Postmodernism and Popular Music in Los Angeles," *Cultural Critique* 5 (1986): 157–77.

[61] On the significance of both texts in drug cultures, see Raymond Knapp, *The American Musical, and the Performance of Personal Identity* (Princeton, NJ: Princeton University Press, 2006), 134–36.

[62] Matthew Tinkcom, "'Working Like a Homosexual': Camp Visual Codes and the Labor of Gay Subjects in the MGM Freed unit," *Cinema Journal* 35/2 (1996): 24–42; Steven Cohan, *Incongruous Entertainment: Camp, Cultural Value, and the MGM Musical* (Durham, NC: Duke University Press, 2005), 41–87.

As discussed previously, moreover, Garland's ability to overplay the drama while at the same time projecting an attitude of amused detachment has been widely understood as signifying camp.[63]

The recognition of a potentially (although not *necessarily*) subversive camp subtext in *Dark Side of Oz* should not be viewed as depending solely on knowledge concerning the reception history of one of its source texts. A large subsection of "users" will inevitably take both source texts at face value (children's cinema meets serious rock), or indulge in one of the several available conspiracy theories. Still, I maintain that the unstable nature of the audiovisual contract, combined with some of the evidence on reception, points toward a proclivity for reading against the grain, thereby transforming the intentions of creators. The motives for this are likely to be manifold. A subtext of jocular resistance will in all likelihood be picked up on by those familiar with existing "misreadings" of *Wizard*, those whose feelings toward *Dark Side* are ambivalent—like "Great Gig" singer Clare Torry, who initially found the idea of the project "pretentious"—or those who are otherwise predisposed toward deconstructive strategies (or "paranoid" strategies, to borrow Sedgwick's terminology).[64] For these audiences, the inclusion of Dorothy, the Tin Man, and the Munchkins alongside Floyd's musical evocations of existential angst might be seen as camping up and thereby dethroning a piece of popular culture that is often held to take itself too seriously. By intentionally misreading the album's serious content, audiences become complicit in an act as violently irreverent as the cyclone that lifts Dorothy from the ground and dumps her in the alien yet effervescent domain of Oz. (It is possible, I should add, to partake of such subversive pleasures while viewing Pink Floyd's achievements with considerable affection.)

Notwithstanding the motives of those who have authored websites on subject, the most common reaction I have encountered when lecturing on *Dark Side of Oz* is one of wry amusement. The synced up—or pimped up—hybrid work is perceived as a deliberate misprism of artistic intention that transforms originals, in spirit and form. Vacillating between the sublime and the ridiculous, representation and its transcendence, the effects produced resemble those investigated by Žižek in his analysis of David Lynch's *Lost Highway*.[65] Gender is implicated in any consideration of the Burkean and Kantian sublime, since this quality has conventionally been associated with masculinity, in contrast with the beautiful, which is assumed to be feminine. An element of ridicule can decamp the premises of this binary construct. Camp is the operative word here, since the qualities discussed in the previous chapter are equally germane in this context. Camp is expressed through an emphasis

[63] Richard Dyer, *Heavenly Bodies* (Basingstoke: Macmillan, 1986), 178–86; Cohan, *Incongruous Entertainment*, 25–27.

[64] Whiteley, "Prismatic Passion," 150.

[65] Slavoj Žižek, *The Art of the Ridiculous Sublime: On David Lynch's Lost Highway* (Washington: University of Washington Press, 2000).

on aesthetic stylization and the obvious artifice of the recombined forms. It seeps through the conventional genre assumptions surrounding opera and the film musical, which are present in the source and "destination" genres we have been discussing.

Coda Number 3: Resurrecting the Wizard in Popular Song

This is the third consecutive chapter where I consider it instructive to extend the terms of the discussion in a final section to encompass phenomena belonging more broadly to the dominion of alternative popular music. Conspicuously similar in spirit to the *Dark Side of Oz* is the burlesque pop group the Scissor Sisters' satirical cover version of the Pink Floyd song "Comfortably Numb." In this arrangement, Bee Gees-styled falsetto harmonies, dampened guitar patterning from Floyd's "Another Brick in the Wall," sinking surf-sound chords and a relentless "four-to-the-floor" disco beat all play havoc with the lyrical content and musical connotations of the original song, imposing on it a highly camped up and sexually suggestive übertext.[66] *Wizard* allusions otherwise abound in Scissor Sisters' creative output: their debut album includes the song "Return to Oz," while its sleeve art shows a present-day Dorothy following a double-yellow line to a neon-lit Emerald City. In addition, their subsequent DVD release includes reenactments of several *Wizard* scenes, including the notorious crossroads scene where the Scarecrow tells Dorothy "people do go both ways." Unsurprisingly, Scissor Sisters front man Jake Shears endorses *Dark Side of Oz* wholeheartedly:

> Have you ever tried watching *Wizard of Oz* with *Dark Side of the Moon* playing over the top? It's very uncanny and strange, the movie is set up perfectly with all the songs. It's one of my favourite things. You really should try it out.[67]

And why shouldn't he like it? Like the band in which Shears made his name, *Dark Side of Oz* mocks conventions. And it does so in a manner that conjoins not only with camp aesthetics but also with the technological conditions of contemporary life. In both *Dark Side of Oz* and *La Belle* the technological apparatus through

---

[66] Hawkins offers a perceptive discussion of Scissor Sisters that places the band in the context of male queering in mainstream pop. See Stan Hawkins "On Male Queering in Mainstream Pop," in Sheila Whiteley and Jennifer Rycenga, eds., *Queering the Popular Pitch* (New York and London: Routledge, 2006), 279–94, 287–88.

[67] "Cut from a Different Cloth", *The Age*, 2004, http://www.theage.com.au/articles/2004/05/19/1084917648430.html, retrieved October 23, 2005.

which performances are articulated becomes the primary mechanism of artistic transformations. Weaving a narrative web of social divergence and euphoric convergence, (mis)syncing practices thereby subvert the teleological imperative of existing forms by binding them to the mechanised flow of the unfolding present.

In the introduction to this chapter, I situated practices of remix, mashup and loose synchronization in the context of broader tendencies in digital culture in the information age. The practices in question evidence the intersection of the avant-garde concern to erode the boundaries between art and life and a structurally similar tendency in vernacular cultures of the past few decades to treat existing recorded performances like the material objects (and commodities) that they actually are. In this respect, the structures of feeling at work here come to resemble those found in other areas of life in advanced capitalism, where the impetus to repackage or reinvent familiar things for public consumption is a definitive feature of our time. Above all, the fractured nature of these two examples reminds us how synchronization works in daily life. Just as synchronization in the instances considered in this chapter does not always work, so members of the audience recognize such temporally and technologically marked points of tension in their own lives: the struggle to keep in step with the multiple and often contradictory temporalities of current life; the (Oedipal) creative "struggle" between the creative artist and his (or her?) forebears; the incongruity of melodramatic expression in ordinary life and the correlative impetus to "stage" everyday forms of expression by invoking something that transcends the workaday self (Umberto Eco's famed lovers' quotation marks; in *La Belle*, historical selves that tower above their contemporary doubles). All of these factors play a part in the broader resonance of these art forms, which could be considered special instances of incongruous entertainment, by which I mean performances that somehow refuse to work, but because of this apparent reluctance they end up doing effective cultural work.

6

The Surrealism of Virtual Band Gorillaz: "Clint Eastwood" and "Feel Good Inc."

"They're here." (dir. Tobe Hooper, *Poltergeist*, 1982)

"They live." (dir. John Carpenter, *They Live*, 1988)

"They're us." (dir. Zack Snyder, *Dawn of the Dead*, 2004)

Unpacking the Idea of the Virtual Band

The Brit Awards since their inception have been regarded as one of the most reliable barometers of the popular music Zeitgeist in the UK. Witnessed by millions, popular music awards ceremonies have turned into increasingly lavish spectacles. Their opening moments serve a crucial framing function, priming the audience for what is to come and providing terms of reference that will inform audiences' understanding of the ensuing performance. So it was at the opening of the 2002 Brit Awards in London's Earls Court Arena. The houselights were lowered and an aerial tracking shot surveyed the venue before homing in on a darkened stage. Kick-drum simulations of a heartbeat triggered the illumination of four towering screens. The silhouetted image of 2D, the aptly named animated front man of the "virtual band" Gorillaz, emerged out of the primal matter of television static in a manner resembling a key scene in the classic suspense film *Poltergeist*. Three additional figures materialized on separate screens before the muscular arms of animated hip hop powerhouse Russel smashed out the four-beat introduction to the hit song "Clint Eastwood."[1]

---

[1] An earlier version of sections of this chapter on authorship and the analysis of the song "Clint Eastwood" was first published in 2005. See John Richardson, "'The Digital Won't Let Me Go': Constructions of the Virtual and the Real in Gorillaz' 'Clint Eastwood,'" *Journal of Popular Music Studies* 17/1 (2005): 1–29. This article has strongly influenced at least two scholars working on Gorillaz, although formal acknowledgement of indebtedness has not been forthcoming. This seems strangely ironic in light of the contentious issues surrounding authorship in the song "Feel Good Inc.," addressed in this chapter. Just as my influence is invisible in these scholars' work, so they shall go unnamed in this context; virtual authors all of us.

I had the good fortune to attend this event. I mention this not to imbue my account with the empirical authority of ethnographic work, although witnessing in person the juxtaposition of live and animated performers in this situation undeniably brought home something essential about Gorillaz' mode of a address. Still, the true locus of empirical inquiry in this case is spread across the diverse media in which the band disseminates its artistic messages: "live performance," television, the Internet, recorded and printed media. My approach will attend to these diverse channels of dissemination, employing methodological tools such as Internet ethnography, constructive reading of sounds and images, and the application of cultural theory.

On a primary level, then, the Brit Awards performance was a mass media event witnessed by millions on national television. Attending it could not afford privileged access to the Benjaminian "aura" of live performance. After all, the band itself was physically absent (unlike Kylie, Dido, Sting and others), replaced by animated caricatures of real musicians. Indeed, poor sound quality in the venue, frequent disjunctions in narrative flow (edited out of the television coverage), and overt articulations of social hierarchy all served to accentuate the socioculturally constructed nature of the event and to undermine any sense of authentic or unmediated communion between artists and audience. It was in this context, of an event already replete with unintentional alienation effects and the potential for deconstructive gesture that Gorillaz took the stage, towering over the standing audience and countering the gazes of the privileged many, seated in expansive restricted areas of the venue, with their own blank stares.

This ambitious audiovisual spectacle, reported to have cost more than £170,000, came at the zenith of a period of high exposure for the band.[2] The music press in both Britain and the United States had embraced Gorillaz, seeming to take inordinate pleasure in joining them in their satirical mixed-media games by interviewing cartoon character surrogate band members rather than the "real musicians." The band's flash-media-encumbered website gorillaz.com, which serves as the primary publicity vehicle for the group in lieu of more conventional celebrity appearances, had more than 500,000 hits a month in 2001.[3] Add to this platinum record sales on both sides of the Atlantic, a lucrative contract with PlayStation for the video game *MTV Music Generator 2*, plans for a feature-length animated film and related concept album (which probably gave way to the touring theater and circus project, *Monkey: Journey to the West*), negotiations with the Cartoon Network for airings of the band's promotional videos, and the scale of the band's burgeoning influence begins to take shape. All of this at a time when

    [2] "Gorillaz Planning Giant Video Performance for Brits," musicgoeson.com, August 1, 2002, www.musicgoeson.com,. retrieved January 24, 2004.

    [3] Sheryl Garrat, "'Hey, hey, we're the Gorillaz.' The Observer Profile: Damon Albarn," *The Observer*, September 7, 2001, www.guardian.co.uk/arts/, retrieved January 24, 2004.

"manufactured" pop acts were riding high in the UK charts; when reality TV shows filled the channels; and when the language of spin, simulation, and make-over was reaching into all areas of the popular imagination from politics to play. The calculated irony of the Gorillaz' Brit Awards performance was that some of the key architects of manufactured pop watched from the audience as animated caricatures of the acts they created paraded cockily before them with vacant eyes and mocking smirks.

To perceive critical intent in the Gorillaz' ostensibly shallow and unapologeti-cally juvenile multimedia art is not to impose the falsifying lens of cultural theory on intellectually naïve pop artifacts. Interviews and other promotional parapher-nalia tell of the band's wish to resist pop commodification by denying access to the real musicians while exaggerating traits associated with pop stardom. For UK audiences in particular, this critical message is inseparable from the star persona of Blur front man, Damon Albarn, widely known to be the musical founder of Gorillaz, whose voice is instantly recognizable as the same as his animated counterpart 2D, and whose highly publicized critiques of manufactured pop have been the subject of much debate in the UK music press. In a rare personal interview on the band, Albarn commented: "We—I mean they—are a complete reaction to what is going on in the charts at the moment…Everything is so manufactured these days…Gorillaz are different. They may only appear in cartoon form but, believe me, they are larger than life."[4] The most obvious index of this reaction is in the apparent withdrawal of the "real band" from public life, which stands in stark con-trast to the fly-on-the-wall perspective on the pop industry and the "real people" who populate it, offered by reality TV shows like *Pop Idol* and its North American offspring *American Idol*. Albarn's critique of the cult of personality in pop is unam-biguously stated in the title of Gorillaz' first DVD release, *Phase One: Celebrity Take Down* (henceforth *POCTD*). Shortly afterward, in 2004, the band launched a "culture jamming" campaign, in which visitors to the official Gorillaz website were encouraged to buy or download "Reject False Icons" stickers, which could then be used to deface existing media images. Finally, and in a more satirical mode, the band launched an online talent contest in the same year as a way of find-ing (token?) collaborators to work on a remix album. Hinging on the idea of virtual as immanent critique, the subversive potential of the band's evasive strategies was destined to be compromised by Albarn's iconic status in British popular culture. Add to this the large number of famous musicians, actors and the like that Albarn has brought in as guest artists on Gorillaz' various album releases and the idea of subverting the cult of celebrity can easily be understood as unintentionally ironic. The project nevertheless represents an earnest attempt to eschew the usual trap-pings of the pop industry that evokes a variety of musical and visual precursors. At

---

[4] Nick Duerden, "Gorillaz in Our Midst," *The Observer*, March 11, 2001, www.guardian.co.uk/arts/, retrieved January 24, 2004.

the most austere end of the scale, artistically ambitious pop/rock musicians have consistently shunned media attention in the domain of pop performance. Bands like Steely Dan, Tangerine Dream, Pink Floyd and the later-day Beatles all strived in different ways for anonymity, thereby allowing the music to function in a Kantian sense as art that "speaks for itself." The Beatles substituted live performances with animated ones in *Yellow Submarine* and a live band for a fictional one in *Sgt. Pepper's Lonely Hearts Club Band.* Along similar lines, artists working in the genre of electronic dance music will often retain pseudonyms or nicknames, including Moby (Richard Melville Hall), Aphex Twin (Richard James), Gorillaz producer Danger Mouse (Brian Burton), Gnarls Barkley (Brian Burton and Cee Lo Green), and Handsome Boy Modelling School (brainchild of another Gorillaz producer, Dan "The Automator" Nakamura). Alternative or indie-styled bands like Kraftwerk, Devo and The Residents have all operated behind fictional fronts ranging from the cyborgian to the surreal. At the lighter end of the scale, the pastiche television act The Monkees projected in their 1960s television show a largely fictional identity based upon the escapades of the Beatles and the surrounding hippie culture. Spoof bands such as Spinal Tap and The Rutles took this principle a step further in their outright satires of existing acts. Animated bands such as The Archies and Josie and the Pussycats have something in common with Gorillaz, albeit without the critical edge. Similarly, the Bugaloos and the Banana Splits offer a cartoonlike take on band buffoonery that resembles some of the animated antics of Gorillaz' characters. Gorillaz' performances resemble most closely those precursors that have operated at the more serious end of the expressive scale, albeit with an appreciation of how the sublime and the ridiculous can coexist in the context of recent avant-pop expression.

Looking beyond the immediate contexts of genre and geographical location, the emergence of Gorillaz coincided with a fascination with Japanese anime cartoons across the technologically advanced world. This influence can be attributed in part to the pervasiveness of gaming culture (Game Boy, PlayStation, Wii, etc.), the rapid influx in Europe and North America of Japanese cartoon series (including *Pokémon, Digimon,* and *Sailor Moon*), and the growing popularity of feature-length animated movies produced for adult consumption (e.g., dir. Hideki Takajama *Legend of the Overfiend,* 1989; dir. Hayao Miyazaki, *Spirited Away,* 2001; dir. Peter Chung et al., *Animatrix,* 2003). Such imagery has unsurprisingly found its way to the visual representations employed in recent pop, including extracts of erotic anime in performances on Madonna's Drowned World Tour; a concept album of sorts by the Flaming Lips based on a fictitious anime heroine named Yoshimi (*Yoshimi Battles the Pink Robots,* 2002); a feature-length anime "house musical" by French dance outfit Daft Punk (*Interstella 5555,* 2003); and a growing number of music videos, including Björk's "Hyperballad" (dir. Michel Gondry, 1996) and "I Miss You" (dir. John Kricfalusi, 1997). Common to all of the above is a fascination with technology expressed both visually and in sound; an interest in lo-fi sound textures juxtaposed with the possibilities of digital sound production; a post-punk, deconstructive sensibility; and an engagement with disposable youth culture ("bubblegum pop") that resists notions of good taste and flaunts commercial intent. More specifically, some form of parodic coding would seem to be implied, which in its rejection of transparent discourse resembles camp expression.

VIRTUAL REALITY OR REAL VIRTUALITY?

In much of Gorillaz' popular reception the band has been described as purveying a form of virtual reality that reflects and critiques some of the dominant forms of audiovisual expression in modern life. The band's breakthrough came within a decade of the popularization of theories of postmodernism in university programs in the United Kingdom and elsewhere. Baudrillard's ideas about simulation and hyperreality were the taste of the day, chronicling a ubiquitous virtual reality that has taken the place of epistemological depth and substance in contemporary experience.[5] Whether this had any influence on the creators of Gorillaz is debatable, but it is worth remembering that these ideas circulated freely in academic research and were beginning to infiltrate the discourses of popular culture at the time when the project was conceived.

At the center of Baudrillard's ideas is the proposition that reality has changed qualitatively for the worse in the age of digitally mediated production. Instead of originals, we are confronted with copies and simulations at every turn, leading to distorted perceptions of reality, which is replaced by an experientially barren *hyperreality*, a stratum of pure reproduction that transcends signification and in this way signals a crisis of signification.[6] The seriousness of Baudrillard's claims belies an impish sense of humor and taste for hyperbole that his detractors have often chosen to disregard. He is, of course, one of a long line of principally Marxist critics, including Theodor Adorno, Guy Debord and Raymond Williams, who have subjected popular mass media and consumption culture to this type of critique. Most distressing to critics of Baudrillard is the vagueness of his formulations about ontology, which reflects a Lacanian lineage. The real in Lacanian parlance is everything that is excluded by this theorist's other central concepts: the symbolic and the imaginary. As such it signifies a traumatic split in the symbolic order that can nevertheless ultimately be understood as emerging out of—and is therefore implicated within—symbolically framed knowledge. Most detractors would accept that Baudrillard is an ardent critic of the simulated hyperrealities his work exposes. As with Lacan's theories, however, there appears to be

---

[5] Jean Baudrillard, *Simulations*, trans., Paul Foss, Paul Patton and Philip Beitchman (New York: Semiotext, 1983).

[6] Ibid., 146–47.

no way out of this hypothetical zone in his theorizations, and hence no escape from the cultural logic of the mass media and consumerism that defines his view of postmodernism.[7] At bottom this is a pessimistic view, with little room reserved for personal agency, or for naïve or reductive (phenomenological) opting out of the symbolic matrix. This is viewed here as a significant shortcoming, although it does not detract from the value of his theorizations as heuristic tools in the present discussion. As an aside, it should be noted that Baudrillard drew favorable attention to the potential of surrealist forms to subvert mediated hyperreality.[8] It is debatable whether Gorillaz' audiovisual strategies should be considered surrealist, although I argue that they should.

Baudrillard is relevant to discussions of Gorillaz to the extent that the band's founders furnish audiences with a metadiscourse on their activities that resembles his line of thinking. This comes out in interviews with the two founding members of the group. According to Jamie Hewlett (responsible for the band's animated imagery and co-author of the *Tank Girl* comic books), "delivery of misinformation is as valid as the delivery of information."[9] And from Damon Albarn: "The people who work on Gorillaz are there because they love the idea of experimenting in the mainstream."[10] Given his celebrity status, it is of course moot whether Albarn could experiment anywhere but in the mainstream. Nevertheless, the intentions implicit in these statements reveal a desire to subvert the iconography of commercial pop (culture) from within—a strategy that because of its emphasis on pilfering from existing forms resembles postmodernist forms of montage (as well as those found in Dada and surrealism). In such circumstances, commercial ends are no longer seen as precluding artistic worth. Indeed, this layer of the Gorillaz' "message" is wholly contingent on the exploitation of existing codes saturated with an explicit commercial agenda.

---

[7] A different view of postmodernism and the realities it produced is found in the writing of critics Robert Venturi and Charles Jencks, who consider the American cityscapes of cities like Las Vegas and Los Angeles to be shaped more by social heterogeneity than by the blanket dictates of corporate social engineering or an all-encompassing hyperreal In these analyses, the emphasis on signs (or codes) more than form is not held to preclude everyday realities and productive agency among inhabitants. See Charles Jencks, *What Is Post-Modernism?* (New York: St. Martin's, 1986); Robert Venturi, "The Duck and the Decorated Shed," in Thomas Docherty, ed., *Postmodernism: A Reader* (New York: Columbia University Press, 1993), 295–307. This line of thinking has something in common with those strains of postmodernist thinking that emerged in feminist and postcolonial areas of research, which placed an emphasis on hybridity, personal agency, social mobility and embodied experience. Admittedly, theses facets were downplayed in much of the research on postmodernism.

[8] Baudrillard, *Simulations*, 142.

[9] Quoted in *POCTD*.

[10] Quoted in Steve Baltin, "Albarn Going Ape over Gorillaz: Blur Frontman Prefers Animated Life 'in the shadows,'" *Rolling Stone*, July 25, 2001, www.rollingstone.com/, retrieved January 24, 2004.

To align Gorillaz images and musical sounds with Baudrillard's hyperreal, a concept akin to what some writers loosely call "virtual reality," is not however to deny the ontological standing of images (by which I mean crossmodal sensory images, sound as well as vision) that are obviously mediated.[11] From a phenomenological standpoint experiences of so-called virtual reality are every bit as real as experiences of extra-medial reality.[12] They are secondary only insofar as they are experienced as secondary and therefore somehow reductive or disenchanted.[13] Manuel Castells strikes a necessary balance on this question when he dubs the modes of experience available through new media technologies in the information age as "real virtuality."[14] He qualifies this statement, however, with the constructionist assertion that "all realities are communicated through symbols"[15]; there exists no uncoded plane of experience to precede current mediated forms. Nevertheless, Castells recognizes, like so many other social commentators of our time, that an element of disembodiment characterizes interpersonal relations in the network society. This is an outcome of the replacement of historically and geographically stable "spaces of places" with what he calls "spaces of flows," implying interactions that are not as reliant on direct human contact as in the past.[16] Time as well becomes virtual in the new world order, in which the logic of timelessness and instant communication substitutes for the traditional emphasis on chronology and temporal sequence. We will see shortly how this impacts on the temporal organization of Gorillaz' music.[17]

To the extent that virtual reality (or, more properly, real virtuality) is understood to be a codified representation of a real world that lies beyond its borders, it possesses potential to reflect back on that world (in other words, it does not completely eclipse that world).[18] As Gabriella Giannichi observes: "The virtual has become the main theatre of the real—the place from where the real can be viewed,

---

[11] Two recent collections address uses of "virtual reality" in new media: Michael Ayers, ed., *Cybersounds; Essays on Virtual Music Culture* (New York: Peter Lang, 2006); and Jamie Sexton, ed., *Music, Sound and Multimedia: From the Live to the Virtual* (Edinburgh: Edinburgh University Press, 2007).

[12] Gabriella Giannachi, *Virtual Theatres: An Introduction* (London and New York: Routledge, 2004), 124. Martin Lister, et al., *New Media: A Critical Introduction* (London and New York: Routledge, 2003), 360–61.

[13] My understanding of the virtual is unrelated to that of Deleuze. The philosophical definition according to which "the virtual is that part of the real that is not actual" has little relevance to the present discussion and diverges from vernacular understandings of the term. Lister et al., *New Media*, 361–92; see also Brian Massumi, *Parables for the Virtual: Movement, Affect, Sensation* (Durham, NC: Duke University Press, 2002), 133–43.

[14] See Manuel Castells, *The Rise of the Network Society: The Information Age: Economy, Society and Culture,* vol. 1 (Oxford: Blackwell, 1996), 403.

[15] Ibid., 404.

[16] Ibid., 407.

[17] Ibid., 491–94.

[18] Manovich similarly refers to "fake realities" in recent audiovisual expression. Lev Manovich, *The Language of New Media* (Cambridge: MIT Press, 2001), 3.

a space for critique, art and politics."[19] The question of difference, rather than sameness or imitation, therefore lies at the heart of how virtual realities work in recent art forms. From this perspective, it is the tension between lived reality and mediated reality (which is equally true in ontological terms) that is responsible for bringing about some of the most striking effects in recent artistic forms. As Giannichi writes:

> The most exciting experience of virtual reality is not so much the one that totally alters the viewer's perspective on the real as the one that is able to expand, augment and enlarge the real. In other words, it is in the *relationship* with the real, rather than its attempts to substitute itself for the real, that the most original use of virtual reality is found.[20]

It is this no man's land between reality and fiction, therefore, that offers the greatest potential for critical responses to events in the "real world." Since we know in advance that virtual worlds are fictitious, the places where they converge with or augment lived reality are those in which a productive discourse on the nature of that reality becomes possible. Moreover, even when virtual realities articulate a notion of performance that is "posthuman" and therefore critically detached (see Harraway and Katherine Hayles[21]), they connect to the human and embodied experiences of audiences—who feel and respond to the beat.[22]

If this is the case, what do we mean when we talk of Gorillaz' audiovisual performances as disembodied or virtual? The Gorillaz' artistic agenda is transmitted in their music and its attendant visual representations in parodically marked "real virtualities" that operate on several embedded planes. The remainder of this chapter is concerned with tracking the movement between these planes and elucidating meanings thus afforded in the songs "Clint Eastwood" (*Gorillaz*, 2001) and "Feel Good Inc." (*Demon Days*, 2005).

---

[19]   Giannachi, *Virtual Theatres*, 123.

[20]   Ibid., 125.

[21]   Katherine Hayles offers an especially useful adjustment to theories of the posthuman in her use of the concept "embodied virtuality." Hayles is unwilling to relinquish aspects of agency and choice that are traditionally associated with liberal humanism. Arguing for a more critical stance on posthuman aesthetics in which the fleshiness and complexity of experience are restored, she outlines a view "that embraces the possibilities of information technologies without being seduced by fantasies of unlimited power and disembodied immortality, that recognizes and celebrates finitude as a condition of human being, and that understands human life is embedded in a material world of great complexity, one on which we depend for our continued survival." N. Katherine Hayles, *How We Became Posthuman: Virtual Bodies in Cybernetics, Literature, and Informatics* (Chicago: University of Chicago Press, 1999), 15.

[22]   For more on embodiment and its relationship to the concept of virtual reality, see Frances Dyson, *Sounding New Media: Immersion and Embodiment in the Arts and Culture* (Berkeley: University of California Press, 2009).

VIRTUAL BAND GORILLAZ AND ITS AUTHORIAL DOUBLE

It is commonplace in the reception of popular music for listeners to look and listen for authorial points of reference. Certain styles and modes of performance to some extent challenge this point of view, by drawing attention to collaboration or by concealing agency, but traditional views of creative activity would seem still to exert a powerful influence over the popular imagination.[23] Given this apparently built-in response to look for an author, it is hardly surprising that some of the strongest criticism of Gorillaz has targeted the perceived human progenitors of the band more than their virtual creation. For audiences and critics alike, it would seem, the authorial reconstruction of the "real band" in large part conditions perceptions of its animated counterpart. To the extent that the real band too is a construction, a highly mediated version of reality produced for public consumption, the idea of an authorial "virtual band" that is a shadow or double of its animated counterpart easily emerges. Revealingly, Albarn characterizes his role in the band in precisely these terms:

> I want to make another Blur record, but then again, whether you'd ever be able to see Blur again—whether I'll be prepared to step out of the shadows...I don't know, because I like it in the shadows. It's so much more fun to see stuff from the side of the stage, so to speak...I could be in the audience with Gorillaz.[24]

Shadows in this context are more than a mere metaphor. In early live performances, Albarn and his musical collaborators appeared as shadows moving behind an opaque screen, thereby deflecting attention from the animated images and in so doing arguably subverting some of their more subversive intentions. A shadowy presence is a presence nonetheless, which in this case points toward a prominent figure on the British musical landscape whose solo escapades have received substantial coverage in the UK music press. Music journalists and Blur aficionados alike have understood Albarn's animated adventures as one in a series of side projects by the former Britpop star, including collaborative work with Malian musicians, composer Michael Nyman and, most recently, ex-Clash members Paul Simenon and Mick Jones. Much of this work has been well received. Enthusiasm seems to have waned, however, when it came to Gorillaz' early "live" performances. In the shadowgraph concerts that coincided with the release of

---

[23] See David Brackett, *Interpreting Popular Music* (Cambridge: Cambridge University Press, 1995), 14–17; Will Straw, "Authorship," in Bruce Horner and Thomas Swiss, eds., *Key Terms in Popular Music and Culture* (Oxford: Blackwell, 1999), 199–208, 200.

[24] Quoted in Baltin, "Albarn Going Ape."

Gorillaz, widespread dissatisfaction among critics and audiences was registered.[25] This could be attributed to the power of conventional modes of representation over the popular imagination, or to a simple breakdown in communication between the band and its target audience(s). At any rate, the problem of the absent authors in live performances was quickly addressed in various ways in subsequent incarnations of the band.

Gorillaz' shadowy double extends beyond live performances to numerous discursive texts, including interviews as well as apocryphal and authoritative inside stories on the "real band." Notably, audiences are permitted more explicit glimpses of Albarn and Hewlett in mock interview photographic materials included on the first DVD release, *POCTD*. In these images, the two men display bandages and bruises while telling of their latest violent run-in with their animated progeny. Such cameo appearances resemble walk-on performances by Hitchcock, Lynch, Linklater and others in their work in film and television and underline the license granted to the auteur to play with reality—to insert into the diegetic frame characters we know are not "actors," thereby creating a kind of authorial signature while simultaneously bringing into sight the artifice that is his or her creation. Undoubtedly such strategies work against any pretense of anonymity in the reception of the band, encouraging more than destabilizing the attribution of agency to these "key players," arguably at the expense of even less visible collaborative agents. A self-reflective twist is added, however, by the acknowledgement that all is not right in Gorillaz' diegetic world. These are wounded and therefore "distanced" authors.[26] They are not, however, Barthesian *deceased* authors—phantoms of a bygone era whose influence over readers has diminished to the extent that agency has been relinquished to newly activated "readers." Far from it: Albarn and Hewlett's agency is never seriously challenged.

The inclusion of the "band behind the band" is not restricted to these personal appearances. Several critics have commented on resemblances between the animated characters and members of the "real band," which arguably foregrounds further the creative roles of authors in absentia Albarn and Hewlett (at the expense of the full creative cast). Albarn clearly resembles zonked out, post-punk pretty-boy 2D in both physical appearance and body language, and the chiseled features of bass player Murdoc could easily be mistaken for those of the more diminutive Hewlett. The white ethnicity of these two characters, moreover, reinforces the

---

[25] Karen Bliss, "Rocky Start to Gorillaz Tour: Tight Quarters Prevent Crowd from Enjoying Music/Animation Project," *Rolling Stone*, February 25, 2002, www.rollingstone.com/, retrieved January 24, 2004; Caroline Sullivan, "Damon Albarn Monkeys Around," *The Guardian*, March 24, 2001, www.guardian.co.uk/arts/, retrieved January 24, 2004; Tony Naylor, "Gorillaz: Manchester Academy." *NME*, n.d., www.nme.com/, retrieved January 24, 2004.

[26] See Roland Barthes, *Image—Music—Text*, trans., Stephen Heath (New York: Hill and Wang, 1977), 145.

associations. In contrast, virtual drummer Russel embodies the hip hop connection, while the techno-Orientalism that is so central to the band's aesthetic is anthropomorphized in guitarist Noodle.

An enigmatic line on the *POCTM* sleeve artwork states "an ego is a dangerous thing to feed." This tallies with the band's explicitly stated anti-celebrity agenda. But egos can be fed in different ways. A sublimated authorial role, such as that enjoyed by many musicians working in classical, contemporary avant-garde and contemporary dance idioms, can confer greater approbation on producers than one based on celebrity.[27] The kind of stardom enjoyed by Albarn in the heyday of Blur has been relinquished but something more valuable—in terms of subcultural capital—has been gained in the process. Albarn and Hewlett speak in self-deprecating terms of their creative roles in early interviews, but personal appearances such as these became increasingly pivotal in the marketing of the band. This suggests that the Gorillaz must on some level engage with the music industry on its terms (real, human terms) if they are to achieve their goals. Albarn's apparent dilemma brings to mind earlier attempts to escape the trappings of celebrity, such as John Lydon's PIL, in which the erstwhile Sex Pistols singer jettisoned his band, stage name and widely recognized musical style in favor of a form of dub-influenced deconstructive pop that in many respects prefigures the Gorillaz' music. Ex-Clash guitarist Mick Jones's Big Audio Dynamite is a similar case, this time featuring early uses of sampling such as those that are employed or mimicked in Gorillaz' musical style. Such ventures articulate the deconstructive wishes of the alternative artist to ditch the trappings of pop stardom while simultaneously benefiting from the status achieved through earlier work in an iconic band. The ascription of authorship in such cases is undoubtedly more complicated than is usual, which makes it judicious to view claims about authorial anonymity and democratic collaboration that are often allied to "anti-commercial" endeavors of this type with at least initial skepticism.

Pauline Reay makes the plausible point that Albarn may have turned to film soundtracks in the late 1990s in part because of the unwanted attention he received in Blur due to his boyish good looks. A comment in a 2003 *NME* article that Albarn "is still ludicrously pretty" highlights the nature of the problem.[28] The desire to garner the right kind of recognition by distancing himself from more obviously commercial contemporaries while aligning his activities with the serious side of pop, could well have been a motivational factor in the creation of Gorillaz. When further considering questions of authorship and agency, the relationship between perceived primary and secondary creative roles in Gorillaz should not be overlooked. For the present, let it suffice to flag a discrepancy

---

[27] Straw, "Authorship," 207; Timothy Taylor, *Strange Sounds: Music, Technology and Culture* (New York and London: Routledge, 2001), 140.

[28] Quoted in Pauline Reay, *Music in Film: Soundtracks and Synergy* (London: Wallflower, 2004), 85.

between the apparent replaceability of Gorillaz collaborators (everyone from rap performers to studio engineers) and the more elevated positions occupied by the two primary auteurs, particularly Albarn. The nature of textual incorporations in more recent Gorillaz music further raises questions that impinge on issues of authorship and agency, something I will return to in the section on "Feel Good Inc."

Whatever conclusions one draws concerning the "real band" (the musicians), it should not be forgotten that a subsection of Gorillaz' audience has no interest in matters of authorship. Fans can go online, "meet" the fantasy characters and in a limited sense communicate with them, join the fan site (fans.gorillaz.com) and add a virtual identity to a list of fans whose identities are similarly veiled behind cartoon characters of their own making. This is a big part of what Gorillaz is about, particularly for those who are unable or unwilling to look beyond the enticing bubblegum imagery of the animations, the catchy melodies and infectious beats of the songs, and the faux-naïf surrealism of the lyrics. For the majority of pop consumers, however, *another* virtual band exists that the creative forces behind the representations, despite strenuous efforts, exert less control over. It is appropriate, therefore, to talk of two "virtual bands," the animated band and its authorial double, the duplicity of which makes special demands on audiences and critics. This underlying double coding permeates all communicative layers of Gorillaz' artistic messages, not least of which is the musical text, which I will now consider in greater detail.

Virtual Worlds in Gorillaz' "Clint Eastwood"

TEMPORALITY AND THE VIRTUAL WORLD OF MUSIC PRODUCTION

The recorded popular song is invariably made up of its own "virtual realities" that to varying degrees support or challenge notions of emotional and performative naturalism.[29] Foremost in multitrack recordings is the illusion of discretely recorded parts coalescing to form a single time-bound performance. This impression is supported by various means, not least of which are production techniques

---

[29] Toynbee addresses the question of naturalism and its alternatives by dividing the musicians' relationship to the "technosphere" into three categories: the naturalism of recorded concert hall performances; the ventriloquism of electrified performance, which nevertheless conforms to an extended notion of naturalistic aesthetics; and what he calls "the far side of the technosphere," in which the virtual space constructed in recordings extends beyond the bounds of the naturally possible. The song "Clint Eastwood" occupies a discursive space between the second and third of these categories. Jason Toynbee, *Making Popular Music: Musicians, Creativity and Institutions* (London: Arnold, 2000).

that mimic the sonic effects of spatial proximity, distance, size, as well as the physical characteristics of the performance space, all of which anchor the illusion of a simultaneous unfolding performance conducted by real musicians in an undivided performance space.[30] In recent years, new forms of music are being made that suggest the emergence of revised notions of performative space and time or which extend or play with listeners' expectations in these regards. In popular as in experimental genres, first analog then digital technologies have been employed as tools to assist the creative artist to break down dominant naturalistic assumptions and in this way deflect attention toward the mediating roles of people like producers and DJs. This mediation gives rise to new temporalities, in which the musical text is no longer held to be a static object but an encapsulated process that becomes the subject of multiple transformations during the various stages of production and performance. This temporal coding has definite ideological implications, although elucidating these is not straightforward.

The song "Clint Eastwood" belongs to a new generation of recordings that could not have come into existence without the assistance of digital recording technology. Just as the onset of analog multitrack recording left an indelible watermark in the music of the late sixties and seventies,[31] production techniques distinctive to digital media have since their inception informed the musical end products that populate today's music charts.[32] This does not imply a narrow technological determinism. Human actions and interventions invariably come into play where technologies employed in contemporary pop are concerned, whether in the production and development of new technologies or in uses made of existing ones.[33] These practices are, moreover, bound up with the culturally, geographically and historically situated actions of individuals. How music technologies call forth expressive meanings that connect with broader social formations is best illustrated with the help of an example. Allusions in the sounding

---

[30]   See William Moylan, *The Art of Recording: Understanding and Crafting the Mix* (Woburn, MA: Focal Press, 2002); and Steve Jones, "A Sense of Space: Virtual Reality, Authenticity, and the Aural," *Critical Studies in Mass Communication* 10 (1993): 238–52.

[31]   Michael Chanan, *Repeated Takes: A Short History of Recording and Its Effects on Music* (London: Verso, 1995), 143–50.

[32]   See Andrew Goodwin, "Sample and Hold: Pop Music in the Digital Age of Reproduction," in Simon Frith and Andrew Goodwin, eds., *On Record: Rock Pop and the Written Word* (New York: Pantheon, 1990), 258–73; Stan Hawkins, "Joy in Repetition: Structures, Idiolects, and Concepts of Repetition in Club Music," *Studia Musicologica Norvegica* 27 (2001): 553–78; Kay Dickinson, "'Believe'? Vocoders, Digitalised Female Identity and Camp," *Popular Music* 20/3 (2001): 333–47.

[33]   See Richard Middleton, *Studying Popular Music* (Milton Keynes: Open University Press, 1990); Jonathan Sterne, *The Audible Past: Cultural Origins of Sound Reproduction* (Durham, NC: Duke University Press, 2003), 338; René Lysloff and Leslie Gay, "Introduction: Ethnomusicology in the Twenty-first Century," in René Lysloff and Leslie Gay, eds., *Music and Technoculture* (Middletown, CT: Wesleyan University Press, 2003), 1–22, 16–18; Taylor, *Strange Sounds*, 26–28.

music to technologies that serve as markers for a particular musical style or genre (e.g., the use of tape echo in dub reggae) invoke broader cultural formations and practices (those of the Caribbean diaspora and related subcultural groups), which in turn sheds light on the individual motivation for choices of a given style (Damon Albarn's choice of this musical style) and the cultural significance of the music (connotations of hedonistic escape and subcultural opposition). It is only by paying heed to each of these levels within a broader discursive network that a convincing reading of the cultural meanings of music technologies might be assembled.

All of the above processes of course take place in reference to a star text that has its own connotative impact on audiences' understanding of the music. The biographical background of Gorillaz' musical front man Damon Albarn is especially germane in this respect. Albarn rose to celebrity status as lead singer of the band Blur, whose music is often associated with the suburban southeast of England. In the mid-1990s, this band and Manchester-based Oasis, who fostered a more overtly working-class image, developed a rivalry that helped propel both bands to the forefront of the Britpop movement. As the name suggests, Britpop was concerned with the search for a quantifiably British musical identity in response to the Acid House movement of the late 1980s and the growing influence of North American grunge bands of the early 1990s. The movement extolled a return to the songwriting values and traditional rock arrangements of the 1960s and 1970s. For Albarn these musical influences ran parallel with an early interest in psychedelia, stylistic plasticity and theatricality (including the influence of David Bowie and Kurt Weill) that would become more prominent still later in his career. Blur's later albums would also evidence a more pronounced eclecticism than previously, including the incorporation of stylistic elements from grunge ("Song 2" from *Blur*, 1997); dub reggae ("Death of a Party" and "Theme from Retro," also from *Blur*); gospel ("Tender" from *13*, 1999); and electronic dance music (much of *13*). This eclecticism facilitated access to the highly lucrative North American market, as evidenced by the chart success of "Song 2," the "whoo hoo" hook of which is now heard at countless sporting events across the United States. Gorillaz offered Albarn an opportunity to push this envelope further, essentially starting his musical escapades with a clean slate. Moreover, it would give the star the opportunity to ditch the relatively parochial stylistic baggage of the Britpop movement, in favor of a style with broader international appeal.

In order to better understand the significance of this musical sea change, it is helpful to turn to matters of musical production. While there is some evidence of production techniques resembling those employed by Gorillaz on recent Blur albums, such as *13*, produced by EDM guru William Orbit, and *Think Tank*, produced by Blur with Ben Hillier, in most songs the band retains the sonic identity of a guitar rock band whose dominant mode of expression is that of the traditional song.[34] The majority of songs on these albums were recorded in traditional fashion, albeit with the help of digital recording software such as Pro Tools and Logic. In most cases this meant the recording of a core performance of a precomposed song in the studio, which was then embellished with overdubs. The Gorillaz' eponymous first album, in contrast, was composed and recorded in a more fragmented way, involving the manipulation of musical materials on a computer screen rather than in rehearsals prior to recording. Producer Jason Cox recalls the parallel production and composition process as follows:

> I think the reason why we worked in a different way is because we've got this whole Logic thing going on,[35] so instead of working in a linear world where you're using tape, you've got a hell of a lot more flexibility…It just gives you a chance to experiment, basically chuck a whole load of paint at the canvas and see what sticks, and weed out all the drips of paint that you don't want![36]

This approach would permit greater flexibility when recording but would also lead to some unexpected musical repercussions. Indeed, the "copy and paste" mentality that is widely associated with work in digital media became so deeply ingrained that in this case musicians and producers alike had difficulty distinguishing the tracks they were working on from one another.[37]

Focusing on the versions of "Clint Eastwood" found on the *Gorillaz* album and single mixes, the confluence of technologies and sonic practices found in the song might be charted as follows:

1. In light of the producers' comments concerning the recording process, it is unsurprising to find a high degree of apparent interchangeability between musical parts within and between tracks. Sounds are very similar across album tracks and similar musical materials are found in several songs. This results in a partial corrosion of narrative directionality in favor of extranarrative flow, due to

---

[34] For more on the production of the album *Think Tank*, see David Greeves, "Ben Hillier: Recording Blur, Tom McRae and Elbow," *Sound on Sound*, July 2003, www.soundonsound.com/sos/Jul03/articles/benhillier. asp, retrieved May 1, 2009.

[35] Emagic's Logic Audio Platinum software, now owned by Apple and renamed Logic Studio.

[36] Cox quoted in Sam Inglis, "Tom Girling and Jason Cox: Recording Gorillaz's Clint Eastwood," *Sound on Sound* (September 2001). Available at www.sospubs.co.uk/, retrieved May 20, 2002.

[37] The following quotation illustrates this point: "At the beginning loads of songs merged into each other…Say if we had four tunes, all those four tunes would be made up of all the same bits…We'd keep swapping bits round, and whatever it sounded best in, we'd leave it in that song and take it out of the other song…The confusing thing was the names changing all the way through. We would have our name for a song, Damon would have his…and we'd be sitting there for ages having to listen to all the songs again to find out what he was calling it!" quoted in Inglis, "Tom Girling."

the interpolation of events that are apparently only loosely bound up with the surrounding musical milieu, and the relinquishment of the idea of the song as a unique and self-contained whole. The song in this light takes on a markedly depersonalized or posthuman character.

2. This interchangeability extends to the concept of "remix," whose genealogy here owes as much to the influence of dub reggae (mediated by late 1970s to 1980s UK punk) as it does to the influence of recent dance styles. While in a limited sense the *Gorillaz* version of "Clint Eastwood" could be regarded as the primary text, listeners with an interest in UK garage have tended to prefer Ed Case's two-step "refix," while the "Phil Life Cypher version" has received more exposure in clubs and radio programming where reggae and related styles (such as drum'n'bass and jungle) are favored (*G Sides*, 2001).

3. A structural analysis of the different musical elements of "Clint Eastwood" reveals the concrete impact of an aesthetic of "copy and paste," which is in part attributable to the use of music-editing software. When working in the "arrange windows" of software packages such as Logic, structural relationships that may not be immediately apparent when listening can easily be recognized visually on the computer screen, such as rhythmic layering that does conform neatly with the dominant hypermetric structure of the song. This can be seen in Figure 6.1, where the spatial layout resembles the appearance of music production software packages. Particularly salient is the part labeled "psychedelic string synth," which cuts across the underlying hypermetric and strophic structure of the backing track (measure 67), and slices again through one of the song's main macro-structural blocks (measure 83), before eventually dovetailing with the hypermetric organization of the song (measure 93). However, by this time Albarn's lead vocal and melodica are willfully disregarding the song's macro-structure, precipitating a gradual slide into the relative incoherence of the song's dub section, in which the simulated analog technology of tape delay (simulated because it is digitally reproduced) takes over from its digital counterpart in the looping of the synthesizer part.

4. The most immediate sense in which technologies are implicated in the music of "Clint Eastwood" is in the choice of sounds. When compared to Albarn's earlier music, a different aesthetic of sound pervades here, which emphasizes microlevel transformations and interpolations rather than stable sonic forms embedded within a fixed discursive macrostructure. Sounds distinctive to recent digital technology include bass sub-notes (see Figure 6.1.), the harmonizer applied to sections of Albarn's lead vocal (a simulation of vocal harmonies), and a variety of effects including reverse reverb (measures 14 and 49–56), band pass filtering and panning effects (prominent in the coda and dub sections, after measure 67). Many of these effects are extensively employed in recent dance genres, but as indicated above much of this track makes conspicuous reference to the analog sound world of 1970s and '80s dub reggae at the same time as it is more transparently

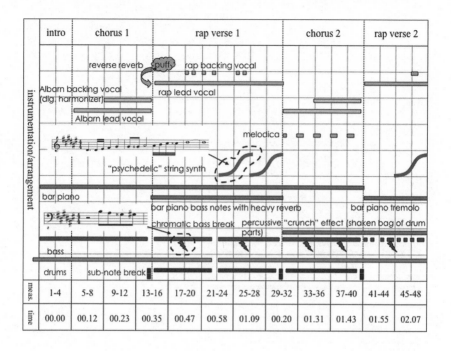

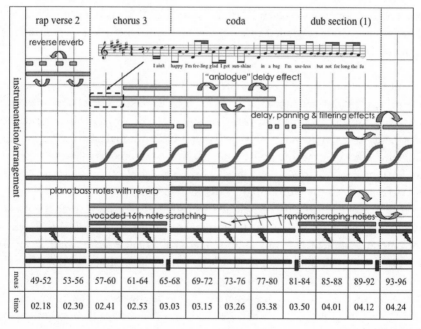

Figure 6.1

(continued)

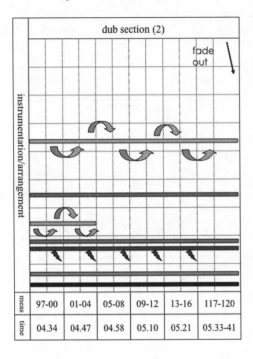

Figure 6.1 (continued) Graphical representation of arrangement and musical form in "Clint Eastwood" (*Gorillaz* mix).

marked as belonging to the era of digital recording. This juxtaposition between parallel sonic worlds encoded as "contemporary" and "historical" (or outmoded) is integral to the semiotic workings of the song.

"Clint Eastwood" is characterized therefore by its general piecemeal feel and by the principle of interchangeability that finds its expression on several interlocking levels. Given this shift away from the more tightly circumscribed sonic landscapes of Britpop toward an eclectic approach to materials incorporating influences from reggae, hip hop, punk, dub, and contemporary dance styles, it is understandable that critics of Albarn's earlier musical output have responded more favorably to the Gorillaz. The crossmarket potential of the band is, moreover, maximized in the diverse audiences catered to in the various remixes of "Clint Eastwood," just as it is in the band's parodic cartoon imagery, which incorporates influences from anime, Western, science fiction and suspense genres, not to mention appropriations of hip hop's ubiquitous culture of graffiti and textual appropriation. Gorillaz' crossover appeal would not be possible were it not for the band's penchant for parody, which allows for the emergence of ambiguous encodings of musical and visual texts that are available to both mainstream and "alternative" audiences. This opens the music up to several generations of listeners and to diverse cultural groups, who recognize in the musical text technologies that sound like their own.

SPATIALITY AND THE VIRTUAL WORLD OF MUSIC PRODUCTION

"Virtual realities" are invoked also in terms of spatial representations of the musicians in the mix, which intersect in significant ways with attendant visual representations. In most recorded music, the spatiality of live performance is simulated to varying degrees.[38] The emphasis on DJing and remix in club cultures over the past couple of decades has challenged these conventions to some extent, but even in hip hop, rap, and dance genres the live encounter between performers (or surrogate performers: DJs) and audiences is still largely upheld as ideal.[39] Gorillaz' music adheres, for the most part, to these conventions, although there is evidence of a deconstructive sensibility in the combinations of music and visual materials in the recorded and live performances discussed here.

In the 2002 Brit Awards performance, each of the animated musicians was projected onto a separate screen. (When using the *POCTD* DVD, the viewer is permitted to choose between "virtual," or computer generated, and "real" performance spaces). As might be expected, the position of the projected figures approximates the spatial locations of the sounds associated with them in the mix (see Figure 6.2.) The lead singer and rapper occupy positions "close" to the listener: little reverb has been added and the onset of reflections is long; both are panned to center.[40] Backing singers (including Albarn's harmonized "backing vocal") are panned slightly to the left, approximating the conventional positions of performers on the stage. Conventional positions are occupied also by other instruments: bass sounds fill the center area, along with bassier percussion sounds, including a crunching sound produced by shaking a bag full of metallic drum parts;[41] the piano is located right of center with an ethereal synthesizer characteristically floating in a large area slightly to the left and in the distance. A haunting melodica similarly occupies a large area in the distance and panned to the left. Special effects, such as scratching, are panned hard left and right. As the song progresses, however, the virtual fingers of the producer enter the equation and

---

[38] Jones, "A Sense of Space." Also Jeremy Gilbert and Ewan Pearson, *Discographies: Dance Music, Culture and the Politics of Sound* (London and New York: Routledge, 1999), 131. Moore interprets the spatiality of sound in terms of a visualized "sound box," a heuristic model that has long been recognized in sound production and mixing practices. Allan Moore, *Rock: The Primary Text* (Buckingham: Open University Press, 1993), 106; also Moylan, *The Art of Recording*, 48–59.

[39] Toynbee overstates his case that the orientation of the DJ or electronic performer evidences an "inward aesthetic." Toynbee, *Making Popular Music*, 162. The fact is that musicians in dance genres perform live and they receive interpersonal "payback" in a similar way to rock musicians. As in other "intelligent" genres, however, EDM artists work hard to *efface* the ideological work that goes into putting on a performance.

[40] This applies to the Dolby Digital surround sound recording as well, where the surround sound channels are used predominantly for ambient sound.

[41] Inglis, "Tom Girling."

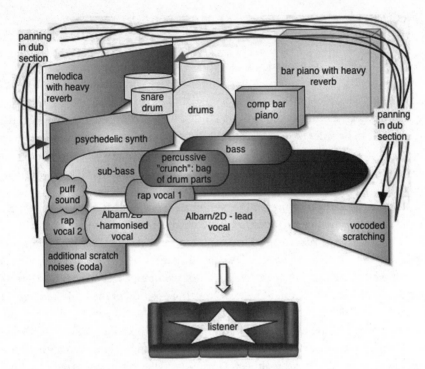

Figure 6.2 Implied spatial relations in Gorillaz' "Clint Eastwood" (*Gorillaz* mix, stereo).

panning pandemonium is gradually unleashed. Here playfulness in post-production replaces sensory realism as the decentering influence of the DJ-producer is felt. Namely, scratching, piano and melodica parts all go walkabout, swinging alternately hard to the right and left (see the arrowed lines in Figure 6.2.). The resulting sensory disorientation has its historical roots in roots reggae and can be attributed in part to an agenda related to conventions of psychedelic coding in the lyrics and music.[42]

The disruption of virtual locations just described corresponds to the obvious artifice of the visual pseudo-performance to draw attention to the constructedness of spatial location in this particular song and by extension more generally in pop. In terms of Manuel Castells's theorization of spatial relations in the

[42] Panning conventions are discussed most notably by Tagg, for example, Philip Tagg, "Analysing Popular Music: Theory, Method, and Practice," in Richard Middleton, ed., *Reading Pop: Approaches to Textual Analysis in Popular Music* (Oxford: Oxford University Press, 2000), 71–103, 97. Tagg's interpretation of Abba's "Fernando" draws attention to the ideological significance of situating the Western European lead vocalist center-front in the mix while "ethnic" quena flutes are located at the periphery.

information age, it might be stated that the apparently stable naturalistic spaces of the initial sections of the song gradually accede to virtual and randomized "spaces of flows."[43] The mirroring of these auditory conventions in the visuals reveals the arbitrary nature of realist performance conventions. The band's cartoon characters are initially unable to break out of their individual projection screens (the "cages" referred to in the lyrics), whose frames indicate the rigidity of recording conventions, although in the dub section of the song this is precisely what happens musically. Visible tension between the "virtual" (or computer generated) visual performance of Albarn and his fellow musicians and the "real performance" of the rappers further amplifies the growing sense of incongruity. Although, as suggested earlier, this raises problems of authorship and ownership: which musicians are the real creative force behind the band and which are the "hired help"? The physical absence of Albarn and his team would seem to imply a different relationship to the audience than that of the rappers, who are required to "sweat it out" on stage and whose performances are ultimately regarded as replaceable (in other performances, different rappers have been employed). Rapper Del Tha Funky Homosapien, as his name suggests, is a real person and not a member of Gorillaz, who despite their resemblance to human beings are not cast as essentially human. Aside from underlining qualitative differences between live and electronically mediated parallel performances, not unlike the cases studies discussed in the previous chapter, this juxtaposition between real and virtual performers can be interpreted as an ironic and potentially destabilizing inversion of racial stereotypes.[44]

Evident in the illocutionary force of these gestures is a degree of confusion between layers of experience that might be dubbed hyperreal and fictional. At least this is the understanding a Baudrillardian reading would offer. Both sets of performers have to them a degree of fictionality, insofar as they are both stereotyped cultural constructions, although both are real to the perceiver in ontological terms. They are both sensorily "larger than life." The amplified reality of the animated performers invokes Benjamin's category of secondary aura more than is the case with the human performers, who, for their part, call to mind aura in his

---

[43] Castells, *The Rise of the Network Society*, 407.

[44] For a discussion of the cultural implications of the use of the word "gorilla" and its homophone "guerrilla" in hip hop culture, see Russel A. Potter, *Spectacular Vernaculars: Hip-Hop and the Politics of Representation* (Albany, NY: SUNY Press, 1995), 76–79. Originally conceived of as a racist slur on African-Americans, the term has been knowingly signified on by rappers, who invest it with positive connotations of streetwise toughness and exoticism. Albarn's appropriation betokens a wish to partake of these subversive qualities in a way that accentuates the alienated, dehumanized qualities of the band's animated figures.

original sense: as implying physical proximity.[45] One has a profound physical impact through the size and nature of the reproductive apparatus; the other has the benefit of the human dimension (the imprint of human embodiment on the recording medium). Insofar as both are mediated to audiences though television screens, the distance between the two is eroded in a way that heightens ambiguities between performers who are larger than life literally (and therefore surreal) and those who are larger than life only figuratively.[46] Both become virtual insofar as they mediate images that are social constructions.

Connected to the spatiality of the musicians in the mix, the type of performance this implies, and the corresponding actuality of the Brit Awards stage performance, are the roles these different layers of spatialization play in the semiotic encoding of the music and the relationship this indicates to corresponding cultural formations. Most noteworthy in this respect is the fact that the song alludes crossmodally (by linguistic, visual and musical means) to Westerns in general and the Morricone/Leone spaghetti Westerns in particular. An interview with the studio technicians who worked on the project suggested that the choice of title was motivated by the song's general "Western feel."[47] Albarn's melodica (strongly reminiscent of reggae artist Augustus Pablo's) and a stereotypical detuned bar piano, referred to by the producers as a "cheesy upright," are both ambiguous genre synecdoches, as Philip Tagg would call them, of the Western film genre; they are parts of an outside genre that stand in for the larger whole.[48] The melodica is timbrally close to the harmonica, prominent in Morricone soundtracks, while the tremolo effect of the upright piano in the rap sections is reminiscent of the piano styles heard in Western bar scenes. Simulated tape delay applied to several

---

[45]   Mechanical reproduction for Benjamin robs perceived objects of their tactile qualities by subtracting from them the impression of distance that physical proximity brings. When reproduced on film, images of actors lose the aura of the photographed person due to the distracting influence of the star text and the commodified quality of the experiences relayed by film. And yet, something of value can be retrieved from the encounter with film because of the possibilities afforded in techniques such as montage, close-ups, zooms, tracking, slow motion, and so on, to draw the perceiver's attention to the physical details of an object as well as to the mediated and contingent nature of the represented reality. Just as a vestige of auratic presence can be preserved in still photographs of absent or deceased subjects, so the surgical strategies of the director open up the cinematic text to second-order auratic impressions. In contrast to the activities of the painter, which Benjamin likens to those of a magician, insofar as they maintain distance from the perceiver, the filmmaker is able to convey a sense of captured physical proximity, which translates into mediated auratic perceptions of distance. Walter Benjamin, "The Work of Art in the Age of Mechanical Reproduction," in Hannah Arendt, ed., Harry Zohn, trans., *Illuminations: Essays and Reflections* (New York: Schocken, 1968), 217–51.

[46]   For a similar understanding of Gorillaz' live performances, see Jem Kelly, "Pop Music, Multimedia and Live Performance," in Jamie Sexton, ed., *Music, Sound and Multimedia: From the Live to the Virtual* (Edinburgh: Edinburgh University Press, 2007), 105–20, 112.

[47]   Inglis, "Tom Girling."

[48]   See Philip Tagg, "Towards a Sign Typology of Music," www.tagg.org/articles/trento91.html, retrieved August 20, 2010.

instruments in the dub section, although in reality achieved only in narrow can-yons with high walls, is conventionally associated with the wide open spaces of the Wild West, such as the desolate landscapes depicted in Gorillaz' video and CD artwork.[49] Musically, the final section is obviously inspired by dub, with a probable allusion to reggae toaster Clint Eastwood embedded in the song's title. Michael Veal considers the vast echoing soundscapes of reggae to be an attempt to simulate precolonial African space. This simulation served as an antidote to the harsh realities of diaspora life in the 1960s and 1970s; a fantastical space in which the powers of the postcolonial imagination could be deployed as means of recon-structing cultural identity.[50] This imaginary space was readily adopted by British punk rockers in the late 1970s, whose experiences of urban decline and mass unemployment gave grounds for identification with those from the Caribbean diaspora.[51] It is this lineage that finds its expression in the Gorillaz song, whose spatialized sonic representations call forth images of the "precivilized" Wild West (which of course is a colonial construction, insofar as Native Americans are accorded only the role of adversary in such images) intermingled with the utopian landscape of precolonial Africa.

UTOPIAN ESCAPISM AND PSYCHEDELIC CODING

Invocations of utopian postcolonial soundscapes in the dub section of "Clint Eastwood" suggest an additional way in which the song invokes "virtual realities." Of further interest is how these connect with discursive formations from the his-tory of British pop. The song's lyrics are intentionally indeterminate, calling forth a plethora of loose associations to drug culture, punk sensibility and dub reggae that locate the music in the British alternative tradition. This indeterminacy extends to the temporal coding of the music, which invokes dub reggae and the expansive soundscapes of spaghetti Westerns while bringing into play the sub-woofers and bass-boost buttons of contemporary hi-fi systems. In the musical syntax as well the genre coding is ambiguous: the slow tempo and upbeat chop of reggae (implied in the second upbeat) are seasoned in parts of the song with

---

[49] A strong tradition of similar uses of sound technology can be identified in film Westerns, including the classic movies *Shane* and *High Sierra,* in which exaggeratedly echoing voices symbolize both the character's heroic isolation and the sublime power of Nature. The incorporation of an imaginary Western expansiveness through the use of echo and reverb in dub reggae is not exclusive to this genre but is prefigured in several decades of production practices in country western music, where the image of the lonesome cowboy was a common stereotype. See Peter Doyle, *Echo and Reverb: Fabricating Space in Popular Music Recording 1900–1960* (Middleton, CT: Wesleyan University Press, 2005), 95–119.

[50] Michael Veal, *Dub: Soundscapes and Shattered Songs in Jamaican Reggae* (Middletown, CT: Wesleyan University Press, 2007), 198–99.

[51] Ibid., 225–27.

syncopated sixteenth-note scratching, produced not with turntables but digital vocoder software.

An element of escapism here warrants further commentary. Melodically, the sections sung by Albarn are characterized by a lazy aeolian/pentatonic oscillation between the tonic and the dominant in the first two measures, giving an aimless or nondirectional feel, the dysphoric atmosphere of which is heightened by the presence of passing minor thirds. The song melody sinks lethargically down to the subdominant in the third measure and the low tonic in the fourth. The final step incorporates a minor third descent, which brings a sense of disillusionment or submission. Finally, the melody rests on the simple alternation of the aeolian seventh degree and the tonic, coinciding with the echoing line "it's coming on, it's coming on." The singer's apathy is reinforced in his slurred articulation and references in the lyrics to his own uselessness; a situation we are told will change. The line "sunshine in a bag," the main hook of the song, is ambiguous: it could refer to something the character has done that will eventually pull him out of his malaise—this song, for example, if an author-centered reading is privileged; or it could imply the prospect of drug-induced bliss.

Interpretations of the lyrics are likely for many listeners to be conditioned by concomitant musical coding. The carnivalesque (and fairground-organ-like) chromatically ascending synthesizer line is significant in this regard. Add to this the disorientation brought about in the dub section as the discursive structure of the song disintegrates while conventions of performative realism are knowingly subverted and a clear set of cultural references is mobilized. The strategies employed here resemble those discussed by Sheila Whiteley in her writing on Jimi Hendrix. Rising musical movement (getting high); nondirectional or "floating" movement (feeling spacey); smudged, unclear or distorted timbres (disorientation); and chromaticism (shifts in perceptions of reality) are all conventional markers of the psychedelic.[52] Here the hallucinatory effects of marijuana are loosely connoted through the association with dub reggae, although the reference to "sunshine" could be understood to refer to Californian Sunshine, a form of LSD, or acid, widely available in the 1980s, which was often sold in small plastic bags. In the context of pop and rock subcultures, these allusions serve a fairly conventional function, working against the taken for granted structures of "uncool" mainstream culture while endorsing an escapist, undeniably masculine ideal of freedom.

Michael Veal alludes to what he calls the "ganja factor" when discussing the presence of psychedelic coding on dub reggae. Coding of this type in dub

[52]   Sheila Whiteley, "Progressive Rock and Psychedelic Coding in the Work of Jimi Hendrix," in Richard Middleton, ed., *Reading Pop: Approaches to Textual Analysis in Popular Music* (Oxford: Oxford University Press, 2000), 235–61.

represents an aesthetic coincidence more than being directly indebted to psyche-delic practices in the 1960s.[53] Regarding the cultural significance of dub reggae, Veal aligns the disjunctive techniques employed in the style with those used by collage artists in Dada and surrealism.[54] An additional productive line of inquiry in his analysis points toward similarities in how reality is configured in the litera-ture of the South American "magical realist" authors and those of dub reggae musicians. Several theorists have argued that elements of this literary style can be understood as a mode of "ontological resistance" to the dominant structures and strictures of life under colonial rule. The gaps and inconsistencies with which nar-rative forms are interpolated in dub reggae suggest a deconstructive impetus in which dominant or residual cultural formations are "remixed" into new hybrid identities that articulate local concerns. According to Veal's reading, dub reggae's broken soundscapes speak to an agenda of distancing with respect to the cultural forces behind colonial repression, while articulating in sound the nature of the historically violent encounter between industrial capitalism and preindustrial cultures. Dub reggae thus gives voice to structures of feeling that expose a subtext of resentment toward colonizing forces, but it nevertheless rechannels these sen-timents in socially productive ways.[55] It re-enchants them in a manner directly comparable to the surrealists' fascination with the found object.

The rappers' dynamic performances in "Clint Eastwood" articulate similar sentiments. 2D's (Albarn's) vocal disenchantment contrasts sharply with rapper Del Tha Funky Homosapien's more proactive stance. Within the overall world-within-a-world of the song, then, two virtual spaces vie with one another. When release comes, it is engendered by means of musical and linguistic initiatives located in the rap sections of the song. It is the combative and energized world of this musical genre ("finally someone let me out of my cage"), therefore, that even-tually provides the required antidote to Albarn's lyrically languid choruses (Albarn: "I'm useless, but not for long, the future is coming on"). The release of energy is substantial and has the impact of a genie let out of its bottle (an image from the music video). In the lyrics too animate and inanimate forces are unleashed or "let out of their cage" as the song progresses, a line that is anticipated by an eerie reverse reverb culminating in an ambiguous "puff" sound. The musical catalyst for this transformation is rhythm, located by the rapper "under each snare." In summary, if there is a political agenda in "Clint Eastwood," it is to be found not only through semantic means, but primarily through surrealist strategies of appropriation and disruption and their embeddedness in a musical style that sig-nifies noise—which audiences recognize on a primary level because they feel it and know it from past experiences.

[53] Veal, *Dub*, 80–85.
[54] Ibid., 207.
[55] Ibid., 203.

Reproducing Success: Gorillaz' "Feel Good Inc."

OF DAMON'S DAYS AND DANGER MOUSE

In the next chapter of Gorillaz' history, music videos and live performances would become more finely textured and technologically sophisticated. Released in the summer of 2005, the album *Demon Days* would once again feature a flagship single release, "Feel Good Inc." Crafted in much the same way as its predecessor, with a spoken-word first verse, catchy melodic refrains and two high-energy rap sections, the single achieved a significant level of commercial success. The chiseled figure of Clint Eastwood would feature again on *Demon Days*, this time in the guise of "Dirty Harry," the album's third single release. Masterminded again by Damon Albarn, Gorillaz' second album relies heavily upon the talents of Brian Burton (Danger Mouse), producer of the controversial *Grey Album* (a mash-up of the Beatles' *White Album* and Jay-Z's *Black Album*).[56] His task on *Demon Days* was similar to that of *bricoleur*-producer Dan the Automator on *Gorillaz*: to meld together the song-form elements composed by Albarn with the dance, rap and remix elements brought in by guest artists. These included the rap trio De La Soul, Ike Turner (a piano solo on "Every Planet We Reach Is Dead"), actor Dennis Hopper (the spoken-word section on "Fire Coming Out of a Monkey's Head"), and hip hop performing songwriter Neneh Cherry (on "Kids With Guns").

Awards ceremonies featured prominently again in the promotion of the album's first single release. At the 2005 MTV music awards and the 2006 Grammy Awards, Gorillaz used state of the art hologram technology in performances of the song "Feel Good Inc." to achieve previous unrealizable levels of immersive experience. In both awards shows, life-sized holographic images were projected from high-definition projectors onto transparent foil to produce the illusion of three-dimensional movement in space. The so-called eyeliner technique, developed by London-based Musion Systems, is based on the principles of the Pepper's ghost optical illusion.[57] Both of the awards ceremonies performances employed angled screens, one running the length of the stage, the other erected atop the drummer's podium. This can be seen in the image reproduced on the front cover of this book, which is taken from a rehearsal of the MTV music awards. Essentially a remediated version of the "Feel Good Inc." music video (discussed later), this performance featured animated extracts from the video projected onto a large back-screen, which provided narrative context for the

---

[56]　See Michael Ayers, The Cyberactivism of Dangermouse," in Michael Ayers, ed., *Cybersounds; Essays on Virtual Music Culture* (New York: Peter Lang, 2006), 127–36.

[57]　Details of the "Musion Eyeliner" technique and its various applications can be found at the official Musion website: www.musion.co.uk/, retrieved December 11, 2010.

Figure 6.3 A holographic Madonna dances with Gorillaz at the 2006 Grammy Awards.

actions of the holographic musicians. In this performance the animated musicians interacted more realistically with one another than in the Brits show
because of the relative invisibility of the technical apparatus—which in turn
facilitates immersive consciousness over alienation effects.

A second holographic performance, at the 2006 Grammy's, incorporated a
leotard-clad projection of Madonna weaving between cartoon band members in
the song "Feel Good Inc.," before the Gorillaz remix segued into her hit song,
"Hung Up" (see Figure 6.3.). In contrast to the 2002 Brit Awards performance,
the cartoon figures in these performances were similar in stature and appearance
(appearing to be three-dimensional) to human performers, thus taking suspension
of disbelief to a new surreal level. This aspect was heightened and the boundaries
between augmented virtual reality and live performance eroded further by the
physical appearance of Madonna onstage following the disappearance of her identically clothed hologram. This exploration and exposure of intermedial boundaries yields a level of sensory confusion that wields considerable subversive
potential. As I noted earlier, real virtuality is at its most effective *and affecting*
when it augments everyday experiences rather than simply imitating them. That
was certainly the case in these two performances. The irony of the cartoon characters' appearances at these events alongside popular icons, when these too
appeared at their most flamboyant and cartoonlike, would not have been lost on
more media-savvy audio viewers. Each reflects favorably on the other: the presence
of human artists renders the animations more credible, more *real*, while the

disruptive presence of Gorillaz in the midst of popular peers imparts a level of avant-garde reflexivity and black humor, which a growing number of popular artists strive to achieve.

On the same night as the MTV Europe Music Awards in Lisbon, the real musicians behind the project performed songs from *Demon Days* in one of a series of shows at Manchester's Opera House. These performances took place beneath projected images of the cartoon band, although the performing musicians ended up being the main focus of attention. Much the same formula would be repeated in performances on the Escape to Plastic Beach World Tour in 2010. As Gorillaz' reputation has grown, it would appear that its creators have learned something from earlier experiences by giving the audience more of what they want: more ingeniously realized fantastical elements *and* closer contact with physically embodied musicians. The success of this strategy has been reflected in the critical reception of more recent Gorillaz projects. Synergetic diversification is a central principle in any successful (anti)capitalist enterprise in the digital age, which can be witnessed also in the music theater work, *Monkey: Journey to the West*, a Gorillaz franchise spin-off and stage show featuring a troupe of Chinese dancers, actors and singers. Most striking about *Monkey* is a subtle shift in musical direction for Albarn, toward a more through-composed and musically complex sonic idiom. Ironically, it is an idiom based in large measure on the compositional techniques of minimalist music combined with the sampled timbres of traditional Chinese music. This more studious approach allowed Albarn and his creative partner, Hewlett, to call the new venture an opera and to garner some of the prestige this designation accords.

"FEEL GOOD INC.": THE MUSIC VIDEO AND THE CULTURE INDUSTRY

The song "Feel Good Inc." achieved much of its impact through its cross-media packaging as the soundtrack to a visually opulent music video. Directed by Hewlett and Pete Candeland, the video consists of a mixture of computer-generated imagery, two-dimensional animation and filmed footage. It would win two MTV music awards, as well as become the most-played video on the channel in 2005.[58] Inspired by Hayoa Miyazaki's *Castle in the Sky*, the video's music and visual imagery juxtapose two imaginary landscapes, representing dystopic and utopian perspectives on a surrealistically modified modern world.[59] The video's *mise en scène* is described thus in a book co-authored by the Gorillaz creative team:

---

[58] "Feel Good Inc." controversially became the first recording to enter the UK singles charts on the basis of Internet sales alone, a fact that seems apposite in light of Gorillaz' reputation as a virtual and digital era band. Cass Browne with Gorillaz, *Rise of the Ogre: Gorillaz* (London: Penguin, 2006), 215.

[59] Ibid., 214.

The video opens on a vast sprawling metropolis, a grimy dystopia over which the Feel Good Tower surveys. It is this building that houses three of the Gorillaz—Murdoc, 2D and Russel—plus a whole host of liggers and burnouts... Outside, Noodle is seen sitting on the edge of a floating island, which appears to be powered by a windmill positioned on top of the island. However, she is being monitored by the ominous presence of two black helicopters... Inside the tower, 2D remains apparently unable to free himself from this state. To make matters worse, the ghostly apparitions of De La Soul appear to taunt 2D.[60]

In the light of Gorillaz' media-skeptical agenda, such imagery is best understood as an allegorical portrayal of the exploitation of consumers by an ethically impoverished entertainment industry. At the same time, the video raises questions about the environmental, social, and psychological costs of consumer-orientated urban life.

The video's narrative design is closely aligned to the content of the lyrics. An establishing shot reveals a dreary urban vista that bears more than a passing resemblance the grimier residential areas of London. The "camera" pans toward the base of the Feel Good Tower before tilting upwards toward its upper stories. Visually and conceptually the tower is a conglomeration of a factory chimney (representing industry), London's BT Tower (representing the domain of telecommunication), and the Capital Records Tower in Los Angeles (representing Adorno's "cultural industry"). The same rundown urban landscape is referred to obliquely in the lyrics of the first verse: "City breaking down on a camel's back" and "In a melancholy town where we never smile."

Shots of the song's fantasy domain, a windmill-powered airborne island inhabited by guitarist Noodle, are synchronized with the melodic refrain. In the first half of this section, the arrangement is largely acoustic, the main focus being on Albarn's lead vocals and the accompanying acoustic guitars. In the second, a powerful beat takes hold, which bridges the (mostly) acoustic refrain and the (mostly) electrified verses (which are driven by a strident bass guitar riff). The lyrics of this section strike a chord with the nostalgic and utopian tone of the music, speaking of forces of nature, stoic acceptance, and the rewards of interpersonal attachment: "Windmill, windmill for the land, turn forever hand in hand." However, the last two lines of the section strike a more menacing tone, with references to "fallin' down" and the enigmatic question, "is everybody in?" Rapping takes place over the dystopic verses (A sections), which feature the only filmed action of the video: shots of De La Soul taunting 2D on multiple video screens. These images are compared in the Gorillaz book to scenes from *Poltergeist* (dir. Tobe Hooper, 1982) and the Japanese film, *Ring* (dir. Hideo Nakata, 1998).

[60] Ibid.

Verses of the song are saturated with hysterical, mocking laughter, which corresponds loosely with themes of captivity and psychological torment that are obliquely expressed in the lyrics. The juxtaposition of "live" rappers and animated musicians works in much the same way as it does in the live performances discussed previously: both serve as allegories for something that lies beyond the videos and the actors, and both in different ways represent Benjamin's second order understanding of aura (implying alienated and disembodied experiences).

Readers familiar with the basic works of critical theory will recognize an affinity between these narrative machinations and Adorno's influential concept of the culture industry.[61] Feel Good Inc. is a near synonym of Adorno's term, suggesting the pseudo-industrialized production of pleasures that are designed to intoxicate the masses and thus to reproduce the socioeconomic status quo.[62] Aptly, the opening shots of the video closely resemble the urban topography described in Horkheimer and Adorno's *Dialektik der Aufklärung*, where they write of "a mass of gloomy houses and business premises in grimy, spiritless cities." The imprisonment of 2D along with his fellow band members and entourage of "liggers and burnouts" fits the Adornian picture of pernicious corporate powers exerting cynical control over an urban landscape filled with disenchantment. In the song's choruses, a glimmer of hope is offered as 2D turns his gaze longingly toward Noodle's sunlit utopia (a verdant lump of earth fashioned after a Gibson Flying V guitar). The same is true when this character, in the last line of an album suffused with darkness, implores the listener to "turn...around toward the sun" ("Demon Days," *Demon Days*). This optimism is quickly stamped out, however, by the ominous presence of two corporate-controlled helicopters, which monitor every move made by the island's inhabitants.

"ONLY THE COPY APPEARS...": FURTHER MUSINGS ON REPETITION AND ARTISTRY

As I have discussed in previous chapters, Theodor Adorno is notorious for his bad-tempered musings on popular music and jazz, which take issue with an element of repetition he perceived in the musical structures of Tin Pan Alley styled pop.[63] This

---

[61]   Max Horkheimer and Theodor Adorno, *Dialectic of Enlightenment* (London: Allen Lane, 1972 [1944]), 120–67.

[62]   See the chapter "The Culture Industry: Enlightenment as Mass Deception," in Horkheimer and Adorno, *Dialectic of Enlightenment*.

[63]   The text "only the copy appears" is taken from the first chapter of Horkheimer and Adorno's *Dialectic of Enlightenment* and encapsulates their bleak vision of contemporary life under consumerism and Fordist mass production: "The fusion of culture and entertainment that is taking place today leads not only to a depravation of culture, but inevitably to an intellectualization of amusement. This is evident from the fact that only the copy appears: in the movie theater, the photograph; on the radio, the recording." Horkheimer and Adorno, *Dialectic of Enlightenment*, 143.

he aligned with the alienated modes of production found in the Fordian production line, whose relevance in the contemporary socioeconomic climate is fast becoming moot. Stereotyped images of the industrial nevertheless make a strong statement that can be turned toward critical artistic ends. A brief look at the music of "Feel Good Inc." reveals an element of repetition that seems to make most sense when viewed through the lens of Adornian exegesis. The music in question is a two-syllable iteration of the line "Feel Good" set to a descending major second interval and intoned by Albarn/2D in a mechanical, emotionally stilted falsetto voice (Adorno might have called it a castrated voice). What sounds like a digital sample is detached from the naturalized context of vocal production that would ordinarily nourish it with meaning. Played no fewer than twenty-one times in the course of the dystopic song verses, this element is responsible for conveying the irony behind the lyrics. 2D is reduced to the status of an automaton, churning out the party line with an obvious lack of conviction. In the video these interpolations are illustrated with close-ups of 2D's face, which betray his obvious disaffection with his surroundings. Musically, the sample can be read as a representation of mass-produced material culture—a musical equivalent to Andy Warhol's endless silk-screen reprints of media icons like Marilyn Monroe and Elvis Presley. Transferred to a musical context, repetition of this type becomes a satire of manufactured pop, the feel-good factor of which has been overcooked, boiled dry until the music is drained of its expressive power—revealing the strained order of posthuman expression. In the lyrics, Albarn/2D remarks: "And all I want to hear is the message beep," a typically inscrutable message, which nevertheless hints at the narrator's withdrawal from salutary human contact. In this context, his musings become a reflection on the hollow digital dystopia that surrounds him, which is returnable to an endless stream of naughts and ones, bleeps and intervening silences—the digital sublime.

2D in this video (and elsewhere) is obviously dehumanized—as are many of his fellow actors. Which raises questions about the prominence of such imagery in the Gorillaz' creative output. Zombies (the living dead) feature prominently in the band's fictional world, and it might plausibly be surmised that this fate has befallen 2D, not to mention the groupies in the dystopic sections of video. Hewlett comments:

> The whole zombie thing is an obsession of mine. I love zombie films. Once, I looked out the window where I work and realized that everybody was walking around in circles with their mobile phones attached to their heads— it reminded me of that scene from *Dawn of the Dead* in the car lot.[64]

Zombies, then, stand in allegorically for alienated human subjectivity in an increasingly mediatized and consumption-orientated world. This assertion can be related to Marx's classic argument from the first volume of *Capital*, where he described the

---

[64] Gaiman, "Keeping It (Un)real," 2.

alienation of consumers from the material circumstances of industrial production. Widely associated with a species of technological determinism, this argument was extended by Frankfurt-school theorists like Adorno to address how industrial mass production casts a long shadow over contemporary life, including such expressive spheres as music and cinema. The association of zombies with a consumption-critical stance is addressed in some detail in academic writing on films like *Dawn of the Dead* (dir. Snyder, remake, 2004; dir. Romero, original, 1978).[65]

Provocatively, Hewlett directs his criticism of consumption-driven media culture toward audiovisual contexts that are conspicuously similar to those found in this video: "Everybody on TV's a fucking zombie, right? I mean, watch a 50 Cent video where he's in the middle of a club, and he's just surrounded by zombies."[66] In this way, the taunting rappers in "Feel Good Inc." become messengers from the media netherworld of MTV, an association that is not unproblematic given the degree of similarity in the audiovisual codes employed by De La Soul and 50 Cent. Albarn is generally more cautious in statements about his musical peers. He would probably subscribe to Hewlett's view, however, insofar as hip hop enthusiasts also differentiate between the "gangsta rap" of 50 Cent—with its apparent glorification of violence, homophobia and sexism—and the more liberal and eclectic approaches of "alternative rappers" like De La Soul. In this section of the video, the personae adopted by the rappers are stereotypically ardent, to such a degree that it is possible to understand these parts of the video as an ironic "take" on gangsta rap. Bullied into compliancy by the rappers' derisive laughter and their overbearing presence on multiple screens, Albarn's animated mouthpiece, 2D, can do little more than to reiterate his fixed sampled line. Entrapped in this dead-end world of base pleasures and deceptive gratification, the character is compelled to turn elsewhere in search of sanctuary. But where does he look, in terms of the narrative world of the video and beyond it? And is escape possible in light of the all-enveloping nature of his the condition, which would seem to be inseparable from the condition of advanced capitalism itself?

The utopian world 2D turns to for relief is the sanctuary of "acoustic music," a concept that the following chapter will demonstrate is not the same unreconstructed entity it might once have been. The refrain of "Feel Good Inc." is marked as acoustic through the presence of acoustic guitar layering, diegetic sounds (including the creaking sounds of the windmill) and 2D/Albarn's "untreated" voice. Contrasting with this, however, are a number of indeterminate electronic bleeps and an underlying synth pad wash. This is the only melody in the song, as the first verse introduction comprises only the clipped Feel Good sample and a spoken-word verse, performed by Albarn/2D on megaphone. Rapped lyrics and the chopped up Feel Good sample dominate verses 2 and 3. Demarcating this

---

[65] See Stephen Harper, "Zombies, Malls, and the Consumerism Debate: George Romero's *Dawn of the Dead*," *The Journal of American Popular Culture (1900–present)* 1/2 (Fall 2002), available at www.americanpopularculture.com/journal/articles/fall_2002/harper.htm, retrieved December 11, 2010.

[66] Gaiman, "Keeping It (Un)real," 2.

structural shift, as well, is a conspicuous change in sound quality when comparing the first verse with the vocal refrain section. 2D speaks through a megaphone in the first verse and this is reflected in the sound quality of Albarn's singing (or vice versa): the signal has been passed through a strong high band pass filter that emphasizes upper partials while distorting the tone of the voice. In contrast, the sung refrain is more naturalistic. This naturalness is relative, however, as careful listening reveals that it, too, has been equalized with an emphasis on high-end frequencies. This results in a sonic emulation of 1960s pop—particularly that of the so-called British invasion bands, whose vocal sound was also rich in upper partials.

The point of musical focus in the refrain is an ascending melodic line that is instantly recognizable as being strongly derivative of the Kinks's "Sunny Afternoon." The line "Taxman's taken all my dough" in Albarn's rendition becomes "Windmill, windmill for the land." This choice of referent will not surprise listeners familiar with Albarn's early career. The Kinks were among his most audible influences even in the days of Britpop. Albarn's voice resembles Kinks singer Ray Davies at the best of times, but here the resemblance is truly uncanny because the melodic extract he sings is audibly "lifted" from Davies' most famous hit. The stepwise minor ascent followed by a perfect fourth jump and subsequent drop to the dominant tonal function leave little doubt about the origin of the musical incorporation. A clear example of a hook, the phrase is repeated eight times in total, four in each refrain.[67] If formal resemblance were not enough, the subject matter of the two songs is remarkably similar. In "Sunny Afternoon," Davies relates the story of a decadent pop star whose life appears to be crumbling around him, but he is able to take solace in the simple pleasures of life, attainable by "sailing away" to the utopia of sunny afternoon. Albarn's song and video similarly document a desire to escape the trappings of pop stardom by utopian escape to a sunny day. (See Examples 6.1a and 6.1b.)

Example 6.1a Extract from the Kinks, "Sunny Afternoon."

Example 6.1b Extract from Gorillaz, "Feel Good Inc."

---

[67] Gary Burns, "A Typology of 'Hooks' in Popular Records," *Popular Music* 6/1, (January 1987): 1–20.

Asked to comment on Albarn's textual incorporation, Ray Davies responded:

> What can I say? He's a bit of an upstart. That is not just inspiration, it's bla-
> tant. I think some people do that kind of thing and they don't know they're
> doing it. I met him at some awards last year—and I'd just heard that song
> because it was one of the most successful songs of [2005]—and I was just
> too shocked to say anything to him. Oh well. These things happen...But
> I get fed up with affectionate nods to me. I'd rather they just paid up.[68]

The ethical issues at stake here are similar to those that have often been raised in discussions of sampling practices in rap, hip hop and contemporary dance styles; although, in sampled music the "duplication" of materials is usually easier to prove, since the source materials are demonstrably more present in the destination text. The incorporated materials here remain relatively unchanged, however, which invites comparison with sampling practices. Albarn himself is well aware of the direct nature of the textual incorporations in his music:

> If I hadn't spent all those years learning how to play instruments, I'd be
> using a sampler to put all these pieces together. Instead, I use a song-
> writing method that's a lot like sampling without actually digitally sam-
> pling. Gorillaz is how I take everything I hear and filter it. It's been really
> helpful having Danger Mouse onboard for that aspect of it.[69]

This approach is typical of music in the digital age, which has little to do with "copying" as the term is historically understood. Nevertheless, when Oasis "lifted" a melody, almost note-for-note, from Manfred Mann's "Yellow Flamingo" in "Don't Look Back in Anger," or Damon Albarn "borrows" from The Kinks in this song, the action performed is something other than the innocent use of a common musical currency.[70] The incorporation is more in the nature of a citation, not least because it is formally marked as distinct from the surrounding musical and sonic

---

[68]   Davies quoted in Sylvia Patterson, "What Happened When Ray Davies Wrote a Song for His Daughter's Band?" *The Word* 39 (May 2006): 32–34, 32. In an interview published in the same month, Davies is more generous: "I saw Damon when we got the UK Hall of Fame award. We even talked about working together on something this year. With Britpop, I was concerned about 'Why pick on me?', but at the same time very flattered. It's good to be embraced. And I found it all to be a return to innocence, in some ways. It was a nice time for music." Davies quoted in Nick Hasted, "An Audience with Ray Davies: Interview," *Uncut*, May 2006, 53.

[69]   Albarn quoted in Gaiman, "Keeping It (Un)real."

[70]   For a deconstructive reading of the Beatles that argues that musical incorporations were equally direct in their music as they are in contemporary forms, see Derek Scott, "(What's the Copy) The Beatles and Oasis," in Yrjö Heinonen et al., eds., *Beatlestudies 3* (Department of Music Research Reports: Jyväskylä, Finland, 2001), 201–11, 204.

environment. This type of incorporation is not what semiotician Robert Hatten would call a *stylistic* inclusion. The said technique is by far the most common form of intertextual incorporation to be found in popular music preceding what I will call the digital age (whose impact started to be felt in the 1980s). In contrast, Britpop, electronic dance music and hip hop acts of the past couple of decades have all taken an interest in *strategic* inclusions: those that are "marked" as distinct from the music style into which they are incorporated. In "Feel Good Inc." the act of marking is accomplished on several levels: in sound production, instrumental arrangement, formal musical content and textual subject matter. Because the music was not actually sampled, however, an element of uncertainty remains as to whether this might be considered a direct incorporation. No "quotation marks" are present to spell out the nature of the textual "borrowing," even though the music is *implicitly* marked for those with sufficient knowledge of popular music's history and its emerging codes. It is in this light that we should understand Davies' indignation, a vintage recording artist who hails from an age when such incorporations were frowned on.

The current aesthetic climate is characterized by the widespread use of *bricolage* (implying the use of found sonic objects) as a constructive principle to a degree that simply was not true for earlier generations of composers. This does not mean that contemporary musicians' creative faculties are somehow stymied compared with before. As Mark Katz notes in reference to digital sampling practices, collage-like uses of materials and the techniques of sound manipulation they are subjected to in recent styles suggest an activity that is "most fundamentally an act of *transformation*."[71] Unavoidably, this "challenges our notions of originality, of borrowing, or craft, and even of composition itself."[72] Academic writing on sampling and other conspicuous intertextual practices has generally agreed with this view, although ethnomusicological writing has flagged some problematic instances of power relations overlapping with long standing cultural imbalances.[73] Ray Davies could be forgiven for thinking in a similar way, although the cultural distance indicated in this case is generational rather than geopolitical.

Quite conspicuously, the "Sunny Afternoon" textual incorporation indicates a similar expressive purpose in the semantic content of the song to that of the source text, while at the same time articulating longing on Albarn's part for a coherent English identity that is in part mythological. As much as indignant over unacknowledged creative indebtedness, Davies might have been equally vexed at being

---

[71]   Mark Katz, *Capturing Sound: How Technology Has Changed Music* (Berkeley: University of California Press, 2004), 156.

[72]   Ibid., 156.

[73]   See Taylor, *Strange Sounds*.

consigned to the past by Albarn's strategic inclusion. Albarn is a different kind of composer to Davies: a surrealist collage artist of the digital age as much as the romantic image of the creator-artist trading in authenticity; a craftsperson as much as an artist; in other words, one who obviously compiles music out of existing materials rather than concealing his influences behind a transparent idiolect.[74] The emotional tenor of recent digital culture is strongly inscribed in almost all of his recent musical activities, as is an assumed cultural hybridity that Albarn's generation of songwriters takes for granted but which more senior musicians, on occasion, struggle to comprehend.

Afterthoughts

What sense can be made of Gorillaz' multimedia performances? Is this a playful deployment of Derridean deferral, where semiotic slippage brought about by listeners' inability to locate the band makes a mockery of the very act of representation, thus foregrounding spectacle and pleasures of the lower register? Perhaps this deployment has a critical edge, with the partial withdrawal of the "real band" from the public eye allowing audiences to re-examine their relationship to acts that employ more conventional modes of representation, and to recognize their own alienated condition as propagated by a nonbenign and dehumanizing music industry. When viewed in the light, the larger than life projected characters of the band and the unseen forces that guide them raise similar questions to those articulated in avant-garde music and theater.

Similar issues have been addressed also in recent cinema. At the end of a key scene in *The Truman Show* (1998), the creator of a fictional-reality TV series warns its hero not to step outside of the simulacrum he has lived in since birth: "There's no more truth out there," he piquantly observes, "than there is in the world I created for you." This quotation, with its obvious Baudrillardian resonance, is paraphrased in a comment of Hewlett's: "Gorillaz may not be real but they are no less so than the caricatures that are Marilyn Manson and Eminem."[75] It is possible, however, to overlook the parodic side of Gorillaz, in which case the crunching rhythms and towering figures of the virtual musicians might resemble more than they deconstruct existing modes of representation.

Unsurprisingly, long-time Blur antagonist Noel Gallagher is unconvinced. When first asked about the band, he commented:

---

[74] Susan McClary, *Conventional Wisdom: The Content of Musical Form* (Berkeley: University of California Press, 200), 141.

[75] Duerden, "Gorillaz in Our Midst."

"Is there a bandwagon passing? Park it outside my house." He'll be in a heavy metal band next year when it's fashionable... [I]t's fitting that he ended up a cartoon. He always was a cartoon.[76]

Here Gallagher seems to recognize both Albarn's troubling complicity with the culture industry and the apparent futility of his idealistic attempts to step outside of its symbolic apparatus. But by placing *himself* on the outside, the Oasis singer does little more than remind audiences how tropes of authenticity are traditionally understood to be the exclusive property of the rebellious male rock star. Returning to Albarn, there can be little doubt that in this project he has taken a disconcerting step toward the lucrative youth market on the one hand and the post-countercultural hedonism of dance on the other. His new audiovisual environment, created using the nonlinear, object-orientated logic of Logic and a semi-anonymous wealth of collaborative talent is infuriatingly flexible, apparently impossible to pin down to a fixed ideological agenda, preoccupied with production techniques and presentation rather than the serious business of writing and performing songs. In the spaces between the flickering of the animated figures and a booming synthetic bass, however, an agenda of sorts can be recognized that is closely bound up with the technological keystones of the music.

"The digital won't let me go," Albarn sings in the refrain of the song "Tomorrow Comes Today" (*Gorillaz*), which brings to mind Adorno's controversial comments regarding the impact of industrial technology on popular styles.[77] For Adorno, popular music was so saturated with the rhetoric of oppression, as conveyed most obviously in its repetitive form, so that even the most politically reactionary song became an unintentional affirmation of technocratic servitude. Throughout his career, however, Adorno's blind spot was his failure to understand how transforming the material conditions of oppression musically might lead to a form of emancipation. In Gorillaz' music, the source of greatest anxiety might also be the source of listeners' greatest pleasure. A powerful subtext in the words, music and visual representations of their songs points to the alienation of a technologically savvy, post-apocalyptic "lost generation" embracing a life of pointless pleasure and streetwise skepticism. Technology is inextricably bound up with the band's musical world as well. While the music of "Clint Eastwood" makes nostalgic reference to the analog technologies of punk-era dub reggae, the song would not have turned out the way it did had it not been produced in a contemporary digital setting incorporating a wide array of current styles. This is conveyed both in the choice of sounds and in the structural properties of the music. It results in a

---

[76] Quoted in Michael Odell, "The Oasis Interview," *Q magazine*, May 2002, 92–100, 100.

[77] Theodor Adorno, *Prisms* (Cambridge, MA: MIT Press, 1981 [1967]), 121–32; Theodor Adorno, "On Popular Music," in Frith and Goodwin, eds., *On Record*, 301–14.

form of temporal stratification between "outmoded" and "contemporary" styles that leads to the partial rebuttal of narratives of technological progress. More important, it allows listeners to track changes in personal and collective identities in parallel to changes perceived in the music.

Gorillaz' music sounds (and *looks*) as though it were composed in the cultural context of modern-day multicultural Britain. This apparent celebration of hybridic cultural identity in contemporary urban Britain does not *feel* as though it is fake, no matter how painstakingly constructed other aspects of the band's real and virtual messages might seem to be. However, the audiovisual imagery the band employs does seem to articulate some residual anxieties about post-imperialist Britain. We can see this in the way the group of rappers frightens the white emo singer in "Feel Good Inc."[78] By juxtaposing the rap sections of the song with its utopian island, occupied by East Asian rhythm guitarist Noodle and acoustic music that harks back to the golden age of British songwriting, Albarn sets up a dialectical circuit that is nowhere broken down into a more explanatory discourse. And yet, there is nothing to suggest that Albarn's multicultural references are disingenuous. Because of the skillful melding of styles in Gorillaz' "songs," their music imports a deep appreciation of rap artistry and the subversive potential of hip hop noise that elevates the music above parodic condescension.[79] African-American rhythms and subsonic sounds are the gravitational force that bonds the band's fragmented musical textures. This is reflected in the African-American identity of Gorillaz drummer, Russel. Moreover, the dissolution of musical coherence in the dub sections of "Clint Eastwood" and countless other Gorillaz songs is heavily indebted to Afro-Caribbean models of escapism alloyed to cultural narratives of post-imperial resistance.

Paul Gilroy's misgivings about postcolonial melancholia occupying a dominant affective position in the Britpop movement are justified.[80] In Gorillaz, however, Albarn has largely discarded this problematic cultural baggage. Even an obvious incorporation from (ethnically cleansed) British popular music from the swinging sixties, although it is not without a residue of postcolonial anxiety, seems celebratory of cultural hybridity in contemporary Britain more than it is nostalgic. For the most part, Gorillaz' audiovisual representations feel like sonic articulations of Gilroy's "principled internationalism" and "cosmopolitan conviviality";

---

[78] I am grateful to Carol Vernallis for prodding me to recognize this aspect.

[79] A seminal consideration of black identity and the politics of noise as resistance in rap music is found in Tricia Rose, *Black Noise: Rap Music and Black Culture in Contemporary America* (Hanover, NH: Wesleyan University Press, 1994).

[80] Paul Gilroy, *There Ain't No Black in the Union Jack* (Abingdon, Oxfordshire: Routledge, 2002), xxiv. For more on the cultural aspects of Britpop, see Kari Kallioniemi, "'Put the Needle on and Think of England'— Notions of Englishness in the Post-War Debate on British Pop Music," (Ph.D. dissertation, University of Turku, Finland, 1998).

ideals that pop consumers in the British capital and elsewhere will increasingly recognize as belonging to everyday experience in cultural circumstances that are increasingly intercultural and multiethnic.[81]

The affective power of Gorillaz' music can only be explained when all of this cross-referencing is inscribed within the context of a carefully crafted and deceptively simple pop song, which in no small measure is attributable to the handiwork of Albarn. The auteur in the age of digital pop, although wounded does not seem to be willing to lie down and die. This is decidedly not, however, a 1960s-style singer-songwriter auteur. If the running call of that generation was Timothy Leary's catch phrase "turn on, tune in, drop out," a reversal of these sentiments might be indicated by 2D's final act at the Brit Awards. In a gesture as self-empowering yet evasive as man-without-a-name Damon Albarn's reluctance to take center stage in the early years of this project, his animated-double approaches the camera with haughty indifference at the end of the Brit Awards performance to extinguish his own projected image. This measured response to his "overexposure" may find a parallel in pop consumers' growing skepticism toward the overexposure of manufactured pop acts, as indicated by the recent plummeting sales in the music industry. Perhaps the critics are right and pop has no need for soapboxes, as each generation critiques itself in music and music sales.

[81] See Paul Gilroy, *After Empire: Melancholia or Convivial Culture?* (Abingdon, Oxfordshire: Routledge, 2004), 9. This, at least, was my experience when teaching the materials presented in the chapter at City University in London in the early 2000s. Gorillaz turns up in a wide range of social and media contexts at the time of this writing. The Japanese surrealist writer Haruki Murakami listens to Gorillaz when jogging, as does the protagonist of the TV show *House M.D.* (played by British actor, Hugh Laurie) in the first episode of series two. The song played in the opening moments of this episode is "Feel Good Inc." The ironic tone of the music in this audiovisual context comments eloquently on the protagonist's uncharacteristically cheerful disposition.

7

Performing Acoustic Music in the Digital Age, or a Surreal Twist of Fate

In the previous chapter, I indentified "acoustic music" as a discursive category that stands for the apparent sanctuary of unmediated experience in a world where technological mediation is ubiquitous.[1] It is this opposition that lies at the heart of this chapter, which tracks how a group of artists working at the fringes of popular music have engaged with a range of discourses fanning out from the idea of "the acoustic." I should stress that it is *the idea* of the acoustic that is my primary focus here: acoustic music as a discursive construct. "Acousticness" obviously has a distinctive phenomenal imprint: a sonic quality arising from the performance of unamplified instruments in close proximity to listeners. That said, much of what passes today for acoustic music involves elements of compromise or even fakery, not least because of how the acoustic signal is modified electronically and digitally in the majority of recordings and live performances. Furthermore, a case could be made that even acoustic music in the traditional sense of unamplified performance is conditioned in part by the prevalent modes of production and dissemination of the digital age, as repertories and performing styles are increasingly dominated by practices that have come to prominence in new media contexts.

In close readings of performances by KT Tunstall, The Blue Nile, Suzanne Vega, and Sigur Rós, I will grapple with the question: what is the relevance of

[1] An earlier version of the section on KT Tunstall was first published as John Richardson, "Televised Live Performance, Looping Technology and the 'Nu Folk': KT Tunstall on *Later…with Jools Holland,*" in Derek B. Scott, ed., *The Ashgate Research Companion to Popular Musicology* (Farnham and Burlington: Ashgate, 2009), 85–101. Sections of this chapter have benefited from the comments of numerous colleagues, including Philip Auslander, Derek Scott, Stan Hawkins, and Susanna Välimäki. The sections on The Blue Nile and Sigur Rós were presented as a lecture, "Back to the Garden? Performing the Disaffected Acoustic Imaginary in the Digital Age," at the International Institute for Popular Culture (IIPC) Debates series, University of Turku, March 2, 2010, see http://iipc.utu.fi/iipcdebate3.pdf, retrieved May 22, 2011.

acoustic forms in an age of unprecedented technological sophistication and communicative indirectness? This will entail identifying how acoustic performance is different today than it was in the past—in previous folk revivals and 1960s counterculture—to which the new acoustic music is sometimes (simplistically) compared. Several threads will emerge, including how semiotic marking directs and modifies musical affects, how the migration of forms (or their "remediation") from visual to sonic media and vice versa articulates tensions in daily life, and the usefulness of reflection as an analytical category in discussions of the emerging acoustic forms.

As I implied above, the notion of acoustic music retains significant ties to earlier ideas about the nature and politics of unamplified performance. The folk protest song era, the 1960s counterculture, and the singer-songwriter movement—which extended into the 1970s and beyond—are commonly held to be the glory days of what is now called acoustic music. The title of this chapter implies both continuity and difference in the passage from the heyday of acoustic folk to the present day. The lyrical content of each of the artist's songs discussed in this chapter speaks to something other than the kind of political activism that has been traditionally associated with folk. If there is a politics in the "nu-folk," and I would contend that there is, then it is implicit and embodied in sounds and actions more than it is semantically explicit.

There are important differences as well in the cultural meanings ascribed to the music as they relate to the technologies used in recordings and performances. Ever since the advent of folk-rock in late 1960s, uses of electronic technology have met with a mixed reception. This is epitomized by the urban myth of Pete Seeger literally pulling the plug from Dylan's first electric performance at the Newport Folk Festival in 1965. My primary intention is not to rehearse the debates on authenticity that have circulated since that time. Suffice it to say that the alignment of folk with an idealized agrarian past ("we've to get ourselves back to the garden," as Joni Mitchell sang in the hippie anthem "Woodstock" [*Ladies of the Canyon*, 1970]) and notions of community founded on interpersonal communication between equals encountering one another in intimate spaces was strongly problematized in the passage from folk to folk-rock, where individual expression and savvy articulations of city life displaced earlier ideas about what was considered "real" or relevant.[2] Both folk and rock artists shared an attitude of derision toward pop consumerism, which continues to some extent in the statements of

    [2] For more on these debates, see Simon Frith, " 'The Magic That Can Set You Free': The Ideology of Folk and the Myth of the Rock Community," in Richard Middleton and David Horn, eds., *Popular Music. Vol. 1. Folk or Popular? Distinctions, Influences, Continuities* (Cambridge: Cambridge University Press, 1981), 159–68; and *Performing Rites: Evaluating Popular Music* (Oxford: Oxford University Press, 1996). See also Keir Keightley, "Reconsidering Rock," in Simon Frith, Will Straw and John Street, eds., *The Cambridge Companion to Pop and Rock* (Cambridge: Cambridge University Press, 2001), 109–42.

"nu-folk" artists today (KT Tunstall is quite ardent about this). These boundary lines are proving harder than ever to defend, however, as nu-folk artists increasingly dabble with the semiotic codes of mainstream pop and electronica. As I maintained in the preceding chapter, the technological foundations of styles may well be crucial in determining the cultural meanings styles are equipped to carry. More than electrification, which might have been the crunch issue to those making popular music in the 1960s, the modes of production and aesthetic understanding we have absorbed from digital culture in recent years impinge directly on the musical examples to be discussed. Surpassing old distinctions between the urban and the agrarian, digital aesthetics can be seen as infiltrating musical production and consumption in ways that are more fluid and which are certain to redefine the relationship between individuals and communities. Folk revivals in such contexts are undoubtedly not what they used to be.

A chapter on the (conspicuously absent or present) visual in acoustic music might seem like a red herring in view of the central concerns of this project. Yet, it reflects back on the other chapters in a negative dialectic that brings the remainder of the book into sharper relief. Arguably, acoustic music illuminates better than much of the music discussed in this book how imagination is key in responses to recent forms, which implies the potential for crossmedial negotiations even in the absence of an obvious or deliberate visual "text." It is because the visual in acoustic music comes so heavily freighted with anxieties that rebound on experiences of modern life that it is of particular interest. Furthermore, as I will argue in the final section of this chapter, the new acoustic music requires from audiences a kind of "night vision": the ability the step across the threshold that separates categorical consciousness from sensory experience, the auditory from the visual. In doing this, it gives license to the imagination and what Benjamin calls the mimetic faculties to usurp the position conventionally held by restrictive rationalizing forces in shaping subjectivity.

Instance I. KT Tunstall on *Later . . . with Jools Holland*: Visualizing the Recorded Song

Authenticity in folk and rock genres has long been premised upon what some theorists have called "the demonization of the visual."[3] By this they mean the impulse to distinguish folk/rock performance sharply from those (commercially

---

[3] Christopher Martin, "Traditional Criticism of Popular Music and the Making of a Lip-Synching Scandal," *Popular Music and Society* 17/4 (1993): 63–81, 67; Philip Auslander, *Liveness: Performance in a Mediatized Culture*, 2nd edition (London: Routledge, 2008), 91.

sullied) forms that depend on visual reinforcement in order to court a popular following.[4] But there are limits to even the most insistent rock critics' disdain of the ocular. When it comes to authenticating musicianship, the question of liveness is frequently pushed to the fore, an aspect that is enforced through the principle "seeing is believing."[5] The role played by visual reinforcement is not, of course, new, or exclusive to electronic and digital technologies. As long as music has been performed, it has had a corresponding visual component. Moreover, the advent of the recording age did not put an end to this state of affairs. Just how visually codified auditory experience has been throughout the twentieth century, a time when acousmatic listening has prevailed, is apparent from research into consumption practices associated with gramophone records.[6] What is more, traces of visual experience are frequently retained in auditory forms: including the placement of musicians in the stereo or multichannel mix; the semiotic encoding of instruments to imply spatial effects (horns for wide open spaces, acoustic guitar for intimacy); the spatial qualities of the acoustic environment (as determined by natural acoustics or simulated reverb, delay and compression); and other factors relating to the tactile and visual bases of auditory memory.[7] Regardless of the impetus to bury the visual dimensions of auditory

[4] I hold rock authenticity to be the transformation of folk authenticity, in line with the research since Simon Frith's article "'The Magic That Can Set You Free,'" (see note 2). While folk aesthetics advocated the effacement of the individual and a return to agrarian values, rock aesthetics saw the individual performer as a focus for self-identification in the context of mediatized, industrial society. See Keightley, "Reconsidering Rock," in Frith, Straw and Street, ed., *The Cambridge Companion to Pop and Rock*. It is easy to agree with Gracyk's insistence that authenticity "is not on the wane in the rock community." Theodore Gracyk, *Rhythm and Noise: An Aesthetics of Rock* (London: I.B. Tauris, 1996), 222. But his endorsement of Kurt Cobain as the model authentic performer brings into view the extent to which narratives of stardom (and in this case also martyrdom) impinge upon perceptions of the music. Above all, authenticity in rock and other genres is bound up with perceptions of creative agency and authorship and how these are mediated in different musical and multimedia settings.

[5] See Auslander, *Liveness*, 85. Whether a performer can "cut it live" is a question frequently broached in rock criticism and in the digital age it is no longer easily answered. See Andrew Goodwin, "Sample and Hold: Pop Music in the Digital Age of Reproduction," in Simon Frith and Andrew Goodwin, eds., *On Record: Rock, Pop and the Written Word* (London: Routledge, 1990), 258–73, 268, for a consideration of how performers, including the Pet Shop Boys, have employed different tactics of legitimation by authenticating their performances more through their actions as pop auteurs than through conventional channels.

[6] See Dave Laing, "A Voice Without a Face: Popular Music and the Phonograph in the 1890s," *Popular Music*, 10/1 (1991): 1–9, 7–8; Jonathan Sterne, *The Audible Past: Cultural Origins of Sound Reproduction* (Durham, NC: Duke University Press, 2003), 215–33; and Andrew Goodwin, *Dancing in the Distraction Factory: Music Television and Popular Culture* (Minneapolis: University of Minnesota Press, 1992), 8.

[7] See Chapter 6 on Gorillaz. Also Auslander, *Liveness*, 85; Peter Doyle, *Echo and Reverb: Fabricating Space in Popular Music Recording* (Middletown, CT: Wesleyan University Press, 2005); Evan Eisenberg, *The Recording Angel: Music, Records and Culture from Aristotle to Zappa* (New Haven, CT: Yale University Press, 2005), 53; Denis Smalley, "Space-Form and the Acousmatic Image," *Organised Sound* 12/1 (April 2007): 35–58; Philip Tagg and Bob Clarida, *Ten Little Title Tunes: Toward a Musicology of Mass Media* (New York and Montreal: The Mass Media Musicologists' Press, 2003), 217–70.

experience, whether in deference to rock ideology[8] or with a view to debunking bourgeois spectacle,[9] the visual has a tendency to resurface, much like the Freudian unconscious and with all of the libidinal force of the repressed. Contrary to the prevailing theoretical bias, this need not be understood as detrimental to performances. Like Kay Dickinson, I am distrustful of "theoretical assumptions that...only...recognize unitary, fenced in modalities," a theoretical line that stretches back at least as far as Eisenstein in audiovisual theory and Hanslick in music theory. The Kantian assumptions behind such theories are challenged in my theorization.[10]

The visual authentication of performers is strongly inscribed in the format of BBC television's *Later...with Jools Holland* (henceforth *Later*), a program that in the British context continues the legacy of shows like *The Old Grey Whistle Test* (1971–1987) and *The Tube* (1982–1987). By advocating live performance, programming of this type has long stood in opposition to the widespread use of playback on *Top of the Pops* (1964–2006) as well as the pre-recorded audiovisual "distractions" of music video channels. The role of Holland himself in the series is symptomatic; a virtuoso boogie-woogie and blues-style pianist, the show's *compère* is regularly called on to prove his credentials as a live performer in cameo appearances with top performers, thereby asserting his authority to front the show. Recently, the status of television programming that endorses live (rock) musicianship has nevertheless been eclipsed somewhat due to the popularity of the—highly commodified and tightly formatted—*Idol* franchise, as well as other forms of "reality" programming. The popularity of such shows could be attributed in part to their incursions into rock territory through an emphasis on live performance, just as rock values have been eroded at the other end of the spectrum by the willingness of rock artists to flirt with visual spectacle, from Pink Floyd to the Arctic Monkeys—albeit ironically in the case of the latter. And yet, these might be considered exceptions that prove the rule. Recognized pop acts known for their showmanship are still inclined to tone down their performances when appearing on *Later*, including Robbie Williams and the Scissor Sisters, while acts that self-identify as rock have long been inclined to introduce an element of parody into their lip-synching and miming actions when appearing on

[8] Lawrence Grossberg, "The Media Economy of Rock Culture: Cinema, Post-Modernity and Authenticity," in Simon Frith, Andrew Goodwin and Lawrence Grossberg, eds., *Sound and Vision: The Music Video Reader* (London: Routledge, 1993), 185–209, 204–05; Gracyk, *Rhythm and Noise*, 75–79.

[9] Theodor W. Adorno, *Introduction to the Sociology of Music*, trans. E.B. Ashton (New York: Continuum, 1976), 81–84; also Guy Debord, *Society of the Spectacle* (London: Rebel Press, 2004).

[10] Kay Dickinson, "Music Video and Synaesthetic Possibility," in Roger Beebe and Jason Middleton, eds., *Medium Cool: Music Videos from Soundies to Cellphones* (Durham, NC: Duke University Press, 2007), 13–29, 15.

Top of the Pops (*TOTP*).[11] Perhaps the truth of the matter is that greater pressures are being brought to bear on artists across the pop-rock divide to prove their mettle in the live arena; a matter that is certainly highlighted in KT Tunstall's debut appearance on *Later*.

Tunstall's métier is live performance, a point she has made relentlessly in interviews. And yet, as Theodore Gracyk has noted, the primary activity for many contemporary recording artists is not live performance but rather the labor undertaken in the studio beforehand.[12] Moreover, an element of "remediation" is present in live performances of rock, which can easily be perceived as reworkings of recordings produced for consumption in different formats and media—such as CD, compressed digital audio (MP3, AAC), or music video.[13] What happens, one might ask, when the very act of remediation is spotlighted through the incorporation of multitrack recording techniques as an integral aspect of live performance in a way that inscribes the musician's performativity? This question, I will argue, goes to the heart of Tunstall's breakthrough performance of "Black Horse and the Cherry Tree" on *Later*, televised by the BBC on October 22, 2004 (later released on the DVD, *Best of Later...with Jools Holland: 2000–2006*). The choice of this performance is justified because it encapsulates a cluster of issues that have come to a head in recent popular culture, relating to the changing nature of live television, the cultural meanings ascribed to repetitive music, and the interface of digital technology with creativity in emerging audiovisual forms.

SITUATING "BLACK HORSE"

Tunstall appeared on *Later* only because of a last-minute cancelation by the rap artist Nas. Prior to her performance, she was a virtually unknown aspiring "nu-folk" artist performing in small venues to a scattering of enthusiasts. Some indication of the perceived strength of the *Later* performance can be surmised from its immediate impact on her career. Tunstall surpassed established acts like The Cure and Jackson Browne in the popularity poll for the episode posted on the show's website, winning more than half the votes.[14] Her debut album, *Eye to the Telescope* (2004), was quickly released just a month later with the newly popular "Black Horse" appended to it; it jumped to number seven on the UK charts before

---

[11] For a comprehensive list of spoofing practices on (and of) *TOTP*, see the relevant Wikipedia site http://en.wikipedia.org/wiki/Top_of_the_Pops, retrieved June 19, 2008. The introduction of the *Later* spin-off show, *Later Live*, in 2008, could be understood as an attempt to reclaim the initiative from reality shows in live television programming.

[12] Gracyk, *Rhythm and Noise*, 69–98.

[13] Jay Bolter and Richard Grusin define remediation as "the representation of one medium in another." "Remediation," *Configurations* 3 (1996): 311–58, 339. See also Auslander, *Liveness*, 6–7.

[14] Fiona Shepherd, "Live and Proud," *The Scotsman*, June 11, 2005, http://news.scotsman.com/kttunstall/Live—proud.2634231.jp, retrieved June 19, 2008.

peaking at three.[15] In the months that followed, Tunstall was engaged for similar solo spots on the French live music program, *Taratata* (May 12, 2005),[16] and several North American talk shows, as well as headlining at Glastonbury. The pinnacle of exposure for Tunstall's music, if not the artist herself, came when *American Idol* contestant Katharine McPhee covered "Black Horse" in the final of the 2006 season, which resulted in a quantifiable peak in record sales.[17] This is ironic in light of Tunstall's scathing criticism of the show—criticism consistent with her outspoken comments on a variety of issues, including the influence of the mass media, environmentalism and performers she does not wish to be compared with, including Dido and Katie Melua.[18] A conspicuous thread running through this commentary is her stalwart commitment to the ethos of "liveness" as it has been understood in the context of folk-rock ideology.

Technology figured prominently in Tunstall's performances during this time. Prior to the *Later* appearance, she had completed a three-month solo tour of small venues where she beefed up her live sound using one of a new generation of digital looping pedals, the Akai E2 Headrush, which allows the simulation of multitracking studio techniques in "real time."[19] A further rationale for its inclusion in her live act was the simple fact that she could not afford a supporting band.[20] Several folk artists at the time were experimenting with looping technology, including Howie Day, David Ford and Foy Vance, and it is possible that Tunstall took

[15] Editorial, Charts.us website, http://acharts.us/album/14298, retrieved June 20, 2008.

[16] "KT Tunstall: Black Horse and the Cherry Tree," My Taratata official website, http://video.mytaratata.com/search/?q=KT+Tunstall, retrieved June 30, 2008.

[17] Chris Rolls, "KT Tunstall: Slightly More Esoteric," http://www.mp3.com/news/stories/10018.html, retrieved June 19, 2008.

[18] "Tunstall Apologies to Dido," contactmusic.com, http://www.contactmusic.com/new/xmlfeed.nsf/mndwebpages/tunstall%20apologies%20to%20dido, retrieved June 19, 2008. Following unfavorable reactions to her comment, "Dido can't fucking sing," Tunstall made the following retraction: "I was slightly ashamed the other day, I responded in a very virile manner. It just sometimes gets very frustrating, particularly when it comes to playing live, because that is my domain. If there is one thing I can blow my own trumpet about it's that I can let rip at a live show." See also the Editorial, "Tunstall Hates Melua Comparison," http://www.contactmusic.com/news.nsf/article/tunstall%20hates %20melua%20comparison_1041625, retrieved June 19, 2008.

[19] Chris Rolls, "KT Tunstall: Slightly More Esoteric." The Akai E2 Headrush, used by Tunstall in "Black Horse," is one of a new generation of devices that features this functionality. The pedal is no longer in production at the time of writing and has been surpassed in its specifications by the Digitech Jamman and the Boss RC-20 Loop Station. New technologies will undoubtedly have replaced these by the time this book is published. Other songs performed by Tunstall with the pedal include The Jackson Five's classic hit "I Want You Back," Tunstall's own "Stoppin' the Love," Bob Dylan's "Tangled Up in Blue" and Missy Elliot's "Get Ur Freak On."

[20] Quoted in the editorial, "KT Tunstall: Refusing to Be 'The Suicidal Girl With A Guitar,'" UltimateGuitar.com, November 6, 2007, http://www.ultimate-guitar.com/interviews/interviews/kt_tunstall_refusing_to_be_the_suicidal_girl_with_a_guitar.html, retrieved June 23, 2008.

inspiration from one or more of these musicians.[21] The fact that she refers to the Akai Headrush as Wee Bastard opens up intriguing avenues for interpretative inquiry, along with the songwriter's self-description as "a robbing gypsy bastard."[22] Setting aside the potentially offensive stereotyping in this statement (which I do not underwrite), it is evident that Tunstall identifies on a personal level with the pedal.[23] An adopted child of mixed Scottish, Irish and Cantonese descent, in statements such as these she projects a road-hardened nomadic identity onto the mechanical apparatus that facilitates her performances, which in turn becomes a form of commentary on musical production. Of particular interest in this respect is contemplating how her use of digital looping technology and, more generally, her approach to songwriting might be informed by self-perceptions of this nature.

Tunstall's work is bound to contemporary performers primarily though her interest in looping technology. Narrowing the focus further, it is easy to recognize an affinity with musicians associated with the label "folktronica," a catchphrase for all manner of artists who combine mechanical dance beats with elements of acoustic rock or folk, such as Múm, David Gray, Tunng, The Books, Björk and the Blue Nile. Productive though the category might be, Tunstall's music is something of a square peg in relation to this round hole. Her reliance on traditional blues-based forms in tandem with the catchy guitar-pop side of her musical identity set her apart from those working in more marginal aesthetic places. Her uses of looping in solo live performances produce similar sonic end results to some of her more experimental or avant-pop peers, however, and it is this aspect that I will focus on.

LOOPING THE LOOP—PERFORMING CONTROL

Early shots of the *Later* performance capture the solitary figure of Tunstall stooped over the looping pedal while immersed in the labor of setting down the song's initial groove. Such an elevated degree of concentration is necessary because inaccuracies in timing can lead to a flawed underlying groove that will repeat embarrassingly throughout the duration of the song.[24] A distinctive feature

---

[21] Another artist to employ live looping on *Later* was the French singer Camille in the song "Au Port," televised on May 12, 2006.

[22] Quoted in Sylvia Patterson, "I'm a Robbing Gypsy Bastard," *The Word* 37 (March 2006): 74–78, 76, 78. In a similar vein she describes herself in the same interview as "a magpie" and one of a group of "folk tart[s]" who use "folk music as a bed—and then sleep[s] with other things." Ibid., 75.

[23] In one interview, she commented: "I have this theory that I can name and blame…Often, I press the wrong button to record stuff, and I just thought if I called it something derogatory that people would assume that it was because it was temperamental, not me." Quoted in "KT Tunstall: Refusing to Be 'The Suicidal Girl With A Guitar.'"

[24] In her performance of "I Want You Back" on the French live music show *Taratata*, Tunstall was distracted by the audience clapping along with the beat and was forced to scrap her first attempt at setting up a groove.

of this performance is the attention the singer-songwriter pays to laying down a complex multipart groove. The ratio is somewhat different in other performances of "Black Horse" in which Tunstall plays five verses. In the *Later* version she plays only three; consequently more than half of the song is taken up with the piece-meal construction, abrupt dissolution and reconstitution of the arrangement in audible processes that resemble those found in musical minimalism (measures 1–26 and 61–79; DVD timings can be extrapolated from Table 7.1).[25] In addition, a family resemblance to contemporaneous forms such as electronic dance music (EDM), remix practices and gaming music is likely to inform many listeners' experiences.[26]

Consequently, the viewer becomes privy to processes of assembly that are usually conducted in private, rather than in the presence of a studio audience and television cameras. This aura of privacy is accentuated when a handheld camera encircles Tunstall, when else but during the "turnaround" chord sequence of the song's chorus, which engenders a tangible sense of intrusion. Only in those sections that are sung and where no new loops are introduced does the performer engage with the audience more directly, although even here she makes a conspicuous show of multitasking by stomping a tambourine with her left foot while her right remains free to control the looping pedal. Contrary to the received wisdom on looping and other repetitive practices—which portrays them as "passive" and, when sampling is involved, "parasitical"—the evidence of this television footage points toward a heightening of agency through the performer's immersion in the act of composition, which is compounded by the fact that her role overlaps with that of the studio engineer. For this reason, I consider the gerundive form of the verb "looping" to be a more accurate descriptor of her activity than the noun "loop." The loop, in this instance, must be looped: the musical sample does not simply repeat; Tunstall must *repeat it*.[27] Furthermore, the process of looping must be visually authenticated if agency is to be correctly assigned.

---

[25] John Richardson, *Singing Archaeology: Philip Glass's Akhnaten* (Hanover, NH: Wesleyan University Press, 1999); K. Robert Schwarz, "Steve Reich: Music as a Gradual Process, Part 1," *Perspectives of New Music* 19 (1981): 374–92; Dan Warburton, "A Working Terminology for Minimal Music," *Intégral* 2 (1988): 135–59; Robert Fink, *Repeating Ourselves: American Minimalism as Cultural Practice* (Berkeley: University of California Press, 2005).

[26] Luis-Manuel Garcia, "On and On: Repetition as Process and Pleasure in Electronic Dance Music," *Music Theory Online* 11/4 (2005), sections 1.1–7.4. Available at http://www.societymusictheory.org/mto/issues/mto.05.11.4/mto.05.11.4.garcia.html, retrieved December 17, 2010; Stan Hawkins, "Feel the Beat Come Down: House Music as Rhetoric," in Allan Moore, ed., *Analyzing Popular Music* (Cambridge: Cambridge University Press, 2003), 80–102; Karen Collins, "An Introduction to the Participatory and Non-Linear Aspects of Video Games Audio," in John Richardson and Stan Hawkins, eds., *Essays on Sound and Vision* (Helsinki: Helsinki University Press/Yliopistopaino, 2007), 263–98.

[27] See Garcia, "On and On," 39; also Christopher Small, *Musicking: The Meanings of Performing and Listening* (Hanover, NH: Wesleyan University Press, 1998).

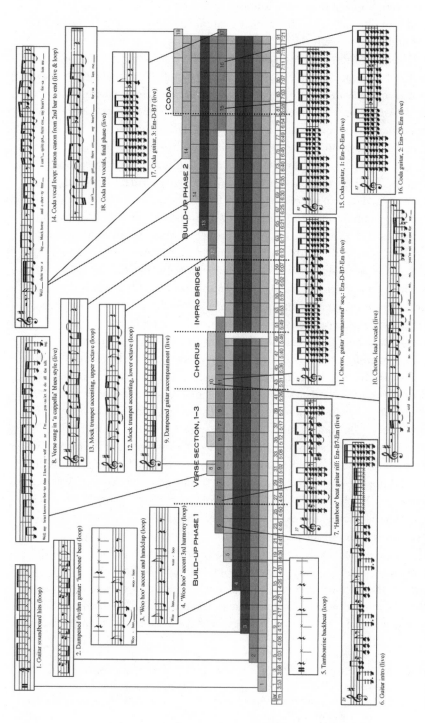

Table 7.1 KT Tunstall's "Black Horse and the Cherry Tree" on *Later...with Jools Holland*: Transcription Showing the Organization of Tracks and Loops

In the song's initial moments, Tunstall lays down a brisk "um pa" beat with repeated soundboard hits on the acoustic guitar (measures 1–4). This pattern is quickly embellished with dampened rhythmic chopping, which establishes a skeletal groove for the verses (measures 5–8). The resulting pattern is recognizable as the "hambone" (or Bo Diddley) rhythm, with its New Orleans styled syncopations pulling against the first two beats prior to two emphatic unsyncopated accents.[28] An element of bluesy soul enters the picture with the incremental addition of catchy woo-hoo accents, the "hoos" falling on the downbeat—the "woo" upbeat and trailing melodic line spelling out the singer's blues credentials through vocal "smears" on the third and seventh degrees. The first such loop, centered on the E minor tonic, is lent percussive edge by strident handclapping, a gesture designed to evince a response from the studio audience (measures 9–14). The second loop reinforces the initial pattern through harmonizing on the third (measures 15–17). With the song's basic groove in place, the accompaniment is filled out by the addition of live acoustic guitar. Some initial riffing high up the neck of the instrument precedes a dramatic downward slide in search of a resounding open-position E minor chord (measures 23–26). It is as if this chord cues the beginning of the performance proper, although the setting of the musical stage that has gone on beforehand is only nominally secondary to "the song."

David Brackett has addressed the sensory and symbolic significance of the open E chord in folk-rock styles in a probing discussion of Elvis Costello's "It's Time."[29] For Brackett, use of the instrument's open strings in this chord and coincidences in its pitch organization with the overtone series are factors contributing to the unique power and resonance it is felt by many performers to have. In the context of folk-rock composition, he further argues that the "sonic emblem" of the open E (in his discussion, E major) has mostly been exploited by singer-songwriters from the mid-1960s, the cultural affiliations evinced by this gesture effectively marking off such "magic moments" from perceived African-American influences. In "Black Horse" the articulation of this gesture, or something resembling it, is characteristically celebratory and resounding, an affective conditioning the presence of the minor third does little to dispel. Undoubtedly, Tunstall's jaunty oscillation between minor tonic and dominant seventh chords, both in resonant open-position voicings and striking up a spirited Bo Diddley beat, contributes to the euphoric charge of the song's opening dispatches (measures 27–30). The overriding affective message Brackett distills from earlier instances of the gesture is one of "defiance, strength and resolution," often "in the face of

[28] On the history of the Bo Diddley beat, see Charles Keil and Steven Feld, *Music Grooves* (Chicago: The University of Chicago Press, 1994), 104–06. It is possible to hear Tunstall's signifying on the beat as one in a line of "mechanical participatory discrepancies" that characterize music in the post-disco and boom-box era.

[29] David Brackett, "Elvis Costello: The Empire of the E Chord, and a Magic Moment or Two," *Popular Music* 24/3 (2005): 357–67.

adversity, yearning [and] sneering."[30] This assessment resonates with Tunstall's strident performance.

An important difference between this usage and those discussed by Brackett lies in the evocation of blues tradition through the use of the open G string (instead of the stopped G♯ of the major chord) in combination with the sung "blues third." If these techniques seem sufficient to indicate an overriding sense of "African-American" parentage, a caveat or two should be noted. First, this is a minor blues, a form with a more flexible identity than its major counterpart due to its popularity in jazz. Second, while the song indisputably relies upon blues-based (therefore, African-American) expressive tropes, these come to Tunstall secondhand via the mediating hand of the British blues revival, as strains of Fleetwood Mac's "Oh Well" and Led Zeppelin's "Black Dog" are perceptibly woven into Tunstall's call-and-response alternation of densely worded a cappella and instrumental phrases (measures 29–40).

Tunstall is an accomplished blues-rock vocalist, her gravelly and improvisatory style ticking all the right boxes for the "edgier" female performer working in these genres. Moreover, her ability to "deliver the goods" by recording near-perfect overdubs in "real time" speaks to her professionalism as a musician,[31] at the same time reinforcing narratives of authenticity that have long been a part of blues-based and folk-rock idioms. In this respect, reactions shots play an important role in the format of the series. During Tunstall's performance, the camera dwells for an inordinate amount of time on veteran soul singer Anita Baker's responses to Tunstall's blues-inflected vocals—a shot that coincides with the most impressive vocal layering in the song. Whether intentional or not, the *choice* of reaction shots and how they coincide with the structures of the music underlines an aspect of aesthetic "profiling" that is moderated in ideas about color and musical authenticity. Moments after the image of Baker, indie-rock approbation is bestowed upon Tunstall via a group shot of the British guitar band Embrace, whose responses coincide with the dramatic second entry of the acoustic guitar, culminating on the resonant open E chord, with all of its "invocations of bohemian discourses around alternative practices of accreditation."[32] In this way, Tunstall's performance is authenticated visually on two fronts: in the approval she receives from a seasoned soul singer and in terms of the "cool factor" garnered through association with members of the alt-rock establishment. This would mean very little were it not underscored by music that draws on codes established on both sides of the Atlantic and which is characterized by a fundamental duality

---

[30] Ibid., 362.

[31] Recorded time is just as real ontologically as live time. The expression could be compared to the use or the division between "reality" and "real virtuality" made in chapter 5.

[32] Brackett, "Elvis Costello," 362.

(almost a schism) between the style of performance, which is traditional, and the way it is organized, which could be considered experimental or alternative.

The chorus (measures 43–49) is a timely reminder of Tunstall's investment in the pop mainstream. It employs an energetic four-measure turnaround that is as effective as it is stereotyped. The i–$\flat$VII–V^7 sequence repeats several times before terminating on an accented $\flat VI^7$ chord, a typical feature of minor blues. Insistent "no, no, no" exhortations in the vocals add little in the way of narrative substance, serving primarily as a foil to the already established groove.

An emphasis on musical construction returns following an abrupt one-measure *tacet* in all the looped instruments that, above all, evidences Tunstall's control over the technological parameters of her performance (see Table 7.1; measure 50). This dramatic solution is typical of loop-based forms, from electronic dance music to minimalism, and is a way of toying with listeners' expectations,[33] much like what follows, a second accumulation of instrumental capital culminating in the presence of no fewer than eleven simultaneous tracks (see Table 7.1). The accumulative process resumes with the recording of a two-part mock-trumpet fill, performed vocally in parallel octaves, thus reinforcing the kinetic impact of the rhythmic phrasing while simultaneously defusing some of the seriousness of the performer's introspective actions (measures 61–68). The songs bravura move occurs shortly afterward, as Tunstall crafts one of the song's most memorable vocal lines into a four-measure loop ("big black horse in a cherry tree / I can't quick get there cos my heart's forsaken me"), before superimposing over this a unison canon of the same phrase, offset by two measures (see Table 7.1; measures 65–76). This musical gesture, which would not be out of place in a Bach fugue or a process composition by Steve Reich, serves as further evidence of the performer's control over the performance situation, both in terms of her ability to "cut it live" and to mix or "DJ" it live. The impact of this sonic accumulation is strengthened by the dramatic reinstatement of the acoustic guitar in an elaboration of the earlier chord sequences that now incorporates the denser sonority of C^9 (measures 87–91). Tunstall jams over this vocally for several cycles before dovetailing with the looped vocals in the very last phrase, which leads to a sudden cessation of all of the loops and the cheeky a cappella line "my heart's forsaken me." (See Figure 7.1.)

Notwithstanding the folk-revivalist aspects of Tunstall's performances and the cultural capital she acquires through investment in this tradition, what is most remarkable about this mode of performance is the performer's ability to capture "takes" from her performances in "real time" (without breaks and retakes) and to reorganize these into larger forms that resemble those found in differently accredited musical genres. Mark Spicer sheds light on technological factors behind the proliferation of "accumulative forms" in pop-rock styles, showing how changes in technologies—from the early days of multitrack recording in the 1960s to the use

---

[33] See Hawkins, "Feel the Beat Come Down," 91.

Figure 7.1 Transcription of last four measures of the *Later* performance of "Black Horse": in its final moments the song features as many as eleven overlaid tracks.

of sequencers and drum machines in the 1980s—channeled the compositional possibilities available to pop-rock musicians in hitherto unforeseen ways.[34] Significantly, the new tools available to musicians permitted them to lay down overdubs with a high degree of precision and reproducibility from one take to the next, opening new expressive pathways that would mark the music as distinctive to its time. Similar forms had existed before, such as the characteristic "terraced instrumentation" of Baroque music or thematic techniques employed by North American composer Charles Ives, but not with the same combination of sounds and formal precision as would be afforded by the new technologies.[35]

This sense of the term *accumulative form* is consistent with the nomenclature used in reference to early minimalist music. A founding figure in minimalism, Terry Riley, described the technique of running tapes between two recorders in his early compositions, *Mescalin Mix* (1960) and *Music for the Gift* (1963), as "accumulative technique" and "time-lag accumulation."[36] This approach, which characterizes Riley's work at the San Francisco Tape Music Centre in the early 1960s,

[34] Mark Spicer, "(Ac)cumulative Form in Pop-Rock Music," *Twentieth-Century Music* 1/1 (2004): 29–64.

[35] Ibid., 29.

[36] See Keith Potter, *Four Musical Minimalists: La Monte Young, Terry Riley, Steve Reich, Philip Glass* (Cambridge: Cambridge University Press, 2000), 107; and Terry Riley quoted in Thom Holmes, *Electronic and Experimental Music: Technology, Music and Culture*, 3rd edition (New York and Abingdon: Routledge, 2008), 132.

would provide the inspiration for his early minimalist output that is constructed around repeated musical cells, including the seminal *In C* (1964). Riley's looping techniques directly inspired Steve Reich to undertake similar tape-loop experiments in compositions like *It's Gonna Rain* (1965) and *Come Out* (1966), and his experiences with two out-of-sync tape recorders helped this composer develop his trademark phase-shifting technique. Accumulative form aptly describes the processes at work in the two build-up sections of "Black Horse." Nevertheless, I consider it unlikely that early minimalist experiments with analog-looping technology directly influenced Tunstall.[37] It is more likely a result of the combined influence of similar technologies and similar structures of feeling.

The interest of a growing number of folk artists in mechanized dance rhythms and looping practices indicates another productive line of inquiry, as do Tunstall's comments concerning the hybridized and stylistically promiscuous foundations of her approach. Tunstall is no stranger to the attractions of the dance floor, as is perhaps best illustrated by her tendency to produce electrofolk covers of disco and contemporary dance tracks in live performances, including the Jackson Five's "I Want You Back," Chaka Khan's "Ain't Nobody" and Missy Elliott's "Get Ur Freak On." It might be instructive, therefore, to look toward writing on contemporary dance styles to learn more about the pleasurable foundations of her approach. Luis-Manuel Garcia's research on repetition in EDM offers a useful window onto the pleasurable foundations of looping in "Black Horse."[38] Drawing on the psychoanalytical work of Karl Bühler, Garcia proposes a three-point model of repetition that counters the prevailing Freudian emphasis on regression and compulsion with the more positively coded categories of satiation pleasure, process pleasure, and the pleasure of creative mastery. Key to his analysis of EDM are the last two categories, process pleasure referring to an artist's immersion in the moment-by-moment constitution of the work in accumulative tasks, creative mastery to the sense of accomplishment the accumulative technique gives rise to, as expansive sonic edifices are compiled from humble material origins.

The distinctive process-based pleasures of loop-based forms are deftly realized in the accumulation of loops in the build-up sections of "Black Horse." Tunstall's overlaying of parts defies expectations of what is possible for the unaccompanied "folk singer," or anyone for that matter, in the context of live performance. Her repetitive but, in terms of the combinatory effect of the song's layers, constantly evolving approach (even between performances, as Tunstall rarely configures her

[37] The idea of an indirect influence is plausible when one considers the number of popular artists who have drawn on the musical language of minimalism, including Mike Oldfield, Pete Townsend, Brian Eno, Suzanne Vega, David Bowie, and The Orb.

[38] Garcia, "On and On." The usefulness of Garcia's approach is limited by his dismissal of what he calls "reflection theories," a factor that causes him to view sonic production in EDM looping practices in isolation from technologies in related artistic forms, not to mention the entirety of contemporary media culture.

loops identically) redirects attention toward the phenomenal qualities of the sounds in a way that is equally true of minimalist music or EDM. At the same time, listeners' expectations are rewarded or confounded as the groove is pieced together bit by bit (the digital implications of this expression are intentional), eventually culminating an orchestral tapestry of textures—an electroacoustic "wall of sound"—that belies the modest instrumental means available to the performer.

"SUDDENLY I SEE": EXHIBITING MASTERY, PARODYING PRODUCTION

The idea of pleasure in creative mastery is also relevant when it comes to evaluating Tunstall's live persona. At stake is an exhibition of the performer's mastery over the performance in a way that challenges expectations. In the past, it might have sufficed for multi-instrumentalist authors of popular-music compositions (from Mike Oldfield to Prince) to assemble the fruits of their creative labor in private by meticulously overdubbing parts in the studio—the concealment of these activities in the private sphere adding an aura of seriousness and mystery to the artist's achievements.[39] Some musicians have adapted their studio overdubbing practices for "live authentication" by moving between different instruments in rapid succession when performing on stage. Stevie Wonder is one such musician. *Record Breakers'* Roy Castle perhaps best exemplifies a vaudevillian strain within such practices during a performance in the 1970s, when the intrepid presenter played as many as forty-three instruments within the span of a four-minute song. Tunstall is not averse to this type of showmanship, as can be seen in her second *Later* performance, where she switches from electric guitar and vocals to drums in the final moments of "Suddenly I See," a gesture that could easily be perceived as overdetermined and gimmicky in its insistence on telescoping the performer's agency. In the *Later* performance of "Black Horse," Tunstall brings the folk concept of the one-(wo)man band to bear on this set of practices, in such a way as to demystify prevailing assumptions about musical production and its economic foundations, i.e., the idea that overdubbing is a time-consuming, expensive and ultimately invisible process. She achieves comparable (if perhaps not as enduring) artistic end results to some of her pop-rock composer-auteur precursors, in real time and with the sole assistance of her relatively inexpensive Wee Bastard looping pedal.

---

[39] Toynbee writes of the socially empowering effects of multitrack recording in the context of early developments in tape recording technology. Jason Toynbee, *Making Popular Music: Musicians, Creativity, Institutions* (London: Arnold, 2000), 90. The effect is magnified in the case of Tunstall's live performances, where all of the parameters of the performance are visibly controlled by the artist.

I noted how "Black Horse" bears a family resemblance to tape loop experiments conducted by experimentalists in San Francisco in the early 1960s. In terms of its theatrical slant, Tunstall's performance coincides more with the interest of Dada and Fluxus artists in performance, expressed above all in a refusal to separate private and public activities, as well as through the incorporation of technologies and the bodies operating them as constitutive of the aesthetic encounter.[40] Experimental music of all stripes is commonly thought to be exclusively about "the music," a view that was not accepted by one of its leading exponents: "Theatre is all around us," John Cage commented, "and it has always hung around music—if only you let you attention be 'distracted' from the sounds."[41] Visual "distractions" in the performances of Fluxus composers Cage and Riley commonly drew attention to the technological means of musical (re)production, such as radios and tape machines, just as the visual identification of such means is integral to Tunstall's performance.

Tunstall undeniably possesses a keen sense of performative occasion, which may owe something to her training in music and drama at the University of London's Royal Holloway College. A question that might be asked is, to what extent these priorities conflict with those raised concerning the demonization (or suppression) of the visual as a linchpin of folk-rock credibility? Intimations of this are found in *The Word* magazine's characterization of Tunstall as "mainstream folk-rock pin-up";[42] her reduction to the status of glamour icon an ever-present danger for female artists in a marketplace dominated by traditional values. But it is a danger the performer apparently embraces, given the extravagant mode of self-presentation she has adopted at least since her third album, *Drastic Fantastic* (2007), the visual iconography of which gives a wide berth to traditional "folk values." Similarly, the title of its immediate predecessor, *Acoustic Extravaganza* (2006), is oxymoronic to upholders of folk-rock semantics because of the obvious staginess of the concept extravaganza. In other words, there is something theatrically camp in Tunstall's manner of presentation, which is not entirely accidental.[43]

Tunstall's conspicuous use of technology might be understood as an extension of her theatrical propensities. Electronic technology has, of course, long been a sticking point for folk artists, as discussed previously. Like Dylan's electrification

---

[40] See Rose Lee Goldberg, *Performance Art: From Futurism to the Present* (London: Thames and Hudson, 1988), 123–38.

[41] Michael Nyman, *Experimental Music: Cage and Beyond*, 2nd edition (Cambridge: Cambridge University Press, 1974), 22.

[42] Joe Muggs, "The Family That Plays Together," *The Word* 63 (May 2008): 50–51, 50.

[43] Tunstall's status as something of a gay icon would seem to confirm such an interpretation. The inclusion of rainbow-colored braces on her first album sleeve is just one of many gestures that audiences have interpreted as indicating an affinity with marginal sexual constituencies.

at the Newport Folk Festival, looping in "Black Horse" embodies *while it signifies* one of the dominant cultural forms of our age, an approach that is at odds with traditional folk aesthetics, which idealizes preindustrial technologies. More pressingly, Tunstall's practices draw attention to themselves through an element of performativity that contaminates the audiovisual contract. As Robert Wechsler notes, a big part of the attraction of technological media in live performance lies in the "how'd they do it?" factor, which causes spectators to divert attention to how the previously unseen (and unheard) was achieved, thereby pushing the media itself to the fore.[44] Auslander reiterates this point by arguing that the current fascination with technologically mediated spectacle and novelty derails artistic communication through a failure of audiences to attend either to expressive content or deconstructive intent.[45] Undoubtedly some spectators of the *Later* performance will privilege the novelty factor by concentrating on how the multitracking effect was achieved technically. It remains a matter of contention, however, to what degree such "distractions" can be though to monopolize spectators' consciousness.

Arguably, what rises to the surface is not the technological apparatus of the performance *as such* but Tunstall's mastery over it. In a sense, she becomes a present-day counterpart to the mythological figure of Echo, while going beyond the conventional passive role ascribed to this figure through the sheer force of her personality combined with her impressive "remixing" abilities.[46] By this I mean that she takes existing musical elements that might be considered outmoded or clichéd in different contexts (a classic "turnaround" chord sequence, a Bo Diddley rhythm, a half-remembered melody from Peter Green) and incorporates them as building blocks in musical processes that underwrite a different temporal logic than that which has prevailed in the dominant forms of Western music since the Renaissance.[47] Without wishing to downplay Tunstall's instrumental and vocal abilities, it is how she handles these "raw materials" in her use of looping that allows her to make some of her most original and compelling artistic statements. Of course, this notion of originality has undergone considerable revision since the dawn of the digital age. As Mark Katz suggests, sampling practices in the digital era are only coarsely described in terms of technological

[44]   Robert Wechsler, "Artistic Considerations in the Use of Motion-Tracking with Live Performers: A Practical Guide," in Susan Broadhurst and Josephine Machon, eds., *Performance and Technology: Practices of Virtual Embodiment and Interactivity* (Basingstoke: Palgrave Macmillan, 2006), 60–77.

[45]   Auslander, *Liveness*, 41. McLuhan made a similar point several decades earlier when stating that fascination with technological gadgetry could be regarded as an (alienated) extension of the human nervous system that leads irrevocably to experiences of "numbness." Marshall McLuhan, *Understanding Media* (London and New York: Routledge, 1964), 95–121.

[46]   See Doyle, *Echo and Reverb*, p. 40.

[47]   See Philip Tagg, "From Refrain to Rave: The Decline of Figure and the Rise of Ground," *Popular Music* 13/2 (1994): 209–22, 219.

"quotation." Sampling—and by implication, its temporal reproduction in looping—is in his view "most fundamentally an art of *transformation*."[48] Tunstall's aesthetic of "robbing" and "stealing" is something she shares with countless current artists (see the discussion of Damon Albarn in the previous chapter). This works well for her in the context of live performance, although questions have been raised about how convincing she is as a studio artist. Tunstall's LPs gravitate toward a reiteration of classical values, raising questions about how dependent her creative work is on visual authentication. In live performance, we have seen, she remediates existing forms and is therefore able to comment, on some level reflexively, on the dominant cultural practices of our time. Her recorded music has been perceived as doing little more than to reiterate the tried and trusted formulas of popular music; in other words, she is perceived as being too transparent, too derivative. A contrast can be drawn between her recorded work and that of recording artists such as the duo Gnarls Barkley, comprising the rapper-vocalist Cee Lo Green (Thomas Callaway) and renowned multi-instrumentalist producer Danger Mouse (Brian Burton). Positioned alongside musical arrangements whose technological estrangement points toward a twenty-first century pop-remix aesthetic, Brown's frenzied soul-styled vocals are made to rebound in unexpected ways against listeners' expectations. The same might be said of the recently deceased media icon Amy Whitehouse's collaborative work with producer Mark Ronson; this duo's lucrative retro-aesthetic to some degree reconditions existing forms—albeit while reinforcing tropes of authenticity relating to the troubled pop diva.

A useful light is cast on Tunstall's looping practices by comparing them to those found in experimental film. Jaimey Hamilton writes on how the phenomenal effects of repeated spectacle can affect our understanding of the mediated self.[49] For this writer, video loops in works by Bruce Nauman, Nam June Paik and Paul Pfeiffer, provide a continual oscillation that encourages the viewer to contemplate how similar images function at large in mediated society. In this way, looped forms serve as eddies in the media flow of contemporary life, whose deleterious influence has been recognized in writing from Williams to Debord.[50] By temporarily diverting attention away from ubiquitous narratives of progress and productivity, the relentless flow of the media, and toward smaller units of encapsulated time that inhabit the media, Hamilton argues that looping practices can unleash considerable transformative potential.

---

[48] Mark Katz, *Capturing Sound: How Technology Has Changed Music* (Berkeley: California University Press, 2004), 156.

[49] Jaimey Hamilton, "The Way We Loop 'Now': Eddying in the Flows of Media," *Invisible Culture: An Electronic Journal for Visual Culture* 8 (2004): 1–24.

[50] Raymond Williams, *Television* (London: Routledge, 1974), 77–120; Debord, *Society of the Spectacle*, 86–92.

Undoubtedly some of this potential is harnessed in Tunstall's *Later* performance, not every aspect of which is "revisionist" or deserving of critical endorsement. Indubitably, though, Tunstall's performance resonates with contemporary experience, offering a model, of sorts, for coming to terms with new technologies, for struggling to assert agency in an increasingly prefigured world, and for the ability to concentrate on the unfolding moment in unlikely material circumstances. Much could be said, of course, about how the format of (recorded) live television favors artists with Tunstall's theatrical leanings, and how the contradictions inherent in her approach are less flatteringly manifested in different formats and media. In this performance, though, she might be said to have succeeded in rewriting at least part of the script for her mythological precursor, Echo.

Instance II. The Blue Nile's "Because of Toledo": Recording Disaffection

THEORIZING THE AFFECTIVE TERRAIN OF THE ACOUSTIC

The lessons to be learned from KT Tunstall's performances seem clear enough: defining "acoustic performance" in the present mediatized and digitized age can be complicated; secondly, the constructions of authenticity it supports are heavily dependent on visual legitimation. Her example is in some ways atypical, however. The mechanical, digital and audiovisual spirit of our age has for some time infiltrated musical styles in more subtle ways than Tunstall's performance evidences. In addition, acoustic music is caught up with crossmodal modes of understanding in ways I have yet to adequately consider. In other words, acoustic performance always exceeds its material conditions and the idealistic intentions of producers because it is perceived and conceived in the mind. It is always something more and something other than what it appears to be.

In the previous section, I commented how the medium becomes the message in a specific performance by Tunstall. I referred in particular to aspects such as her physical presence as a performer—the body as a medium for audiovisual communication—the digital looping technology that was the precondition for shaping the performance, and the televisual medium that established the conditions in which that performance could take place. All of these factors mediated the performance and to some extent dominated its affective tone. Otherwise, Marshall McLuhan's statement begs the question: what is the message of the medium? In chapter 5, I discussed how the Romantic trope of the sublime combined with a subtext of camp subversion both inform how loosely synced hybrid forms have been understood in mainstream and more marginal interpretive contexts. Here, too, the affective coding of performances deserves closer attention than I've given it thus far.

Affectivity has been debated extensively in cultural studies and philosophy during the past decades by theorists such as Deleuze and Gauttari, Spinoza, Bergson, Massumi and Sedgwick, partly in polemical response to poststructuralism's linguistic constructionism as this was understood in postmodernist theory and partly unfolding from poststructuralist thinking itself, with all of its emphasis of immanence, grain, *jouissance*, fragmented narratives, flows and surfaces. The extent of this interest is such that some scholars have gone so far as to announce with some fanfare an affective turn in scholarly practices.[51] Many theorists hold the concept of affect to be a way of addressing the neglected sensory and corporeal aspects of the human interface with art. Even before the newfound popularity of this term, Philip Tagg used it in popular musicology in a manner resembling the *Affektenlehre* taxonomy of musical figures in Baroque music: to account for the semiotic means by which music communicates specific discursive content (with reference to an implicit network of intertextual relations). Tagg's approach closely resembles research on topic theory in the semiotic study of classical music (practiced by scholars like Raymond Monelle, Kofi Agawu, Robert Hatten and Eero Tarasti). This approach was flirted with in the first section of chapter 5. This line of study provides researchers with valuable tools to investigate the specific meanings encoded within musical works by attending to significant details.

Another music semiotician, Naomi Cumming's use of the term comes closer to the current interdisciplinary research and is the primary sense in which I employ the term. Cummings describes music as conveying emotional potentialities through a synthesis "of different elements … [which] add up to an emergent affect that is complex and subtle yet in some sense singular."[52] The literary critic Sianne Ngai has discussed literature in much the same way, employing concepts like "mood" or "tone," the latter of which should not be confused with the more restrictive musical sense of the word. For Ngai, tone is a cultural artifact's "global or organising affect, its general disposition or orientation towards its audience and the world."[53] This sense of the word encompasses "the formal aspect of a literary work that makes it possible for critics to describe a text as 'euphoric' or 'melancholic'"; and, importantly, how these and other more subtle designations can be related to "a holistic matrix of social relations."[54] Affects do not exist in

---

[51]   Eve Kosofsky Sedgwick and Adam Frank, eds., *Shame and Its Sisters: A Silvan Tomkins Reader* (Durham, NC: Duke University Press, 1995); Brian Massumi, *Parables for the Virtual: Movement, Affect, Sensation* (Durham, NC: Duke University Press, 2002); Patricia Ticineto Clough with Jean Halley, eds., *The Affective Turn: Theorizing the Social* (Durham, NC: Duke University Press, 2007); Tia DeNora, *Music in Everyday Life* (Cambridge: Cambridge University Press, 2000), 21–45.

[52]   Naomi Cumming, *The Sonic Self: Musical Subjectivity and Signification* (Bloomington: Indiana University Press, 2000), 216–24, 217.

[53]   Sianne Ngai, *Ugly Feelings* (Cambridge, MA: Harvard University Press, 2005), 28.

[54]   Ibid.

isolation from discursive and semiotic layers of meaning; they are invariably channeled within and modified by these layers. As Richard Dyer writes:

> When we attend to the extra-semiotic, amodal dimension of an artwork, we are never entirely within extra-semiotic or amodal reality precisely because we are in art and discourse, we are in what is already only analogous to affect, what is always already worked, historical, contingent. Art can never quite get affect, partly because it can never actually be affect, only its formalized and conventionalized objectification. I believe everyone knows this intuitively; everyone knows that art falls short of the real. Yet still we respond, still we are moved.[55]

Along similar lines, Ngai notes how "affects are *less* formed and structured than emotions, but not lacking form or structure altogether; *less* 'sociologically fixed,' but by no means code-free or meaningless; *less* 'organized in response to our interpretations of situations,' but by no means entirely devoid of organization or diagnostic powers."[56] Drawing on the strengths of both of these propositions, I will argue that each of the musical and audiovisual instances discussed in this chapter articulates a dominant affective mood (or ground-tone) that is inflected by culturally contingent expectations and responses. These can be triggered or modified by the specific textual details of performances. For this reason, discussions of affect do not render more analytical, semiotic or intertextual considerations of audiovisual performances null and void. They simply realign the priorities of analyses, their aims as well as the means by which those aims might be achieved. Analysis in this sense becomes one of several means of charting experiences—secondary perhaps to phenomenological observations about the nature of experience. Significant details can inflect meaning, but a large part of what makes audiovisual texts meaningful resides in the physical unfolding of sonic and visual events. This is where affect comes in. Ngai refers to affective tone as a *noisy* concept, by which she means that it is abstract and indeterminate. In this respect it resembles Lawrence Kramer's equally indeterminate notion of emerging "structural tropes," or Raymond Williams's idea of "structures of feeling."[57] The strength of these terms lies in their malleability, their indeterminacy, which mimics how affective meanings are shaped around experiences. Their weakness inheres in the danger that structure might be perceived as a static "thing" more than an emerging "character."

---

[55] Richard Dyer, "Side by Side: Nina Rota, Music, and Film," in Daniel Goldmark, Lawrence Kramer and Richard Leppert, eds., *Beyond the Soundtrack: Representing Music in Cinema* (Berkeley: University of California Press, 2007), 246.259, 256.

[56] Ngai, *Ugly Feelings*, 27.

[57] On structures of feeling, see Raymond Williams, *Marxism and Literature* (Oxford: Oxford University Press, 1977), 128–35.

The affective character, mood or tone that is most central in this chapter is what I call the disaffected acoustic imaginary. It is imaginary because it is a discursive construct, an idea, whose boundaries spill over strict ontological definitions. My discussion largely bypasses, therefore, the debates over authenticity that have dominated discussions of folk music, which prioritize one ontological view over another (the ontology of the acoustic over the electrical). I prefer the term disaffected to any implication that the phenomena I discuss are entirely without affect. Undoubtedly, this concept echoes what Jameson refers to as the waning of affect under postmodernism.[58] However, I do not believe affect can simply be dismissed because it has been negated. Rather it becomes strengthened in a certain way, seeping up from between the cracks of the discourse rather than constituting it. Affect in this sense is different to conventional narrative impulses, which track experiences closely and to some extent coercively. The affective strategies taken in the nu-folk forms discussed here track them more loosely and comprise cumulative and modificatory mechanisms of intensification and disintensification that thereby provide a rubric for different structures of feeling. These planes of shifting intensity do not, pace Jameson, imply the relinquishment of affective consciousness. Silvan Tomkins' concept of "affect amplification" seems especially apt when it comes to one of the central question of this work.[59] The fact that electrical amplification could be said to modify and to mediate the intensities of pop and rock music is widely accepted. However, this relationship also reflects back onto practices of acoustic music, which is not as innocent as some commentators have thought in the digital age. Fundamentally, the acoustic in popular music is a discursive entity that is defined in terms of a negative dialectic. In other words, it seeks to offer audiences something different from dominant (electrified) discourses but at the same time is implicated within those discourses.

APPROACHING THE DISAFFECTED IMAGINARY IN BLUE NILE'S "BECAUSE OF TOLEDO"

Released in 2004, the song "Because of Toledo" (*High*, 2004), composed and performed by the Glaswegian singer Paul Buchanan and his band The Blue Nile, presents a number of challenges to the analyst interested in elucidating its expressive meanings. Namely, there is something introverted and refractory about this recording, which seems designed to fend off identification with the singer and the song. Despite Buchanan's defining vocal presence in the song, an impersonal

---

[58]   Fredric Jameson, *Postmodernism or, The Cultural Logic of Late Capitalism* (Durham, NC: Duke University Press, 1991), 10.

[59]   Sedgwick and Frank, eds., *Shame and its Sisters.*

element is articulated in its acoustic guitar accompaniment. Played in strict metronomic time, Buchanan's mode of performance resembles the prepro- grammed drum-machine parts found in The Blue Nile's early electronic work (from the late 1980s) more than it does the expressive performance styles ordi- narily associated with the instrument. Not only is the guitar played with a distinct lack of embellishment and expressive contouring, but the way the musical syntax is put together highlights the blandly repetitive nature of the unfolding musical terrain. Throughout the entire duration of the verses, changes result from incremental bass movement alone, which hints at conventional tonal functions without every really convincing.[60] With the exception of the chorus, which intro- duces two additional chords, there is only really one chord in the song, which supports my contention that it is dominated by a single musical affect. Built on a thirdless, and consequently hollowed out (or disaffected), voicing of G, each var- iant of the chord outlines the same angular trajectory. A hint of polymeter in the 3 + 3 + 2 patterning of the arpeggios strains against the surrounding 4/4 time sig- nature, suggesting a push toward ternary time, which does eventually happen in the chorus. Functionally, the chord sequences of the verse revolve around movement between the tonic (G) and its relative minor (E), effectively establish- ing the latter as an alternate or proxy key center. At the beginning of the chorus the progression is "misdirected" toward an "interrupted cadence" onto the super- tonic (A), the most obviously tonal procedure in the song. Understanding the music as tonal, however, in the ordinary sense of the term is misleading, because, with the exception of the bass movement, an element of implacability defines how the song works. In addition, a constant abrasive yet resonant minor-second disso- nance is folded into the texture of the guitar patterning through the simultaneous presence of g^1 and $f\sharp^2$, suggesting an inner wound or scar in the subjectivity of the performer (see Figure 7.2.).

My point resembles one that is made by Naomi Cumming in her writing on the Adagio's of Bach's Sonata in G minor for Solo Violin.[61] Starting out from an affective ground-tone of minor pathos, she shows how a major-seventh disso- nance enfolded within the Adagio's inner voices gives rise to a grating sense of melancholy, which is nevertheless contained within a harmonic schema that is suggestive of poise, reflection and—because the music is performed *rubato*— spontaneity. Reflection, in Cumming's account, is a quality that "emerges when

---

[60] Were one to assign jazz/rock designations to the chords generated in the arpeggio patterning, this would look like a difficult piece of music, with more than its fare share of extended and indeterminate disso- nant sonorities. A: Verse: G (no 3) maj 7–or E minor add 2 (or E/G [no 3] maj 7)–C (no 3) add 2 ♯11–B minor 6 (G maj 7, 3rd inversion)–E minor sus 2. B: Chorus: A7 (no 3)/13 sus 4–A7 (no 3) sus 4–C sus 9–C–C maj 7://E minor sus 2–C (no 3) add 2 ♯11–G (no 3) maj 7. C: Bridge: G (no 3) maj 7–E minor add 2–C (no 3) add 2 ♯11.

[61] Cumming, *The Sonic Self*, 216–24.

Figure 7.2 "Because of Toledo": extract from the first verse, Paul Buchanan and the Blue Nile, *High* (2004). Author's transcription.

someone dwells on a point, and looks at its many sides, without seeking quick progression, peremptory 'answers,' or revolutionary change";[62] an aspect that emerges through the use of a familiar chord progression. Bringing into play the idea of musical form as articulating "virtual personae," Cumming extrapolates from her analytical observations a view of one "who plays with his or her own melancholy, with some moments of spontaneity and others of containment and restraint."[63] She attributes an impression of mediated agency to the music's inner as well as its outer voices, surmising that that "these movements can be heard quite literally as examples of 'inward' pain, momentary expressed and then contained."[64] The same is true of the guitar accompaniment in "Because of Toledo," where Buchanan, too, plays with his own melancholy, although the musical and cultural contexts are different: Bach's dissonance is contained within a tonal context that deals with

[62] Ibid., 219.   [63] Ibid., 238.   [64] Ibid.

pain by framing it within the rubric of Enlightenment rationality; Buchanan's suggests the barren yet luminous backdrop of twenty-first century urban life, in which technological containment is an unavoidable fact.

All things considered, it seems clear that the primary affective modality of "Because of Toledo" is melancholic, even depressive. This is accentuated in lyrical content, which addresses the theme of object loss, and which from the standpoint of Freudian exegesis would also imply partial loss of the self.[65] Little sense of pathos associated with this loss is communicated in the guitar part, however, as one would expect in Romantic representations of melancholy. The accompaniment seems almost indifferent to the affections of the singer, as it continues along a mechanical course, bringing to mind both the insistent rhythmic drive underlying Baroque aesthetics and the techno-subjectivity of musical styles like techno, minimalism, Krautrock and British synthpop (the stylistic movement from which The Blue Nile originally emerged). This mechanical conditioning seems to suggest an absence of individual agency that interconnects with markers of melancholy in the instrumentation. In this way, the guitar accompaniment becomes the implacable (mechanized) environment to the song's self. In her writing on the classical repertory, Cumming repeatedly addresses subjectivity that is impersonal, emotionally distant, disembodied or Other.[66] The extent of musical othering in this song exceeds anything this writer discusses, however. The idea of musical experience as somehow standing in relief against the self, even while it is constitutive of the self, has special resonance in this instance, where the primary locus of the expressive self is the human voice. The guitar accompaniment is knowingly dehumanized. Buchanan himself frequently refers to his music as "industrial" and in visual terms as depicting cityscapes.[67] It follows that an element of impersonal disaffection connected with urban experience is intentionally encoded into his musical structurations.[68]

Given the implacability of the guitar part, attention is easily diverted toward the vocals. After an initial statement of the song's main hook ("Because of Toledo"), the melody rises up to an emotionally labored d^2 concomitant with the loaded line "I got sober and stayed clean." At the same time, the bass line and

---

[65] See Susanna Välimäki, *Subject Strategies in Music: A Psychoanalytical Approach to Musical Signification*, Approaches to Musical Semiotics 9 (Imatra: International Semiotics Society of Finland, 2005), 237. On object loss, see also Melanie Klein, *The Selected Melanie Klein*, Juliet Mitchell, ed. (New York: The Free Press, 1986), 117–18; 173–74.

[66] Cumming, *The Sonic Self*, 130, 204, 224; also Välimäki, *Subject Strategies*, 342.

[67] Numerous interviews with Buchanan and other members of The Blue Nile underline this conception of the music. See, for example, Brown's impressively written biographical account of the band: Allan Brown, *Nileism: The Strange Course of the Blue Nile* (Polygon: Edinburgh, 2010), 88, 233.

[68] By "structurations," I am referring to Julia Kristeva's concern to go beyond descriptive considerations of structures to consider how those structures came into being: what are their intertextual referents?

bass guitar plummet to an affectively charged E. Thereafter the singer soars to a vertiginous e^2, before descending in a series of carefully weighted meandering phases. The last of these culminates on the emotionally fraught line ("I live here but I don't really live anywhere"), which is colored musically by ending on the dissonant major seventh of G. Technically speaking, the song might be major (although this is debatable, given that E minor is an equally viable alternative key center); it nevertheless comes across as melancholic due to the enfolded dissonances of the guitar part, the descending arpeggiation (vaguely homologous with falling rain, referred to in the lyrics), the mournful melody, and the pitches Buchanan highlights in his setting of the lyrics. The line "another faded waitress dressed in pink," for example, sounds bleak because it comes to a halt on an extended a^1, a dissonant second above the tonic. As if to confirm the desolate mood, the bass line falls again to a brooding open E following this phrase (root note of the related minor chord).

Nevertheless, the vocals are distinguished by an element of stylistic distancing, which to some extent counteracts the dominant impression of melancholy. In short, Buchanan's singing is characterized as much by affectation as it is by affection. I am referring to the influence of 1950s-style jazz crooning on his vocals (from Frank Sinatra to Nat King Cole),[69] including the use of stylized portamentos, Tin Pan Alley mannerisms including a tendency to dwell on the major seventh, and a rubato, speech-driven approach to vocal phrasing.[70] Such stylization can be understood as a form of parodic distancing, an interpretation that finds support in the sonic environment of the music, where the voice is left to reverberate across empty spaces, a solitary subject in inhospitable surroundings.

Buchanan's evocation of the jazz crooner intersects with a construction of masculinity that is romantic in its juxtapositioning of the hardboiled and solitary male in opposition to the unattainable and irrational female. It can be related in some measure to Glaswegian Americanophilia and local ideas about manliness as arising from an existential battle in which the starkness of ordinary life is used to justify an irrevocable downward spiral toward depression and alcoholism, from which the singer must extricate himself ("I got sober and stayed clean"). However, that is not all. As I indicated, the music is executed with considerable performative swagger and historical awareness, implying an appreciation of style that transports the music into a more reparative register. An unlikely point of reference, but one I maintain is relevant, is Tom Waits's parody of Americana in much of his musical output, evidenced particularly in his ironic portrayal of Frank

---

[69] Buchanan speaks in numerous interviews of the influence of North American music of his father's generation. Sinatra is commonly cited as an influence. See, for example, Brown, *Nileism*, 112.

[70] John Potter, *Vocal Authority: Singing Style and Ideology* (Cambridge: Cambridge University Press, 1998), 55.

Sinatra on the album, *Frank's Wild Years* (1987).[71] This nostalgic landscape of guys and broads, whiskey and diners is executed with a gravelly voice, occasionally rising to emotive heights, and a sympathetic twinkle of the eye. It harks back to the post–World War II era, a time of Tin Pan Alley tunes and fraught but erotically heightened gender roles, such as those found in film noir. In short, the vocal style is evocative of courtly heterosexual love and an affective terrain of inner turmoil that remains bottled up rather than finding outward expression. Essential to the songs affective identity is the distance inscribed between its contemporary and implied geographical setting and the psychological landscape it alludes to. This distance, doubly inscribed, turns the song into a performative rendering of archetypal gender positions rather than their direct expression. Buchanan is known to be a Scottish man interpreting (re-presenting) the actual and psychological American landscape; just as he is understood to be a modern man reflecting on how the old tunes used to sound (those of his father's generation).

WORDS, MUSIC AND IMAGES

Buchanan's approach to music-text relations is characterized by close attention to mood, often conveyed through descriptions of the material world more than references to the narrator's feelings.[72] An icy luminosity infuses his vivid verbal descriptions, which brings to mind the approaches of imagist poets like Ezra Pound and T.S. Eliot, the new novels of Alain Robbe-Grillet, or the painting style of Edward Hopper. In all of these, the "thingness" of objects becomes concentrated. Meaning is implicit in lyrics like "another faded waitress dressed in pink," a character who becomes a sign of romantic disaffection projected onto disaffected consumerism more than being a real person. The theme of facelessness, spelled out in the chorus, permeates the rest of the lyrics: everything from the mediatized real virtuality of the "early morning news" to "shadows dancing" on the prairies, an ingenious double entendre that links up with the preceding reference to "picks ups," inferring both a popular form of transport in rural America and inconsequential relationships: one-night stands.

---

[71] Brown (a Glaswegian) considers the more problematic side of this construction of masculinity to be distinctive to local Glaswegian sensibilities. Particularly the "the bourbon-drinking, straight-talking, roughly sentimental America of Sinatra," which conveys a fantasy of "a city of guys and dolls, of wry stoicism and urban night." This construction, he notes, is repeated in the music of The Blue Nile. Brown, *Nileism*, 144. The performative side of such a persona is illustrated in Buchanan's comments about hats (in relation to the title of the second Blue Nile album), which "become a synonym for people in all their faded glory. A hat gives them character and comes to represent the individual." Ibid., 130.

[72] The attention to lyrical content in Buchanan's songwriting might owe something to his background as an English Literature graduate from the University of Glasgow in the 1970s; just as keyboard player Robert Bell's degree in electronics might be understood as playing a part in his contribution to The Blue Nile.

In light of Buchanan's imagistic (or cinematic) approach to lyric writing, it should come as no surprise that a form of "imaging" is likely to have been involved in the songwriting process. The musician comments:

> There's always a kind of touchstone for us somewhere, be that in a scene that we're all familiar with or a mood that everybody knows, and we tend to talk about the songs in these terms. And we'll become slightly more abstract, we'll say, it's got to be red in the background, or green or whatever it is. It might not mean a lot to anyone else, but for us it's a language that we can use and understand.[73]

Implying a mode of synaesthesia, the ability to generate musical images by summoning recalled visual stimuli that come freighted with an emotional component requires a holistic and "affective" sensibility that rationalizing discourses on audiovisual theory have long distrusted. By first determining a mood and then fleshing out his sonic imagery with words that are as bleakly descriptive as they are emotionally resonant, Buchanan is able to conjure an atmosphere that is audiovisual by implication. Imaging in this context implies mental rather than purely visual "depictions."[74] When translated across media, a metaphorical relationship based on resemblance (or mimesis) more than linguistic differentiation is implied.[75] Kay Dickinson has commented on how processes such as this are related to ideas about synaesthetic transference across the senses, which is metaphorical by nature. In her view, the ability of metaphors to transfer images from one sense to another "allows for their realignment in new 'assemblages'... that evade the restrictive impulses of established modes of consciousness."[76] As commented on in chapter 2, the metaphorical impulse and its role in emancipating the imaginative faculties was a core principle of surrealist aesthetics. Surrealism's imagery was not conjured out of thin air; it had its origins in a metaphorical extension of the experienced object—allowing it to be experienced afresh. Because of this metaphorical emphasis, surrealism was always more phenomenological than it was perceptual or cognitive in its outlook. It was (and is) about feeling through resemblance more than simply perceiving, and in this way

[73] *The Blue Nile: Flags and Fence,* television documentary, Virgin Records and BBC Scotland, 1990.

[74] See Antonio Damascio, *The Feeling of What Happens: Body, Emotion and the Making of Consciousness* (London: Vintage, 1999), 318.

[75] For more on how resemblance is implicated in the production of metaphors, see Paul Ricoeur, *The Rule of Metaphor,* trans. Robert Czerny (London and New York: Routledge, 2003), 229–36. Tagg and Clarida approach this matter by means of the concept of "gestural interconversion." Their analysis of what I will call crossmodal translation in musical constructions of pastoralism is pathbreaking. Tagg and Clarida, *Ten Little Title Tunes,* 253–67.

[76] Dickinson, "Music Video and Synaesthetic Possibility," in Beebe and Middleton, eds., *Medium Cool,* 13–29, 19.

creating new bridges in consciousness—new alliances of understanding. Lawrence Marks notes that while the senses are specialized to modally specific tasks, "sensory domains [also] overlap, for the world about which the senses inform us is, in itself, a unitary one, and so is our conception of it."[77] Might the nondifferentiated domain of affect be the arena where crossmodal negotiations typically take place—caught up in a preemotional wash of feeling in which it matters little which sensory stimulus is foremost? In The Blue Nile's music, crossmodal awareness is implicated as a compositional strategy, but the manner of musical production could also explain why so many listeners report hearing the music as "cinematic" or "visual."

Like much of the digital-era music I discuss in this book, the structure of "Because of Toledo" is shaped by a constant flow of beats divided into fields of varying intensity. The most significant transformation happens in the chorus, when a simple subtractive music procedure, the removal of an eighth note from each measure, results in a transformation of the time signature from 4/4 to 6/8. This brings about an overall heightening, or amplification, of affectivity, which in addition to meter is indicated by Buchanan straining to reach to highest note of the song and by a corresponding thickening of musical texture. Notably, amplified instruments are introduced at this point, the electrifying presence of other musicians serving to dispel some of the lonely disaffection of the verses. The sense of plenitude brought about by this reinforcement is transitory, however, just as images relating to the lost object of affection referred to in the lyrics are fragmentary—like forensic evidence at a crime scene, these material traces (of lipstick and cocaine) stand in for but cannot replace the woman to whom they belonged. The function in question resembles what is involved when encountering the part objects found in surrealist photography—a means of signifying a mode of abstraction from humanity that imparts to the objects an uncanny afterlife. Our memories of these objects carry an emotive residue that activates powerful crossmodal effects (we know how lipstick looks, feels, and tastes; we recall those to whom it belonged). Echoes of Romantic orchestral music (Wagner or Mahler) can be heard in the 6–5 suspension that spans the first and second measures of this section, while voice leading in the second chord (C) moves restlessly along a dissonant trajectory without resolving (ninth, tonic and major seventh). These are mere echoes, however, heard in the context of a repetitive musical patterning, which liberates musical procedures from the formal obligations of the past but in so doing creates its own kind of (digital or mechanized) trap. Escape from this cycle (or loop) of Romantic yearning comes abruptly through rhythmic addition and a harmonic shift to the darkest sonority of the song, E minor.

[77] Lawrence Marks, *The Unity of the Senses: Interrelations among the Modalities* (New York: Academic Press, 1988), 185. See also Charles Spence and Jon Driver, eds., *Crossmodal Space and Crossmodal Attention* (Oxford and New York: Oxford University Press, 2004).

Though the dominant affect may be one of bleakness, the final verse does bring a modicum of relief. Here a trumpet obbligato joins the singer in unison, a traditional way of signifying the presence of a transcendental other—a projection perhaps, but a comforting presence nevertheless. In these final moments, the singer announces how he would like to return to Toledo, a gesture that is underwritten in the music as he joins himself in a harmonization that scoops up to the (positively affected) major third—the missing link in the broken harmony of the verses. Overall, Buchanan's song summons forth an image of the tortured artist, which audiences traditionally respond to. Intertextually, the song recalls a time when gender roles were sharply differentiated and the image of the lonesome stranger was heavily romanticized in North American popular fiction (from cowboys to hardboiled detectives). Hedonistic and humorous, the figure of the crooner, as represented by Sinatra and the Rat Pack, is subjected to a more world-weary rendition that encourages critical reflection. Essential to this impression of reflexivity is how Buchanan constructs his singing persona performatively in relation to a musical accompaniment that connotes technological disaffection.

Instance III. Suzanne Vega's "Night Vision": Where Perception Ends and Imagination Begins

The New York based singer-songwriter Suzanne Vega approaches the song "Night Vision" (*Solitude Standing,* 1987) in a remarkably similar fashion to Buchanan's approach in "Because of Toledo." Based on a tribute to Cubist painter Juan Gris by one of the luminaries of surrealism, the poet Paul Éluard, Vega's adaptation of the original poem highlights a principle at the core of the surrealist aesthetic: the impetus to explore the blurry regions of experience where perceptions ends and imagination begins. Éluard's ascetic style of poetry is easily translated into Vega's curt minimalist style (Éluard: "Table guitare et verre vide"; Vega: "the table, the guitar, the empty glass"). In line with surrealist thinking, the poem explores the dialectic of darkness and light, the conscious and the unconscious (Éluard: "De jour merci de nuit prends garde / De douceur la moitié du monde / L'autre montrait rigueur aveugle"; Vega: "By day give thanks / By night beware / Half the world in sweetness / The other in fear"). Éluard's poem interprets Juan Gris's cubist paintings as occupying a kind of twilight zone in which ordinary objects are perceived as possessing haunting shape-shifting qualities. Vega's lyrics similarly extol luminous experience, an outlook that is achieved by replacing perception with imaginative projection as the world fades into invisibility at the end of the day. The lines of such objects "blend together" after dark when the listener is implored to "Find the line / find the shape / through the grain" (the lyric here is

Vega's rather than a translation of Éluard). Although the emphasis on lines and shapes is vaguely reminiscent of the cubists' preoccupation with geometric forms, Vega seems more interested in following Éluard's example by exploring the surreal and psychological implications of cubism. Her song parts company most clearly with the original in the bridge and final verse. Here she personalizes the poem in a lyric that resembles a lullaby sung mother to child. Darkness (and its auditory corollary, silence) is an unavoidable fact. The best the narrator can do in such circumstances is to enjoin the addressee to turn her look inwards ("I would shelter you / Keep you in light / But I can only teach you / Night vision").

The song is built on the foundation of Vega's unorthodox guitar part. It is this that brings it to life, or more accurately that leaves it suspended half way between waking life and slumber. Repetition is key to understanding Vega's minimalist style. Over several patterns of chord changes, a continuous repetitive current is maintained in the instrument's upper voices, the open e^2 and b^1 strings either resonating or conflicting with the surrounding harmony. Only in the short refrains does the accompaniment stray away from this formula when it is replaced with an adjacent pair of tones, g^1 and b^1, both chord tones of G6. Both the song's verses and its choruses are constructed from chords whose dissonance make them difficult to understand in terms of conventional harmonic movement or the symbolic conventions of jazz/rock lead sheets. The verse alternates between tonic and dominant but is colored with trademark hues for Vega, an added second dissonance in the chord of A minor and a disaffected thirdless sonority in E minor 7 (no 3rd). The tonic here is weighed down with traces of inner conflict, intimated through the presence of a major second dissonance, much as it is in "Because of Toledo." But the relentless rocking movement of the accompaniment, combined with the conspicuous absence of major/minor marking, deprives the pattern of goal directedness. Harmonic movement in the chorus, too, is linear more than it is horizontal, a stepwise melodic line (VI– ♭VII–VI–V) providing the impetus for harmonic change rather than tonal functionality. When repeated, the sequence culminates in a suspended dominant chord that resolves from the fourth degree to an affectively conditioned major third before shifting to the A minor tonic. This is one of the few concessions to tonic functionality in the song, which for the most part has a meandering, dreamlike quality. Dissonance does not, therefore, motivate change, but rather it serves as a form of affective shading which elevates the impersonal and unchanging nature of the guitar accompaniment. As with "Toledo," the metaphor of an impassive, audibly constructed (urban) environment is never far away. The unrelenting twang of the upper voices imparts to the music a mood of disaffection, but in the context of a mesmerizing flow of ideas. Vega pioneered this guitar style and it can be heard on almost every track of the album *Solitude Standing*, with the exceptions of "Tom's Diner," which has no accompaniment, and the uncharacteristically lyrical and anthemic "Gypsy." Buchanan's guitar style on "Because of Toledo" is conspicuously similar to Vega's; a principle that could be extended to many contemporary guitarists working at the "alternative" margins of acoustic genres. Such accompaniments have an angular and relentless quality that is more akin to the repetitive patterning produced with midi sequencing and sampling software than the organic feel we ordinarily associate with acoustic instruments. In short, the relentless pulse of minimalism is never far away in Vega's songs of this period. (Indeed, she was strongly influence by New York downtown minimalism and has collaborated with Philip Glass.)

This aspect is keenly felt in the bridge, where the song pseudo-modulates to the relative major key of C, a move that is akin to slipping into a dream. In the melody this movement is negotiated by means of an ascending diatonic line that vaguely evokes the Baroque topic of *ascensus*, signifying a movement toward transcendence or elevation.[78] The line repeats twice and is underscored by a complementary move in the guitar harmony. Both melody and accompaniment culminate on C♯, a dissonant minor (or Phrygian) second above the new key signature of C major. In the context of the song's dominant key of A minor, however, it demarcates a melodic shift to the major mode. Without wanting to pin the musical procedure down to a specific semantic meaning, structural shifts from minor to major have long been thought to suggest an unveiling of consciousness or transcendence. The narrative and imagistic context of the song hints at a more secular interpretation, however. As the ascending line repeats, Vega enunciates in breathy tones the lines, "Now I watch you falling into sleep" and "watch your fist uncurl beneath the sheet." A soothing synthesizer pad and humming bass tones support the meditative mood of the guitar in conveying subjective drift, but not in an entirely comforting direction as the tritone coloring embedded within the new tonic chord (C maj7 add♯4) reminds the listener. Dangers lurk in the relinquishment of consciousness (and agency), a matter that is addressed directly in the lyrics of the final verse. Harmonic slippage (G maj 7–F maj 7–E7 sus 4–E7), common also in minimalist music, accompanies a descending line that carries the narrative irrevocably toward the end of the bridge. The spatial metaphor of *falling* asleep is an apt description in light of the descending trajectory of vocal line, which eventually "comes to rest" uncomfortably on the major third of the dominant chord (G sharp), the dissonant leading tone of the song's home key.

Vega "would comfort" and "lead into light" the song's addressee in the final verse, her use of the conditional tense saying it all. Despite good intentions, both "comfort" and "light" are qualities beyond her powers to bestow. This human warmth, however, in the face of an outwardly indifferent environment constitutes the dominant mood of the song. This comment requires further elucidation. Namely, in many of Vega's songs both musical production and compositional strategies elevate the tactile qualities of the musical environment over discursive

---

[78]   Dietrich Bartel, *Musica Poetica: Musical-Rhetorical Figures in German Baroque Music* (Lincoln: University of Nebraska Press, 1997), 179.

or lyrical "meanings." In connection with Paul Buchanan's song, I discussed how mechanical patterning was suggestive of a relentless mechanical flow that conditions the narrator's perceptions. In Vega's music the intensity of the repetitions is such that attention is stolen away from their function in the song. It is almost as if these gestures are meant to signify touching, plucking and stroking of substances that do not yield to the touch. By this I mean that there is a distinct haptic quality to how Vega approaches her instrument, the use of closely miked open strings and repetitive patterning apparently resisting the performer's efforts to mould it into organic continuities, thereby exposing a subtext (or contratext) of existential tension between the performer and her instrument. In the lyrics, Vega advises listeners to "Find the line / find the shape / through the grain"; grain in the Barthesian sense of the word is surely close at hand if these principles are applied to the perception of sounds in the song. Vega's trademark half-whispered vocal style and the way it is digitally sculpted in studio production, by placing an emphasis on diction through the elevation of high frequencies, accomplishes this in the vocals. But the guitar part does this just as effectively by the use of repetition and close miking, the sum effect of which could be compared to the use of the extreme close-up in film. Indeed, Vega's approach to her instrument is strongly reminiscent of the audiovisual techniques discussed in connection with Glover Gill's score to the Richard Linklater film, *Waking Life* (see chapter 3, pages 80–82), where extreme close-ups of hands on instruments and close miking produce an aggregate effect of intensified realism. To the extent that the mimetic faculty is invoked in this approach, it activates the imagination in a way that brings to mind childhood experiences as well as producing a level of intimacy that verges on the erotic.[79]

In this way, Vega's songs work crossmodally by emphasizing the multisensory dimensions of experience. Ostensibly, the song would appear to comment on how dependent individuals and communities have become upon visual perception. So much so that when deprived of sight we experience a sense of privation that Burke aligned with the ambivalent pleasures of the sublime and Lyotard later identified as a defining feature of the postmodernist avant-garde (see chapter 5, page 189); hence the compulsion to fill the perceptual gaps.[80] This can happen through projection, where the imagination is called upon to create a surrogate or "virtual"

---

[79] As Barthes writes, "the word can be erotic on two opposing conditions, both excessive: if it is extravagantly repeated, or on the contrary, if it is unexpected, succulent in its newness...In both cases the same physics of bliss, the groove, the inscription, the syncope: what is hollowed out, tamped down, or what explodes, detonates." Roland Barthes, *The Pleasure of the Text*, trans. Richard Miller (New York: Hill and Wang, 1975), 42. Both repetition and a sense of language hollowed out (through the use of strange, disaffected chords) are characteristics of Vega's guitar style. On haptics and visual erotics, see Laura Marks, "Video Haptics and Erotics," *Screen* 39/4 (Winter 1998): 331–48.

[80] See Jean-François Lyotard, "The Sublime and the Avant-Garde," in Thomas Docherty, ed., *Postmodernism: A Reader* (New York: Columbia University Press, 1993), 244–56.

audiovisual world.[81] Or it can happen by means of sensory transference and compensation, where tactile experience, as well as the senses of taste and smell, comes to stand in for the missing visual experiences. In fact the two go hand in hand, since the crossmodal function opens up vistas onto sensory perceptions that exist principally in our memories of things. Thus we are encouraged to *see music*, to *hear images*, to *touch sounds*, to *smell colors*, to *taste the beat*, *smell the timbre* and so on. This is what Vega means by night vision, or perhaps it is what I want her to mean, which might well be one and the same thing. To summarize, this is a song that contains the visual even while it negates it.

Not by chance does Vega invoke an avant-garde ancestry that draws on elements of surrealism. A pop avant-garde (or avant-pop) sensibility is seldom far away in how she shapes, reflects and reflects on the audiovisual environment in her music. Perhaps "acoustic music" has privileged access to such modalities because of its phenomenal closeness to the elusive category of "silence," just as electronic styles have privileged access to noises that are not yet fully assimilated into our musical vocabulary. These styles suggest that altering our understanding of the world depends greatly on recognizing potentialities already there in the first place—perception implies activation. There might be something campy and unwitting in KT Tunstall's excursions into avant-garde performance, but the same qualities are present in her music, which is related to how her use of technology opens up a gap between what came before in recording technologies and what is yet to be. In this way and in the passage between the audiovisual and whatever lies beyond, a space is cleared for reflection within the relentless flows and contraflows of mediatized life.

Instance IV: "Heysátan" Performed Live by Sigur Rós: On Silence and the Pensive Listener

In my concluding comments, I would like to return to a central idea in folk ideology, that of getting back to the garden, a line from Joni Mitchell's "Woodstock" that conjures up both the hippie ideal of flower power and folk's rejection of the alienated discourses of electrified modernity. It is an impulse that underlies traditional ideas about "the acoustic," suggesting pre-ideological directness and auratic immediacy in an age when these qualities are thought to have been lost. The examples I provided suggest a different dynamic, in which the reach of the digital is

---

[81]   Virtual here refers to the sense in which this word is employed in Derridean theory, which implies anything that lies beyond the perceived "now." See, e.g., Brian Massumi, *Parables for the Virtual: Movement, Affect, Sensation* (Durham, NC: Duke University Press, 2002), 133–43.

understood to have permeated even the virginal sanctuary of the acoustic, bringing about a tangible state of disaffection. This incursion results in what I refer to in the title of this chapter as a surreal twist of fate, itself a surrealistically tinged reimagining of the electroacoustic Bob Dylan song "A Simple Twist of Fate" (*Blood on the Tracks*, 1975). Some of the most productive models for analyzing the acoustic are, paradoxically, to be found in research on the audiovisual. While ostensibly resisting the mediatized nature of current life, acoustic music is a discourse that relies on visual authentication in order to do its cultural work. This is especially true in discussions of folk. We see ample evidence of this in KT Tunstall's *Later* performance, which requires visual authentication in order to confirm that her actions are parodic of traditional recording practices. Folk authenticity is ultimately proven in audiovisual performances, even in cases when the performativity of acoustic performance threatens to destabilize those very constructions of authenticity. In Tunstall's case, gender becomes an issue to the extent that Tunstall's example of the recording performer repeats while transforming the approaches taken by male precursors.

Other theoretical ideas from research on audiovisuality might usefully be brought to bear on the "problem" of acoustic music. In her recent book, *Death 24x a Second: Stillness and the Moving Image*, Laura Mulvey draws on the theories of Roland Barthes and Raymond Bellour to construct a theoretical apparatus on moments of stoppage in cinematic flow that seems relevant to the issues discussed in this chapter. Mulvey is especially concerned with attending to the gaps and discontinuities that lurk between the serial static images of the filmic medium, which in the various chapters of her study are brought into the sphere of consciousness either through directorial intervention or by strategies of viewer activation.[82] Mulvey interprets freeze-frames in cinema, for example, as an index of death, particularly in the case of the "death-drive endings," such as those found in the films *Butch Cassidy and the Sundance Kid* (1969) and *Thelma and Louise* (1991). In her understanding, reversions to still imagery in film are effective because of how they are embedded within the ostensibly life-affirming medium of film.[83] Mulvey directs attention to how the standard celluloid film is made up of 24 static images per second, a factor that when it is consciously attended to or subverted in radical filmmaking techniques can elevate concerns about the nature of the medium and how material consciousness impinges on conventional modes of understanding though seeing. This takes various forms, including the ability of film icons to strike static poses, the grainy techniques of video artists and experimental filmmakers, and the use of freeze-frames. Moments of stillness in film are capable of

---

[82] See Laura Mulvey, *Death 24x a Second: Stillness and the Moving Image* (London: Reaktion Books, 2006), 181–96.

[83] Ibid., 81.

taking on a heightened significance, which locks the images into a kind of audiovisual purgatory between reality and fiction, ordinary life and the afterlife—a zone that is nothing if not surreal.[84]

If the auditory equivalent of the visual gap in film is silence, we approach an understanding that could prove helpful when theorizing acoustic music; one that understands this musical idiom as saturated with media consciousness rather than as an idealistic escape from such consciousness. For Mulvey, moments of stillness (for our purposes, silence) in cinema create "a 'pensive' spectator who can reflect 'on the cinema.'" She continues: "Not only can the 'pensive' spectator experience the kind of reverie that Barthes associated with the photograph alone, but this reverie reaches out to the nature of cinema itself."[85] For Mulvey, this allows two kinds of time, narrative time and its cessation, to cross-contaminate one another. The new acoustic music articulates a similar sensibility, allowing the imaginary construct of "musical time" to be audibly infused with soundscapes and silences that exist outside its formal borders.

This sensibility surfaces most recognizably when distinct breaks are indicated in the unfolding musical discourse. Two abrupt silences take on a heightened significance in Tunstall's performance of "Black Horse." These are located at its middle and end points. These sonic lacunae direct listeners' attention toward the split between the digital looped time of song structure and external everyday time, allowing each to reflect on the other. This allows us to hear the loops *as loops* and not as narratively configured musical discourse. It furthermore directs attention toward Tunstall as the causative agent responsible for looping the loops.

A third example illuminates this principle more vividly. Performed outdoors in the Icelandic wilderness, the Sigur Rós song "Heysátan" (meaning "haystack"; featured on the DVD *Heima*, dir. Dean DeBlois, 2007) incorporates several silences, which seem to convey not only a conspicuous absence of sound, but also something that it is difficult to express in words about what it means to experience Nature in the digital age. All of this imbues the music and the corresponding images with an atmosphere of melancholic reverie. Directorial choices in the film dwell on this point by drawing the viewer's attention to images of gravestones and what looks like a derelict building (in fact, it is an architectural "folly" designed by the naivist Icelandic artist Samúel Jónsson and set in the desolate outpost of Selardalur on the island's picturesque western coast).[86] Outside and apparently

---

[84] Susan Sontag shared this interest in the relationship between still images and death. See Sontag, *On Photography* (London: Penguin, 1971), 70. Mulvey's formulation is in certain respects an elaboration of Barthes's writing on the secondary *punctum* in photography; not the photographic detail, which was his primary concern, but the haunting quality of images that results from the passing of the photographic moment. See Roland Barthes, *Camera Lucida: Reflections on Photography* (London: Vintage 1993), 96.

[85] Mulvey, *Death 24x a Second*, 186.

[86] See the official *Heima* website, "Iceland Tour Diary, Day Two," http://www.sigur-ros.co.uk/tour/diary/?p=781, retrieved December 12, 2010.

mingling with the performing musicians are a group of uncanny (because they are inanimate) life-sized statues representing seals and people. An ecological impulse would seem to be at work in both images and sounds. Environmental sounds blend with the performed music, while moving clouds seem to match up with the atmosphere created in the song's static harmonies and resonant sonorities, thereby providing a subtle aspect of continuity between the musicians and their physical setting.

Musically, the song comprises individual chord strikes that concentrate on the core functional areas of G major (tonic, subdominant and dominant; G, C, and D) as well as their adjacent minor sonorities (mediant and submediant; B minor and E minor). Notably, the gaps between the strikes are so protracted that the musicians can be seen to visibly count out time while rocking to an unsounded beat. Gaps in the continuity of the song seem to occur almost arbitrarily on any degree of the scale. This is apparent in the instrumental introduction, where the rhythmic patterning conforms to a mechanical order in which beats are subtracted with each repetition of the chord sequence (initially, G – G – Bm6 – E minor – D). In the first cycle of the sequence, each chord is sustained for a full measure (four beats in a slow tempo). In subsequent cycles these relations become more dynamic as minimalist reductive processes are implemented: first E minor and D major are compressed into a single measure, with two beats sounding on each chord; then, in the final two cycles, several chords are held for a single beat, including the above chord change and shifts between the tonic, subdominant and mediant chords. At one point, the dominant chord is held over an asymmetrical count of nine beats in a half cadence whose inconclusiveness is conspicuous.

As in the examples of nu-folk discussed previously, an uncanny opposition is posited between sounds we recognize as organically produced and traditional and musical organization that implies dehumanized mechanization. "Heysátan" has a distinct hymnal quality, an aspect reinforced in the use of the harmonium, including church-organ-like pedal tones. But the music is drawn out to such an extent that the tonal directionality of these chord changes is at key moments divested of all temporal animation. This is especially striking in the final verse when the musicians stop performing for almost two measures (it is difficult to count this accurately as the musicians treat it as an extended fermata). This interruption comes to rest on the dysphoric submediant, E minor, during the sounding of which we see extended shots of rusting gravestones standing amid overgrown grass. Environmental sounds impinge on the music during these silent moments, including birdsong and the white noise of wind hitting a microphone, reminding us that the music and the musicians are also transitory and part of a greater environmental continuity.

The drones in the music provide a similarly large canvas to the physical environment where the musicians perform; in fact, the music becomes homologous (and sonically continuous) with this environment. If the harmonium part sounds hymnal, the electric guitar produces chords that resemble those played by Paul McCartney in the Beatles' "Blackbird": characterized by movement in parallel tenths (an octave plus a third), with the tones b^2 and g^2 humming sympathetically through the changes. In "Heysátan," however, the predominant direction of the music is descending and the tempo slow, which steers it away from the chipper mood of McCartney's song. The songs share an appreciation of open spaces, largely conveyed by airy chord voicings combined with an unchanging chordal backdrop (note that the outdoors is also implied in the lyrics of both songs). A densely orchestrated crescendo in the bridge carries the song effectively toward its apex, but it is the barren atmosphere of the verses that establishes its dominant affect; which once again connotes (urban) disaffection.

Most distinctive about this song is the fact that there is something arbitrary, *even mechanical,* about the places where the music is made to come to rest. In this way, the musical discourse is removed from the teleological impulse that ordinarily determines how it moves in time. This imbues the song with a sense of stasis and contemplative reverie that belies the conventional tonal qualities of the harmony. So unusual is the manner in which the music repeatedly stops in mid-flow that it is tempting to interpret "Heysátan" as expressing a deconstructive attitude.[87] That is, attention is directed away from the song's conventional connotative "meanings," which take on a retrospective or haunted quality as a result of the numerous acts of interruption. With lyrics in Icelandic about an aging farmer watching over his fields while contemplating his approaching demise, it is no surprise that the music is expressive of similar qualities (detachment and wistful reverie). This is achieved by a halting reflectiveness in which musical actions are divested of their expected consequences. The music no longer sounds "religious" or "folky," and seems to go nowhere. Instead, it moves the listener differently, most notably by means of sonic motion itself.

The corporeality of the music is underlined in at least two ways: First, the song cannot be performed effectively without physical movement and eye contact between the musicians; it is too loosely configured rhythmically to hold together in the absence of a visualized beat. Second, its corporeality can be attributed to the sonic properties of the instruments: the initial percussive strikes on a vibra-

---

[87] Suzanne Vega's song "Tom's Diner" (*Solitude Standing,* 1987) includes three such rhetorical gaps, situated as fermatas (pauses) along a schenkerian $\hat{5}\,\hat{4}\,\hat{3}$ Urlinie. Because it is sung a cappella, the song is otherwise infused by silence. I have argued elsewhere that this song evidences a strong deconstructive impulse that facilitates participatory strategies among listeners. This is one reason why so many remixes and cover versions of "Tom's Diner" have appeared since the initial recording. John Richardson, "Vieraannuttamisefektejä ja arkeologisia strategioita Suzanne Vegan lauluissa 'Tom's Diner' ja 'Luka.'" ("Alienation Effects and Archaeological Strategies in Suzanne Vega's Songs 'Tom's Diner' and 'Luka,'") *Musiikki* 4 (1996): 450–68.

phone and the ensuing warm vibrato afterglow; the deep sound of an electroacoustic bass guitar; the sharp onset of plucked guitar chords; the dark and fat
tones of a brass quartet comprising two trombones and two flugelhorns (note that
these instruments both occupy low registers). This instrumental emphasis engenders sonic beats and knots that seem to arise not so much as a result of gestural
contact with the instrument or dynamic chord movement, but out of the intrinsic
properties of the sounds (in this respect, a presumed ontological distinction between acoustical and electrical sounds is misleading, since both types of sound
occasion a similar complement of knots and flows in the musical texture). The
emphasis on sound as such creates musical entanglements that seem bound up
with the physical qualities of moving air more than discursive "musical" logic.
The resulting sonorous fullness (and implied semantic vacuity) leaves abundant
room for the imaginative faculties.

Above and emerging out of this sonic mass (mass also in the religious sense,
because of the hymnal quality of the instrumentation and musical syntax) soars
Jónsi Birgisson's ethereal countertenor voice, conveying its own "nonsensical
truth."[88] Like the accompanying music, the voice of the male falsetto singer directs
attention outward from a semantic and onto a prosodic and ecological plane. It
does this also in terms of gender coding, because the singer's voice refuses to be
subsumed in the binary gender order. By offering an open window onto a naïve
and (phenomenologically) bracketed domain of experience, Jónsi and his fellow
musicians provide something that resonates with the priorities of surrealism,
where spectral meanings collide with instant attraction in a dialectic that cannot
be easily resolved. This sensibility infuses the outdoor performance, carrying its
tones onward in time and space, across the flow spaces of the digital age and into
the privatized sonic spaces where we reside. It is above all the corporeal qualities
of sounds that permit these recorded audiovisual spaces to come into contact
(nondialectically) with our personal lived spaces. The music moves listeners,
quite literally, in a manner that relies on but seems to transcend its technological
mediation.

Might this be considered a straightforward audiovisual representation of folk
authenticity, in which performers and audiences alike are returned to a lost
utopian garden? The music does not support such an interpretation. For one thing,
several of the instruments are amplified, thus complicating the relationship between the acoustic and its electrified Other. Moreover, the music is structured in
such a way that it is recognizably a product of a digital sensibility. Even the silences
seem mechanized and posthuman—in the sense that Hayles employs the term:

---

[88]   See Edward D. Miller, "The Nonsensical Truth of the Falsetto Voice: Listening to Sigur Rós," *Popular
Musicology Online* 2 (2003), http://www.popular-musicology-online.com/issues/02/miller.html, retrieved
28 August, 2010. For more on uses of the countertenor voice in contemporary opera and its cultural significance, see Richardson, *Singing Archaeology.*

virtual insofar as they imply detachment from the human, but nevertheless resulting from performed physical gestures and evincing embodied responses.[89]

Highly significant here is the fact that in optimal conditions (which are fast
becoming the norm in home hi-fi set-ups as well as in theaters) the film offers an
impression of continuity between the depicted silences of the filmed world and
those silences that are part of the audience's immediate listening environment.
Michel Chion offers a useful theorization of the issue in his essay "The Silence of
the Soundspeakers."[90] Because of the technological advances brought about by
the use of technologies such as Dolby Digital and THX surround sound, silences
in recent cinema can make audiences more aware of corresponding and contiguous silences in their immediate environments. The two can never merge seamlessly: we cannot fully immerse ourselves in Sigur Rós's prefilmic reality as we are
always more closely connected with our own environmental reality, but the
images and sounds of this film present audiences with the illusion of continuity
between these two domains, resulting in a silence that seems to be listening to us
(while audibly enveloping us). This is not always an entirely comfortable sensation, but it does encourage a degree of reflection that was not so easily accomplished in the predigital age, when silence in audiovisual media was a scarce
commodity. Mediatized "acoustic music" of this type encourages the adoption of
such a listening position: a quietness that leaves greater space for reflective experience. The discontinuities and lacunae in the Sigur Rós performance, in this way,
articulate a sensibility that closely resembles what Mulvey addresses when she
discusses cinema's pensive spectator. Avant-gardist techniques in the filming of
Heima offer something analogous, but it is the music and surrounding environmental sounds that probably have the greatest impact in this instance. It is justified, therefore, to speak of this performance as facilitating a pensive or reflective
listening attitude.

As we have seen, silence in the examples elucidated in this chapter seems to
connect with two different types of cultural coding, which roughly speaking
might be divided into deconstructive and environmental functions. Roland
Barthes has distinguished between two such modalities in the section of his post-
humously published collection of lectures, *The Neutral*. The form of silence he
calls *tacere* resides in discursive gaps and might be considered rhetorical or deconstructive. That which he calls *silere*, on the other hand, implies a stillness resulting
from the absence of movement and corresponding noise, which thereby gives rise
to a more contemplative and restorative affective tone.[91] An environmental agenda

[89] N. Katherine Hayles, *How We Became Posthuman: Virtual Bodies in Cybernetics, Literature, and Informatics*
(Chicago: University of Chicago Press, 1999).

[90] Michel Chion, *Film, A Sound Art*, trans. Claudia Gorbman (New York: Columbia University Press,
2003).

[91] Roland Barthes, *The Neutral* (New York: Columbia University Press, 2005), 21–23.

is implicit in perceptions of the latter kind. Both modalities are present in the Sigur Rós performance, which can be understood as representing the cessation of the mechanized flow of media, the ubiquitous discourses of the digital age, and a second silence that flows into and out of an ecological discursive space. In the digital age, we are never truly at one with Nature, but rather with an idea of what Nature has become in an age of media flow and digital surround sound. I suspect that this is why the new acoustic music resonates so deeply with contemporary experience—the fact that it touches on both levels of understanding.

8

Concluding Thoughts: Of Liquid Days and Going Gaga

*A traditional scholar does not believe in ghosts—not in all that could be
called the virtual space of spectrality…[Another] would be capable,
beyond the opposition between presence and non-presence, actuality and
inactuality, life and non-life, of thinking the possibility of the specter, the
specter as possibility. He would know that such an address is not only
possible, but that it will have at all times conditioned, as such, address in
general.*

—Jacques Derrida, *Specters of Marx*

*I'll be your one stop (one stop)
Candy shop (candy shop)
Everything (everything)
That I got (that I got)
I'll be your one stop (one stop)
Candy store (candy store)
Lollipop (lollipop)
Have some more (have some more)*
—Madonna, "Candy Shop" (*Hard Candy*, 2008)

*Does anyone know what I hate almost as much as I hate money? Yes,
I hate the truth. The French call it la verité. Je déteste la vérité! In fact
I hate the truth so much, I prefer a giant dose of bullshit any day over
the truth.*

—Lady Gaga, *Monster Ball Tour* (2010)

This book started from the premise that traits of surrealism are found in some of the most provocative and critically salient forms of audiovisual expression currently in circulation. Admittedly, this is just one of several possible courses my research could have taken. Several examples discussed in this book can be regarded either as extending or contesting ideas that initially surfaced in the sphere of postmodernist cultural production. While recognizing some degree of continuity with postmodernism, I would insist on the necessity of situating these practices in a contemporary rubric in which assumptions imported from earlier eras and practices are never taken for granted. In the current age of ubiquitous and rapidly proliferating media, the responses a recorded performance will evince are increasingly difficult to predict. Performances interface with audiences on a constantly changing basis. All of which highlights the importance of not investing unreservedly in any given explanatory framework, be it postmodernism, digital culture, or that which I have chosen to spotlight in much of my exegetical work: (neo)surrealism. Even in a case like Glass's *La Belle et la Bête*, where a good half of the work could be said to be rooted in the mindset of the historical surrealists (due to the incorporation of Cocteau's original film), to invest too eagerly in a historical view of the subject (and in this case it would be merely a *viewing*, not a *hearing*, since the original work is silenced) would be to ignore the transformations the original cinematic artifact was subjected to under Glass's authorial direction. The case studies presented in these pages have supported a claim that is made persuasively in both poststructuralist philosophy and phenomenology: that every repetition is at the same time a transformation.[1] As stated in the introduction, surrealism in the present evaluation is at best a productive analogy. My intention in formulating these conclusions is to maintain a cautious distance with respect to earlier surrealisms in light of the ample evidence my case studies have divulged concerning the impact of localized and historically specific cultural marking on audience understanding. This is why surrealism in the sense of the historical movement can never be more than a touchstone for interpretations. Surrealism is a satisfactory interpretative framework in reference to this corpus of materials only when it is combined with theoretical and historical perspectives that arise out of experiences in the digital or information age.

Flows

One way of understanding the discursive and affective nature of recent cultural production is as conveying a character of relentless unfolding and subjective becoming that different thinkers in different ways have associated with the

---

[1] To assume otherwise is to engage in Hegelian abstraction at the epistemological level of the "concept." The view of repetition as always giving expression to difference is found principally in Gilles Deleuze's extensive philosophical study, *Repetition & Difference*. It is rooted, moreover, in Kierkegaardian ideas about the singularity of experience set against his assumptions concerning personal agency and volition. Derrida's idea of iterability rests on similar assumptions, as does the related notion of performativity, as set out in this writer's work and that of many others. All of these views are commensurate with a phenomenological attitude. See Gilles Deleuze, *Repetition & Difference*, trans. Paul Patton (London: The Athlone Press, 1994 [1968]), 220–26, 105, 221; Jacques Derrida, *Writing and Difference*, trans. Alan Bass (Chicago: University of Chicago Press, 1978).

concept of flow. Manuel Castells in his magisterial opus on the changing nature of experience in what he calls the information age has noted how this era is distinguished from previous ones is by its concentration around spaces of flows rather than spaces of places.[2] The current cultural climate is distinguished by a more distant sense of interpersonal communication and access to more flexible and open-ended communicative networks in both leisure and labor. If this is the case, the famous dictum from Marx and Engel's *Communist Manifesto*, "All that is solid melts into air," may well be in need of revision. In the digital age, all that is solid, arguably, no longer melts into air *but into water* (although the word "melt" suggests "dissolve" or "liquefication"); a transformative medium that has been invested with ameliorative associations in recent cultural studies and philosophy, including metaphors of free-flow, fluidity, liquidity (of assets), and streaming (including stream-of-consciousness writing and digital streaming). At least in the dissident margins of current practices, the ear would appear attuned to sounds of "songs from liquid days"[3] and of ecologically astute but economically complicit "hydraulic power" (to the extent that power relations are implicated in this new economy of flows, which they are). The feminist philosopher Luce Irigaray considered liquid consciousness to be an appropriate model for the nondualistic, sensually heightened and regenerative modes of being that she associated with femininity, progressive sexual politics and salutary interpersonal relations in general rather than those static structurations that are customarily associated with the "masculine" *Logos*.[4] Deleuze's writing on philosophy and cinema is similarly saturated (drenched, flooded, awash—the metaphors go on) with allusions to flow consciousness, implying a mode of experience that might be "tapped into" (yet another aquatic metaphor) as a means of resisting dominant narrative means of structuring time in mainstream audiovisual forms. Those filmmakers who concentrated on the preverbal qualities of physical action and free-flowing movement in time invariably came out on top in his evaluations. Perception for Deleuze has an essential liquid component, a facet that comes out most clearly in his discussion of the early French experimental cinema of Grémillon and Vigo.[5] In the present study, an aqueous subterranean stream surfaces most tangibly in reference to the metamusicals of auteur-directors Sally Potter and Tsai Ming-Liang in chapter 4, and Richard Linklater in chapter 3. For the first two directors, water signifies love, (com)passion, regeneration, reparation, satiation—it is an agent of

[2] Manuel Castells, *The Rise of the Network Society: The Information Age: Economy, Society and Culture*, vol. 1 (Oxford: Blackwell, 1996), 442.

[3] "Songs from Liquid Days" is the title of a song cycle by Philip Glass (1986) composed to texts by popular artists including Paul Simon, Laurie Anderson, David Byrne and Suzanne Vega.

[4] Luce Irigaray, *This Sex Which Is Not One*, trans. Catherine Porter (Ithaca & New York: Cornell University Press, 1985).

[5] Gilles Deleuze, *Cinema 1: The Movement-Image*, trans. Hugh Tomlinson & Barbara Habberjam (London: Continuum, 1986), 76–84.

change in a world that is all too often deprived of this valuable and easily squandered resource.

And yet, flow is a metaphor that a previous generation of cultural theorists distrusted. In critical theory, the constant flow of discourses in the mass media is regarded as entrapping the distracted Western subject in patterns of repetitive continuity whose seductive power is hard to resist. Media flow as theorized by Raymond Williams thus anesthetizes audiences to the material circumstance of their lives as well as those of the people represented on their television screens.[6] This line of reasoning strongly resembles that of Adorno when it comes to popular music, in which the hypnotic beat of popular music is understood to instill a kind of complacency in socially disenfranchised consumers by hoodwinking them into believing that they have a voice. One could of course argue that both Williams and Adorno are missing something essential when it comes to understanding the reparative pleasures of media flow, in the case of the former, or those of the groove, the beat, the funk (including the erotic connotations of these concepts), in that of the latter. To do so is to question the classical Freudian view of repetition as importing only infantile regression and to replace it with a view in which the visceral, process-driven and participatory pleasures (including participatory discrepancies, following Keil and Feld)[7] of syncing and missyncing bodily actions against a rhythmic constant is understood to court sparks, to occasion collisions and to correlate convergences in a manner that is instructive about the conditions of modern life. Two chapters of this book seem to articulate these dialectical principles more directly than the others. Practices of (mis)syncing, discussed in chapter 5, remind us of the mechanical constraints that dominate the cultural ground-tone in the digital age, not to mention the pleasures they can afford, even while the dominant affective tone of these artifacts and performances harks back to "anachronous" industrial technologies (industrialization being one of the great repressed Others of Western civilization in the digital age). Let it not be forgotten that industrialization has not magically vanished in the "postindustrial age"; it has simply been shipped farther from home.

These very digital technologies, however, would seem to offer consider potential for appropriative interventions. Namely, a kind of euphoria, signaling desubjectification (or dehumanization) combined with the reinstatement of subjective agency (through acts of ingenuous and disingenuous appropriation) is present in instances where someone *does something* with technologies they were never supposed to do. An aspect of remediation is implied in such cases, which in turn might imply a performative realignment of conventional positions. Glass's misuse of an historical film brings this deconstructive function into sight (a term he himself uses); as does KT Tunstall's mis(s)use of looping as a means of interrogating the

---

[6] Raymond Williams, *Television: Technology and Cultural Form* (London & New York: Routledge, 1974).

[7] Charles Keil and Steve Feld, *Music Grooves: Essays and Dialogues* (Chicago: University of Chicago Press, 1994), 96–108.

encoded temporalities of the recorded popular song. Deconstruction in these cases does not refer to a dry intralinguistic exercise. Rather, it is a means of releasing the phenomenological and aesthetically rich potential of audiovisual performances.[8] Tunstall's stage(d) performance rises with each added loop to ever higher plateaus of euphoric intensity, and her obvious manipulation of the technological means at her disposal signals agentic interpolation in an age when our understanding of what it means to "compose" is changing drastically. Sally Potter signals a similar sense of auteurist agency in the effortless manner in which she weaves together vocal dialogue, music and the musicality of moving images with a view to transporting audiences on a seductive audiovisual wave. This is the author as producer (as critic), to follow Benjamin's line of reasoning.[9] Linklater aims for something similar in his treatment of digital animated imagery, which is entangled in the independent film *Waking Life* with seductive nuevo-tango refrains and the (hard to ignore) embodied physical actions of performers. The tone of these artistic interventions is strongly affirmative, as the titles of both Linklater's and Potter's films evidence. Both films direct attention toward a form of "aestheticism" that has little to do with those musty forms of autonomy by which the classical Romantic subject was constructed. The social construction of this subject required the individual be considered in relief against other subjects, whose status as Other would open them to various forms of subjugation, just as the notion of the aggrandized Romantic subject, over and above Nature, is symptomatic of an instrumental rationality that was later to be regarded as at best narrowly egotistical and at worst socially irresponsible.[10] An aestheticism made up of ebbs and flows (of water and desire), of lucid dreaming and streams of consciousness (as found in surrealist automatic writing) instead represents, for many commentators, a view of reality that is constituted as one quality flows freely into the next. This change in outlook heralds a dissident attitude when it comes to the binary oppositions on which classic aestheticism was founded. The mode of experience in question resembles those forms of camp aesthetics that Sedgwick aligns with an exuberantly modern disposition

[8] Aitken comments on the phenomenological impact of surrealism in much the same way, in a treatment that leans heavily on the earlier work of the film theorist Siegried Kracauer. Kracauer's theorization closely resembles that which I advanced in this book. Starting from the premise that film and photography correspond structurally with the fragmented condition of modernity, and in this way might be considered "realist" forms, he goes on to consider the redemptive function of filmed images to disclose the "sensuous and ephemeral aspects of reality." Ian Aitken, "Distraction and Redemption: Kracauer, Surrealism and Phenomenology," *Screen* 39/2 (Summer 1998): 125. See also Siegried Kracauer, *Theory of Film: The Redemption of Physical Reality* (Oxford: Oxford University Press, 1960), 299.

[9] See Walter Benjamin, "The Author as Producer" in Peter Demetz, ed., trans. Edmund Jephcott, *Reflections: Essays, Aphorisms, Autobiographical Writings* (New York: Schocken, 1978), 220–38; and "The Work of Art in the Age of Mechanical Reproduction," in Hannah Arendt, ed., trans. Harry Zohn, *Illuminations: Essays and Reflections* (New York: Schocken, 1968), 217–51.

[10] See Terry Eagleton, *The Ideology of the Aesthetic* (Oxford: Blackwell, 1990): Theodor Adorno and Max Horkheimer, *Dialectic of Enlightenment* (London: Verso, 1979).

(or was it postmodern? Does it matter?). At stake is an aestheticism attuned to the affective powers of performances, but always in balance with critical priorities.[11] In this view, both rhythmic flow and its cessations can be invested with redemptive transformative powers.

Interruptions

The idea of interruption has received more than its fare share of attention in the course of this study. It is present above all in the materials themselves and it is duly attended to in the study's methodological apparatus. In the Sigur Rós performance of the song "Heysátan," filmed in the Icelandic wilderness, the music is constantly interrupted by silences. Interruptions in general seem to serve a dual function that correlates with the categories of silence Barthes names *tacere* and *silere*.[12] His first form of silence draws attention to the conditions of discourse itself, to its mortality or ephemerality *as* discourse (and ours as affiliating subjects). Silence as *tacere* (or *tacet*, in orchestral terminology), for its part, brings exterior realities into contact with interior ones in a manner that *neutralizes* the discursive or conventional function of language but does not strip expression altogether of "meaning." This neutrality imparts a ghostly pallor to the codes and meanings embedded in conventional forms (does that music *really* sound like a hymn?), while diverting attention to the phenomenal aspects of the performance. This sets up a dialectic between the two levels that is most illuminating when it comes to the gendered qualities of the voice (Jónsi Birgisson's high falsetto), which incorporates qualities of both masculine and feminine as constructed, while nevertheless implying a phenomenal quality that seems to transcend the gender divide. Barthes's second modality of silence, *silere,* denotes an aspect of heightened ecological awareness through the admission of environmental sounds, which can draw attention both to the limitless expanse of that which evades categorization (which in turn evokes the Romantic category of the sublime; as discussed in chapter 5), while further indicating the precarious balance that holds that external order in place.

Silence can evoke death, but it can also signpost a discursive opening that facilitates agentic engagement. Laura Mulvey wrote extensively on this subject in her investigation into the different forms of interruption to be found in the visual filmic text.[13] Auditory interruption can produce similar results, allowing greater potential for the emergence of a pensive listener. Chion's writing on the impact of digital technologies in cinema, as unveiling silence and thereby activating audi-

---

[11] See Eve Kosofsky Sedgwick, *Touching Feeling: Affect, Pedagogy, Performativity* (Durham, NC: Duke, 2003), 149–51.

[12] Roland Barthes, *The Neutral* (New York: Columbia University Press, 2005), 21–23.

[13] Laura Mulvey, *Death 24x a Second: Stillness and the Moving Image* (London: Reaktion Books, 2006).

ence response, implicitly addressed this question.[14] However, Chion has little to say about how formal interruptions in audiovisual discourses are bound up with an attitude to emerging digital technologies that activates cultural memories.

Discussions of surrealism in the visual arts draw attention to similar processes of interruption. Something not commented on in previous research is how the interruption of sound continuities by silences is distinctive to audiovisual surrealism. These temporal suspensions produce the type of displacement along a metaphorical axis that is referred to in the linguistic definitions of surrealism discussed in chapter 2, page 37. When this happens, the textuality of the music cedes to its phenomenal sonic substance, on the one hand, and the sounds and noises of daily life become palpable, on the other. This is the primary means by which surrealism operates, as commented on in a long line of writing that attends to hidden absurdities in everyday experiences—running from Breton and Aragon, through Benjamin's *Arcades Project* and Barthes's interest in the "Third Meaning" of photographs—culminating in the current spate of research on the cultural history of sound. Surrealism is about hearing the sounds of daily life as aestheticized, and, conversely, learning to become more aware of the conventional and historical nature of naturalized musical discourse. Techniques of montage and appropriation resembling those found in Dada and surrealism often provide the rubric for such interruptive techniques. The intermediality of current modes of performance provides a further context for interruptive techniques, as the rules of one discourse give way to those of another (implying an ethos of hybridity, plurality), and discursive understanding as the dominant paradigm for interpretation gives way to metadiscursivity. We hear this in the music of Gorillaz as we pass from British melodic rock to rap in the passage from chorus to verse. It is heard again in Tsai Ming-Liang's *Wayward Cloud* as the listener passes from the audiovisual conventions of hardcore pornography to those of the classic film musical. A gap opens up in these forms that not only signifies their contingency as forms of discourse, but which also allows the assumptions of one set of practices to be projected onto those of the other.

Technologies

As was just discussed, the affective tone of contemporary urban soundscapes is saturated like porous limestone with sonic markers of digital consciousness. It follows that the soundscapes of our lives sound *and resound* with a distinctive posthuman affective tone.[15] In invoking the term "posthuman," I am referring to

---

[14] Michel Chion, *Film, A Sound Art*, trans., Claudia Gorbman (New York: Columbia University Press, 2003).

[15] See Katherine N. Hayles, ed., *How We Became Posthuman: Virtual Bodies in Cybernetics, Literature, and Informatics* (Chicago: University of Chicago Press, 1999).

a mode of understanding that reaches beyond those that were available to the classic liberal humanist subject (whose universality has long been a matter of contention), but which nevertheless gives serious attention to those ameliorative attributes of this subject that still have currency, including such matters as personal agency, choice and embodiment. The musical (and visual) instruments of digital culture have played a part in bringing about this state of affairs (in quite direct ways, such as in the use of quantization, digital affects and looping technologies), but even when these technologies play no obvious role in sound production, we have become conditioned to produce and listen to electronically mediated sounds to such an extent that a digital sensibility contaminates even those forms of production that have conventionally eschewed the trappings of mechanical production. Philip Glass's handling of orchestral instruments and musical conventions speaks to such an orientation, as does the attitude of the electrofolk musician discussed in chapter 7. The strident rhythmic film music of composers like Danny Elfman and Jon Brion are further confirmation of the transformations currently underway in the audiovisual sphere. Films these days are characterized by soundtracks in which symphonic scores alternate freely with incorporated popular music (*Magnolia; Inception*), and, moreover, the transitions between musical styles are negotiated in such a way that audiences are not necessarily aware of the historical weight of what is being traded. A constant beat characterizes the music of both of the aforementioned film music composers, as it does that of minimalists working in the audiovisual sphere (whether in film or in music theater or opera).[16] It is not always clear whether the musical sounds included in these films, and other audiovisual forms, have been digitally sampled (in other words, recorded, electronically manipulated and looped), or whether real musicians recorded them in a "live" studio session (as would have been the case in Hollywood's Golden Age scoring practices). Elfman is just one of many composers who employs digitally sampled orchestral sounds as liberally as he does actual orchestras. Glass similarly uses both real orchestral musicians and sampled sounds (the latter in much of *La Belle*). A similar boundary line becomes blurred when considering the relationship between electronically produced Foley sounds and real environment sounds in films, games and other new media. As these categories mix in increasingly complex and aesthetically evocative ways, it is fast becoming impossible to differentiate a synthetically produced sound that somehow captures the mood of the scene from a corresponding sound that mimics the sonic qualities of physical reality. This can leave audiences wondering which elements of the soundtrack are "merely" emotionally real and which are

---

[16] See Anahid Kassabian, "The Sound of a New Film Form," in Ian Inglis, ed., *Popular Music and Film* (London: Wallflower, 2003), 91–101; also Susan McClary, "Minima Romantica," in Daniel Goldmark, Lawrence Kramer, and Richard Leppert, eds., *Beyond the Soundtrack: Representing Music in Cinema* (Berkeley: University of California Press, 2007), 48–65.

phenomenally real. In such cases, audiovisual expression might be said to have taken a turn in a surreal direction. Of course, the extent to which a performance might be considered surrealist (or neosurrealist) greatly depends on the level of reflection it occasions in audio viewers.

Ghosts

The subtitle of this chapter and its opening epigram both in different ways address a major concern of this study that might at the same time be regarded as a significant finding. Far from being affectively depleted or caught up in a solipsistic play of signifiers that admits no external point of reference, the instances collected together in this book all in different ways resonate with the memories of the musical "objects" that have become their subject matter. Often the audiovisual objects in question were encountered, perhaps cherished, in childhood or in the formative years of a performer's stylistic self-invention. These objects are then appropriated and set free to rebound against the prevailing circumstances of present-day life. Vintage R&B music for Michel Gondry; British blues revival music for KT Tunstall; scratchy localized recordings of North American country music and outmoded "mandopop" film tunes in Tsai Ming-Liang's film; classical music given a contemporary twist in Sally Potter's; echoes of 1960s British pop and classic dub reggae for Gorillaz' Damon Albarn; a surrealist film encountered when studying composition in Paris for Philip Glass; all these artists use their engagements with these once valued audiovisual objects from a generation or two ago to say something poignant or pointed about the present. The historical surrealists took considerable pleasure in investing found objects with an uncanny new life. Breton and Aragon would frequent the flea markets, antique shops and condemned shopping arcades of urban Paris in search of lost treasures whose lingering presence in incongruous present-day settings activated a flurry of connotative meanings that revealed something about the transitory nature of modern life and the rapid turnover of consumable objects and modes of production in capitalism. More than this, the objects thus understood *to be objects* had a consistency, a phenomenal power in the consciousness of their *materia*, that seemed to be lacking in their original incarnations, in which their utility as objects distracted attention from their object status. In much the same way, the emotive power of photography in Roland Barthes's account of the second *punctum* (or rhetorical interruption) could be said to inhere in the sense of a presence conveyed when the image was first registered onto the photographic medium. This implies a mimetic if mediated relationship to the subject of the photograph, but one that is transformed in the act of perception into an unavoidable sense of absence.[17]

---

[17] Roland Barthes, *Camera Lucida: Reflections on Photography* (London: Vintage, 1993), 96.

Such is the melancholic undertone underlying the thinking of the historical surrealists. It is reprised in the attitude of Frankfurt-school Marxist cultural theorists, especially when it comes to their theorizations of surrealism as commentary on alienated social relations in the industrial world.[18] It is reprised yet again in Derrida's theorizations about the loss of *Marx himself* in discourse that resonates with his ideas and yet conspicuously avoids mentioning him by name.[19] This melancholic orientation colors some of the instances discussed in these pages. But the materials discussed in this book disclose more than this. The childlike pleasures of playing with existing materials in films by Linklater, Gondry and Potter, or in music by Albarn, Buchanan or Sigur Rós, attests to a form of engagement that is altogether more affirmative, ebullient, and, on occasion, erotically tinged in its affective character; but nevertheless permitting a critical sting in the tail that can be traced though historical surrealism to the ghost of Marx himself filtered through the discourses of cultural criticism. It is a mode of production (and activated consumption) that recognizes the forces of enchantment that come into play in a world in which commercial goods are able to unleash fleeting pleasures that can be more than mere "distractions."[20] The ability (or imperative?) to recycle is among the most magical qualities of experience available to consumers in the nascent digital world—a world of flows, confluences, sensory close contact, juxtapositions and interruptions that undoubtedly signify the dominant modes of social structuring in the capitalist world order. At the same time, however, the qualitative nature of modern life provides some possibilities for critical agency. It is a world (depicted mimetically in surreal worlds-within-worlds) that is admittedly far from perfect, but in which simple pleasures can signify a mode of being *or becoming* in which change is initiated from below.

I am struck as I attempt to draw together my final reflections on a project that has taken up more of my waking life over several years than is probably good for me by the nagging feeling that something is missing. Numerous ghosts might in different circumstances have taken on material substance in these pages. At least three chapters never made it to the published version of the book. One of these was a consideration of David Lynch's *Twin Peaks* that for a variety of reasons did not seem to match the subject matter of this book.[21] A chapter on audiovisual

---

[18] Theodor Adorno, "Looking Back on Surrealism" (1954), in *Notes to Literature*, vol. 1, trans. Shierry Weber Nicholson (New York: Columbia University Press, 1991), 86–90, Walter Benjamin, "Surrealism: The Last Snapshot of the European Intelligentsia," in Peter Demetz, ed., trans. Edmund Jephcott (New York: Schocken, 1978), 177–92.

[19] Derrida, *Specters of Marx*.

[20] For a similar perspective on these issues, see Jane Bennett, "Commodity Fetishism and Commodity Enchantment," *Theory & Event* 5/1 (Winter 2001), at http://muse.jhu.edu/journals/theory_and_event/v005/5.1bennett.html, retrieved October 31, 2010.

[21] I have published a version of this research elsewhere. It is in acute need of revision, however, in light of the findings of the present study. See John Richardson, "Laura and *Twin Peaks*: Postmodern Parody and the

silence similarly fell by the wayside. Writing on music videos has occupied me in parallel to this project and at least two detailed case studies were omitted only in the final drafts (a study of Peter Gabriel's "Sledgehammer" was one).[22] I originally intended to write more about popular music awards ceremonies than was eventually included in the chapter on Gorillaz, and may do so in future publications. When writing this book, I was absorbed almost to the point of obsession by the literary output of two writers, Haruki Murakami and David Mitchell, both of whose writing makes frequent allusions to music while addressing the pleasures and anxieties of life in the digital age. Both combine elements of surrealism with an appreciation of sensory experience conveyed through vivid descriptions that resemble the approaches to film discussed in chapters 3 and 4. This resemblance highlights the extent to which what I call neosurrealism extends across the current expressive landscape. Audiovisual neosurrealism in popular culture cannot be contained within these pages. A critical discussion of Lady Gaga's spectacular and outlandish performances could easily have become one of the case studies included in this book. The epigram at the beginning of this chapter evidences this artist's commitment to surrealist aesthetics, but this is more directly expressed through just about every gesture, costume and musical refrain in her growing repertoire of videos and stage performances. Gaga's relatively generic musical sound further evidences an outlook that is based on citation and elevated aesthetic style, combined with elements of brash visual incongruity. All of this situates her expressive language firmly in the domain of neosurrealism. Ultimately, I decided that to include a detailed case study on Lady Gaga was overly ambitious for the scope of this book. Other scholars will hopefully take up the slack that undoubtedly remains in my work by giving this artist's provocative performances the critical attention they deserve. Notwithstanding such conspicuous omissions, I would maintain that the practices and forms discussed in this book represent some of the most illuminating examples of the emerging neosurreal.

What would be an appropriate manner to end a discussion on the audiovisual surreal in the current digital age? The path taken by animated Gorillaz front man 2D at the 2002 Brit Awards performance, discussed in chapter 6, is one option: the animated character, who bears more than a passing resemblance to the pop singer Damon Albarn, approaches an oversized video screen to extinguish his own spectral image. An alternative image is that of the pop star Madonna during the final moments of her Hard Candy Promo Tour concerts. The animated

Musical Reconstruction of the Absent Femme Fatale," in Annette Davison and Erica Sheen, eds., *The Cinema of David Lynch: American Dreams, Nightmare Visions* (London: Wallflower Press, 2004), 77–92.

   [22] Published elsewhere, this article can be considered a companion case study to the work presented in this volume. See "Plasticine Music: Surrealism in Peter Gabriel's 'Sledgehammer,'" in Michael Drewett, Sarah Hill and Kimi Kärki, eds., *Games Without Frontiers: Peter Gabriel From Genesis to Growing Up* (Farnham and Burlington: Ashgate, 2010), 195–210.

performer (this time in a corporeal sense) has left the stage and giant screens scattered around the venue replay an animated video sequence of a metallic ball descending along a labyrinthine trajectory. The image is accompanied by rumbling and clinking noises of the digital sublime, which complete the job of bidding the amassed audience farewell. In oversized letters, the legend appears: GAME OVER. A surreal moment if ever there was one.

That makes two false endings. A third? Nothing for me better captures the changing landscape of audiovisual expression than a "music video" by the alternative rock group Arcade Fire that is only available online.[23] Directed by Chris Milk and requiring the use of Google's Chrome web-browser together with Google Maps, the video to the song "We Used to Wait" (the video is entitled "The Wilderness Downtown") is participatory insofar as it instructs the addressee to supply the address of a place where they grew up.[24] During the running of the video, images of this location begin to appear in multiple pop-up screens, at first in aerial and long shots, and then zooming in on the address provided by the user in images that because they move (employing techniques akin to the Ken Burns effect) come across as filmed and therefore more "real" and "live" than static photos. The user is forced to confront emotionally freighted memories in the context of a lyric that addresses change and personal loss ("Our lives are changing fast / Hope that something pure can last"). As the video progresses, the addressee is instructed to write a note to their childhood self in a stylized animated text font (whereafter the text begins to grow like tree branches). This message is then delivered by a murder of crows that circles the multiple screens menacingly in flowing formations that eventually weave their way down to the user's childhood home. The imagery becomes progressively more surreal following the appearance of the flock of birds. As the song reaches its final insistent refrains an unruly forest sprouts up from the (in my case) suburban terrain to engulf all of the onscreen images. It is hard to relate in writing the emotional impact of the video, which is greatly enhanced by music of considerable iterative power and emotional urgency. The experience is surreal in almost every sense of the word discussed in chapter 2, not least because it compels the addressee to confront the gap between what has passed and what is now. It does this more palpably than any of the examples I provided because it requires a greater level of personalization. Nevertheless, the personalized becomes eerily depersonalized or haunted because of the absence of familiar humanizing factors and because of the disconcerting direction of the depicted actions. In this way, the Arcade Fire video encapsulates something essential about the nature of the audiovisual surreal in the digital age.

[23] A student at Åbo Academy in Finland, Oskar Nyman, first drew my attention to this video.

[24] The video can be found at the website, The Wilderness Downtown, www.thewildernessdowntown.com/, retrieved December 13, 2010.

Bibliography

Adorno, Theodor W. *Introduction to the Sociology of Music*. Trans. E.B. Ashton. New York: Continuum, 1976.

———. *Prisms*. Cambridge, MA: MIT Press, 1983.

———. "On Popular Music." In *On Record: Rock Pop and the Written Word*, eds. Simon Frith and Andrew Goodwin, 301–14. New York: Pantheon, 1990.

———. "Looking Back on Surrealism." In *Notes to Literature*. Vol. 1. Trans. Shierry Weber Nicholson, 86–90. New York: Columbia University Press, 1991 [1954].

———. *Quasi una Fantasia*. Trans. Rodney Livingston. London: Verso, 1992 [1963].

Adorno, Theodor, and Hanns Eisler. *Composing for the Films*. London: Athlone Press, 1994 [1947].

Aitken, Ian. "Distraction and Redemption: Kracauer, Surrealism and Phenomenology." *Screen* 39/2 (Summer 1998): 125.

Altman, Rick. *The American Film Musical*. Bloomington and Indianapolis: Indiana University Press, 1987.

Altman, Rick, McGraw Jones, and Sonia Tatroe. "Inventing the Cinema Soundtrack: Hollywood's Multiplane Sound System." In *Music and Cinema*, eds. James Buhler, Caryl Flinn and David Neumeyer, 339–59. Hanover, NH: Wesleyan University Press, 2000.

Aragon, Luis. *Paris Peasant*. Trans. Jonathan Cape. Boston: Exact Change, 1994 [1926].

Auner, Joseph. "Making Old Machines Speak: Images of Technology in Recent Music." *Echo* 2/2 (2000): 32 pars, February 13, 2004. Online. Available at http://www.humnet.ucla.edu/echo, retrieved December 10, 2010.

Auslander, Philip. "Liveness, Mediatization, and Intermedial Performance." *Degrés: Revue de synthèse à orientation sémiologique* 101 (Spring 2000): 1–12.

———. *Liveness: Performance in a Mediatized Culture*. 2nd ed. London: Routledge, 2008.

———. *Performing Glamrock: Gender and Theatricality in Popular Music*. Ann Arbor: University of Michigan Press, 2006.

Ayers, Michael, ed. *Cybersounds; Essays on Virtual Music Culture*. New York: Peter Lang, 2006.

Babuscio, Jack, "The Cinema of Camp (*AKA* Camp and the Gay Sensibility)." In *Camp: Queer Aesthetics and the Performing Subject. A Reader*, ed. Fabio Cleto, 117–35. Edinburgh: Edinburgh University Press, 1999.

Baltin, Steve, "Albarn Going Ape over Gorillaz: Blur Frontman Prefers Animated Life 'In The Shadows.'" *Rolling Stone*, July 25, 2001. Online. Available at http://www.rollingstone.com/, retrieved January 24, 2004.

Bannister, Matthew. *White Boys, White Noise: Masculinities and 1980s Indie Guitar Rock*. Aldershot: Ashgate, 2006.

Barlow, Priscilla. "Surreal Symphonies: L'Age d'or and the Discreet Charms of Classical Music." In *Soundtrack Available at Essays on Film and Popular Music,* eds. Pamela Robertson Wojcik and Arthur Knight, 31–52. Durham, NC: Duke University Press, 2001.

Barron, Lee, and Ian Inglis. "'We're Not In Kansas any More': Music, Myth and Narrative Structure on *The Dark Side Of The Moon.*" In *The Legacy of Pink Floyd's Dark Side of the Moon,* ed. Russell Reising, 56–66. Aldershot: Ashgate, 2005.

Bartel, Dietrich. *Musica Poetica: Musical-Rhetorical Figures in German Baroque Music.* Lincoln: University of Nebraska Press, 1997.

Barthes, Roland. *Camera Lucida: Reflections on Photography.* Vintage: London, 1993.

———. *Image—Music—Text.* Trans. Stephen Heath. New York: Hill and Wang, 1977.

———. "The Metaphor of the Eye." In *Story of the Eye,* by Lord Auch [pseudonym], trans. J. A. Underwood, 119–27. London and New York: Penguin, 1982.

———. *The Neutral.* New York: Columbia University Press, 2005.

———. *The Pleasure of the Text.* Trans. Richard Miller. New York: Hill and Wang, 1975.

Barz, Gregory, and Timothy Cooley, eds. *Shadows in the Field: New Perspectives for Fieldwork in Ethnomusicology.* Oxford and New York: Oxford University Press, 2008.

Bataille, Georges. *Erotism: Death and Sensuality.* San Francisco: City Lights Books, 1986.

———. *The Absence of Myth: Writings on Surrealism.* London: Verso, 1994.

Baudrillard, Jean. *Simulations.* Trans. Paul Foss, Paul Patton and Philip Beitchman. New York: Semiotext[e], 1983.

Bazin, André. *What is Cinema.* Vol. 1. Trans. Hugh Gray. Berkeley: University of California Press, 2005 [1967].

Beebe, Roger, and Jason Middleton. *Medium Cool: Music Videos from Soundies to Cellphones.* Durham, NC: Duke University Press, 2007.

Benjamin, Walter. *The Arcades Project.* Trans. Howard Eiland. Cambridge, MA: Harvard University Press, 1999.

———. *Illuminations: Essays and Reflections.* Ed. Hannah Arendt. Trans. Harry Zohn. New York: Schocken, 1968.

———. *Reflections: Essays, Aphorisms, Autobiographical Writings.* Ed. Peter Demetz. Trans. Edmund Jephcott. New York: Schocken, 1978.

———. *Selected Writings.* Vol.1. Cambridge, MA: Harvard University Press, 1996.

———. *Selected Writings.* Vol. 2, part 1, 1927–1930. Cambridge, MA: Belknap Press, 2005.

———. "The Work of Art in the Age of Mechanical Reproduction." In *Illuminations: Essays and Reflections,* ed. Hannah Arendt, trans. Harry Zohn, 217–51. New York: Schocken, 1968.

Bennett, Jane, "Commodity Fetishism and Commodity Enchantment." *Theory and Event* 5/1 (Winter 2001). Online. Available at http://muse.jhu.edu/journals/theory_and_event/v005/5.1bennett.html, retrieved October 31, 2010.

Benshoff, Harry, and Sean Griffin, eds. *Queer Cinema: The Film Reader.* London and New York: Routledge, 2004.

Birringer, Johannes. *Theatre, Theory, Postmodernism.* Bloomington: Indiana University Press, 1993.

Björnberg, Alf and John Richardson, "Music Videos." *The Grove Dictionary of American Music.* New York: Oxford University Press, forthcoming.

Bliss, Karen. "Rocky Start to Gorillaz Tour: Tight Quarters Prevent Crowd from Enjoying Music/Animation Project." *Rolling Stone,* February 25, 2002. Online. Available at http://www.rollingstone.com/, retrieved January 24, 2004.

Bloom, Harold. *The Anxiety of Influence: A Theory of Poetry.* London: Oxford University Press, 1973.

Bolter, Jay David, and Richard Grusin. "Remediation." *Configurations* 3 (1996): 311–58.

———. *Remediation: Understanding New Media.* Cambridge, MA: MIT Press, 1999.

Bordwell, David. "Intensified Continuity: Visual Style in Contemporary American Film." *Film Quarterly* 55/3 (2002): 16–28.

————. "In Critical Condition." *David Bordwell's Website on Cinema.* May 14, 2008. Online. Available at http://www.davidbordwell.net/blog/?p=2315, retrieved October 19, 2010.

Bourdieu, Pierre. *Distinction: A Social Critique of the Judgement of Taste.* Trans. Richard Nice. Cambridge, MA: Harvard University Press, 1984.

Brackett, David. "Elvis Costello: The Empire of the E Chord, and a Magic Moment or Two." *Popular Music* 24/3 (2005): 357–67.

————. *Interpreting Popular Music.* Cambridge: Cambridge University Press, 1995.

Breton, André. *Manifestoes of Surrealism.* Trans. Richard Seaver and Helen Lane. Michigan: University of Michigan Press, 1972.

————. *Nadja.* Trans. Richard Howard. London: Penguin, 1999 [1928].

Brett, Philip, Elizabeth Wood, and Gary Thomas, eds. *Queering the Pitch: The New Gay and Lesbian Musicology.* New York: Routledge, 1994.

Brown, Allan, *Nileism: The Strange Course of the Blue Nile.* Polygon: Edinburgh, 2010.

Brown, Julie. "Ally McBeal's Postmodern Soundtrack." *Journal of the Royal Musical Association* 126/2 (2001): 275–303.

Brown, Royal. *Overtones and Undertones: Reading Film Music.* Berkeley: University California Press, 1994.

Buhler, James. "Analytical and Interpretive Approaches to Film Music (II): Analysing Interaction of Music and Film." In *Film Music: Critical Approaches,* ed. Kevin Donnelly, 39–61. Edinburgh: Edinburgh University Press, 2001.

Buhler, James, Caryl Flinn, and David Neumeyer, eds. *Music and Cinema.* Hanover, NH: Wesleyan University Press, 2000.

Bull, Michael. *Sounding out the City: Personal Stereos and the Management of Everyday Life.* Oxford: Berg, 2000.

Bürger, Peter. *Theory of the Avant-Garde.* Trans. Michael Shaw. Minneapolis: University of Minnesota Press, 1984.

Burke, Edmund, *A Philosophical Inquiry into the Origin of our Ideas of the Sublime and the Beautiful.* London: Routledge and Kegan Paul, 1958.

Burns, Gary. "A Typology of 'Hooks' in Popular Records." *Popular Music* 6/1 (January 1987): 1–20.

Burns, Lori. *Disruptive Divas: Feminism, Identity and Popular Music.* New York: Routledge, 2002.

Butler, Judith. *Gender Trouble.* London and New York: Routledge 1990.

Case, Sue Ellen. "Toward a Butch-Femme Aesthetic." In *Camp: Queer Aesthetics and the Performing Subject. A Reader,* ed. Fabio Cleto, 185–99. Edinburgh: Edinburgh University Press, 1999.

Castells, Manuel. *The Rise of the Network Society: The Information Age: Economy, Society and Culture.* Vol. 1. Oxford: Blackwell, 1996.

Chanan, Michael. *Repeated Takes: A Short History of Recording and its Effects on Music.* London: Verso, 1995.

Chapple, Freda, and Chiel Kattenbelt, eds. *Intermediality in Theatre and Performance.* Amsterdam: Rodopi, 2007.

Chauncey, George. *Gender, Urban Culture, and the Making of the Gay Male World 1890–1940.* New York: Basic Books, 1994.

Chion, Michel. *Audio-Vision: Sound on Screen.* Trans. Claudia Gorbman. New York: Columbia University Press, 1994.

————. *Film, A Sound Art.* Trans. Claudia Gorbman. New York: Columbia University Press, 2003.

————. *The Voice in Cinema.* Trans. Claudia Gorbman. New York: Columbia University Press, 1999.

Citron, Marcia. *Gender and the Musical Canon.* Cambridge: Cambridge University Press, 1993.

Clayton, Martin, Trevor Herbert, and Richard Middleton, eds. *The Cultural Study of Music: A Critical Introduction*. New York and London: Routledge, 2003.

Cleto, Fabio, ed. *Camp: Queer Aesthetics and the Performing Subject. A Reader*. Edinburgh: Edinburgh University Press, 1999.

Clough, Patricia Ticineto with Jean Halley. *The Affective Turn: Theorizing the Social*. Durham, NC: Duke University Press, 2007.

Cocteau, Jean. *Beauty and the Beast: Diary of a Film*. Trans. Ronald Duncan. New York: Dover, 1972.

Cohan, Steven, ed. *Hollywood Musicals: The Film Reader*. London: Routledge, 2002.

————. *Incongruous Entertainment: Camp, Cultural Value, and the MGM Musical*. Durham, NC: Duke University Press, 2005.

Collins, Jim, ed. *High-Pop: Making Culture into Popular Entertainment*. Malden, MA and Oxford: Blackwell, 2002.

Collins, Karen. "An Introduction to the Participatory and Non-Linear Aspects of Video Games Audio." In *Essays on Sound and Vision*, eds. John Richardson and Stan Hawkins, 263–98. Helsinki: Helsinki University Press/Yliopistopaino, 2007.

Cook, Nicholas. "Analysing Performance and Performing Analysis." In *Rethinking Music*, eds. Nicholas Cook and Mark Everist, 239–61. Oxford and New York: Oxford University Press, 1999.

————. "Music as Performance." In *The Cultural Study of Music: A Critical Introduction*, eds. Martin Clayton, Trevor Herbert and Richard Middleton, 304–214. New York and London: Routledge, 2003.

Cook, Nicholas, and Mark Everist, eds. *Rethinking Music*. Oxford and New York: Oxford University Press, 1999.

Csikszentmihaly, Mihaly. *Flow*. London: Rider, 2002.

Cumming, Naomi. "The Horrors of Identification: Reich's Different Trains." *Perspectives of New Music* 35/1 (1997): 129–52.

————. *The Sonic Self: Musical Subjectivity and Signification*. Bloomington: Indiana University Press, 2000.

Cusick, Suzanne. "Musicology, Torture, Repair." In *Radical Musicology* 3 (2008). Online. Available at http://www.radical-musicology.org.uk/2008/Cusick.htm#_edn6, retrieved December 5, 2010.

————. "On a Lesbian Relationship with Music: Serious Effort Not to Think Straight." In *Queering the Pitch: The New Gay and Lesbian Musicology*, eds. Philip Brett, Elizabeth Wood and Gary Thomas, 67–83. New York: Routledge, 1994.

Damascio, Antonio. *The Feeling of What Happens: Body, Emotion and the Making of Consciousness*. London: Vintage, 1999.

Davison, Annette. "Demystified, Remystified, and Seduced by Sirens." In *Essays on Sound and Vision*, eds. John Richardson and Stan Hawkins, 119–54. Helsinki: Helsinki University Press/Yliopistopaino, 2007.

————. *Hollywood Theory, Non-Hollywood Practice: Cinema Soundtracks in the 1980s and 1990s*. Aldershot: Ashgate, 2004.

De Beauvoir, Simone. *The Ethics of Ambiguity*. New York: Citadel Press, 1994 [1948].

Debord, Guy. *Society of the Spectacle*. London: Rebel Press, 2004.

Deleuze, Gilles. *Cinema 1: The Movement-Image*. Trans. Hugh Tomlinson and Barbara Habberjam. London: Continuum, 1986.

————. *Cinema 2: The Time-Image*. Trans. Hugh Tomlinson and Robert Galeta. London: Continuum, 1989.

————. *Repetition & Difference*. Trans. Paul Patton. London: The Athlone Press, 1994 [1968].

Deleuze, Gilles, and Félix Gauttari. *Anti-Oedipus: Capitalism and Schizophrenia*. Trans. Robert Hurley, Mark Seem, and Helen Lane. Minneapolis: University of Minnesota Press, 1983.

————. *A Thousand Plateaus: Capitalism and Schizophrenia*. Trans. Brian Massumi. London: Continuum, 1987.

DeNora, Tia. *Music in Everyday Life*. Cambridge: Cambridge University Press, 2000.

Derrida, Jacques. *Margins of Philosophy*. Trans. Alan Bass. Chicago: University of Chicago Press, 1982.

———. *Specters of Marx*. Trans. Bernd Magnus. New York and London: Routledge, 1994.

———. *Writing and Difference*. Trans. Alan Bass. Chicago: University of Chicago Press, 1978.

Dickie, George. *Art and the Aesthetic: An Institutional Analysis*. Ithaca, NY: Cornell University Press, 1974.

Dickinson, Kay. "'Believe'? Vocoders, Digitalised Female Identity and Camp." *Popular Music* 20/3 (2001): 333–47.

———, ed. *Movie Music: The Film Reader*. London: Routledge, 2003.

———. "Music Video and Synaesthetic Possibility." In *Medium Cool: Music Videos from Soundies to Cellphones*, eds. Roger Beebe and Jason Middleton, 13–29. Durham, NC: Duke University Press, 2007.

———. *Off Key: When Film and Music Won't Work Together*. Oxford: Oxford University Press, 2008.

Doane, Mary Anne. "The Voice in Cinema: The Articulation of Body and Space." In *Film Sound: Theory and Practice*, eds. Elisabeth Weis and John Belton, 162–76. New York: Columbia University Press, 1985.

Docherty, Thomas, ed. *Postmodernism: A Reader*. New York: Columbia University Press, 1993.

Donnelly, Kevin, ed. *Film Music: Critical Approaches*. New York: Continuum, 2001.

———. *The Spectre of Sound: Music in Film and Television*. London: BFI, 2005.

Doyle, Peter. *Echo and Reverb: Fabricating Space in Popular Music Recording 1900–1960*. Middleton, CT: Wesleyan University Press, 2005.

Duerden, Nick. "Gorillaz in Our Midst." *The Observer*, March 11, 2001. Online. Available at http://www.guardian.co.uk/arts/, retrieved January 24, 2004.

Dunn, Michael. *Metapop: Self-Referentiality in Contemporary American Popular Culture*. Jackson and London: University Press of Mississippi, 1992.

Dyer, Richard. "Entertainment and Utopia." In *Genre: The Musical*, ed. Rick Altman, 175–89. New York: Routledge, 1981.

———. *Heavenly Bodies*. Basingstoke: Macmillan, 1986.

———. "Side by Side: Nina Rota, Music, and Film." In *Beyond the Soundtrack: Representing Music in Cinema*, eds. Daniel Goldmark, Lawrence Kramer and Richard Leppert, 246–59. Berkeley: University of California Press, 2007.

Dyson, Frances. *Sounding New Media: Immersion and Embodiment in the Arts and Culture*. Berkeley: California University Press, 2009.

Eagleton, Terry. *The Ideology of the Aesthetic*. Oxford: Blackwell, 1990.

Eisenberg, Evan. *The Recording Angel: Music, Records and Culture from Aristotle to Zappa*. New Haven: Yale University Press, 2005.

Eisenstein, Sergei. *The Film Sense*. London: Faber and Faber, 1943.

Eisenstein, S.M., V.I. Pudovkin, and G.V. Aexandrov. "A Statement." In *Film Sound: Theory and Practice*, eds. Elisabeth Weis and John Belton, 83–85. New York: Columbia University Press, 1985.

Elsaesser, Thomas, and Warren Buckland. *Studying Contemporary American Film: A Guide to Movie Analysis*. London: Arnold, 2002.

Elsaesser, Thomas, and Malte Hagener. *Film Theory: an Introduction through the Senses*. New York and London: Routledge, 2000.

Eno, Brian. *A Year with Swollen Appendices: Brian Eno's Diary*. London: Faber and Faber, 1996.

Evans, Tristian. "Towards a Theory of Multimedia Integration in Post-Minimal Music." PhD dissertation. University of Bangor, 2010.

Everett, Wendy. "Screen as Threshold: The Disorientating Topographies of Surrealist Film." *Screen* 39/2 (Summer 1998): 141–52.

Ferrara, Lawrence. "Phenomenological Analysis as a Tool for Musical Analysis." *Musical Quarterly* 70 (1984): 355–73.

Ferrara, Lawrence and Elizabeth Behnke. "Music." In *Encyclopedia of Phenomenology*, eds, Elizabeth Behnke, et al., 467–73. Dordrecht and Boston: Kluwer Academic Publishers, 1997.

Feuer, Jane. *The Hollywood Musical.* London: Macmillan Press, 1982.

———. "The Self-Reflective Musical and the Myth of Entertainment." In *Hollywood Musicals: The Film Reader,* ed. Steven Cohan, 229–35. London and New York: Routledge, 2002.

Fink, Robert. *Repeating Ourselves: American Minimal Music as Cultural Practice.* Berkeley: University of California Press, 2005.

Finnegan, Ruth. "Music, Experience and the Anthropology of Emotion." *The Cultural Study of Music: A Critical Introduction,* eds. Clayton Martin, Trevor Herbert and Richard Middleton, 181–92. New York and London: Routledge, 2003.

Foster, Hal. *Compulsive Beauty.* Cambridge, MA: MIT Press, 1993.

———. "What's Neo about the Neo-Avant-Garde?" *October* 70 (Fall 1994): 5–32.

Fotiade, Ramona. "The Slit Eye, The Scorpion and The Sign Of The Cross: Surrealist Film Theory And Practice Revisited." *Screen* 39/2 (Summer 1998): 394–407.

———. "The Untamed Eye: Surrealism and Film Theory." *Screen* 36/4 (Winter 1995): 394–407.

Flinn, Caryl. "The Deaths of Camp." In *Camp: Queer Aesthetics and the Performing Subject. A Reader,* ed. Fabio Cleto, 433–57. Edinburgh: Edinburgh University Press, 1999.

———. "The Mutating Musical." In *The Oxford Handbook of New Audiovisual Aesthetics*, eds. Claudia Gorbman, John Richardson and Carol Vernallis. New York: Oxford University Press, 2012. Forthcoming.

———. *New German Cinema: Music, History, and the Matter of Style.* Berkeley: University of California Press, 2004.

———. *Strains of Utopia: Gender, Nostalgia, and Hollywood Film Music.* Princeton, NJ: Princeton University Press, 1992.

Freud, Sigmund. *The Interpretation of Dreams.* Trans. A. A. Brill. Wordsworth Editions: Ware, Hertfordshire, 1997.

Frith, Simon. "'The Magic That Can Set You Free': The Ideology of Folk and the Myth of the Rock Community." In *Popular Music. Vol. 1. Folk or Popular? Distinctions, Influences, Continuities,* eds. Richard Middleton and David Horn, 159–68. Cambridge: Cambridge University Press, 1981.

———. *Performing Rites: Evaluating Popular Music.* Oxford: Oxford University Press, 1996.

Frith, Simon, and Andrew Goodwin. *On Record: Rock Pop and the Written Word.* New York: Pantheon, 1990.

Frith, Simon, Andrew Goodwin, and Lawrence Grossberg, eds. *Sound and Vision: The Music Video Reader.* London: Routledge, 1993.

Frith, Simon, and Howard Horne. *Art into Pop.* London: Routledge, 1987.

Garcia, Luis-Manuel. "On and On: Repetition as Process and Pleasure in Electronic Dance Music." *Music Theory Online* 11/4 (2005): sections 1.1–7.4. Online. Available at http://www.societymusictheory.org/mto/issues/mto.05.11.4/mto.05.11.4.garcia.html, retrieved December 17, 2010.

Garrat, Sheryl. "Hey, Hey, We're the Gorillaz. The Observer Profile: Damon Albarn." *The Observer,* September 7, 2001. Online. Available at http://www.guardian.co.uk/arts/, retrieved January 24, 2004.

Geertz, Clifford. *The Interpretation of Cultures: Selected Essays by Clifford Geertz.* New York: Basic Books, 1973.

Gendron, Bernard. *Between Montmartre and the Mudd Club: Popular Music and the Avant-Garde.* Chicago: University of Chicago Press, 2002.

Giannachi, Gabriella. *Virtual Theatres: An Introduction.* London and New York: Routledge, 2004.

Gilbert, Jeremy and Ewan Pearson. *Discographies: Dance Music, Culture and the Politics of Sound.* London and New York: Routledge, 1999.

Gilroy, Paul. *After Empire: Melancholia or Convivial Culture?* Abingdon, Oxfordshire: Routledge, 2004.

——. *There Ain't No Black in the Union Jack.* Abingdon, Oxfordshire: Routledge, 2002 [1987]).

Glendinning, Simon. *In the Name of Phenomenology.* Abingdon, Oxon: Routledge, 2007.

Goehr, Lydia. *The Imaginary Museum of Musical Works: An Essay in the Philosophy of Music.* Oxford: Oxford University Press, 1994.

Goodwin, Andrew. *Dancing in the Distraction Factory: Music Television and Popular Culture.* Minneapolis: University of Minnesota Press, 1992.

——. "Sample and Hold: Pop Music in the Digital Age of Reproduction." In *On Record: Rock Pop and the Written Word,* eds. Simon Frith and Andrew Goodwin, 258–73. New York: Pantheon, 1990.

Goldberg, Rose Lee. *Performance Art: From Futurism to the Present.* London: Thames and Hudson, 1988.

Goldmark, Daniel, Lawrence Kramer and Richard Leppert, eds. *Beyond the Soundtrack: Representing Music in Cinema.* Berkeley: University of California Press, 2007.

Gorbman, Claudia. "Auteur Music." In *Beyond the Soundtrack: Representing Music in Cinema,* eds. Daniel Goldmark, Lawrence Kramer and Richard Leppert, 149–62. Berkeley: University of California Press, 2007.

——. "Ears Wide Open: Kubrick's Music." In *Changing Tunes: The Use of Pre-Existing Music in Film,* eds. Phil Powrie and Robynn Stilwell, 3–18. Aldershot: Ashgate, 2006.

——. *Unheard Melodies: Narrative Film Music.* Bloomington: Indiana University Press, 1987.

Gorillaz. *Rise of the Ogre: Gorillaz.* London: Penguin, 2006.

Gracyk, Theodore. *Rhythm and Noise: An Aesthetics of Rock.* London: I.B. Tauris, 1996.

Graham, Bruce. "Bernard Hermann: Film Music and Narrative." PhD dissertation. University of Michigan, 1985.

Greeves, David. "Ben Hillier: Recording Blur, Tom McRae and Elbow." *Sound on Sound,* July 2003. Online. Available at http://www.soundonsound.com/sos/Jul03/articles/benhillier.asp, retrieved May 1, 2009.

Grossberg, Lawrence. "The Media Economy of Rock Culture: Cinema, Post-Modernity and Authenticity." In *Sound and Vision: The Music Video Reader,* ed. Simon Frith, Andrew Goodwin and Lawrence Grossberg, 185–209. London: Routledge, 1993.

Greil, Marcus. *Lipstick Traces: A Secret History of the Twentieth Century.* London: Faber and Faber, 2001 [1989].

Gunning, Tom. "The Cinema of Attraction: Early Film, Its Spectator, and the Avant-Garde." In *Film and Theory: An Anthology,* eds. Robert Stam and Toby Miller, 229–35. London: Blackwell, 2000.

Hall, Stuart. "Encoding/Decoding." In *Culture, Media, Language: Working Papers in Cultural Studies, 1972–79.* Centre for Contemporary Cultural Studies, 128–38. London: Hutchinson, 1980 [1973].

Hamilton, Jaimey. "The Way We Loop 'Now': Eddying in the Flows of Media." *Invisible Culture: An Electronic Journal for Visual Culture* 8 (2004): 1–24.

Hammond, Paul ed. and trans. *The Shadow & Its Shadow: Surrealist Writings on the Cinema.* San Francisco: City Lights Books, 2000.

Harper, Graeme and Rob Stone, eds. *The Unsilvered Screen: Surrealism on Film.* London: Wallflower Press, 2007.

Harper, Stephen. "Zombies, Malls, and the Consumerism Debate: George Romero's *Dawn of the Dead.*" *The Journal of American Popular Culture (1900-present)* 1/2 (Fall 2002). Online. Available at http://www.americanpopularculture.com/journal/articles/fall_2002/harper.htm, retrieved December 11, 2010.

Harris, John. *The Dark Side of the Moon: The Making of the Pink Floyd Masterpiece.* Fourth Estate: London, 2005.

Hasted, Nick, "An Audience with Ray Davies: Interview." *Uncut*, May 2006, 53.

Hawkins, Stan. "Aphex Twin: Monstrous Hermaphrodites, Madness and the Strain of Independent Dance Music." In *Essays on Sound and Vision*, eds. John Richardson and Stan Hawkins, 27–53. Helsinki: Helsinki University Press/Yliopistopaino, 2007.

———. *The British Pop Dandy: Male Identity, Music and Culture*. Aldershot: Ashgate, 2009.

———. "Feel the Beat Come Down: House Music as Rhetoric." In *Analyzing Popular Music*, ed. Allan Moore, 80–102. Cambridge: Cambridge University Press, 2003.

———. "Joy in Repetition: Structures, Idiolects, and Concepts of Repetition in Club Music." *Studia Musicologica Norvegica* 27 (2001): 553–78.

———. "Musical Excess and Postmodern Identity in Björk's 'It's Oh So Quiet.'" *Musiikin Suunta* 2 (1999): 43–54.

———. "Musicological Quagmires in Popular Music: Seeds of Detailed Conflict." *Popular Musicology Online* 1 (2001). Online. Available at http://www.popular-musicology-online .com/, retrieved October 26, 2010.

———. "On Male Queering in Mainstream Pop." In *Queering the Popular Pitch*, ed. Sheila Whiteley and Jennifer Rycenga, 279–94. New York and London: Routledge, 2006.

———. "Perspectives in Popular Musicology: Music, Lennox and Meaning in 1990s Pop." *Popular Music* 15/1 (1996): 17–36.

———. *Settling the Pop Score: Pop Texts and Identity Politics*. Aldershot: Ashgate, 2002.

Hayles, N. Katherine. *How We Became Posthuman: Virtual Bodies in Cybernetics, Literature, and Informatics*. Chicago: University of Chicago Press, 1999.

Heinonen, Yrjö, Tuomas Eerola, Jouni Koskimäki, Terhi Nurmesjärvi, and John Richardson, eds. *Beatlestudies 1: Songwriting, Recording, and Style Change*. Jyväskylä: University Press of Jyväskylä, 1998.

Heinonen, Yrjö, Markus Heuger, Sheila Whiteley, Terhi Nurmesjärvi, and Jouni Koskimäki, eds. *Beatlestudies 3*. Department of Music Research Reports: Jyväskylä, Finland, 2001.

Herzog, Amy. *Dreams of Difference, Songs of the Same*. Minneapolis: University of Minnesota Press, 2010.

Highmore, Ben. *Everyday Life and Cultural Theory*. London: Routledge, 2002.

Holbrook, Morris. "The Ambi-Diegesis of 'My Funny Valentine.'" In *Pop Fiction: The Song in Cinema*, eds. Steve Lannin and Matthew Caley, 48–49. Bristol: Intellect, 2005.

Holmes, Thom. *Electronic and Experimental Music: Technology, Music and Culture*. 3rd edition. New York and Abingdon: Routledge, 2008.

Hopkins, David. *Dada and Surrealism: A Very Short Introduction*. Oxford: Oxford University Press, 2004.

Horkheimer, Max. *Critical Theory: Selected Essays*. New York: Continuum, 1972.

Horkheimer, Max, and Theodor Adorno. *Dialectic of Enlightenment*. London: Allen Lane, 1972 [1944].

Horner, Bruce, and Thomas Swiss. *Key Terms in Popular Music and Culture*. Oxford: Blackwell, 1999.

Hughes, Timothy S. "Groove and Flow: Six Analytical Essays on the Music of Stevie Wonder." PhD dissertation. University of Washington Graduate School, 2003.

Hutcheon, Linda. *The Politics of Postmodernism*. London and New York: Routledge, 1989.

Huyssen, Andreas. *After the Great Divide: Modernism, Mass Culture, Postmodernism*. Bloomington: Indiana University Press, 1986.

Inglis, Sam, "Tom Girling and Jason Cox: Recording Gorillaz's Clint Eastwood." *Sound on Sound* (September 2001). Online. Available at http://www.sospubs.co.uk/, retrieved May 20, 2002.

Irigaray, Luce. *Levinas*. Trans. Margaret Whitford. London: Athlone Press, 1991.

———. *This Sex Which Is Not One*. Trans. Catherine Porter. Ithaca and New York: Cornell University Press, 1985.

Jameson, Fredric. *Postmodernism or, The Cultural Logic of Late Capitalism*. Durham, NC: Duke University Press, 1991.

Jarman-Ivens, Freya. "Notes on Musical Camp." In *The Ashgate Research Companion to Popular Musicology*, 189–203. Farnham: Ashgate, 2009.

Jencks, Charles. *What Is Post-Modernism?* New York: St. Martin's, 1986.

Joe, Jeongwon. "The Cinematic Body in the Operatic Theater: Philip Glass's *La Belle et la Bête*." In *Between Opera and Cinema*, eds. Jeongwon Joe and Rose Theresa, 59–73. New York and London: Routledge, 2002.

Joe, Jeongwon, and Rose Theresa. *Between Opera and Cinema*. New York and London: Routledge, 2002.

Jones, Steve. "A Sense of Space: Virtual Reality, Authenticity, and the Aural." *Critical Studies in Mass Communication* 10 (1993): 238–52.

Kalinak, Kathryn. *Settling the Score: Music and the Classical Hollywood Film*. Madison, WI: The University of Wisconsin Press, 1992.

Kallioniemi, Kari. "'Put the Needle on and Think of England'—Notions of Englishness in the Post-War Debate on British Pop Music." PhD dissertation: University of Turku, Finland, 1998.

Kassabian, Anahid. *Hearing Film: Tracking Identifications in Contemporary Hollywood Film Music*. New York and London: Routledge, 2001.

———. "The Sound of a New Film Form." In *Popular Music and Film*, ed. Ian Inglis, 91–101. London: Wallflower, 2003.

———. "Ubiquitous Listening and Networked Subjectivity." *Echo* 3/2 (Fall 2001). Online. Available at www.echo.ucla.edu, retrieved July 26, 2010.

Katz, Mark. *Capturing Sound: How Technology Has Changed Music*. Berkeley: University of California Press, 2004.

Keazor, Henry, and Thorsten Wübbena, eds. *Rewind, Play, Fast Forward: The Past, Present and Future of the Music Video*. Transcript. Verlag, Bielefeld: 2010.

Kelly, Jem. "Pop Music, Multimedia and Live Performance." In *Music, Sound and Multimedia: From the Live to the Virtual*, ed. Jamie Sexton, 105–20. Edinburgh: Edinburgh University Press, 2007.

Keil, Charles, and Steven Feld. *Music Grooves*. Chicago: The University of Chicago Press, 1994.

Keightley, Keir. "Reconsidering Rock." In *The Cambridge Companion to Pop and Rock*, eds. Simon Frith, Will Straw and John Street, 109–42. Cambridge: Cambridge University Press, 2001.

Kerman, Joseph. *Musicology*. London: Fontana, 1985.

Klein, Melanie. *The Selected Melanie Klein*. Ed. Juliet Mitchell. New York: The Free Press, 1986.

Knapp, Raymond. *The American Musical, and the Performance of Personal Identity*. Princeton, NJ: Princeton University Press, 2006.

———. "Brahms and the Anxiety of Allusion." *Journal of Musicological Research* 18 (1998): 1–30.

Knights, Vanessa. "Queer Pleasures: The Bolero, Camp and Almodóvar." In *Changing Tunes: The Use of Pre-Existing Music in Film*, eds. Phil Powrie and Robynn Stilwell, 91–104. Aldershot: Ashgate, 2006.

Kracauer, Siegried. *Theory of Film: The Redemption of Physical Reality*. Oxford: Oxford University Press, 1960.

Kramer, Lawrence. *Music as Cultural Practice, 1800–1900*. Berkeley: University of California Press, 1990.

———. *Musical Meaning: Toward a Critical History*. Berkeley: University of California Press, 2002.

———. "Music, Hermeneutics, and History." In *The Cultural Study of Music: A Critical Introduction*, eds. Martin Clayton, Trevor Herbert and Richard Middleton, 124–35. New York and London: Routledge, 2003.

Krauss, Rosalind. *The Originality of the Avant-Garde and Other Modernist Myths*. Cambridge, MA: MIT Press, 1985.

Krims, Adam. *Rap Music and the Poetics of Identity*. Cambridge: Cambridge University Press, 2000.

—. *Music and Urban Geography.* New York and London: Routledge, 2007.

Kyrou, Ado. *Le Surréalism au cinema.* 3rd ed. Paris: Le Terrain Vague, 1985.

Laing, Dave. "A Voice Without a Face: Popular Music and the Phonograph in the 1890s." *Popular Music* 10/1 (1991): 1–9.

Laing, Heather. *The Gendered Score: Music in 1940s Melodrama and the Woman's Film.* Aldershot: Ashgate Publishing Limited, 2007.

Lannin, Steve, and Matthew Caley. *Pop Fiction: The Song in Cinema.* Bristol: Intellect, 2005.

Lanza, Joseph. *Elevator Music: A Surreal History of Muzak, Easy-Listening, and Other Moodsong.* New York: Picador, 1995.

Leppert, Richard. *The Sight of Sound: Music, Representation, and the History of the Body.* Berkeley: University of California Press, 1993.

Levinas, Emmanuel. *Totality and Infinity.* Dordrecht: Kluwer Academic Publishers, 1991.

Lipsitz, George. "Cruising Around the Historical Bloc: Postmodernism and Popular Music in Los Angeles." *Cultural Critique* 5 (1986): 157–77.

Lister, Martin, Jon Dovey, Seth Giddings, Iain Grant, Kieran Kelly. *New Media: A Critical Introduction.* London and New York: Routledge, 2003.

Lowenstein, Adam. "The Surrealism of the Photographic Image: Bazin, Barthes, and the Digital Sweet Hereafter." *Cinema Journal* 46/3 (Spring 2007): 54–82.

Lyotard, Jean-François. *The Postmodern Condition: A Report on Knowledge.* Trans. Geoff Bennington and Brian Massumi. Minneapolis: University of Minnesota Press, 1984.

—. "The Sublime and the Avant-Garde." In *Postmodernism: A Reader,* ed. Thomas Docherty, 244–56. New York: Columbia University Press, 1993.

Lysloff, René, and Leslie Gay, eds. *Music and Technoculture.* Middletown, CT: Wesleyan University Press, 2003.

Magdanz, Teresa. "The Waltz: Technology's Muse." *Journal of Popular Music Studies* 18/3 (December 2006): 251–81.

Manovich, Lev. *The Language of New Media.* Cambridge: MIT Press, 2001.

Marks, Lawrence. *The Unity of the Senses: Interrelations among the Modalities.* New York, Academic Press, 1988.

Marks, Laura. *The Skin of Film: Intercultural Cinema, Embodiment and the Senses.* Durham, NC: Duke University Press, 2000.

—. "Video Haptics and Erotics." *Screen* 39/4 (Winter 1998): 331–48.

Martin, Christopher, "Traditional Criticism of Popular Music and the Making of a Lip-Synching Scandal." *Popular Music and Society* 17/4 (1993): 63–81.

Marx, Leo. *The Machine in the Garden: Technology and the Pastoral Ideal in America.* Oxford: Oxford University Press, 1964.

Massumi. Brian. *Parables for the Virtual: Movement, Affect, Sensation.* Durham, NC: Duke University Press, 2002.

Matthews, J. H. *Surrealism and Film.* Ann Arbor: University of Michigan Press, 1971.

McCaffery, Larry. *After Yesterday's Crash: The Avant-Pop Anthology.* New York: Penguin, 1997.

McClary, Susan. *Conventional Wisdom: The Content of Musical Form.* Berkeley: University of California Press, 2000.

—. "Minima Romantica." In *Beyond the Soundtrack: Representing Music in Cinema,* eds. Daniel Goldmark, Lawrence Kramer and Richard Leppert, 48–65. Berkeley: University of California Press, 2007.

McClary, Susan, and Robert Walser, "Start Making Sense! Musicology Wrestles with Rock." In *On Record: Rock, Pop, and the Written Word,* eds. Simon Frith and Andrew Goodwin, 267–92. London and New York: Routledge, 1990.

McLuhan, Marshall. *Understanding Media.* London and New York: Routledge, 1964.

Merleau-Ponty, Maurice. *Phenomenology of Perception.* London and New York: Routledge, 2002.

Mera, Miguel. "Invention/Re-invention." *Music, Sound, and the Moving Image* 3/1 (Spring 2009): 1–20.

Middleton, Richard, ed. *Reading Pop: Approaches to Textual Analysis in Popular Music*. Oxford: Oxford University Press, 2000.

———. *Studying Popular Music*. Milton Keynes: Open University Press, 1990.

Miller, D.A. *Place for Us: Essays on the Broadway Musical*. Cambridge, MA: Harvard University Press, 1998.

Miller, Edward D. "The Nonsensical Truth of the Falsetto Voice: Listening to Sigur Rós." *Popular Musicology Online* 2 (2003). Online. Available at http://www.popular-musicology-online.com/issues/02/miller.html, retrieved August 28, 2010.

Monelle, Raymond. *The Sense of Music: Semiotic Essays*. Princeton, NJ: Princeton University Press, 2000.

Moore, Alan. *Rock: The Primary Text*. Buckingham: Open University Press, 1993.

Moore, Catherine. "Work and Recordings: The Impact of Commercialisation and Digitalisation." In *The Musical Work: Reality or Invention*, ed. Michael Talbot, 88–109. Liverpool: Liverpool University Press, 2000.

Mosco, Vincent. *The Digital Sublime: Myth, Power, and Cyberspace*. Cambridge, MA: MIT Press, 2004.

Moylan, William. *The Art of Recording: Understanding and Crafting the Mix*. Woburn, MA: Focal Press, 2002.

Muggs, Joe. "The Family That Plays Together." *The Word* 63 (May 2008): 50–51.

Mulvey, Laura. *Death 24x a Second: Stillness and the Moving Image*. London: Reaktion Books, 2006.

———. "Visual Pleasure and Narrative Cinema." *Screen* 16/3 (1975): 6–18.

Mundy, John. *Popular Music on Screen: From Hollywood Musical to Music Video*. Manchester: Manchester University Press, 1999.

Naylor, Tony. "Gorillaz: Manchester Academy." *NME*, n.d. Online. Available at http://www.nme.com/, retrieved January 24, 2004.

Ngai, Sianne. *Ugly Feelings*. Cambridge, MA: Harvard University Press, 2005.

Nye, David. *American Technological Sublime*. Cambridge, MA: MIT Press, 1994.

Nyman, Michael. *Experimental Music: Cage and Beyond*. 2nd ed. Cambridge: Cambridge University Press, 1974.

Odell, Michael. "The Oasis Interview." *Q magazine*, May 2002, 92–100.

Patterson, Sylvia. "I'm a Robbing Gypsy Bastard." *The Word* 37 (March 2006): 74–78.

———. "What Happened When Ray Davies Wrote a Song for His Daughter's Band?" *The Word* 39 (May 2006): 32–34.

Pekkilä, Erkki. "Tango, twist ja Tšaikovski: Musiikki Aki Kaurismäen elokuvassa Tulitikkutehtaan tyttö." *Musiikki* 3 (2005): 45–65.

Peirce, Charles Sanders. *The Collected Papers of Charles Sanders Peirce*. Vol. 1. Ed. Charles Hartshorne and Paul Weiss. Cambridge, MA: Harvard University Press, 1931–1935.

———. *The Collected Papers, Vol. 1: Principles of Philosophy* (1931). Online. Available at http://www.textlog.de/charles_s_peirce.html, retrieved December 1, 2010.

Pfeil, Fred. "Postmodernism as a 'Structure of Feeling.'" In *Marxism and the Interpretation of Culture*, eds. Cary Nelson and Lawrence Grossberg, 381–403. Urbana: University of Illinois Press, 1988.

Phelan, Peggy. *Unmarked: The Politics of Performance*. London and New York: Routledge, 1993.

Plasketes, George. "Cop Rock Revisited: Unsung Series and Musical Hinge in Cross-Genre Evolution." *Journal of Popular Film and Television* 32/2 (2004): 64–73.

Potter, John. *Vocal Authority: Singing Style and Ideology*. Cambridge: Cambridge University Press, 1998.

Potter, Keith. *Four Musical Minimalists: La Monte Young, Terry Riley, Steve Reich, Philip Glass*. Cambridge: Cambridge University Press, 2000.

Potter, Russel A. *Spectacular Vernaculars: Hip-Hop and the Politics of Representation*. Albany, NY: SUNY Press, 1995.

Potter, Sally. *Yes, Screenplay and Notes by Sally Potter*. New York: Newmarket Press, 2005.

Powrie, Phil. "The Fabulous Destiny of the Accordion in French Cinema." In *Changing Tunes: The Use of Pre-Existing Music in Film*, eds. Phil Powrie and Robynn Stilwell, 137–51. Aldershot: Ashgate, 2006.

———. "Masculinity in the Shadow of the Slashed Eye: Surrealist Film Criticism at the Crossroads." *Screen* 39/2 (Summer 1998): 153–63.

Powrie, Phil, and Robynn Stilwell, eds. *Changing Tunes: The Use of Pre-Existing Music in Film*. Aldershot: Ashgate, 2006.

Pudovkin, V.I., "Asynchronism as a Principle of Sound Film." In *Film Sound: Theory and Practice*, eds. Elisabeth Weis and John Belton, 86–91. New York: Columbia University Press, 1985.

Ray, Robert B. *How a Film Theory Got Lost, and Other Mysteries of Cultural Studies*. Bloomington: Indiana University Press, 2001.

Reay, Pauline. *Music in Film: Soundtracks and Synergy*. London:Wallflower, 2004.

Rehm, Jean Pierre, Olivier Joyard, and Danièle Rivière, eds. *Tsai Ming-Liang*. Paris: Editions Dis Voir, 1999.

Reising, Russell, ed. *The Legacy of Pink Floyd's Dark Side of the Moon*. Aldershot: Ashgate, 2005.

Richardson, John. "'Black and White' Music: Dialogue, Dysphoric Coding and the Death Drive in the Music of Bernard Herrmann, The Beatles, Stevie Wonder and Coolio." In *Beatlestudies 1: Songwriting, Recording, and Style Change*, eds. Yrjö Heinonen, et al., 161–82. Jyväskylä: University Press of Jyväskylä, 1998.

———. "'The Digital Won't Let Me Go": Constructions of the Virtual and the Real in Gorillaz' 'Clint Eastwood.'" *Journal of Popular Music Studies* 17/1 (2005): 1–29.

———. "Double-Voiced Discourse and Bodily Pleasures in Contemporary Finnish Rock: The Case of Maija Vilkkumaa." In *Essays on Sound and Vision*, eds. John Richardson and Stan Hawkins, 401–41. Helsinki: Yliopistopaino/Helsinki University Press, 2007.

———. "Intertextuality and Pop Camp Identity Politics in Finland: The Crash's Music Video 'Still Alive.'" *Popular Musicology Online* 2 (2006). Online. Available at http://www .popular-musicology-online.com/issues/02/richardson-01.html, retrieved December 4, 2010.

———. "Laura and *Twin Peaks*: Postmodern Parody and the Musical Reconstruction of the Absent Femme Fatale." *The Cinema of David Lynch: American Dreams, Nightmare Visions*, eds. Annette Davison and Erica Sheen, 77–92. London: Wallflower Press, 2004.

———. "Plasticine Music: Surrealism in Peter Gabriel's 'Sledgehammer.'" In *Games Without Frontiers: Peter Gabriel From Genesis to Growing Up*, eds. Michael Drewett, Sarah Hill and Kimi Kärki, 195–210. Farnham and Burlington: Ashgate, 2010.

———. "Resisting the Sublime: Loose Synchronisation in *La Belle et la Bête* and *The Dark Side of Oz*." In *Musicological Identities: Essays in Honour of Susan McClary*, eds. Steven Baur, Raymond Knapp and Jacqueline Warwick, 135–48. Aldershot: Ashgate, 2008.

———. *Singing Archaeology: Philip Glass's* Akhnaten. Hanover, NH and London: Wesleyan University Press and University Press of New England, 1999.

———. "Televised Live Performance, Looping Technology and the 'Nu Folk': KT Tunstall on *Later . . . with Jools Holland*." In *The Ashgate Research Companion to Popular Musicology*, ed. Derek B. Scott, 85–101. Farnham and Burlington: Ashgate, 2009.

———. "Transforming Everyday Life: Analytical Perspectives on Experimental Film Soundtracks." In *Essays on Sound and Vision*, eds. John Richardson and Stan Hawkins, 88–116. Helsinki: Yliopistopaino/Helsinki University Press, 2007.

———. "Vieraannuttamisefektejä ja arkeologisia strategioita Suzanne Vegan lauluissa 'Tom's Diner' ja 'Luka.'" ("Alienation Effects and Archaeological Strategies in Suzanne Vega's Songs 'Tom's Diner' and 'Luka.'") *Musiikki* 4 (1996): 450–68.

Richardson, John, and Stan Hawkins, eds. *Essays on Sound and Vision*. Helsinki: Helsinki University Press/Yliopistopaino, 2007.

———. "Remodeling Britney Spears: Matters of Intoxication and Mediation." *Popular Music and Society* 30/5 (2007): 605–29.

Richardson, Michael. *Surrealism and Cinema*. Oxford: Berg, 2006.

Ricoeur, Paul. *Hermeneutics and the Human Sciences.* Trans. John B. Thompson. Cambridge: Cambridge University Press, 1981 [1972].

———. *The Rule of Metaphor.* Trans. Robert Czerny. London and New York: Routledge, 2003.

Rink, John, ed. *The Practice of Performance: Studies in Musical Interpretation.* Cambridge: Cambridge University Press, 1995.

Ritzer, George and Nathan Jurgenson. "Production, Consumption, Prosumption: The Nature of the Capitalism in the Age of the Digital 'Prosumer'." *Journal of Consumer Culture* 10/1 (1994): 13–36.

Robertson, Pamela. *Guilty Pleasures: Feminist Camp from Mae West to Madonna.* Durham, NC: Duke University Press, 1996.

Rolls, Chris. "KT Tunstall: Slightly More Esoteric." n.d. Online. Available at http://www.mp3.com/news/stories/10018.html, retrieved June 19, 2008.

Rombes, Nicholas, ed. *New Punk Cinema.* Edinburgh: Edinburgh University Press, 2005.

Rose, Tricia. *Black Noise: Rap Music and Black Culture in Contemporary America.* Hanover, NH: Wesleyan University Press, 1994.

Ross, Andrew, "Uses of Camp." In *Camp: Queer Aesthetics and the Performing Subject. A Reader,* ed. Fabio Cleto, 308–329. Edinburgh: Edinburgh University Press, 1999.

Rothstein, Edward. "Not Quite an Opera Transforms a Film." *New York Times,* December 9, 1994, C5.

Rubin, Martin. "Busby Berkeley and the Backstage Musical." In *Hollywood Musical: The Film Reader,* ed. Steven Cohen, 53–61. London: Routledge, 2002.

Rushdie, Salman. *The Wizard of Oz.* BFI Film Classics. London: BFI, 1992.

Savage, Jon. *England's Dreaming: Anarchy, Sex Pistols, Punk Rock, and Beyond.* London: Faber and Faber, 2001 [1991].

Schechner, Richard. *Performance Theory.* New York and London: Routledge, 1988.

Schwarz, K. Robert. "Steve Reich: Music as a Gradual Process, Part 1." *Perspectives of New Music* 19 (1981): 374–92.

Sconce, Jeffrey. "Irony, Nihilism and the New American 'Smart' Film." *Screen* 43/4 (2002): 349–69.

Scott, Derek, ed. *The Ashgate Research Companion to Popular Musicology.* Farnham: Ashgate, 2009.

———. "(What's the Copy) The Beatles and Oasis." In *Beatlestudies* 3, eds. Yrjö Heinonen, et al., 201–11. Department of Music Research Reports: Jyväskylä, Finland, 2001.

Sedgwick, Eve Kosofsky. *Touching Feeling: Affect, Pedagogy, Performativity.* Durham, NC: Duke University Press, 2003.

Sedgwick, Eve Kosofsky, and Adam Frank, eds. *Shame and its Sisters: A Silvan Tomkins Reader.* Durham, NC: Duke University Press, 1995.

Sedgwick, Eve Kosofsky, and Andrew Parker, eds. *Performativity and Performance.* New York: Routledge, 1995.

Sexton, Jamie, ed. *Music, Sound and Multimedia: From the Live to the Virtual.* Edinburgh: Edinburgh University Press, 2007.

Shaviro, Steven. "Emotion Capture: Affect in Digital Film." *Projections* 1/2 (Winter 2007): 37–55.

Shaw, Philip. *The Sublime.* The New Critical Idiom series. Abingdon and New York: Routledge, 2006.

Shepherd, Fiona. "Live and Proud." *The Scotsman,* June 11, 2005. Online. Available at http://news.scotsman.com/kttunstall/Live--proud.2634231.jp, retrieved June 19, 2008.

Shepherd, John, and Peter Wicke. *Music and Cultural Theory.* Cambridge: Polity Press, 1997.

Slobin, Mark, and Jeff Todd Titon. "The Music-Culture as a World of Music." In *Worlds of Music: An Introduction to the Music of the World's Peoples.* 2nd ed. Jeff Todd Titon et al., eds., 1–15. New York: Shirmer Books, 1992.

Small, Christopher. *Musicking: The Meanings of Performing and Listening.* Hanover, NH: Wesleyan University Press, 1998.

Smalley, Denis. "Space-Form and the Acousmatic Image." *Organised Sound* 12/1 (April 2007): 35–58.

Smith, Merritt Roe, and Leo Marx. *Does Technology Drive History? The Dilemma of Technological Determinism.* Cambridge, MA: MIT Press, 1994.

Sobchack, Vivian. *Carnal Thoughts: Embodiment and Moving Image Culture.* Berkeley: University of California Press, 2004.

Sontag, Susan. "Notes on 'Camp' [1964]." Reprinted in *Camp: Queer Aesthetics and the Performing Subject. A Reader,* ed. Fabio Cleto, 53–65. Edinburgh: Edinburgh University Press, 1999.

———. *On Photography.* London: Penguin, 1971.

———. "The Pornographic Imagination." In *Story of an Eye,* by Lord Auch [pseudonym], Georges Bataille, 82–118. London and New York: Penguin, 1982.

———. *A Susan Sontag Reader.* Ed. Elizabeth Hardwick. New York: Vintage, 1983.

Spence, Charles, and Jon Driver, eds. *Crossmodal Space and Crossmodal Attention.* Oxford and New York: Oxford University Press, 2004.

Spicer, Andrew. "An Occasional Eccentricity: The Strange Course of Surrealism in British Cinema." In *The Unsilvered Screen: Surrealism on Film,* ed. Graeme Harper and Rob Stone, 102–114. London: Wallflower Press, 2007.

Spicer, Mark. "(Ac)cumulative Form in Pop-Rock Music." *Twentieth-Century Music* 1/1 (2004): 29–64.

Sterne, Jonathan. *The Audible Past: Cultural Origins of Sound Production.* Durham, NC: Duke University Press, 2003.

Stilwell, Robynn J. "The Fantastical Gap between Diegetic and Nondiegetic." In *Beyond the Soundtrack: Representing Music in Cinema,* eds. Daniel Goldmark, Lawrence Kramer and Richard Leppert, 184–202. Berkeley: University of California Press, 2007.

———. "It May Look Like a Living Room . . . : The Musical Number and the Sitcom." *Echo* 5/1 (Spring 2003): paras. 1–74.

Straus, Joseph. "The 'Anxiety of Influence' in Twentieth-Century Music." *The Journal of Musicology* 9/4 (1991): 430–47.

Straw, Will. "Authorship." In *Key Terms in Popular Music and Culture,* eds. Bruce Horner and Thomas Swiss, 199–208. Oxford: Blackwell, 1999.

Subotnik, Rose Rosengard. *Deconstructive Variations: Music and Reason in Western Society.* Minneapolis: University of Minnesota Press, 1996.

———. "Shoddy Equipment for Living? Deconstructing the Tin Pan Alley Song." In *Musicological Identities: Essays in Honor of Susan McClary,* eds. Steve Baur, Raymond Knapp and Jacqueline Warwick, 205–18. Aldershot: Ashgate, 2008.

Tagg, Philip. "Analysing Popular Music: Theory, Method, and Practice." In *Reading Pop: Approaches to Textual Analysis in Popular Music,* ed. Richard Middleton, 71–103. Oxford: Oxford University Press, 2000.

———. "From Refrain to Rave: The Decline of Figure and the Rise of Ground." *Popular Music* 13/2 (1994): 209–22.

———. "Towards a Sign Typology of Music." Online. Available at http://www.tagg.org/articles/trento91.html, retrieved August 20, 2010.

Tagg, Philip, and Bob Clarida. *Ten Little Title Tunes: Towards a Musicology of Mass Media.* New York and Montreal: The Mass Media Musicologists' Press, 2003.

Talbot, Michael, ed. *The Musical Work: Reality or Invention.* Liverpool: Liverpool University Press, 2000.

Taylor, Timothy D. *Strange Sounds: Music, Technology and Culture.* New York and London: Routledge, 2001.

Tinkom, Matthew. "'Working Like a Homosexual': Camp Visual Codes and the Labor of Gay Subjects in the MGM Freed Unit." *Cinema Journal* 35/2 (1996): 24–42.

———. *Working Like a Homosexual: Camp, Capital, Cinema.* Durham, NC: Duke University Press, 2002.

Titon, Jeff Todd. "Textual Analysis or Thick Description?" In *The Cultural Study of Music: A Critical Introduction*, eds. Martin Clayton, Trevor Herbert and Richard Middleton, 171–80. New York and London: Routledge, 2003.

Torvinen, Juha. "Fenomenologinen tutkimus: lähtökohtia kriittiseen keskusteluun." *Musiikki* 1 (2008): 3–17.

Toynbee, Jason. *Making Popular Music: Musicians, Creativity and Institutions.* London: Arnold, 2000.

Turim, Maureen."Art/Music/Video.com." In *Medium Cool: Music Videos from soundies to cellphones*, eds. Roger Beebe and Jason Middleton, 83–110. Durham, NC: Duke University Press, 2007.

Välimäki, Susanna. *Miten Sota Soi? Sotaelokuva, ääni ja musiikki.*Tampere: Tampere University Press, 2008.

———. "Musical Migration, Perverted Instruments and Cosmic Sounds: Queer Constructions in the Music and Sounds of Angels in America." In *Essays on Sound and Vision*, eds. John Richardson and Stan Hawkins, 177–220. Helsinki: Helsinki University Press/ Yliopistopaino, 2007.

———. *Subject Strategies in Music: A Psychoanalytical Approach to Musical Signification.* Approaches to Musical Semiotics 9. Imatra: International Semiotics Society of Finland, 2005.

Veal, Michael. *Dub: Soundscapes and Shattered Songs in Jamaican Reggae.* Middletown, CT: Wesleyan University Press, 2007.

Venturi, Robert. "The Duck and the Decorated Shed." In *Postmodernism: A Reader,* ed. Thomas Docherty, 295–307. Columbia University Press: New York, 1993.

Vernallis, Carol. *Experiencing Music Videos: Aesthetic and Cultural Context.* New York: Columbia University Press, 2004.

———. "The Kindest Cut: Functions and Meanings of Music Video Editing." *Screen* 42/1 (Spring 2001): 21–48.

———. "Music Video, Songs, Sound: Experience, Technique and Emotion in *Eternal Sunshine of the Spotless Mind.*" *Screen* 49/3 (Autumn 2008): 277–97.

Warburton, Dan. "A Working Terminology for Minimal Music." *Intégral* 2 (1988): 135–59.

Wechsler, Robert. "Artistic Considerations in the Use of Motion-Tracking with Live Performers: A Practical Guide." In *Performance and Technology: Practices of Virtual Embodiment and Interactivity*, eds. Susan Broadhurst and Josephine Machon, 60–77. Basingstoke: Palgrave Macmillan, 2006.

Weis, Elisabeth and John Belton, eds. *Film Sound: Theory and Practice.* New York: Columbia University Press, 1985.

Whiteley, Sheila. "Prismatic Passion: The Enigma of 'The Great Gig in the Sky.'" In *The Legacy of Pink Floyd's Dark Side of the Moon,* ed. Russell Reising, 143–57. Aldershot: Ashgate, 2005.

———. "Progressive Rock and Psychedelic Coding in the Work of Jimi Hendrix." In *Reading Pop: Approaches to Textual Analysis in Popular Music,* ed. Richard Middleton, 235–61. Oxford: Oxford University Press, 2000.

Whiteley, Sheila, and Jennifer Rycenga. *Queering the Popular Pitch.* New York and London: Routledge, 2006.

Whitesell, Lloyd, "Men with a Past: Music and the 'Anxiety of Influence,'" *Nineteenth-Century Music* 18/2 (1994): 152–67.

Williams, Linda. *Hardcore: Power, Pleasure, and the "Frenzy of the Visible."* Berkeley: University of California Press, 1989.

Williams, Raymond. *Television: Technology and Cultural Form.* London and New York: Routledge, 1974.

———. *Marxism and Literature.* Oxford: Oxford University Press, 1977.

Willis, Holly. *The New Digital Cinema: Reinventing the Moving Image.* London: Wallflower, 2005.

Wojcik, Pamela Robertson, and Arthur Knight, eds. *Soundtrack Available. Essays on Film and Popular Music*. Durham, NC: Duke University Press, 2001.

Žižek, Slavoj. *The Art of the Ridiculous Sublime: On David Lynch's Lost Highway*. Washington: University of Washington Press, 2000.

———. "From Courtly Love to *The Crying Game*." *New Left Review* 1/202 (November/ December, 1993): 95–108.

Index